The A. W. Mellon Lectures in the Fine Arts have been delivered annually since 1952 at the National Gallery of Art, Washington, DC, with the goal of bringing "the people of the United States the results of the best contemporary thought and scholarship bearing upon the subject of the Fine Arts." As publication was always an essential part of the vision for the Mellon Lectures, a relationship was established between the National Gallery and the Bollingen Foundation for a series of books based on the talks. The first book in the series was published in 1953, and since 1967 all lectures have been published by Princeton University Press as part of the Bollingen Series. Now, for the first time, all the books in the series are available in one or more formats, including paperback and e-book, making many volumes that have long been out of print accessible to future generations of readers.

This edition is supported by a gift in memory of Charles Scribner, Jr., former trustee and president of Princeton University Press. The Press is grateful to the Scribner family for their formative and enduring support, and for their commitment to preserving the A. W. Mellon Lectures in the Fine Arts for posterity.

Images in this edition may have been altered in size and color from their appearance in the original print editions to make this book available in accessible formats.

THE A.W. MELLON LECTURES IN THE FINE ARTS

DELIVERED AT THE NATIONAL GALLERY OF ART, WASHINGTON, D.C.

1952 Creative Intuition in Art and Poetry *by Jacques Maritain*
1953 The Nude: A Study in Ideal Form *by Kenneth Clark*
1954 The Art of Sculpture *by Herbert Read*
1955 Painting and Reality *by Etienne Gilson*
1956 Art and Illusion: A Study in the Psychology of Pictorial Representation *by E. H. Gombrich*
1957 The Eternal Present: I. The Beginnings of Art. II. The Beginnings of Architecture *by S. Giedion*
1958 Nicolas Poussin *by Anthony Blunt*
1959 Of Divers Arts *by Naum Gabo*
1960 Horace Walpole *by Wilmarth Sheldon Lewis*
1961 Christian Iconography: A Study of its Origins *by André Grabar*
1962 Blake and Tradition *by Kathleen Raine*
1963 The Portrait in the Renaissance *by John Pope-Hennessy*
1964 On Quality in Art *by Jacob Rosenberg*
1965 The Origins of Romanticism *by Isaiah Berlin*
1966 Visionary and Dreamer: Two Poetic Painters, Samuel Palmer and Edward Burne-Jones *by David Cecil*
1967 Mnemosyne: The Parallel between Literature and Visual Arts *by Mario Praz*
1968 Imaginative Literature and Painting *by Stephen Spender*
1969 Art as a Mode of Knowledge *by J. Bronowski*
1970 A History of Building Types *by Nikolaus Pevsner*
1971 Giorgio Vasari: The Man and the Book *by T. S. R. Boase*
1972 Leonardo da Vinci *by Ludwig H. Heydenreich*
1973 The Use and Abuse of Art *by Jacques Barzun*
1974 Nineteenth-century Sculpture Reconsidered *by H. W. Janson*
1975 Music in Europe in the Year 1776 *by H. C. Robbins Landon*
1976 Aspects of Classical Art *by Peter von Blanckenhagen*
1977 The Sack of Rome, 1527 *by André Chastel*
1978 The Rare Art Traditions *by Joseph Alsop*
1979 Cézanne and America *by John Rewald*
1980 Principles of Design in Ancient and Medieval Architecture *by Peter Kidson*
1981 Palladio in Britain *by John Harris*
1982 The Burden of Michelangelo's Painting *by Leo Steinberg*
1983 The Shape of France *by Vincent Scully*
1984 Painting as an Art *by Richard Wollheim*
1985 The Villa in History *by James S. Ackerman*
1986 Confessions of a Twentieth-Century Composer *by Lukas Foss*
1987 Imago Dei: The Byzantine Apologia for the Icons *by Jaroslav Pelikan*
1988 Art and the Spectator in the Italian Renaissance *by John Shearman*
1989 Intermediary Demons: Toward a Theory of Ornament *by Oleg Grabar*
1990 Gold, Silver, and Bronze: Metal Sculpture of the Roman Baroque *by Jennifer Montagu*
1991 Changing Faces: Art and Physiognomy through the Ages *by Willibald Sauerländer*

OLEG GRABAR

The Mediation of Ornament

THE A.W. MELLON LECTURES IN THE FINE ARTS, 1989

THE NATIONAL GALLERY OF ART
WASHINGTON, D.C.

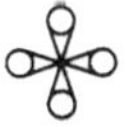

BOLLINGEN SERIES XXXV · 38
PRINCETON UNIVERSITY PRESS

Published by Princeton University Press, 41 William Street,
Princeton, New Jersey 08540
In the United Kingdom: Princeton University Press, Oxford

This is the thirty-eighth volume of the
A. W. Mellon Lectures in the Fine Arts, which are
delivered annually at
the National Gallery of Art, Washington. The volumes of
lectures constitute Number XXXV in Bollingen Series,
sponsored by Bollingen Foundation.

Library of Congress Cataloging-in-Publication Data

Grabar, Oleg.
The mediation of ornament / Oleg Grabar.
p. cm. — (The A.W. Mellon lectures in the fine arts ; 1989)
(Bollingen series ; XXXV, 38)
Includes index.
ISBN 0-691-04099-0
1. Art, Islamic—Themes, motives. 2. Communication in art.
3. Visual perception. 4. Art—Psychology. I. Title. II. Series.
III. Series: Bollingen series ; XXXV, 38.
N6260.G692 1992
709'.17'671—dc20 92-5725

Designed by Jan Lilly

New paperback printing 2023
ISBN (paper) 978-0-691-25276-6
ISBN (ebook) 978-0-691-25277-3

IN MEMORIAM

André Grabar

(1896–1990)

CONTENTS

LIST OF ILLUSTRATIONS

Plates

FIGURES

PREFACE

THIS BOOK IS the transformation into a written text of six lectures delivered at the National Gallery of Art in Washington, D.C., in April and May 1989. The lectures were the annual A. W. Mellon Lectures in the Fine Arts, which have contributed a uniquely distinguished series of volumes on the history, criticism, and, in general, understanding of the arts, most particularly but not exclusively the visual arts.

I felt all the more honored by the invitation to deliver these lectures because twenty-nine years earlier, in 1960, my father, André Grabar, was the tenth lecturer in the newborn series. His book based on the lectures, *Christian Iconography: A Study of Its Origins*, is still a much-quoted introduction to the complicated ways in which a new imagery and a new attitude toward the arts were created. André Grabar died on October 5, 1990, at the age of ninety-four, between the time the lectures were given and the final composition of the book. By the time of the lectures, he was almost blind and certainly was unable to read them, but he requested that I recount them one by one and identify key illustrations for him to recall. He made perceptive comments on approaches and considerations that were not entirely to his liking but that interested and concerned him as unusual directions for the field of the history of art, to which he had devoted his long life. Reflecting his generation and especially a deeply held personal belief in the obligation for scholars to become invisible or to act invisibly behind their arguments and the logic of works of art, he thought these lectures to be more personal than is justified. Whether he was right is for others to judge, but these comments, given a few months before his death, are only the last gestures of help and concern that he had extended to me for decades. For this and many other reasons, which need no further elaboration, I dedicate this book to his memory.

IT IS A pleasure, as usual, to record my gratitude to several categories of friends, colleagues, and associates. First, there is the staff of the National Gallery of Art and of the Center for Advanced Study in the Visual Arts, which so successfully fostered the many ways of the history and criticism of art and at whose creation I was privileged to have participated: Carter J. Brown, director of the National Gallery of Art, who extended to me the invitation to give the Mellon Lectures; Henry Millon and Marianna Shreve Simpson, dean and associate dean of CASVA, who smoothed so many practical problems; Gail

Feigenbaum, curator of Educational Programs, assigned the task of seeing that everything went smoothly on five out of six successive Sunday afternoons; Paavo Hantsoo, in charge of projections in the gallery's auditorium, who saw to it that more than six hundred slides were shown without a hitch; and many unknown guards and attendants from an ever helpful staff who facilitated the presentation of these lectures in dozens of minor ways.

Then, a number of colleagues and friends contributed to the writing of the book by offering comments after the lectures, by reading all or parts of the text of the lectures or of various stages of rewriting, by furnishing specific bits of information, by reacting to questions and queries, and by compelling me to clarify or elaborate my thoughts. Some of these friends have helped me more than once over many years to express better whatever I wanted to argue and say, and I hope that they will recognize in small expressions, in artful rewrites, or in new thoughts the hidden or overt ways in which I have profited from their help. After so many years of writing and of thinking, there probably no longer is a thought not shared at some point with a former student or a younger colleague and, therefore, generated in common with dozens of correspondents. If I have appropriated occasionally ideas that came from others, I console myself with the hope that I furnished as many as I received. The unique friends and colleagues who helped with this particular enterprise are Sheila Blair, Jonathan Bloom, Terry Allen, Renata Holod, Gülrü Necipoglu, Harry Rand, Natasha Staller, William Tronzo, and my colleagues of Harvard's Fine Arts Department, whose reactions to a first draft of what became Chapter 1 were essential in making it more precisely focused, if not crystal clear.

I owe special thanks to Terry H. Grabar. The time of the lectures was a period of sadness for both of us and the time of writing coincided with her retirement after thirty-odd years of teaching, once again the sadness of death, and a move of books and belongings to a new place. Instead of enjoying her newly acquired freedom, she read and reread the new text, bringing to it sympathetic criticism and constant concern for clarity of thought and expression. Her suggestions were not always followed and all of her queries were not answered, but much of what is good in the book is the result of her patient perusals.

Finally, several helpers at Harvard and at the Institute for Advanced Study handled the thankless tasks of typing and retyping, of making and listing slides, of ordering and checking photographs, of verifying notes and occasionally indulging in research on specific topics. They are Catherine McCollum, Maura Donohue, Andrei Molotiu, Peg van Sant, Amy Berridge,

Andras Riedlemayer, and Jeff Spurr. Without their efforts, neither the lectures nor the book would have been completed.

For providing photographs, I am thankful to the following individuals and/or institutions: Hans-Casper Graf von Bothmer, Esin Atil, Walter Denny, Robert Hillenbrand, Robert Morory, Jessica Rawson, Maura Donohue, François Avril, Marthe Bernus-Taylor, Kjeld von Folsach, Nancy Steinhardt, and appropriate authorities in all the collections whose treasures are reproduced, or whose photographic series were utilized. All photographs without specific identification were taken by the author.

For providing the friendliest and most helpful of relationships in transforming words and pictures into a book, I remain most grateful to the staff of the Princeton University Press, automatically entrusted with the publication of the Mellon lectures, and especially to Elizabeth Powers, Timothy Wardell, and Brian R. MacDonald, whose difficult task it was to provide consistency to a text and notes which touch on so many areas and also to question at times the alleged clarity of both text and notes. Transliteration from the Arabic script has been simplified for the sake of presentation and clarity. I trust that all who would wish to do so can figure out the original of all citations.

After the last of the lectures had been delivered, several faithful listeners suggested that I more or less reverse the order of the four intermediary themes—writing, geometry, architecture, nature—discussed in the five lectures that followed the introductory one. The suggestion has a lot of logical merit, as the broadest, most frequent, and best disseminated theme would have come first and the most restricted and most arduous one last. Thinking it over, however, I decided not to follow that suggestion. One reason was my belief that the book, for better or for worse, should reflect the lectures that led to it. The other reason was that the chapter on writing was the one whose scholarly apparatus and conclusions were closest to my own field of the arts of Islamic societies and communities and that I, therefore, felt most comfortable with it in elaborating the broader and more tentative theories and hypotheses of the lectures *and* of the book.

These essays are, therefore, written in the order in which the lectures were delivered with three significant additions, beyond the normal changes from an elocutionary mode to a written one. First, the body of the text has been enlarged and clarified, as only too often the constrictions of sixty minutes per lecture compelled simplifications and elisions hopefully masked by spoken eloquence but glaringly distressing on written pages; in many places, the reasoning required rather significant additions and elaborations in order to be clear. Furthermore, the smaller number of illustrations in the book than of slides during the lectures demanded a certain amount of textual adjustment. Second, a more elaborate introduction than the few words provided at the beginning of the spoken series was necessary to set the key of these essays and I shall return to this key shortly. Similarly, a final chapter picks up the threads of the five essays and weaves them into a conclusion that extends the explanations and procedures of the main chapter to a more elaborate position on the nature of art historical discourse. The third addition is the most important one and consists of a critical apparatus in the shape of notes that are almost half as long as the text. These notes only partly fulfill the traditional functions of referring to sources, to appropriate literature, and to suggestions for further investigations. They form in part a series of small essays, which argue points and hypotheses barely mentioned in or implied by the text and which evaluate opinions and judgments by other scholars and by established traditions of research in the history of art or in Islamic studies.

For, in a sense, this book is, as were the lectures on which it is based, a conscious and deliberate departure from traditional scholarship in the study of Islamic art. It is also different from usual art historical research in that new field, even though similar attempts do exist more frequently among works on western European art after the Renaissance than on most arts of other lands and periods. The ambition of this book is, no doubt, to explain certain features in the classical arts of the Islamic world. But it is also to elaborate and to meditate on issues of the perception, utilization, and fabrication of visually received forms that extend much beyond Islamic art. There are assumptions in this book, which are discussed in some detail, that there are universal approaches to visual behavior and that the experience of one time or of one culture not only can but must be extended to the limits of its possibilities for all arts at all times. The more fundamental assumption, however, is that these universal approaches are not necessarily and automatically derived from the paradigms of the study of western European art as it developed around antique, Renaissance, and post-Renaissance art at the turn of the twentieth century. Nor are these paradigms and the values derived from them necessarily and automatically wrong, as some avant-garde criticism considers them to be. It is rather that, granted an assumption or hypothesis of universal values, the sources and the modalities for that universality have not been investigated within other cultures than Western ones and it has rarely been wondered whether other epochs and other areas have a contribution to make for the elaboration of visual statements or of ideas derived from them that are accessible and meaningful to all viewers and users of art.

Put in such terms, however, the issue could become too easily a sort of accounting of visual or intellectual achievements according to country, region, or culture. Such accounts are usually pointless for anything beyond ethnic publicity and propaganda statements about the greatness of a country. It seemed more important to envisage a series of definable and identifiable visual categories and to explore the perception and understanding of their meaning or meanings as they emerge, without preestablished prejudices or judgments about the operation of works of art. For the point of this book is not merely a matter of defining the universal significance of one historical tradition or of another one. It is also an attempt to deal with the procedures of the history of art without calling into play theories, methods, and paradigms developed in other fields allegedly richer in methodological concerns. After much experimentation, over the years, with many procedures developed in semiology, literature, linguistics, or anthropology, I came to the conclusion that all of these procedures have something to offer, but none is alone capable of dealing with the issues of the history of art. At least they are unable to do so if taken directly—so to speak, transplanted—to the world of visual forms. Before one considers any such transplant, should it be necessary, the ways of the visual arts should become better explained and more fully clarified.

In trying to stay with a coherent and rigorous process of description and of analysis, I was compelled to develop a vocabulary of analysis and of conceptualization that at times uses known words in specific and not necessarily common ways; on a number of occasions I felt the necessity of coining new terms. All of these novelties or idiosyncratic uses are fully discussed in due time, but I thought it worthwhile to list the main ones in one place at the beginning of the book, so that readers may find a place for definitions of neologisms or of apparently original uses of common terms. These words follow, more or less in the order of their appearance:

Artifact or *object:* generic terms for all human creations studied by those who deal with the arts. Both terms include whatever students of art or society have proclaimed to be works of art.

Attribute: any general (that is, different from decoration) characteristic of an artifact that can be defined independently from its carrier. It is a fairly vague category deserving of further investigation and it includes physical features like size, modes like imperial or conventional, and judgments like elegant. (See also under Visual Perception.)

Decoration: anything applied to a structure or an object that is not necessary to the stability, use, or understanding of that structure or object.

Ornament (preliminary working definition): any decoration that has no referent outside of the object on which it is found, except in technical manuals.

Type: a standard that can be identified or proposed as necessary and implied for the creation of artifacts, each one of which is a variant of the type.

Typology: a cluster of types available at a given time or place or around a purpose. A typology can also mean the study of types.

Visual Perception: action of seeing artifacts and leading to their comprehension. Normally perception is of attributes that can be *iconophoric* (carrying otherwise identifiable and nonnegotiable, fully demonstrable, meanings, such as the keys of St. Peter or the arms of Siva), *formal* (involving combinations of shapes, colors, and so on, without normally iconophoric qualities, such as for forceful triangulation of Cézanne's *Card Players*), and *expressive* (leading to a series of judgments, such as the power of Aztec sculpture). In addition, I am proposing the category of *optisemic* attributes; these are perceived themes identifiable before being provided a likely iconophoric, formal, or expressive meaning—such are twelve standing or seated men in long robes who become the Apostles of Christianity or a symmetrically composed figure with hands clasped, which is the Buddha.

Calliphoric: carrying something felt or understood as beautiful.

Terpnopoietic: providing pleasure.

Chronotopic: associated with a specific place and time.

Monoptic: something perceived at one glance.

Taxonomy: the ordering of data (objects or attributes) according to groups that form sets.

Sign: that which denotes something and can usually be demonstrated to be correctly or falsely identified or understood.

Symbol: a term that connotes meanings that are often tied to a time, a place, or a category of patronage, even possibly a single individual, and that are not necessarily acceptable to all.

Style: a term I have avoided except to identify the web of attributes found in a single object.

The point of these terms is not to complicate things without necessity, it is rather to try to maintain rigor and consistency in the frequently complex reasonings that follow.

But, perhaps more important, these terms are meant to reflect a venture, perhaps an adventure. The venture is to study a small number of carefully delineated topics in order to test a hypothesis about the universal phenomenon of the visual perceptions and of the visual judgments made by historians and critics of art. The topics and questions are defined in the first chapter and, then, four test cases are studied in some detail. Answers and further queries are proposed in conclusion. But in a sense the whole enterprise of these essays and of the lectures that preceded them was to reflect almost forty years of professional concerns, which were part of one scholar's intellectual and sensory adventure. Whether it can help in the development of a truly autonomous history and criticism of art is for others to decide. But it would be wrong on my part to hide that, behind the glittering facade of scholarly pursuit, there lies the result of a personal quest more or less visible in the shadow of traditional ways of presenting works of art and the issues raised by them. It is a quest for understanding works of art and the issues raised by them. It is a quest for appropriate meanings given in the past or justified today for the limitless world of visually perceived monuments and artifacts. Such a quest is always partly a personal one. It is successful when what began as an individual's concern becomes of use to the community of scholars and of all those who live with the arts.

The original title of the lecture series was *Intermediary Demons, Toward a Theory of Ornament.* As the end of Chapter 1 will show, I still hold a commitment to the demons who engaged me in this task. But, upon reflection, a more prosaic title seemed more appropriate to what I ended up writing than the flashier one given to the talks.

THE MEDIATION OF ORNAMENT

INTRODUCTION

AFTER YEARS OF research and meditation in a field of expertise, the historian of any art, probably any historian, is enriched by the depth and breadth of that experience, regardless of the time and space limitations that affected his work. Difficulties begin when he seeks to share with other scholars or with the general public views, ideas, information, and interpretations derived from that experience. An almost missionary zeal exists to persuade others of the fascination of one's own field and of its importance for all areas of visual knowledge, learning, and pleasure. But on the other hand there lies the paralyzing fear that endlessly honed subtleties of cultural interpretations and carefully worked out distinctions in chronology or typology must give way to superficial generalities in order to be understandable. The difficulty of communicating properly to other fields the lessons of any one of them is compounded when the world or worlds with which one deals are, in reality or in perception, alien to the mainstream of the history of art and of the prevailing culture of the Western world. It is twice compounded if the world of one's concerns is also remote in time.[1]

Such is the predicament in which I found myself in introducing the topic of the lectures that led, in turn, to this book of essays on and around ornament. Observations and questions about works of Islamic art inspired the investigations and reflections that follow, and nearly every one of the chapters begins with a discussion of objects or buildings from the formative and medieval centuries of Islamic art, from the eighth to the thirteenth, and from the vast area extending from Spain to the frontiers of China through the southern shores of the Mediterranean and across the whole of western Asia, which had become predominantly Muslim after two major periods of expansion, the seventh–eighth centuries and the eleventh–twelfth.[2] At times I will deal with the specific factors and processes that surrounded the creation of these works of art and artifacts or that legitimize the interpretation I shall provide within their own historical context. But the thrust and the ambition of this book are not simply to discuss the character and the meanings of a number of works of Islamic art within the cultural and intellectual constraints of Islamic civilization, but to use them and the experience I have had of them in order to deal with wider questions about the arts as they are created, preserved, and perceived. It has seemed to me that the monuments involved and the questions surrounding them bring up issues that transcend their own time and space and are useful and significant to areas and periods other than those of the medieval Islamic world of western Asia and northern Africa and also to considerations about the visual arts which are not primarily historical.

There are methodological and philosophical difficulties in transferring explanations derived from one historically identified field to another one or even in drawing conclusions from individual works of art that extend beyond the specifics of their history. There is little point in discussing, not to say judging, a Chinese landscape by comparing it with an Impressionist painting or an Indian sculpture according to the canons developed in Hellenistic representations of men and women, because the cultural and historical contexts of classical Greece, traditional China, Hinduist India, and nineteenth-century Paris were so different from each other as to make comparisons irrelevant or gratuitous.[3] It is as though, at least in a traditional reflection upon the arts, each moment is sufficient unto itself and contains within its own time whatever meaning can appropriately be given to any one of its products.

There is, however, another kind of acceptable and reasonable discourse about the visual arts. Instead of beginning with individual works of art clearly identified in space and time, one can start with general questions or problems—for example, how is it that men and women, artists and patrons, view now, or imagined in the past, nature or the human body? No acceptable answer to such general questions will emerge if the experience of certain times or places is ignored. Yet it is also true that the art of some times or places does not enlighten these particular topics. It is unreasonable to discuss the representation of man or of nature without considering classical Mediterranean sculpture or French Impressionism as well as Gupta religious representations or Chinese painted scrolls, but eastern European medieval painting contributes relatively little to meditating on man's physical characteristics and properties, whereas African or Islamic art makes only limited contributions to theories of landscape presentation and of visions of nature.

Conversely, for reasons probably as mysterious as those which explain why all people are differentiated from each other and yet so similar, there hardly is an issue or a question about the arts or about esthetic perception for which some artistic tradition is not more pertinent and more compelling than others. One of our epistemological objectives will be to define that zone of learning, feeling, or understanding which is affected or enriched by the availability of artistic experiences alternate to one's own. It is, of course, true that a viewer fully immersed in Japanese or west central African culture is bound to be affected by and identify with Japanese painting or Benin sculpture in ways inaccessible to others, but this does not invalidate the understanding and empathy individuals without the same immersion may have of Japanese or West African art. Logically and often in the polemical practice of our time, it is possible to argue that interpretative visual experiences by "aliens" are difficult for "natives" to the culture to accept, but this rejection, logical or visceral, does not make the experience wrong or even untrue.[4] Therefore, it will be one of the premises of this book that the knowledge and awareness of the monuments of one artistic tradition, that of classical Islamic times in this instance, can legitimately lead to considerations applicable to other times and other places.

In a general and as yet very crude sense, the examples I have given so far suggest also that the way or ways in which we see or interpret, intellectually or emotionally, sets of images or of types of images may well depend on the questions that are posed. It is one thing to begin with something that exists, a concrete object or the carefully delineated production of a time or space, and to draw as many explanatory and interpretative circles around it as may seem worthwhile. It is quite another task to derive theories and interpretations from a body of visual documents or else to answer queries formulated outside of individual artifacts or of discrete cultures and times by drawing on whatever examples may be necessary.

This book, like the lectures that preceded it, is based almost throughout on all three of these methodological approaches. In nearly every chapter, the study and the contemplation of a very small number of objects will pave the way for the various conclusions and hypotheses of the book. Yet the evaluation and the ingestion over several decades of a vast body of materials from the rich inheritance of the many lands where Islamic art flourished led me, like many scholars and students before me, to identify certain visual characteristics as frequent enough to be typical of Islamic art. These characteristics in turn—for example, the schematization of vegetal or animal shapes—could be understood in several ways. They are part of a precise visual domain, that of medieval Islamic art. But they are also examples of a visual order available elsewhere, perhaps everywhere, and to whose elaboration this book is devoted.

The visual order we shall be exploring is the one loosely called ornament. Ornament, as an initial definition, is differentiated from decoration in the sense that decoration is anything, even whole mosaic or sculpted programs, applied to an object or to a building, whereas ornament is that aspect of decoration which appears not to have another purpose but to enhance its carrier.[5]

Ornament, in this sense, exists everywhere, in every artistic tradition, but it is generally acknowledged that, whatever is meant by the term, its most engaging and best-known examples belong to the arts developed in regions of predominantly Muslim culture. The intricate patterns on imperial Safavid or Ottoman rugs (pls. 21–23), the brilliant geometry of tile work or stucco molding in the Alhambra (pl. 12, fig. 120), the colorful sensuality of Iranian paintings and illuminations (pl. 20), the shining panache of Ottoman ceramic wares (figs. 189, 190), the strongly articulated walls or domes of Timurid Iran or Mamluk Egypt (pl. 15; figs. 123, 124), the ubiquitous cascades of *muqarnas* ceilings from Egypt or Iran (figs. 124, 125)—these are all examples from late Islamic art, the time of the great empires and of the great cities, as the earliest of the monuments I have mentioned is of the middle of the fourteenth century. They illustrate, singly and as a group, treatments of the surfaces of buildings, books, or objects that share two characteristics. One is that the range, expressive impact, and variety of motifs and techniques used to decorate objects and buildings of Islamic art are truly astounding. No category of design, no group of motifs, escaped a kind of treatment that has been called ornamental or decorative, and it is difficult to avoid being affected by the sheer sensuality of most of them. The other characteristic is that nearly every one of these motifs and patterns can also be found in some other artistic tradition, often without demonstrable or even likely impact from or on Islamic art.[6] The art of the Islamic world, it would seem, made more expressive, more tangible, more exclusively its own, aspects of artistic creativity that are found everywhere.

It is, therefore, reasonable to assume that the exploration of the phenomenon of ornamental decoration within a Muslim context is of intellectual and hermeneutic value to decoration everywhere. Some may, of course, argue against this assuredness of universal principles in the perception and explanation of art, primarily on the grounds that such principles are only valid at obvious and elementary levels and that the specificity of a moment in time and space and the historical integrity of a given work of art are far more important matters than the search for elusive universal truths. In fact, however, the search for universals and the integrity of any monument need not be seen as antagonistic expectations, but simply as alternate facets of the visual experience whose elucidation is sought by the historian.

There may be other facets as well and, from the very outset, therefore, I would like to state two premises underlying the essays that follow. One is that I shall try to develop an equilibrium between, on the one hand, observations on and explanations of specific works of art or motifs and, on the other, broader concepts of artistic perception or visual understanding. The second premise is that the methods and procedures I will be expounding are not the only possible ones. They are part of what I see as a cluster of approaches, indefinite in number, to the study of the visual arts. At any one time, within the context of any one book or article, only one or at best two ways can be explored. But in reality there are many mansions for the feast offered to the mind by the eyes. In the contemporary jargon with gourmet connotations of computer programs, many menus are possible and provided for our pleasure and instruction. The menus I have chosen or the mansions that I have explored are neither historical with a concentration on time and space nor critical with the expectation of a personal or collective judgment of quality. They can be called thematic, as they imply or suggest the existence of consistent categories of focus or of perception that are not tied to the time of their execution and, therefore, do not require the contextual breadth and the judgmental appreciation of value required in historical or critical discourse.[7]

In recent years, rich, if at times hermetic and dense, philosophical, anthropological, and semiological (in the widest meaning of the word) discourses have been spun around all our intellectual and sensory involvements with the visual world. As a result, the history and appreciation of art have acquired new dimensions and new requirements, as answers to novel intellectual challenges or to old challenges set in the new language of the waning twentieth century are expected.[8] I shall return to some of these issues in the concluding chapter of this book, but I do want to stress at the beginning one key premise as well as objective of the investigations that follow. I will keep as a backdrop of my consideration of individual works of art or of motifs found on them the firmly held belief that each of them is valuable in itself, as a discrete object, but also that each one is an exemplar of or a beacon toward the complex interactions between the work, life, thought, and emotion of men and women today as well as in the past. Pure theory has its place in a philosophical discourse and the results or paradigms issued from theory can, probably must, be used by historians of art, but no discourse on the arts can avoid the direct, immediate, encounter with objects. The topic of this book is the investigation of some of the intellectual assumptions and visual procedures that make this encounter possible.[9]

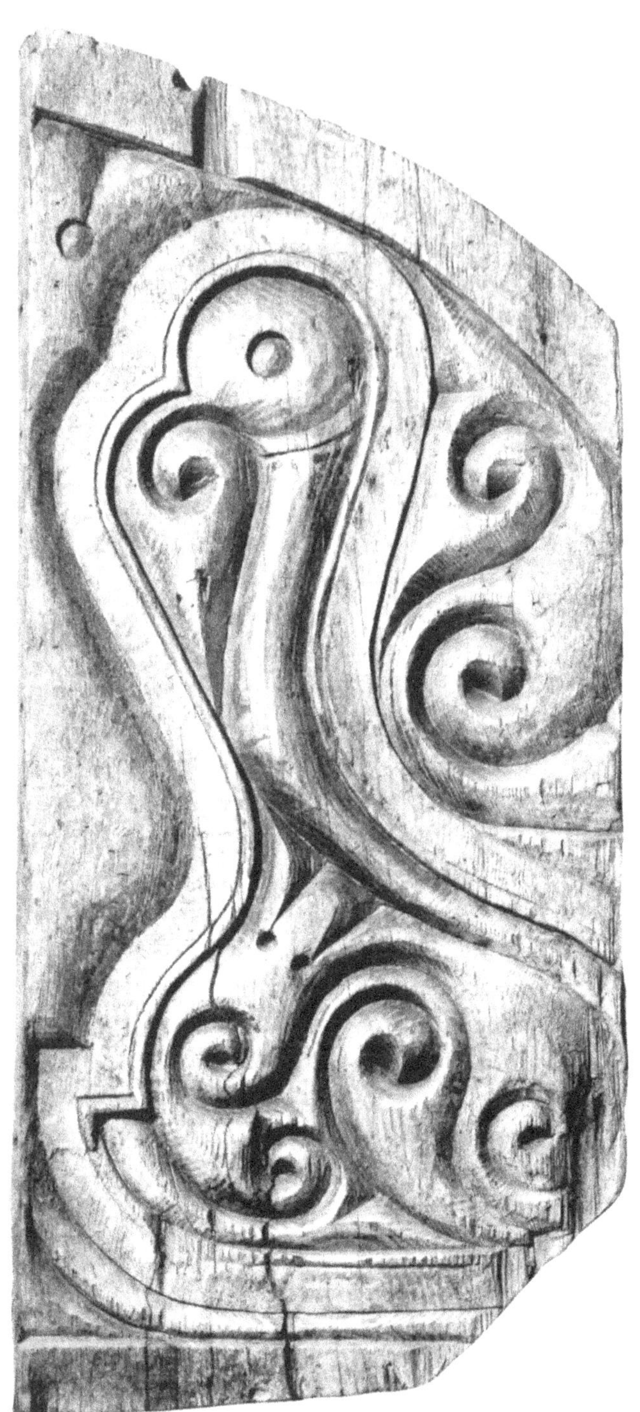

Fig. 1. Wooden panel, representation of a bird (?), Egypt, ninth or tenth century. Paris, Louvre Museum, inv. 6023.

CHAPTER I

A Theory of Intermediaries in Art

THE CLAIMS that certain works of art are decorative and that some of the motifs found on them are ornament derive from two different categories of visual knowledge. One is the general and almost automatic agreement that otherwise identified features—for instance, a rinceau of flowers and leaves or heart-shaped dots set in rows—are decoration rather than representations of something or significant of something else. The second category involves the manner of treating something rather than the nature of what is represented. The colorful patterning of Matisse's representation of dancers, the oval elongation of Modigliani's portraits, or Andy Warhol's serially repeated cans of Campbell soup may, at some level of perception and understanding, be called ornamental, because, at least for the setting of my argument, the transformations of perfectly accessible subjects are not dictated by those subjects and do not alter whatever original quality was the privilege of these subjects.

The aim of this chapter is to elaborate on these definitions, to identify their assumptions and implications, and, in conclusion, to elaborate a hypothesis or a set of hypotheses for further investigation. I shall begin with observations on works of medieval Islamic art and then expand my remarks into considerations affecting other times and other places.

The Louvre Museum owns a very peculiar piece of woodwork, seventy-three centimeters (about two feet three inches) high and thirty-two centimeters (a bit over a foot) wide (fig. 1). It is a flat panel shaped to fit into a tympanum of some sort and decorated with what has usually been called a bird. It is dated to the late ninth century, a dating neither demonstrated nor unlikely. Its physical function is that of a carved wooden panel to be fitted into the walls of buildings or, less likely in this case, into a piece of furniture like a chest or a door. In terms of decorative typology, it contains a motif, which can be unique or frequently repeated, set within a carefully delineated frame, usually a square or a rectangle. Both function and decorative typology are known in Egypt from the eighth to the thirteenth centuries.[1]

The Louvre piece is original in two ways. One is the odd shape of the frame for the principal motif. It probably reflects something in the architectural setting for which it was designed, but I have at this stage no specific explanation for it. The second originality is the agreement to call the motif a bird. Seen objectively, that is to say without prejudice as to meaning, the motif can be divided into several parts: below, a roughly ovoid mass filled with beveled volutes that derive from representations of leaves, then a curved elongated stem, and, finally, a nearly round ball with a smaller ball cut out in its center and terminating with a leaf extending from its lower left. None of these elements is by itself birdlike or even remotely resembles a bird or any part of a bird, but the combination strikes as "sort of" reflecting the outer shape of one. The stem becomes a bird's neck because of the way in which it emerges from the back of what then is the seated body of a bird because the stem has made it so once it is seen as a neck. A narrow band like a collar separates the neck-stem from what becomes then a head with an eye in its middle. The historically sophisticated, or at least knowledgeable, viewer can recall a fairly common textile motif of a bird holding a leaf or something else in its mouth and thus explain the plantlike look of the beak.[2] A historical comparison also explains the beveling of the carving and the tour de force of design that transformed primarily vegetal or neutral motifs into a bird, for in the ninth century beveling became a manner of carving wood or stucco characteristic of the main cultural centers of Islam in and around Baghdad and eventually under the influence of the Abbasid capital.[3] The "birdiness" of the image disappears almost completely once its parts are analyzed separately and only comes back through the apprehension of a silhouette for which no explanation seems to exist except that of a bird.[4] What is, at this stage, quite unclear is whether an artisan wanted to represent a bird, or a patron or a designer ordered one, or whether it is today's spectator who needs to interpret this particular design from a non–western European source in zoomorphic fashion.

There are a few other remaining pieces of carved Egyptian wood with real birds or possible birds, and one of them, in the Museum of Islamic Art in Cairo (fig. 2), has the striking formal qualities of the Louvre piece with the additional complexity of a symmetrical overall design.[5] Other pieces have less clearly identified birdlike features[6] and some (fig. 3) are usually described as

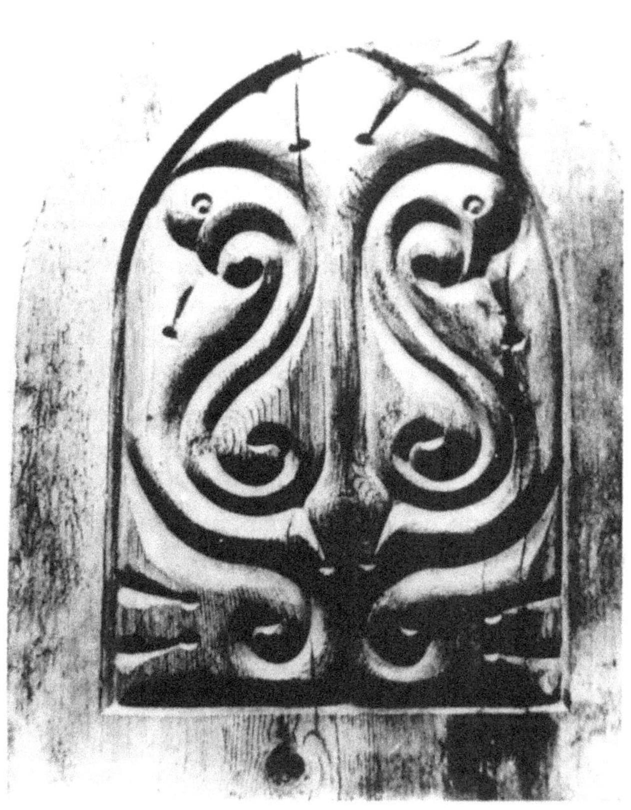

Fig. 2. Wooden panel, representation of a bird (?), Egypt, ninth or tenth century. Cairo, Museum of Islamic Art, inv. 13173.

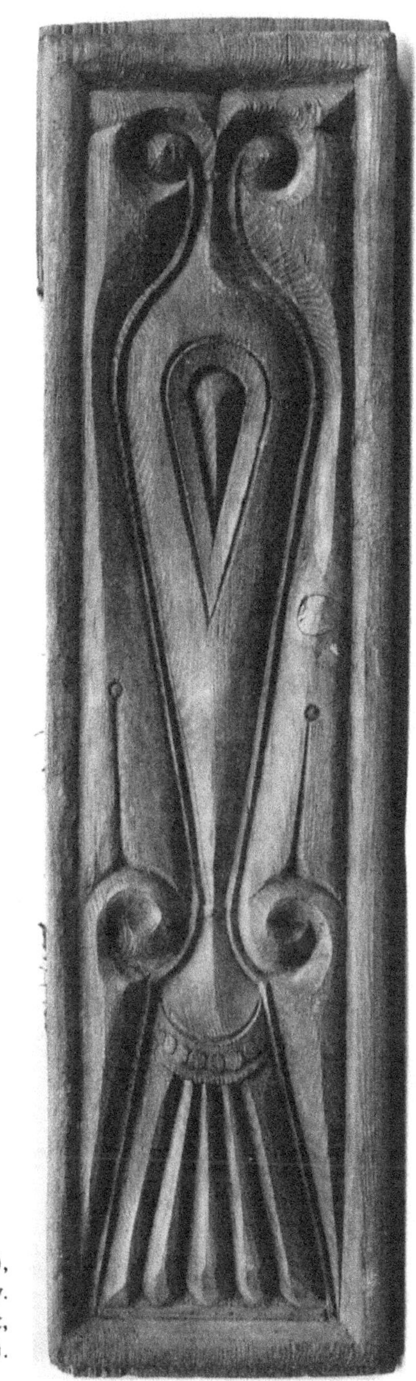

Fig. 3. Wooden panel, vegetal design (?), Egypt, ninth or tenth century. New York, Metropolitan Museum of Art, gift of V. Everit Macy, 1930 (30.112.7).

floral, a "palmette design" according to the label of the Metropolitan Museum, but it *is* possible to see it as an elongated bird with two heads (a common enough motif) carrying leaves. The whole set could probably be put in chronological sequence according to time-honored art historical practices. But the point of my observations is not a historical one of formal development, but the ontological one of an apparent ambiguity between what we see and the meanings we usually give or can give to that which we see.

This kind of interpretation is not peculiar to Egyptian woodwork of the ninth and adjoining centuries. At roughly the same time and continuing into the eleventh century, paintings on ceramics from Iraq or especially from northeastern Iran exhibit decorative motifs that are remarkable for their inventiveness and for their novelty.[7] Very few among them go back to earlier, pre-Islamic times or derive from the better-known vocabulary of designs on contemporary techniques of manufacture like metalworking. All these objects more or less share the same shape. They are bowls and plates with one dominant side visible immediately and, in most cases, simple and minimally enlivened exteriors (fig. 4). All Iranian examples are decorated in the same technique of painting on an opaque slip and under a transparent glaze. The best Iraqi examples, on the other hand, are often covered with luster, which gives a brilliant effect to the surface of the dish or bowl, but they too are meant to be seen primarily from one side.[8] A few objects within this group with decorative patterns that are unique—for example, a bowl in the Freer Gallery of Art (fig. 5) or a plate formerly in a private Iranian collection (fig. 6)—are true masterpieces of design within a circular space.[9] These bowls or plates demonstrate, among other things, that the technique was used for a considerable range of taste and probably financial means.

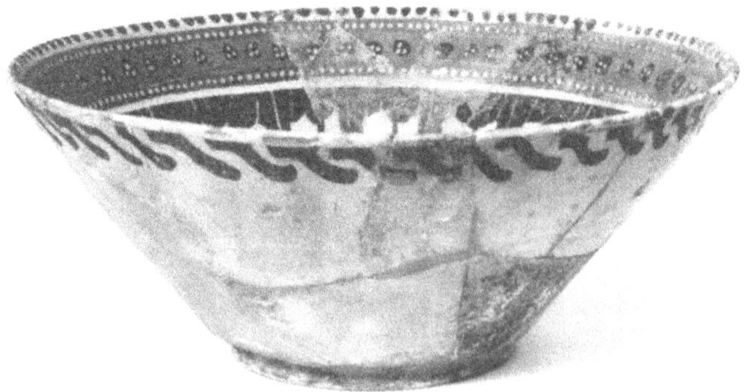

Fig. 4. Ceramic bowl, side view, northeastern Iran, ninth century. New York, Metropolitan Museum of Art, 1939, and Rogers Fund, 1939 (39.40.7).

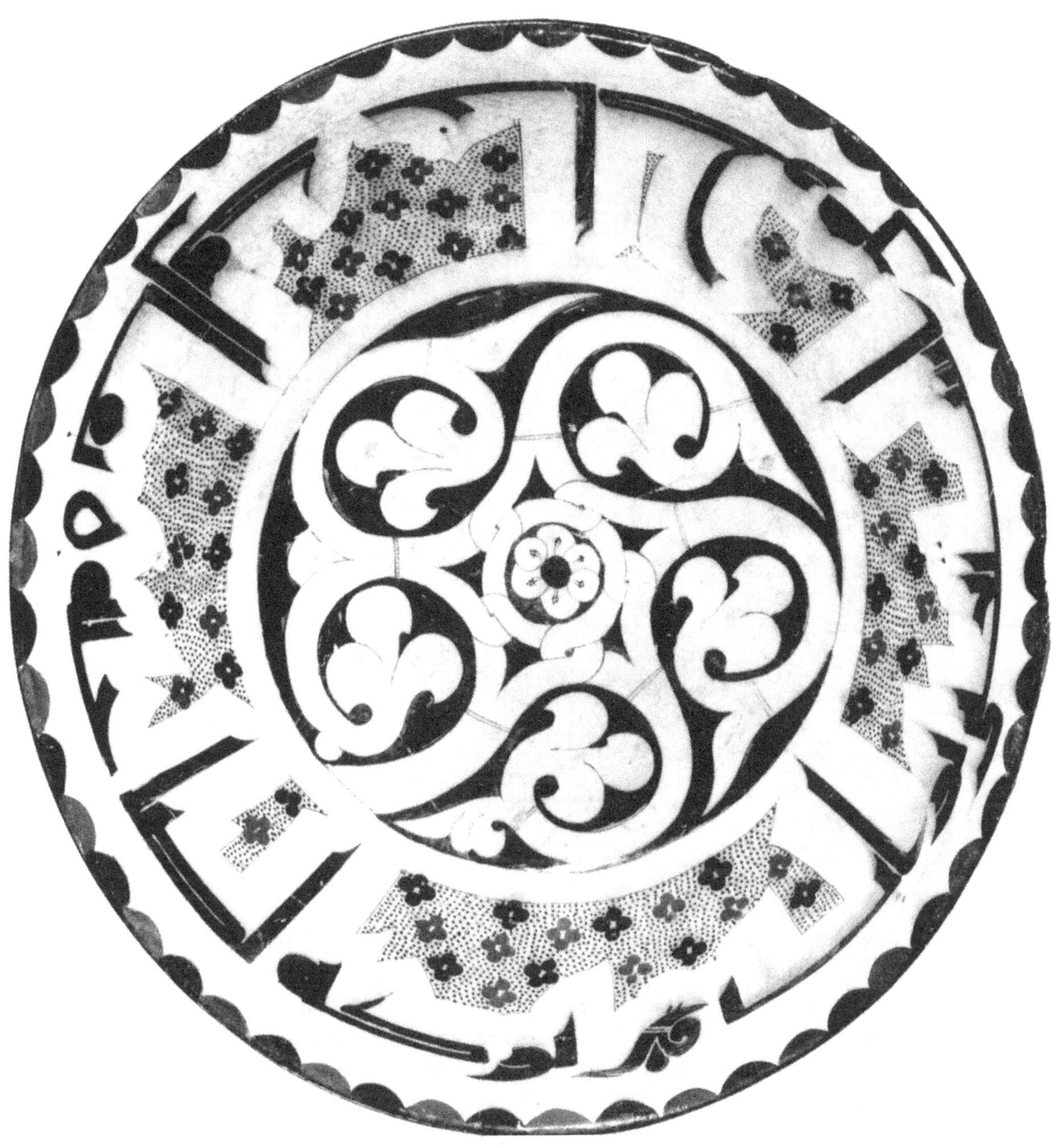

Fig. 5. Ceramic bowl, side view,
northeastern Iran,
ninth or tenth century.
Washington, D.C., Freer
Gallery of Art, 57.24.

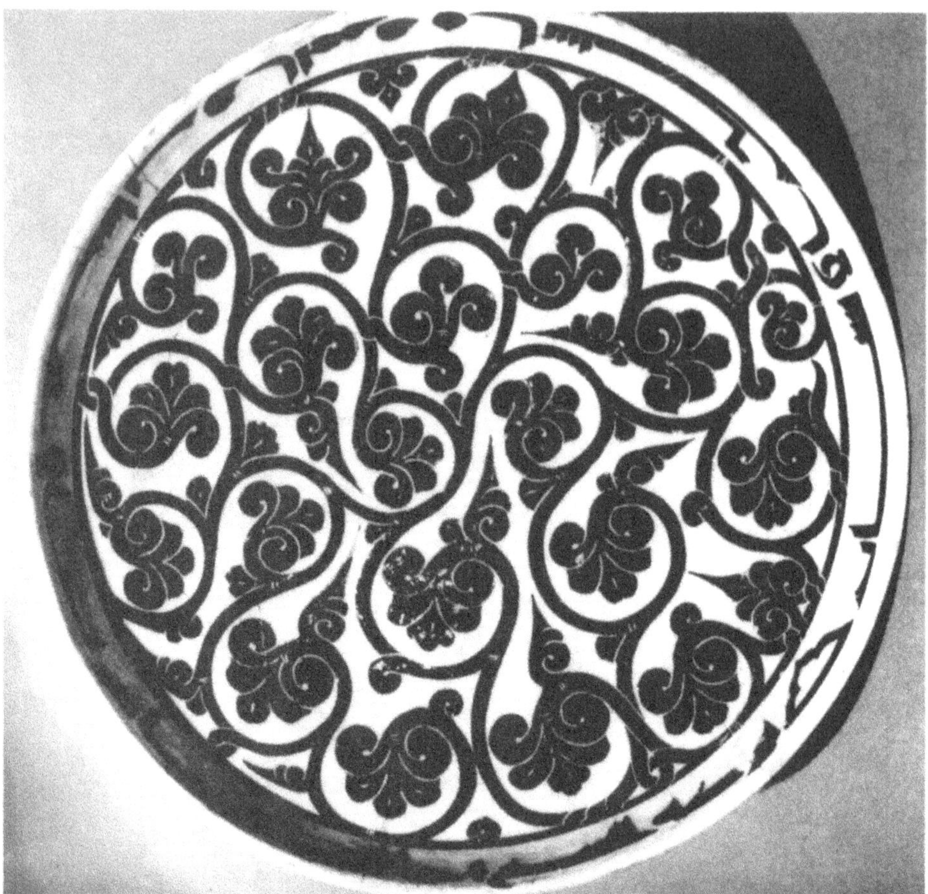

Fig. 6. Ceramic bowl, northeastern Iran, ninth or tenth century. Formerly Foroughi collection, Tehran; present whereabouts unknown.

There is no comprehensive study of the themes and styles decorating these bowls and plates. Some topics, like writing (figs. 5, 7), are perfectly clear and easily relate to external referents.[10] Others are fascinating exercises in composition within a circle in which neutral lines or forms, very remotely and vaguely relatable to traditionally known vegetal or animal motifs, are organized according to very strict (pl. 1, fig. 8) or, equally frequently, very loose patterns (figs. 9–12). Some ceramics have perfectly legible inscriptions and only ask the viewer to transform writing arranged in a circle into a normal right-to-left linear projection (fig. 7), and then to translate it into the simple message of homey proverbs, since the statements put on these bowls are striking for their repetitive lack of personality. But, then, the writing itself can range from utmost simplicity and clarity (fig. 7) to meaningless imitation of

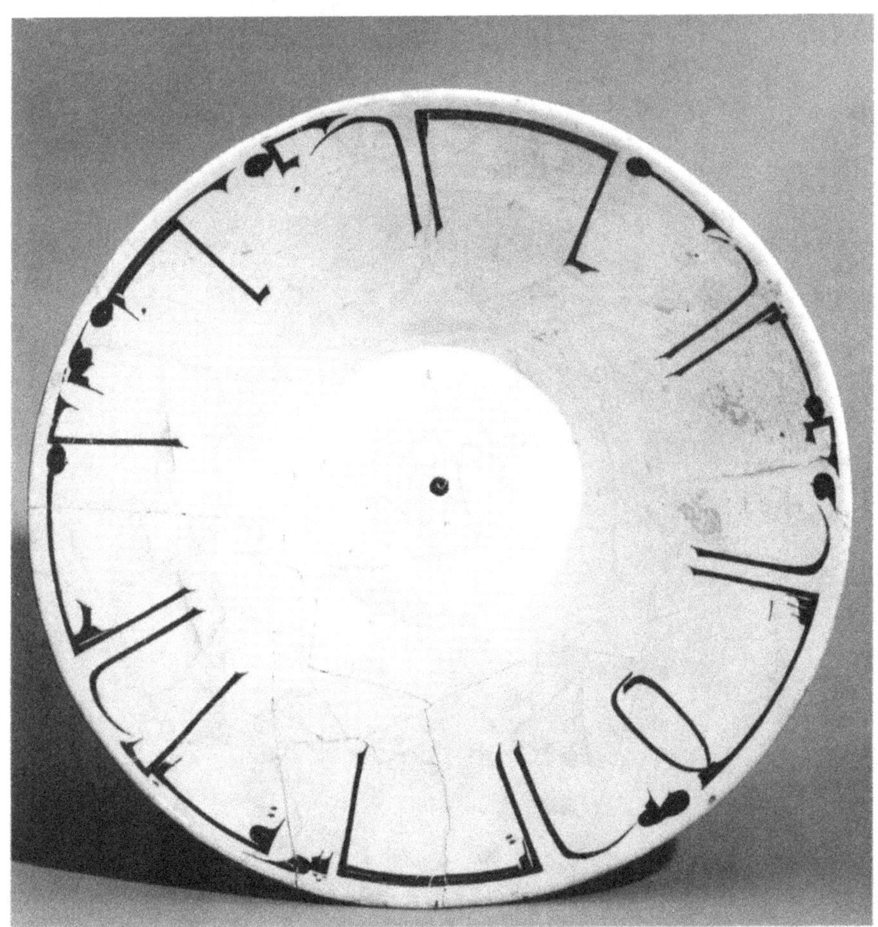

7

Fig. 7. Ceramic bowl, northeastern Iran, ninth or tenth century. New York, Metropolitan Museum of Art, Rogers Fund, 1965 (65.106.2).

Fig. 8. Ceramic bowl, northeastern Iran, tenth century. New York, Metropolitan Museum of Art, Rogers Fund, 1928 (28.82).

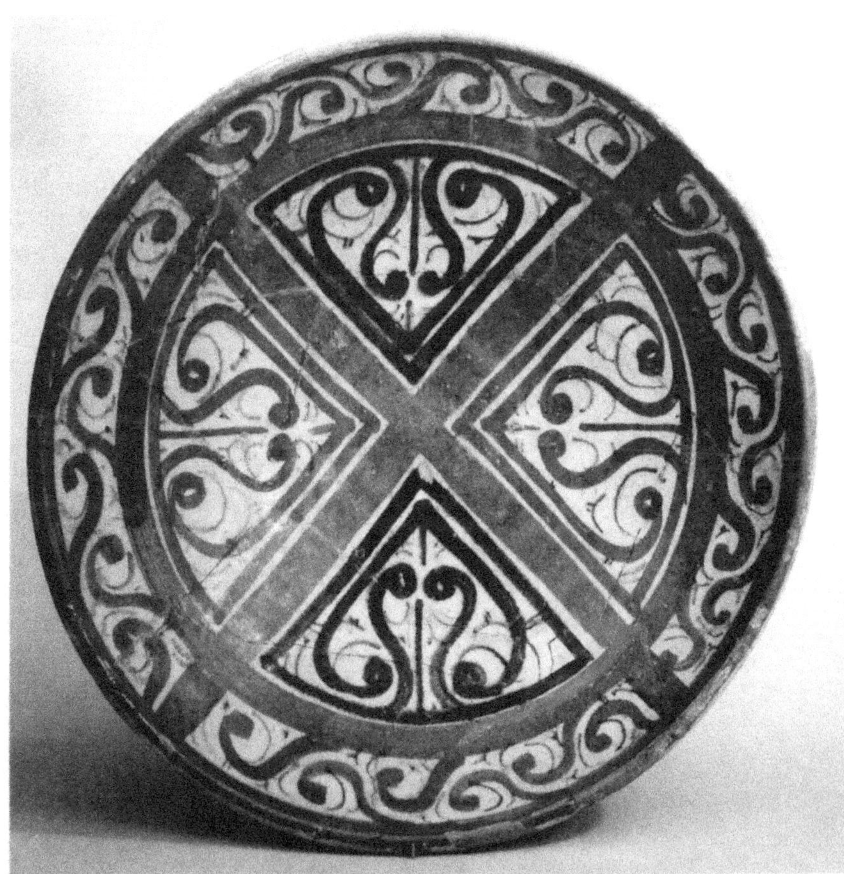

8

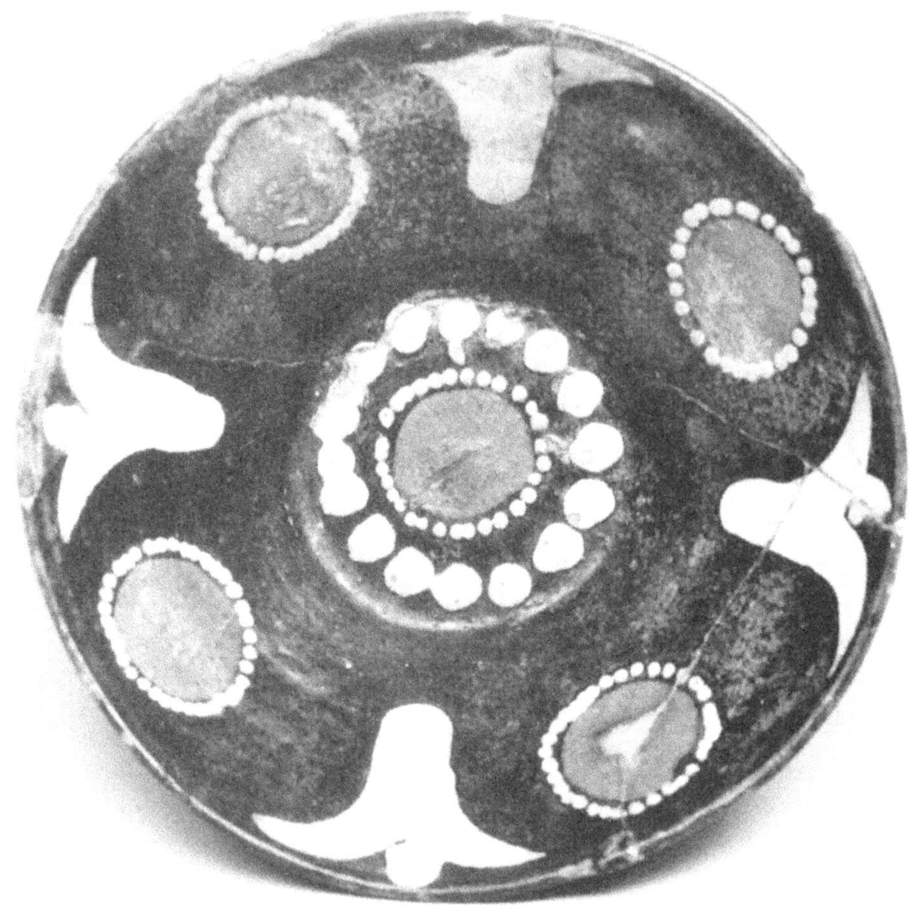

Fig. 9. Ceramic bowl, northeastern Iran, ninth century. New York, Metropolitan Museum of Art, Museum excavations, 1937, and Rogers Fund, 1938 (38.40.120).

writing (fig. 11). Similarly, birds or fish or even vegetal motifs appear in these ceramics reasonably clearly at times but quite often are distorted or altered to the point where their zoological identity is dubious (pl. 2 or fig. 12).

This range of ways to handle motifs within the same set of objects serves to make two points. First, most of the existing objects and designs are unique, with significant exceptions almost entirely restricted to writing. It is, therefore, reasonable to assume that artisans and users or patrons did not simply repeat learned formulas or order by number; they were conscious of what was depicted on these ceramics, even if we do not know which categories of visual perception—iconophoric, formal, or expressive—affected them most. Formal distinctions must have been specifically ordered or, at least, acknowledged as meaningful in one of many possible ways. Second, the explanation for this variety lies somewhere within the complicated cultural and social makeup of Muslim urban society in the early Middle Ages. It may reflect the

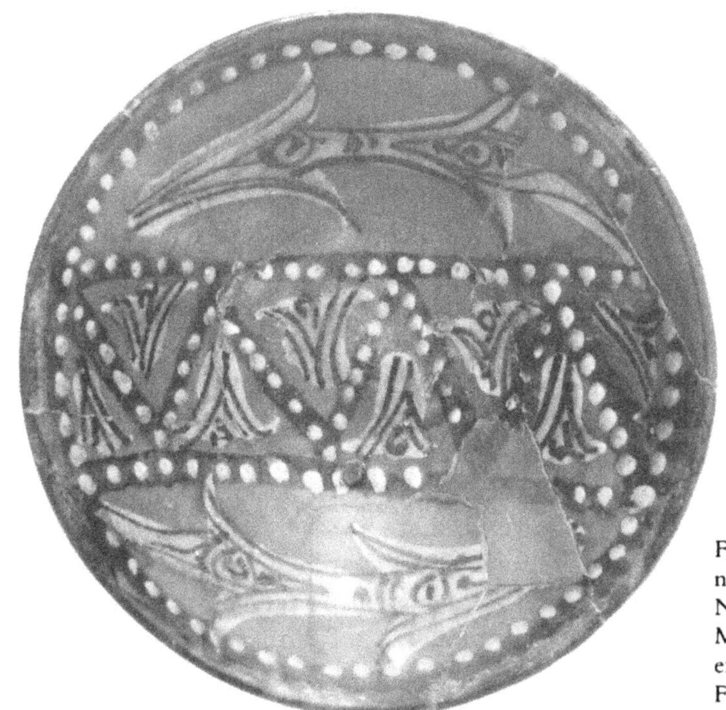

Fig. 10. Ceramic bowl, northeastern Iran, ninth century. New York, Metropolitan Museum of Art, Museum excavations, 1936, and Rogers Fund, 1937 (37.40.16).

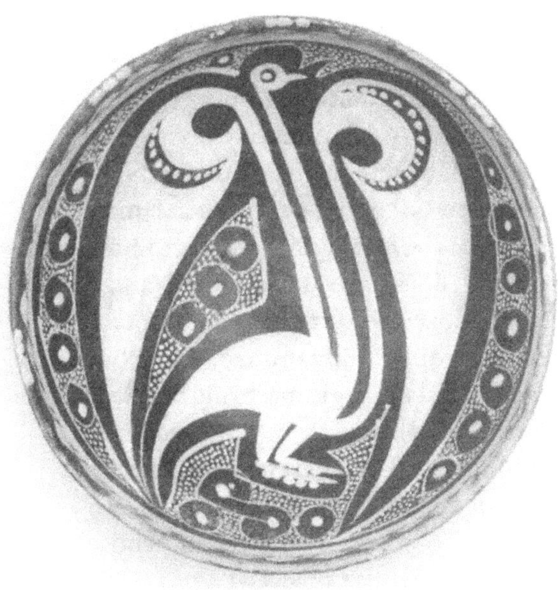

Fig. 11. Ceramic bowl, northeastern Iran, tenth century. Copenhagen, David Collection, 10/1975.

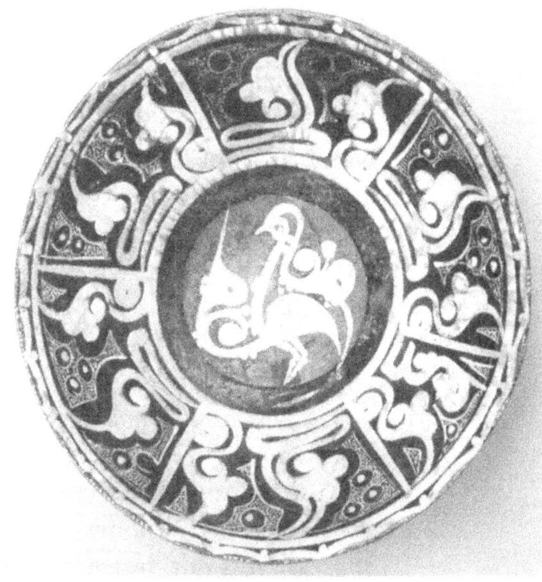

Fig. 12. Ceramic bowl, northeastern Iran, tenth century. New York, Metropolitan Museum of Art, Purchase, Huntley Bequest Fund, 1958 (58.152).

divisions of urban population into ethnic, cultural, religious, or professional groups whose separate individualities are only beginning to emerge. The further elaboration of this particular point lies outside the scope of my present investigations.[11]

The problems which *are* part of my investigation are two. First, what makes us recognize or identify a bird, a fish, writing, or a leaf, when what we see does not bear any real resemblance to what we call it? Once we cannot identify a represented figure as being part of our physical experience of the phenomenal world, what makes us say that it is a fish or a bird? What psychological reactions or modes of behavior appear to require a mimetic interpretation of so many forms, that is to say, an interpretation that assumes all forms are related to an actual physical world or to a potential one, as, for instance, with a unicorn? These questions deal with the way we today comprehend what we perceive. They are directed to the contemporary viewer, the scholar equipped with a mass of comparative material who can provide the functional context of objects or the pedigree of motifs, but also a public attracted by the variety and playfulness of forms and finding in these objects an excitement independent of the object's history and context.

A later example from the realm of Islamic art may serve to focus the issue. The celebrated albums from Istanbul possess a striking fifteenth-century Iranian painting (pl. 3) whose combination of squares of seven different colors separated by black lines inevitably recalls some of Mondrian's best-known and most exciting compositions (pl. 4). It is easy enough to become mesmerized by the richness of color of the Iranian painting, to play with its patterns, and to wonder about the majestic mystery of artistic creativity that would have made so strikingly alike the work of a Dutchman painting in New York toward the end of World War II and of an unknown master at a Turkic court of Iran. At the same time, the pedestrian scholar and those who read the Arabic script can point out that the squares, lines, and dots of the Iranian painting are in fact a sort of whorl repeating dozens of times and in different colors the name of Ali, the son-in-law of the Prophet Muhammad, Ali, from whom alone, according to the Shiʿite branch of Islam, legitimate rule derived, but whose importance in Muslim culture extended much beyond sectarian legitimacy.[12] In other words, it seems appropriate, even necessary, to ascribe to this painting an iconographic or, better, iconophoric meaning—that is to say, an exact and nonnegotiable relationship to an external referent whose expression is not, however, restricted to this particular object. To put it yet another way, once the subject of a representation is identified on a given image, that particular image is no longer the only possible way for the subject to be represented.[13] And, at another level the knowledge of iconographic specificity may in fact modify or even cancel out the initial sensory experience of forms alone. For instance, some may appreciate the painting less or more once they know that it contains a Shiʿite religious message. Others will never understand its visual sensuality, as they are only spiritually affected by its meaning.

In short, as we perceive these various images and try to restate in words what they are and what they mean, two conclusions emerge. One is a set of valid statements ranging from something inalienably true, like an incontrovertible iconographic meaning as well as the presence or absence of the color red, all the way to subjective or ideological truths valid primarily for each observer, such as the excitement provided by a pattern, the association made between a formal unit and a thought or a belief, or the emotional appeal of a design. The other thing we discover is that all these truths can be present simultaneously in any one object. They may even conflict with each other, as is already the case with liking or disliking works of art, and yet they remain both appropriate and accurate.

The second set of questions raised by the Egyptian bird and the Iranian or Iraqi ceramics is directed to the past, to the time of creation and to the people who made, bought, ordered, or otherwise used these objects. What did *they* see or mean to represent? If an intimation of some sort of reality was their aim, why the variety of ways to show it? And why move so far away from physical reality or from obvious signs of literal communication like letters? Could it be that what they meant is not what we see, at least not entirely? That the *transformation* of the mimetic sign is important, not the sign itself? It has been argued, already three generations ago, that the modifications brought to the representation of physical reality by the Muslim world in the ninth century had a religious, even a theological, meaning. By withdrawing from a *re*creation of tangible or visible reality, these modifications, it was argued by the great French scholar Louis Massignon, expressed the impermanence of the visible, an alleged tenet of the Muslim ethos.[14] An alternate but, at this stage of research, much more tenuous relationship may be suggested between the interpretation of visual forms I am sketching and a theory of the linguistic sign metaphorically used that was proposed by al-Jurjani in the eleventh century. That extraordinary philosopher of language and literature argued for the existence in poetic language of transferences of forms, such as groups of letters, which removed them from their original meaning.[15] His theories applied to the visual world would argue that the autonomy of forms from meaning allows for greater freedom in creation than if forms are tied to specific meanings. The thought of this unique personality in early medieval literary criticism is strikingly contemporary, with its concern for structures, but unfortunately little is known about al-Jurjani's actual impact on his time and on theorists or artists, in his time or later on, within the Muslim world. There, as in the Christian Middle Ages, the validity of correspondence between the visual arts and literary criticism still needs to be demonstrated.[16]

I shall return in conclusion to the limits of cultural interpretations for visually perceptible forms and indirectly to the appropriateness of al-Jurjani's or Massignon's explanations for a form issued from the Muslim world. What concerns me at this stage is the assumption of an intellectual or social explanation for a visual phenomenon when there is no identification or suggestion of the process by which society or culture actually affects the making of works of art. Such intimations are automatic and justified for all creations with an iconographic meaning, when one can identify the narrative, the event, or the practice that led to the forms they have acquired. Yet, for the examples from the Muslim world I have given, it can just as easily be imagined, as was done by Kandinsky, Matisse, and a few contemporary Western critics who worried about such issues,[17] that the artists of the ninth to eleventh century in Egypt, Iran, or Iraq engaged in exercises of imaginative freedom more or less tied to iconographic or culturally precise statements.

To choose between sociocultural control with a concrete symbolic or ideological intent for visual creativity and a more romantic vision of free artists at work is nearly impossible on rational grounds. The hypothesis of artistic freedom is an anachronistic transfer to the past of nineteenth-century dreams in western Europe. And cultural control, in the particular case of the woodwork and of the ceramics, is difficult to demonstrate, because it would have affected the *manner* of presenting motifs as much as the motifs themselves.[18] Such a control of process would have required an organization or an ideology for which there is, to my knowledge, no evidence in the social history of the time.[19]

THE THOUGHTS and queries inspired by the rapid observation of a few examples of ceramics and woodwork from Iraq, Iran, and Egypt can be summarized, at least temporarily, into the following statement. In the ninth century and those immediately following, the Muslim world created forms that are not mimetic representations, yet are usually defined by contemporary scholars in mimetic terms. Furthermore, their synchronic (time- and place-bound and, therefore culturally specific) and diachronic (timeless but evolving and universal) meanings vary considerably inasmuch as there is no way to demonstrate how these images were understood in their time or whether our own contemporary explanations and even descriptions are accurate for the past. But it is possible to go even further. We could see a bird or a fish without knowing whether one was intended and we could see pious writing as a colorful formal game, as a metaphor for something or other, or as the mystical expression of a truth. In various permutations, such legitimate and occasionally incompatible interpretations will surface more than once in the pages that follow. What is important at this stage is simply to acknowledge the apparent paradox of forms with a tenuous and at times debatable relationship to outside referents. How is all of this possible?

Traditionally two concepts and two sets of terms were attached—as they still are—to the phenomenon I have been describing. One is abstraction and the other is ornament or decoration, two words frequently used as synonymous, although they should be understood differently.[20] All these terms exist as nouns and adjectives. They also exist as verbs, but the verbs are not as clear as the nouns or the adjectives. "To abstract" does not simply mean to modify something by making it schematic, as in the celebrated sequence of bulls so brilliantly sketched by Picasso (figs. 13 and 14),[21] even though some

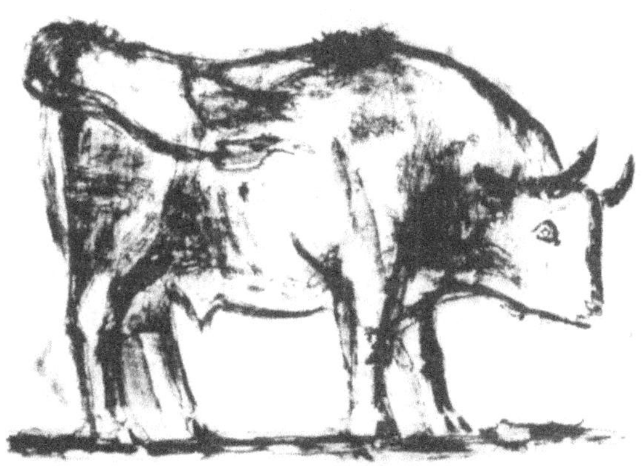

Fig. 13. Pablo Picasso, *The Bull,* first state, lithograph. Washington, D.C., National Gallery of Art, Ailsa Mellon Bruce Fund, 1982.

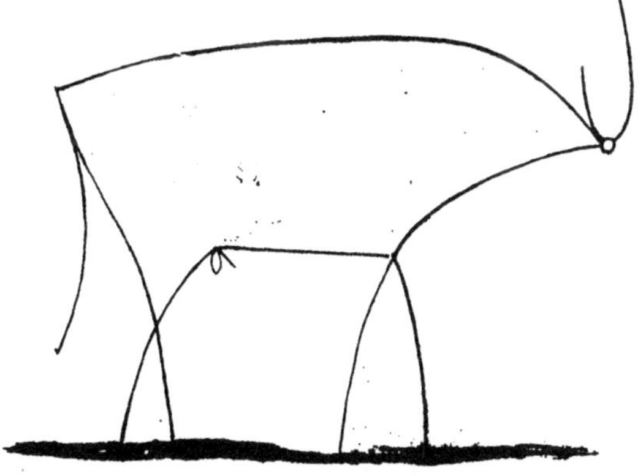

Fig. 14. Pablo Picasso, *The Bull,* eleventh state, lithograph. Washington, D.C., National Gallery of Art, Ailsa Mellon Bruce Fund, 1982.

of the transformations we saw in the early Islamic examples may be imagined as summarized simplifications of a fuller original just like Picasso's. The verb "to stylize" may be more appropriate, but its exact meaning is nebulous, except in the sense of generalizing in a consistent manner from a concrete and differentiated reality, as when Modigliani creates "stylized" versions of upper-class women during the early part of this century.[22] "To ornament" or, better, "to decorate" are verbs with clearer meanings, but they imply the act of putting something on something else rather than describe the nature of what is put.

It is easy enough to give up on the word "abstract" and its derivatives.[23] Its first and simpler definition, as in the *Oxford English Dictionary*, is "separated from matter, practice, or particulars; ideal; abstruse," and in Webster's dictionary it is "considered apart from any application to a particular object or specific instance; separated from embodiment." However one is to interpret these phrases (and the differences between them) in logic or in semantics, they are not appropriate to my purpose, because the historian of art always talks about something that *is* embodied, be it only through the material of its creation, and because our concern has so far been not to exclude something from experience but to understand how it operates within it. An example consists in the series of lines and dots that form the plan or even the section of a building (see fig. 148). A plan is an abstraction in the terms of the simple definitions I have quoted, but it is also the expression of a very concrete building and I shall deal at some length with this problem in one of the subsequent chapters.[24] Except for extremists in schools of architecture who have been known to worship a plan for its own sake, it is the building behind the plan that interests most people and historians.[25]

Thus, the first and simplest definition of the word "abstract" may be appropriate only to the extent that there are indeed instances of forms removed from the specifics of a model through a process of simplification or of alteration. Abstraction, in this sense, becomes one of many possible attributes or avatars of a form. Picasso's celebrated sequence of endlessly simplified bulls (figs. 13, 14) would be an example of this sort of simple abstraction. A pattern like the ninth-century one found in the ruins of the new city of Samarra north of Baghdad and known as Samarra III (fig. 15) is another example. The possible sequence of transformations of floral patterns that led to it have disappeared and it itself is best defined in terms of tension between light and shade or line and volume or else through general words like symmetry, repetitiveness, infinity, and so on. Since the experiments that led to Samarra III are no longer available, we may have to assume the kind of arbitrary yet

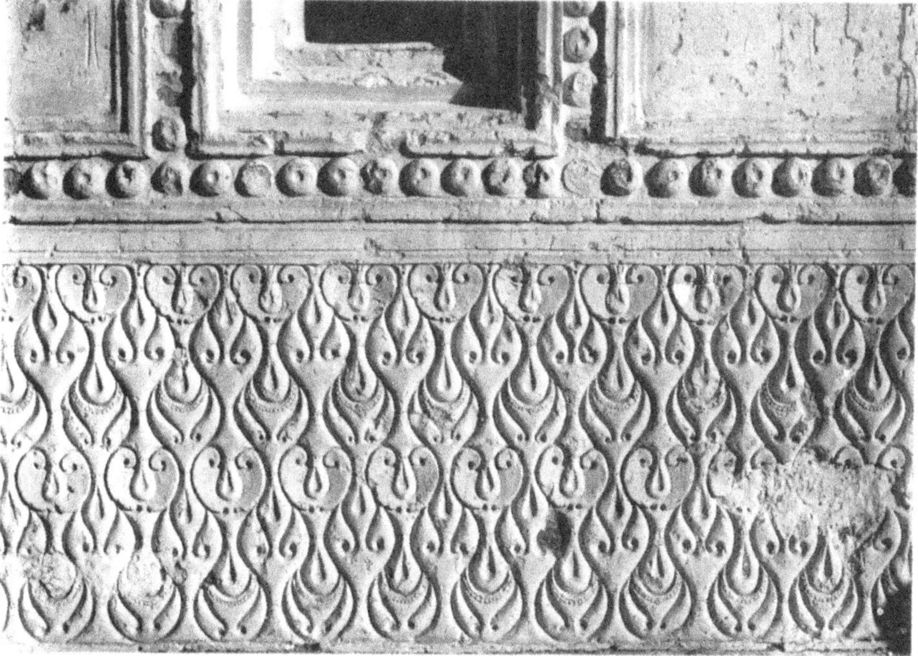

Fig. 15. Samarra, Iraq, palace of Balkuwara, stucco wall covering, ninth century.

mechanical process of simplification illustrated by Picasso. In any event, abstraction is not, in any of these instances, an explanation. To say that the bird from Egypt (fig. 1) or the fish in a northeastern Iranian ceramic (fig. 10) are abstract or stylized may be telling the truth but a useless truth, because the fact itself neither explains the form nor my reading of it. It is only in dealing with architecture that, as we shall see later on, the analysis of this type of abstraction as simplified rendering of a reality may be considered to have been productive for the consideration of meaning in certain types of forms.

The second meaning of the word "abstract" found in dictionaries is directly connected to the visual world. Its long version found in the unabridged Webster's deserves a ministudy on its own right, as it was affected by concrete intellectual or ideological positions of our time.[26] Its shorter form in the Webster's Abridged goes as follows: "having only intrinsic form with little or no attempt at pictorial representation or narrative content." Once again the definition is a negative one, but it is also clear that it is chronospecific—that is, directly affected by its time, as it derives from the development of western European painting since the beginning of the twentieth century, or a decade earlier. At that time artists from several countries consciously created forms that bore little direct resemblance to the commonly experienced world. Many of them, like Kandinsky and Mondrian, saw spiritual values in these forms, and therefore attributed abstract qualities to abstract designs, at times even using the word itself to refer to their paintings. Others, like Barnett Newmann, Jackson Pollock, or Mark Rothko, occasionally entitled their paintings through numbers, thereby acknowledging something of the arbitrariness of their works and certainly asserting their remoteness from the world of mimetic representation. But just as often, they provided their paintings with titles that strike by their concreteness more strongly than the paintings themselves, thus introducing a confusing ambiguity for the viewer. But, then, confusion or ambiguity is part of the message of the picture.[27]

One is tempted to seek in the art of our own times verbal pronouncements from contemporary artists and critics that could provide elements for a terminology to consider abstract forms and their processes everywhere and at any time. But, in reality, the contemporary experience is bound to the questions, anxieties, ideologies, and economics of the twentieth century. It is dangerous to use that experience to explain the past or areas removed from western Europe and America, just as it is often disingenuous to claim that contemporary art discovered or rediscovered values hidden in other or earlier artistic traditions. It is, however, true that we look at the past with today's sensitivity and that we feel and understand contemporary creativity through whatever knowledge or sense of the past has been lodged in us. The pursuit of *that* particular contradiction will not be central to my discourse in these essays, because it derives from another experience than that of the Islamic art of centuries back. In any deeper exploration of our perceptions of art, its further investigation is essential.[28] In the meantime, the word "abstract" should simply be capitalized and restricted to a contemporary movement—at best used only as a temporary lexical purgatory for otherwise nameless motifs as suggested by the first definition of the word. For it is probably all right to say that something "separated from matter, practice, or particulars" is abstract until one discovers that it is really connected to a specific subject.

Let us turn to the terms "ornament" and "decoration." Much has been written about ornament since the early decades of the nineteenth century, as every one of the thinkers, educators, and creators involved in all the arts except perhaps canvas painting had to develop a position or a doctrine on whatever was considered ornament. Ornament played an essential part in the debates surrouning the formation of schools for the industrial, applied, or decorative arts. In their own very different ways, Owen Jones, William Morris, John Ruskin, Carl Semper, Viollet-le-Duc, and Alois Riegl all contributed passionate statements about ornament and, in a far more academic fashion, the echo of these statements permeates and weakens Sir Ernest Gombrich's long and learned treatment of ornament with the programmatic title of *The Sense of Order*. Twentieth-century architects and architectural historians also confronted decoration in which, during the previous century, Ruskin, Viollet-le-Duc, and a less well known German philosophical esthetic tradition going back to Kant and Hegel saw the inner spirit of what they used to call the races of mankind. Architectural modernism rejected the very idea of ornament with passionate vehemence and postmodernists brought it back, frequently as a mere toy to amuse themselves and the spectators around them.[29]

Eventually, in the concluding chapter, I will respond to some of the positions taken over the past two centuries with respect to an ever present and yet so elusive ornament. But, as the approach I am developing is not a historiographic one but a more pragmatic and immediate one dealing with actual practice and immediate observation, it seems more useful to deal initially with the term "ornament" in a more basic, more direct, fashion. In the *Encyclopedia of the Arts*, a standard statement of generally accepted verities, ornament "refers to motifs and themes used . . . without being essential to structure and serviceability, . . . [but] for the purpose of embellishment." The contrast is clear between structure and function, on the one hand, and embellishment on the other, with ornament connected to the expression of the latter but not to the former. Paintings are excluded from most of these definitions, as though a "Virgin and Child" escapes the need for embellishment or the intention of it. Perhaps only a still life may be arbitrary enough to be decoration and, therefore, beautiful. Something is clearly wrong with this and nearly all definitions of ornament found in manuals of art, as they simultaneously imply the secondary side of ornament and, almost as a result of that, its singular and exclusive attribute of beauty.

IT IS INTERESTING to note that the terms "ornament" and "decoration" or their derivatives have been used as literary metaphors or have unusual etymological relations. A wise medieval Jewish saying from the Book of Ben Sirach goes as follows: "A mind settled on an intelligent thought is like the stucco decoration on the wall of a colonnade."[30] The contemplation of something intelligent is compared to what makes a wall beautiful, that is something plastered on it, in a technique prevalent in Iraq whence the saying probably came. Decoration seems to complete an object, a wall or a person, by providing it with quality. In classical Arabic *adab* literature, literary theory, or practice, words like *naqqasha* ("to cover with decoration" in many different techniques), *zawaqa* ("to embellish"), and especially *istiʿara* ("to use metaphorically") have different meanings dealing with artistic or esthetic practice or description; all are positive in their judgment and all imply effective completion and even transfer of meanings from one form to the other.[31]

A related but much more complicated development occurs around the Sanskrit word *bhusati*, which means "to adorn." It too implies the successful completion of an act, of an object, or even of a state of mind or soul. In being applied to the adornment of women, it means the prosperity of the male head of a family or of a household. For a king in battle, the word denotes the sound and sight of his victory, just as it can be an attribute of copulation, which perfects a union in creating life. And, in a most beautiful image, the moon is the adornment of the night, because, without it, the night is incomplete.[32]

The point of all these verbal or metaphysical examples is the apparent agreement, in several highly literate and articulate societies, on the existence of an action that completes something, that makes it perfect. That action is to decorate and the medium of its effectiveness is ornament, independent from but essential to the expression of the action or of the reality. Thus the generalization of the contemporary esthetician writing for the general public and the specifics of cultural contexts as different as medieval Judaism and traditional India both identify ornament as bringing beauty to whatever it adorns, as though this particular attribute was lacking until some last moment of creation. Ornament is, to coin a word, exclusively *calliphoric*; it carries beauty with it.

And yet, in a disquieting passage, the urbane Bassanio from Shakespeare's troubling *The Merchant of Venice* argues, before choosing the casket with Portia's portrait, that "[Thus] ornament is but the guiled shore / To a most dangerous sea; the beauteous scarf / Veiling an Indian beauty; in a word, / *The seeming truth* which cunning times put on / To entrap the wisest." Earlier in the same monologue (act 3, scene 2), he said: "The world is still deceived with ornament / . . . There is no vice so simple but assumes / Some mark of virtue on his outward parts." The beauty and attractiveness of ornament are fully acknowledged, but so is its surfacelike superficiality, its impermanence, and ultimately its evil.

A third verbal example is equally unsettling. Le Corbusier relates that one of his teachers used to preach that "only Nature is inspiring and true," and that one must "penetrate" it, "make a synthesis of it by creating ornamentation." Ornament is like a microcosm of nature and physical reality.[33]

It is not, at this stage, appropriate to debate these statements. What is pertinent is to realize that Shakespeare, a man of the word, makes ethical judgments through the guise of ornament, thus implying, correctly as I shall argue at the end of this series of essays, that morality is never far away from beauty or pleasure. In far less poetical ways and less directly implying ornament, tenth-century humanists from Baghdad, seventeenth-century French architects, or contemporary theologians from Tehran argue the same point of art and beauty as evil, while some Persian mystics saw them as an appearance of the divine.[34]

As so often with verbal reasoning about the arts, the fascination with philosophical or even poetic discourses hides the fact that they rarely help in dealing with individual works of art. As will be evident more than once in the course of these essays, one of the main expectations of words on the history and criticism of art is that they contribute to the understanding of works of art, not merely that they be a sort of poetic or pedantic gloss over them. In order to reach these results, a dialogue must constantly be established with objects and monuments. Let us consider then a few well-known examples of monuments and ask what in them should be considered ornament and especially why are some features so identified.

A first example is the thirteenth-century facade of the cathedral of Amiens (fig. 16). Since my concern is not one of historical connoisseurship but of attitude to what is seen, and inasmuch as I have already alluded to the differences in perception between the time of creation and the moment of viewing, the extensive nineteenth-century restorations are not pertinent to the remarks that follow. The structural skeleton of stone is transfigured, on the facade, by life-size statues (fig. 17), narratives of holy history, local stories, moralizing references, plants, buildings, animals, gargoyles, and even geometric designs, as under the feet of the standing Christ (fig. 18). This decoration, unnecessary to the maintenance of the building or to the celebration of the liturgy, can be read from many different points of view, whether examined as excerpted segments glued on the facade or as a single visual program. It can be seen as grandiose theological statements of a vision of Christianity, as a very local interpretation of the faith in action, as the joyful labor of artists, as chronological sequences of styles, as a form of social and economic domination, and in many other ways as well.[35] But, regardless of the way one chooses, there remains on the facade of the cathedral a hierarchy in the intensity of visual presentation, whereby the apostles in the central west portal (fig. 18) are more forcefully imposed on the viewer than the labors of the month in low relief below them or the lively floral ornament presented at times with acrobatically mauled personages on their pedestals (fig. 18). It is not simply

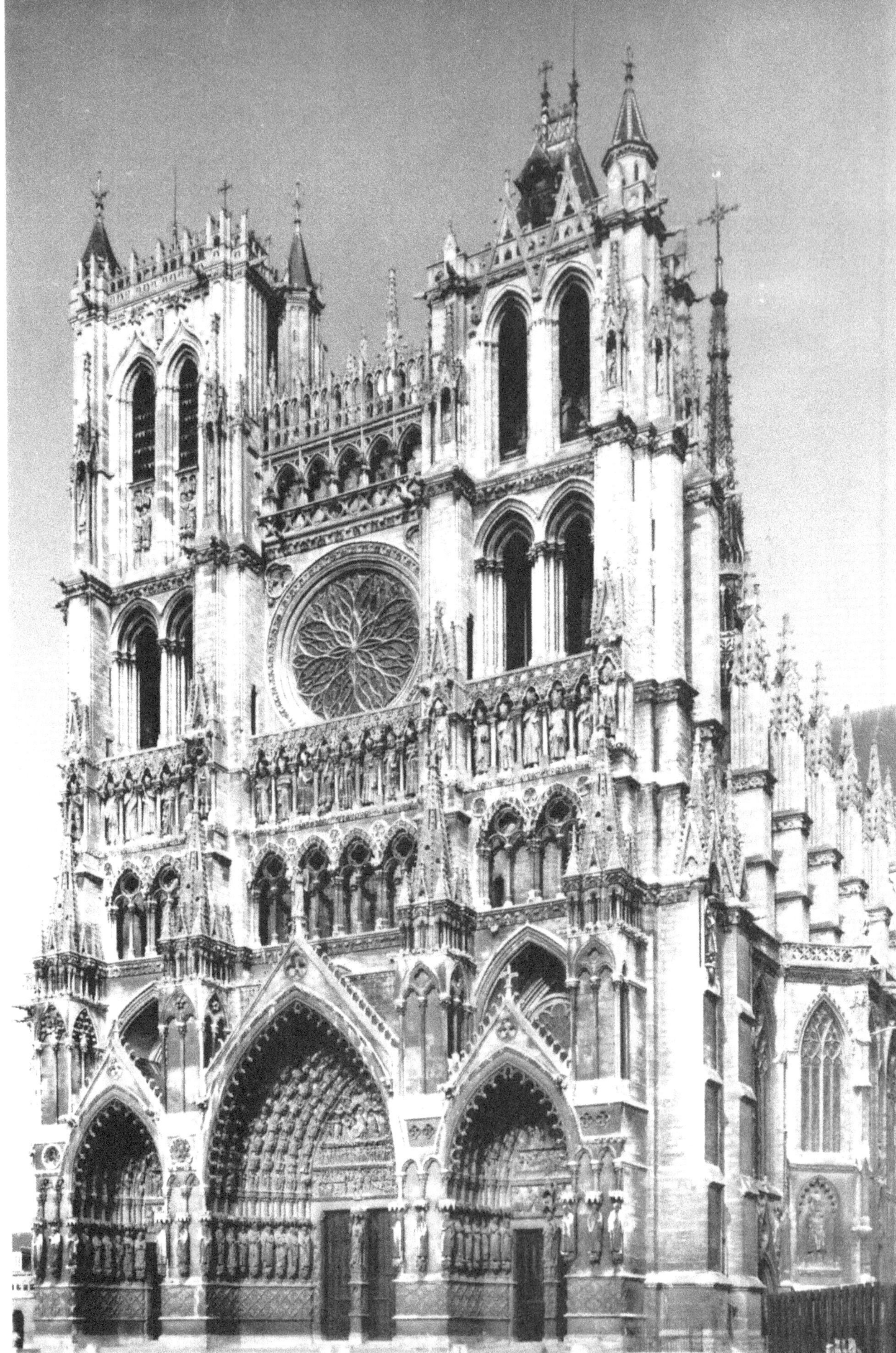

Fig. 16. Amiens, cathedral, thirteenth century, west facade.

Fig. 17. Amiens, cathedral, thirteenth century, west facade, central portal.

Fig. 18. Amiens, cathedral, thirteenth century, west facade, central portal, right side.

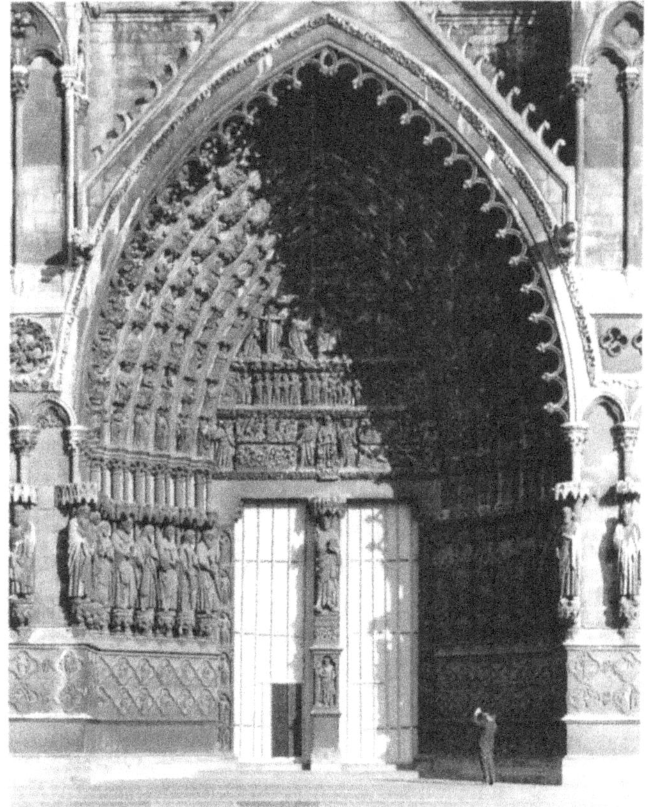

17

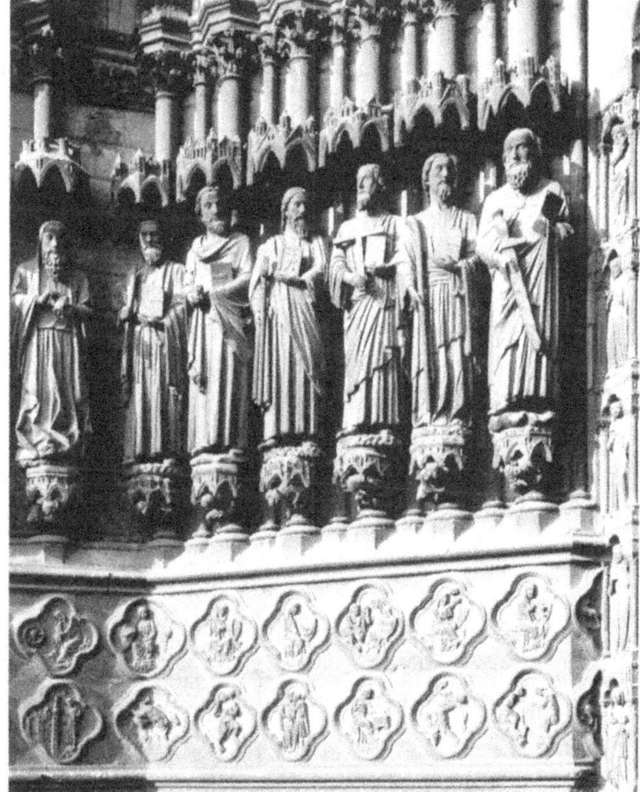

18

the absence or presence of external referents— that is to say, of signs in the memory of viewers identifying Saint Peter among apostles and a Nativity as different from a birth scene—that separates one kind of decoration from another. What may be called the muscular structure of the decorative program is also involved.

The relative size of decorations, the degree of relief, the actual location of different kinds of motifs, and other such organizational or compositional characteristics are attributes of a work of art that are logically independent of the subject matter, yet which allow the viewer to identify, among other things, a hierarchy of importance in the use of motifs and in the shape of designs. Like the muscles of a body, these attributes manipulate the subject depicted *and* the perception of the viewer. There are, of course, perfectly valid theological and religious reasons for apostles to be nearly life-size, three-dimensional sculptures jutting out of the portal, while the narrative illustrations of the labors of the month are in low relief and the delicacy of floral tracery in windows is hardly visible (fig. 19), but these differences are also made visible to those who are not attuned to thirteenth-century Christianity in northern Europe by the manipulation of other attributes than iconographic or cultural ones.

This point could be made for nearly every major monument. It is true of the Sistine Chapel where different sizes of available spaces create a formal hierarchy regardless of the iconographic or expressive content given to these various areas. It is also true of Benvenuto Cellini's salver (fig. 20), where a whole range of types of relief exists. At this stage I am only arguing that the hierarchy exists, not that certain motifs—plants, for instance, or people—tend to be at one end or the other of the level of charge that can be given to forms.

The celebrated Roman altar known as the Ara Pacis seems to have two realms neatly separated by a dry fret (figs. 21, and 22). One is focused on an imperial procession with men, women, and children marching in a disorderly and individualized way. Some of them can, through comparison with contemporary representations on other media, be identified as members of the imperial family of Augustus. Several allegories with fairly obvious and common subjects are also part of this realm dominated by images of people. The second level below has more or less the same height and consists in rich compositions of stems and leaves with an occasional bird thrown in for no immediately apparent reason (fig. 22). The perception of this vegetation does not lead automatically to references in nature then or now but at best to other similar vegetal designs for comparisons of style and of quality. It is, of course,

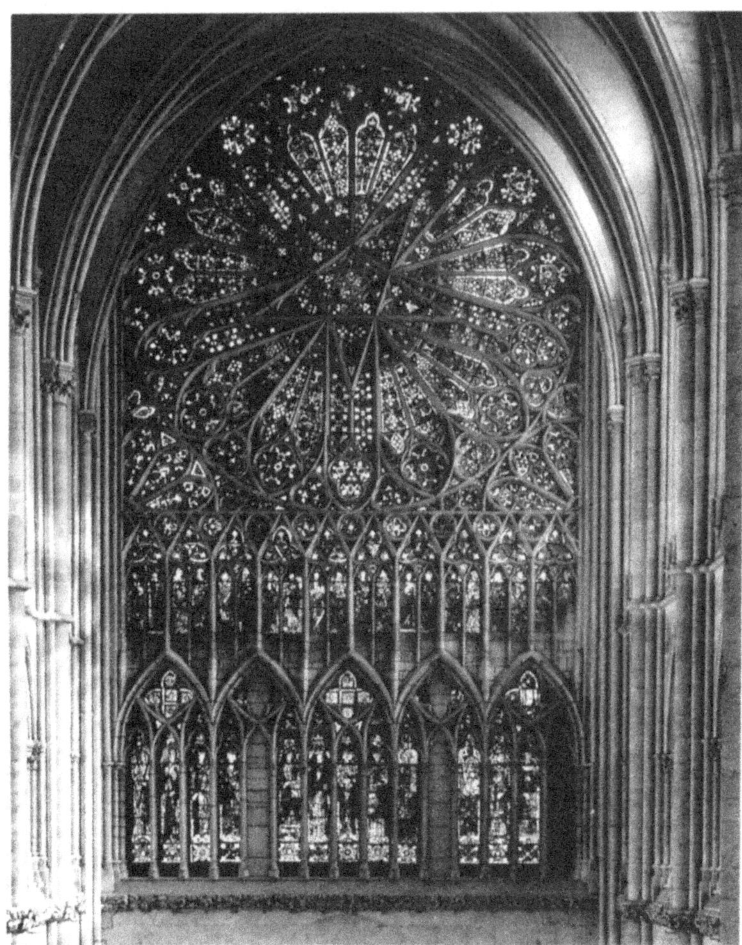

Fig. 19. Amiens, cathedral, thirteenth century, west facade, tracery on windows.

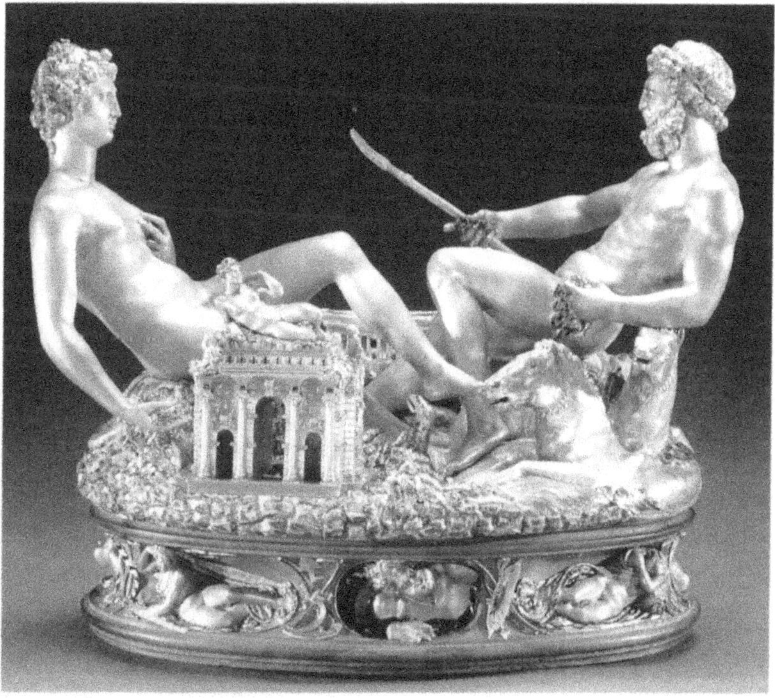

Fig. 20. Benvenuto Cellini, Salver, 1539–1543. Vienna, Kunsthistorische Museum, inv. no. 881.

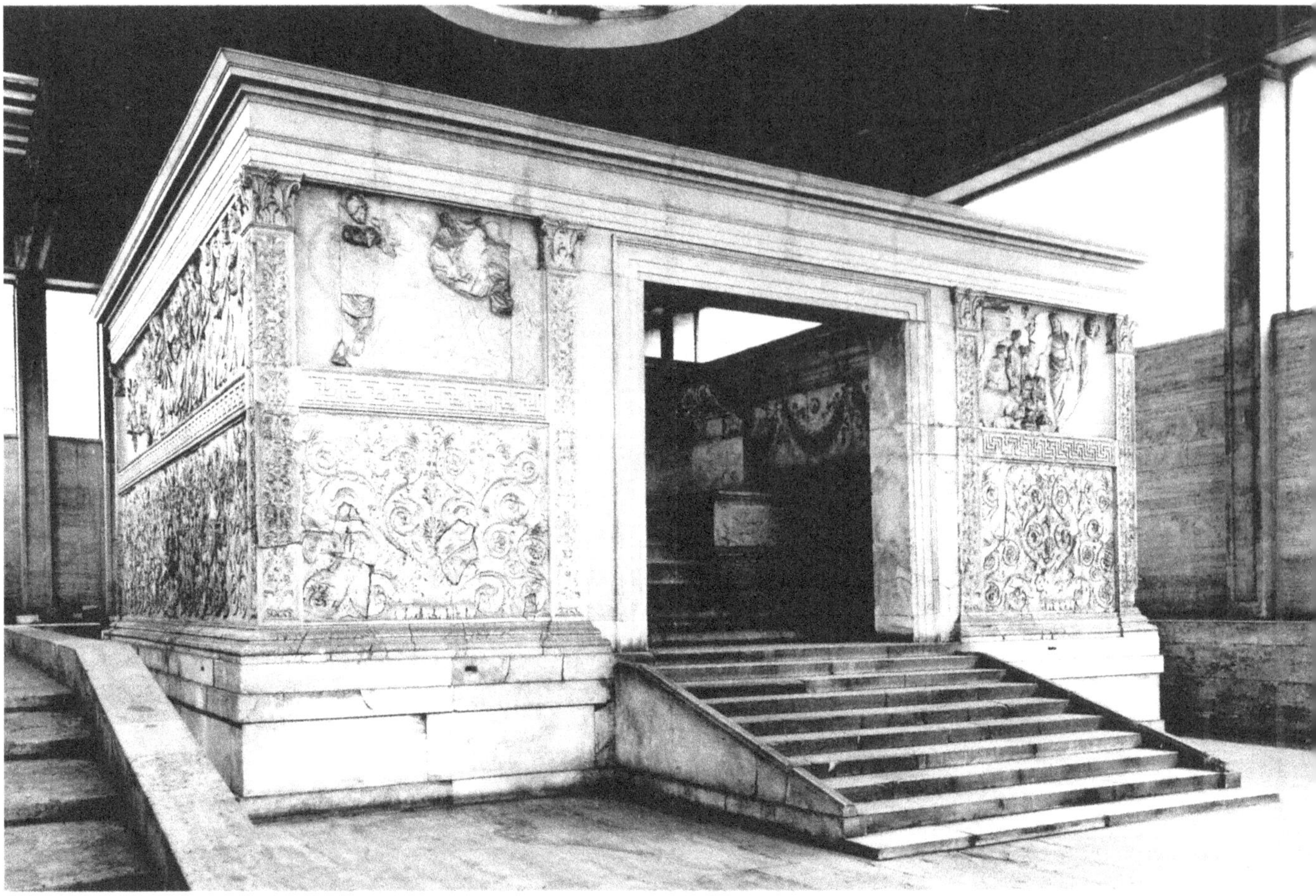

Fig. 21. Rome, Ara Pacis,
first century A.D.,
general view.

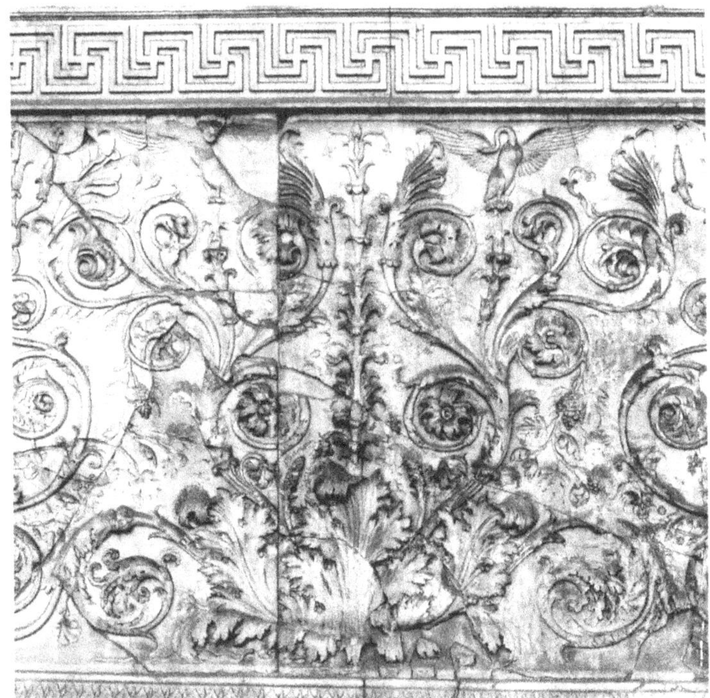

Fig. 22. Rome, Ara Pacis,
first century A.D.,
detail.

true that in recent years an iconographic explanation has been provided for this vegetation. It represents, so it is argued, the harmonious peace and the overall bounty created by the reign of Augustus. Plants like the elegant acanthus leaves and birds like the superb cranes in the vegetation are seen as references to or symbols of ceremonies and ethnic or other identifications.[36] All of this may well be true, at least in the convoluted minds of the altar's designers (or of the scholars of today), but it is difficult not to feel that the procession and the allegories above belong to a different order of meaning from the order with which the vegetal design below should be associated. By suggesting for the vegetal realm a precision of meaning reasonable for the realm of people, contemporary interpreters may have transferred one order of meaning to a realm that does not lend itself to that particular order. Perhaps classical scholarship, so steeped in meanings, hidden or overt, failed to deal with an ornamental realm in which esthetic values prevail. To this issue we shall return shortly. In the meantime, whatever the reason and even if partly contradicted by the cultural context, on the Ara Pacis two different and separate visual worlds are set next to each other.

Just about the opposite reasoning is usually made for the facade of Mshatta (figs. 23, 24), the celebrated unfinished palace of the middle of the eighth century located in contemporary Jordan, whose decor was removed to Berlin early in the twentieth century. There also partly geometricized vegetal patterns hide animals or objects, and iconographic interpretations have been proposed for some of them, although without great success.[37] There are no obvious and easily detectable human beings on Mshatta's facade, but on thirteenth-century inlaid metalwork (fig. 25), personages abound in the midst of vegetation or geometry and one can recognize standard representational sets, such as signs of the zodiac, princely activities, or labors of the month.[38] In these examples of early and medieval Islamic art, specificity of identifiable meaning through representations seems to have been overtaken by an ornament that makes these meanings less immediately accessible. One could, of course, argue that the context of an Islamic culture, uneasy with the very idea of representation, led to what could be called visual obfuscation, whereby a concrete message comparable in intensity to the procession of the Ara Pacis or to the apostles at the entrance of Amiens is being hidden in an ornamental pattern, with the intent that its intensity be diminished or only recognized by those who, as our bureaucracy puts it, need to know. Ornament in these examples from Islamic art would be a sort of cultural thermostat regulating the power and therefore the effectiveness of a visual message, but the message is still present and has the same intrinsic meaning as have the apostles in

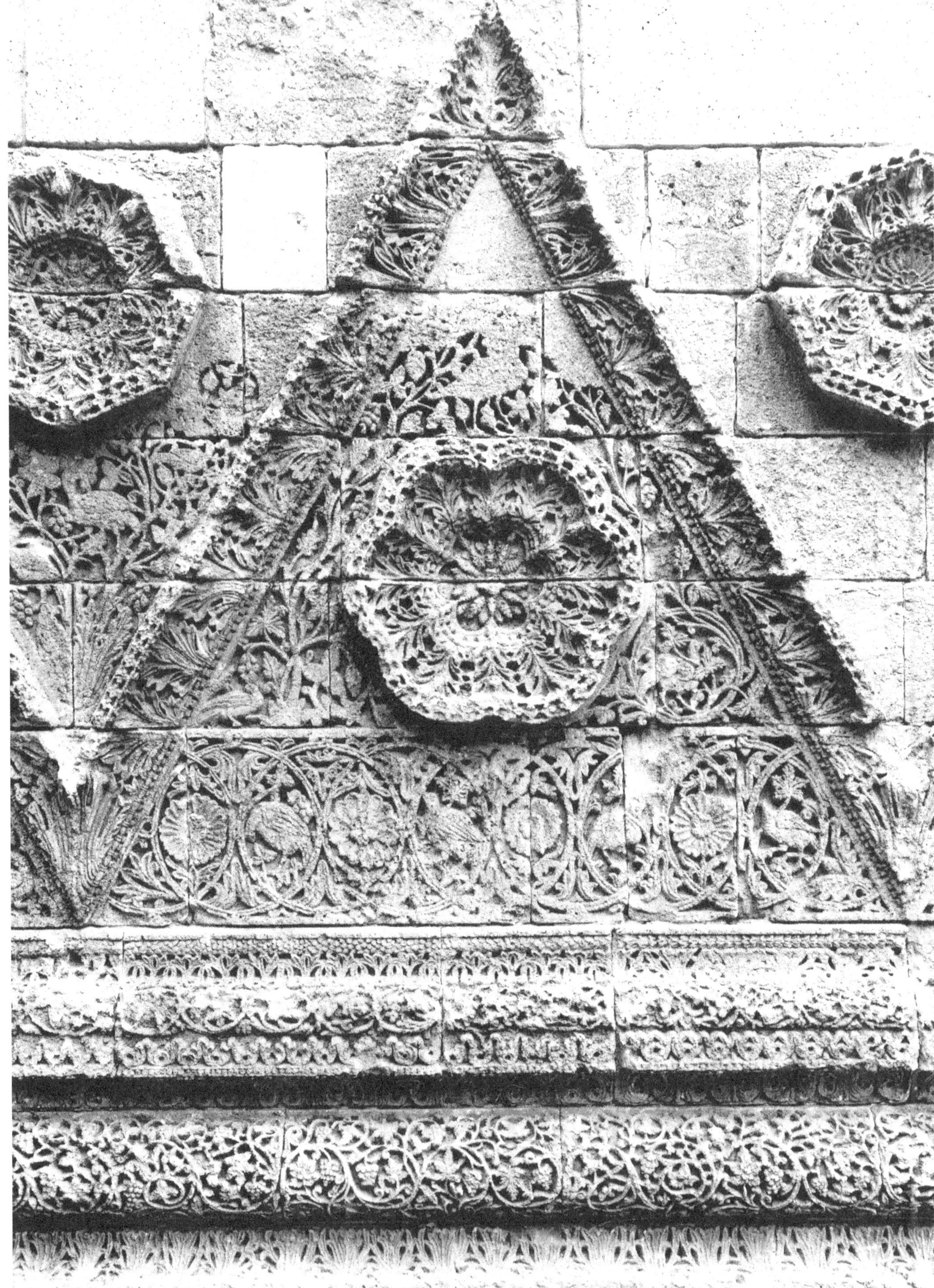

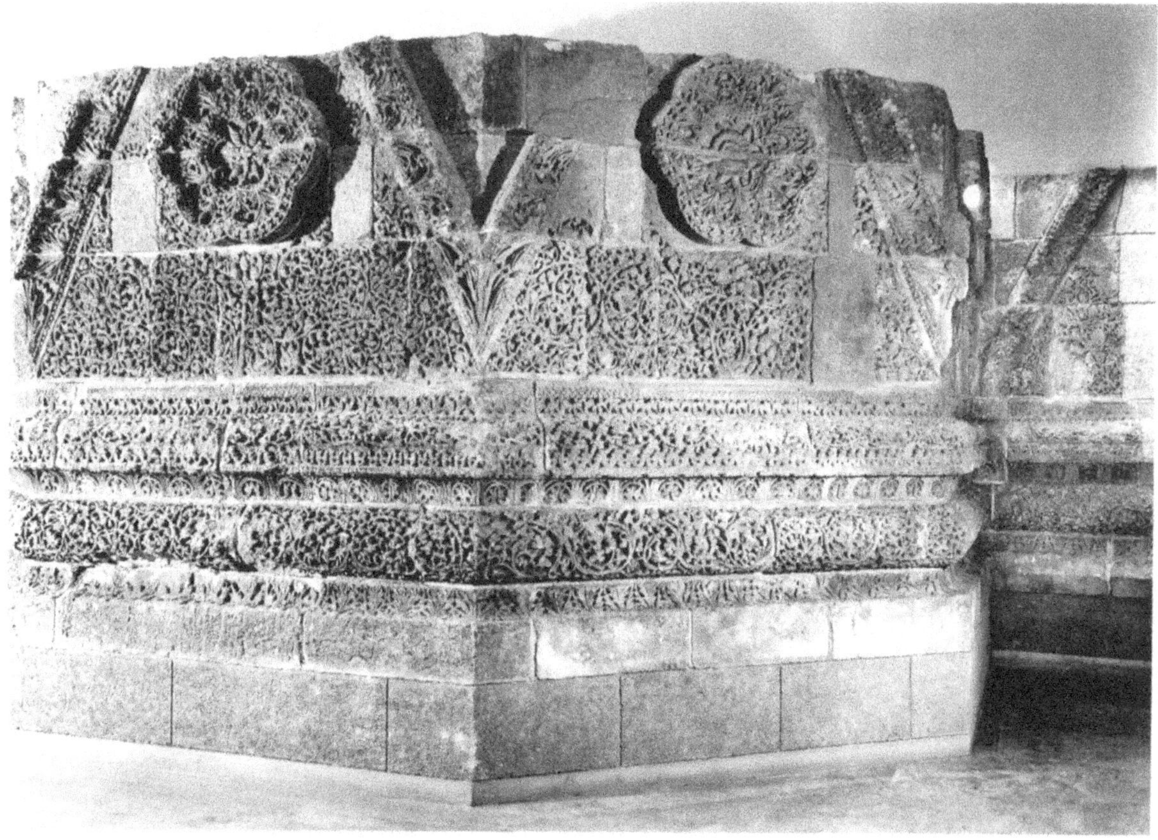

Fig. 24. Mshatta, palace, eighth century, base of frieze.

Fig. 23. Mshatta, palace, eighth century, decorative triangle.

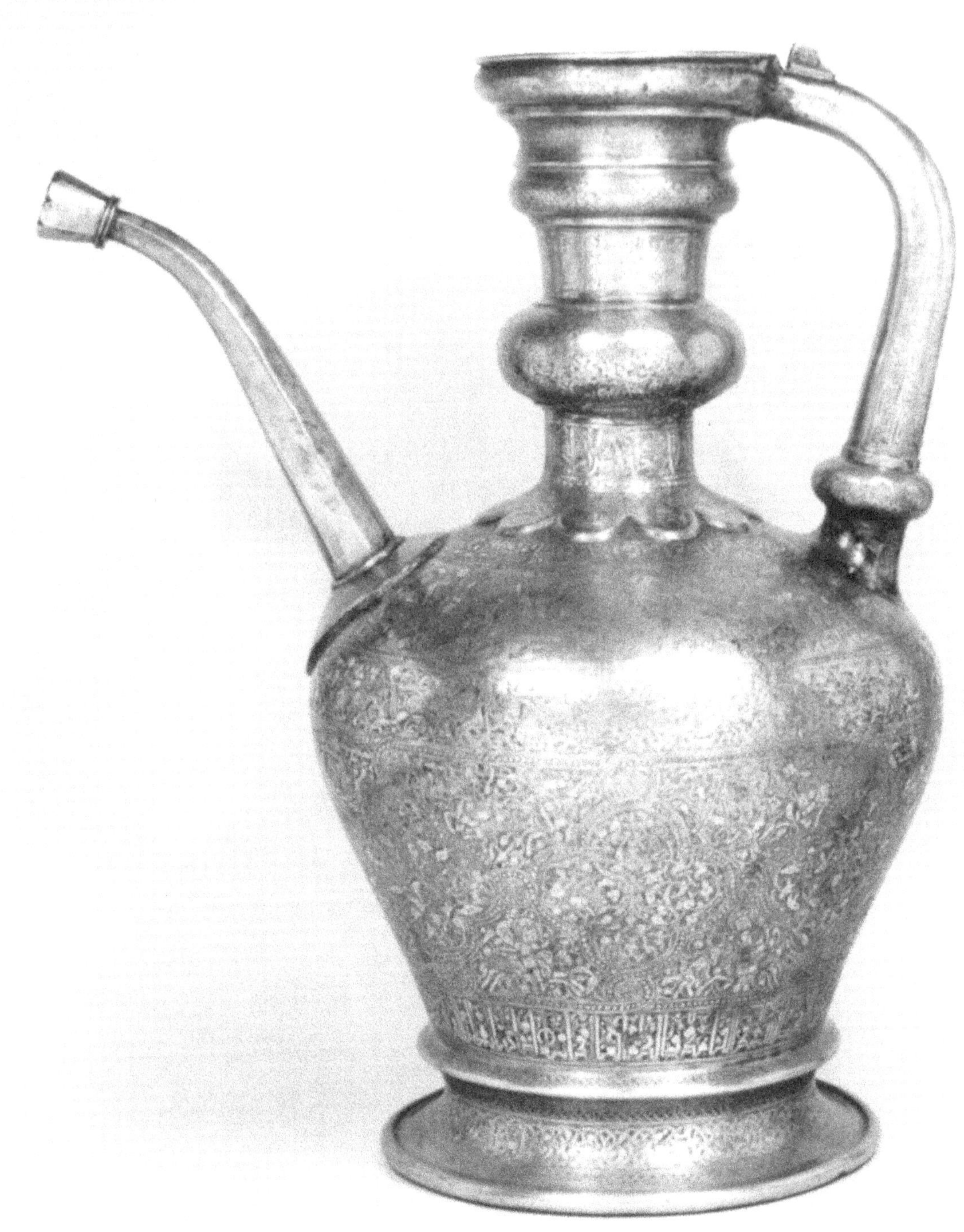

Fig. 25. Ewer, silver inlaid bronze, 1226–1227, signed by Ahmad b. ʿUmar al-Dhakki. New York, Metropolitan Museum of Art, acc. no. 91.1.586.

Amiens. And in an example like Mshatta's we simply have not learned to understand the message in the mass of signs thrown all over the facade. Or, possibly, there was no iconographic message and the ornament was there for its own sake. It alone carries its own message and, since we are unlikely to get fascinated by grapes or pine cones for their own sake, some other purpose, ambition, or expectation has to be acknowledged for the Mshatta facade. The only logical one is that it was meant to attract by providing what, since Plato, has been recognized as a central result of dealing with the arts—that is, *pleasure*. The ornament of Mshatta is *terpnopoietic*, a neologism to mean "providing pleasure," and, until the contrary is proved, this is all it is.

We may by now have moved forward a bit in the sense that what written documents have allowed us to call a "carrier of beauty" is now explained through the pleasure it provides. This conclusion is in part a circular one, as it simply argues that beauty provokes pleasure or pleasure can be acquired from beauty, a point made by nearly every philosopher of art and by nearly every practitioner. Even if one agrees that a theory of pleasure includes much more than agreeable satisfaction, my more immediate point is slightly different: to argue that some monuments are exclusively harbingers of pleasure does not really explain them but only identifies a reaction to them. More important for my purposes, it does not explain how ornament differs from nonornament, as the conclusion seems to apply equally well to all forms of decoration, to nearly anything that we call art.

All we know then is that ornament is not a motif nor is it a manner of presenting motifs, although it could be both. It can include representations and nonrepresentations. It may be the result of an attitude of the viewer or of a decision by an artist. In short, it is perhaps too vague a term, at least at this preliminary level of investigation, for the themes and designs whose operation I seek to elucidate, because it is used simultaneously for a type of design, a process of working, and a final result. As we looked at individual objects, however, in all cases the need arose to define two kinds of information: what are the visual attributes of a given artifact, both the topics it contains and what I called its musculature; and how does one define their meaning, through something provided by the object or by the memory of the user.

The difficulty of using the term "ornament" is further increased by looking at two of the most common or most used statements on ornament: their grammar, styles, or dictionaries and their philosophical interpretation.

Grammars and dictionaries are for the most part lists of designs with appropriately drawn plates (fig. 26) arranged either simply typologically (vegetal, geometric, calligraphic, and so on) or culturally *and* topologically

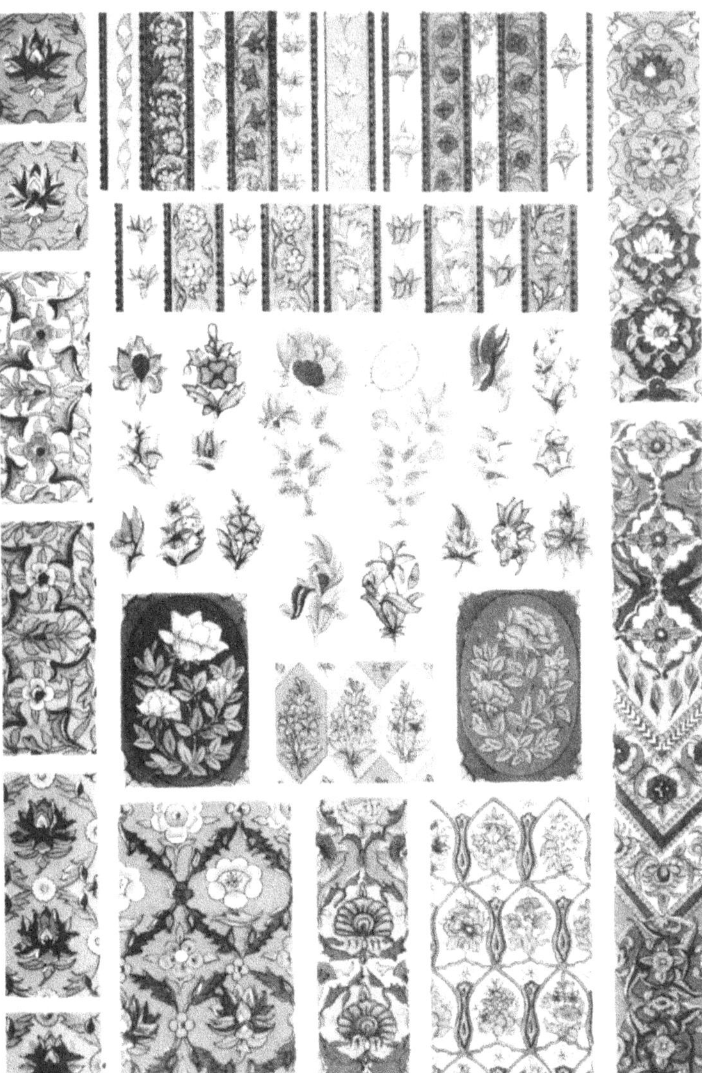

Fig. 26. Table of ornamental designs.

(English, French, Chinese, baroque).[39] Typological definitions by geometric figure or floral origin are descriptive and relatively free of value judgments. They are excellent resources for any designer seeking inspiration, but their only real usefulness to the historian or to the critic is that of providing *the* correct or *a* correct name for some foliage or for a sequence of circles and squares. Typological and cultural definitions are, at first glance, innocuous enough, as nothing seems less threatening than "Mexican fret" or "Persian faience scrollwork." In fact, however, the perusal of plates in Speltz's *Styles of Ornament*, not to speak of discussions by Ruskin, Viollet-le-Duc, Riegl, or Strzygowski, brings into ornament an ideological content that is at times quite virulent. National (Persian) or cultural (Moorish or Islamic) names for ornamental designs are not simply indicative for classification purposes, they imply certain national or racial, occasionally cultural, judgments and values. Such arguments were an accepted part of thinking about art at the turn of the century. Their inappropriateness in our own time is due in part to the possibly temporary, even if justified, diffidence with which we attribute formal qualities to ethnic or national entities.[40] But it is mostly that an explanation of the origins of a motif rarely justifies its presence on any one monument or object, except at times of conscious revivals or of ideological statements tainted with historicism, which have been studied in Western art at great length but which are certainly present everywhere, as one tries to understand the operation of building or of making objects.[41] The study of origins in the manner of Riegl, for instance, who genuinely felt the presence of permanent visual qualities attached to ethnic culture, is not so much premature as it is irrelevant to anything but an abstract fascination with etymologies, unless one shares the historicism behind it.[42]

The philosophical commentaries on ornament are more productive. Three approaches can derive from the more thoughtful essays among them.

The first approach is not one I shall pursue in these chapters. Inspired originally by Riegl, it was used by the first major generation of collectors and curators of Islamic art, including E. Kuhnel, M. Dimand, and G. Flury, and sometimes misused by J. Strzygowski. This approach sees ornament primarily as a diagnostic tool for the elaboration of a monument's pedigree.[43] As in the principles developed by Morelli for attributions and dating,[44] ornament is the detail in which every worker is trained, so that his cultural signature is bound to appear in whatever he does, wherever he goes. It is easy enough to parody and to scoff at an art history that saw in ornamental details stirring cultural and racial connections identifying the presence of workers from one area in another area and therefore contributing to the pernicious vision of the history of art as a bundle of influences.[45] This sort of reasoning bears, I believe, too little relationship to historical reality to need pursuing, although contemporary nationalism may well return to it.

A second approach, eloquently and beautifully illustrated in some of Ruskin's most evocative pages, can be put in somewhat different terms from his. Ornament is to be recognized and praised because it shows (or can show) the pleasure of work. "I believe the right question to ask," writes Ruskin, "respecting all ornament is simply this. Was it done with enjoyment—was the carver happy while he was about it?"[46] The question can obviously not be answered by a scholar, only by a poet or a moralist, perhaps by an artist. But Ruskin's approach does imply that ornament and its perception lead to a sense of what is beautiful and of what is good. Esthetics and ethics are, once again, automatically the issues of ornament, whereas painters and sculptors obfuscate the Beautiful and Good with distracting subjects or idiosyncratic styles. Ornament on objects produced by artisans and on monuments of architecture, on the other hand, is what gives value to the buildings or practical artifacts on which it is found. Labor, cost, and usefulness predominated in the creation of ornament. All three have a human component independent of what is being produced, but the propriety of handling craftsmen, the appropriateness of spending money, and the actual practice of ornament lead to one conclusion. It is that the perception we have of its motifs requires that beauty and morality become the appropriate, in fact almost exclusive, categories for analysis and judgment.

The point that visual impressions of surfaces occasionally lead to the moral evaluation of whatever or whoever bears those surfaces is easy to demonstrate from daily experience. We reject and dismiss ties or dresses much more readily and easily than paintings and other ordained works of art, and we are far more likely to draw conclusions about the moral values of people from the clothes they wear or the interior decoration of their abodes than from their taste in art. The more exciting side to this sensory approach to ornament is its proclamation of joyful forms endowed with the gift of providing pleasure. It implies that decorative forms are alive, that they breathe more easily than ponderous statues and endless Madonnas. This joy permeates Ruskin's drawings and Focillon's "life of forms."[47] But, beyond its value as a first and immediate reaction to artistic forms, this kind of beautifully written outburst may be too personal to have more than inspirational value. It may help to love works of art, but does it explain anything?

The third approach, best demonstrated by Gombrich (although not necessarily with the same emphasis and for the same reasons as mine) avoids the taxonomy of forms as a purely lexical activity and identifies the practical effects of ornament.[48] To Gombrich, the main ones are framing, filling, and linking. These attributes, which are not exclusive, are certainly appropriate definitions of three common features of ornament. In addition, and more important, Gombrich identified ornament through processes in the relationships of maker and user to some object, a picture to be framed or a wall space to be covered. This process, as I understand it, was essential to Gombrich in providing the support needed for an appreciation of what is truly important about art, which is the nonornamental, that grand and grandiose recreation of the natural world that forms, at least within a mainstream art historical tradition, the major achievement of Western painting.

It is at this level that I part company with Gombrich's position. I do so only in part by rejecting the European-centered criticism of a vision of art based so exclusively on Western representations. Within the constraints of these essays, I do it primarily because, as I hope to have shown already indirectly, it is possible for an ornament to be *the* subject of the design. In fact, any artifact, Mshatta's facade (figs. 23, 24) or the Sistine Chapel, is to the viewer (but not necessarily to the maker) only ornamented surfaces until such time as other meanings are provided for them. In the meantime, they are not simply examples of "filling," since they were visibly the reason why a building or an object was made. There is a difference between "filling" a space with a design and transforming an object by covering all or parts of its surfaces with that design. In the first instance, the filling design has no other purpose than to partake of whatever uses its carrier has; in the second one, it can transform the very purpose of its carrier.

Ornament can make a utilitarian woven fabric into an elegant and sensuous rug (see fig. 186), but a similar design on a wallpaper or in a painting does not necessarily have the same effect, because, as I have tried to demonstrate with the facade at Amiens, the hierarchical location of a decorative motif may well modify its impact. One rug design becomes a minor iconographic or descriptive detail in a Dutch painting depicting it once or loses all sense when endlessly repeated on a wallpaper. In this hypothesis of a type of design without semantic charge, without specific and consistent meaning, ornament may only be ornament because of our ignorance, as meanings may well be hidden within delicate curlicues of vegetal scrolls and in animals cavorting amid flowers and leaves (see pls. 21–23).[49] In the world of Nuba body paintings (fig. 27),[50] brilliant geometric decoration is fraught with social and cultural meanings, and the piety of the Ethiopian makers and users of sacred

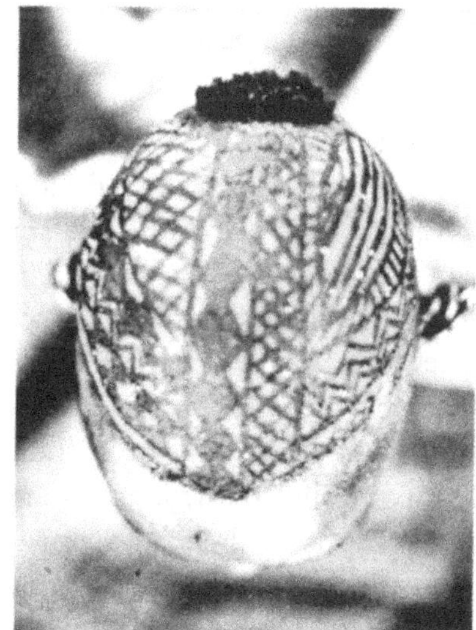

Fig. 27. Geometric painting on shaved head, Nuba culture of southern Sudan.

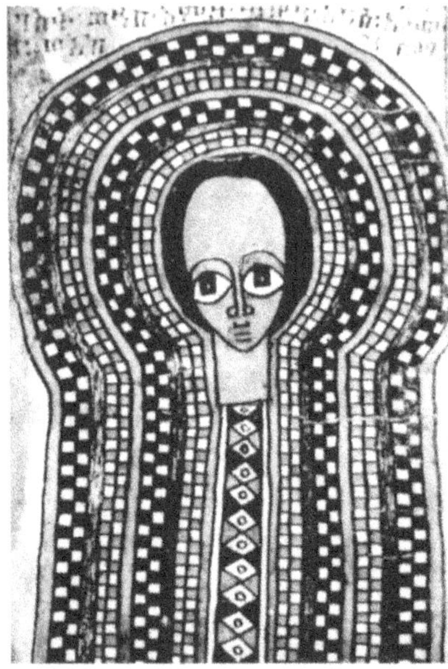

Fig. 28. Ethiopian popular images.

images (fig. 28) is not lessened by the apparent senselessness of their colorful designs.[51] It is indeed to the credit of Gombrich's work that processes of analysis and of creation took over from endless lists of design or from poetic trances, but the constriction of his interpretative sources to the written European, post-Renaissance tradition prevented him, I feel, from fully realizing the potential of his own approach.

My remarks so far began with the assumption that there is an order of forms called, usually indiscriminately, ornament or decoration and with the particular role played by Islamic art in the creation and especially the identification of such forms. Through the discussion of a few examples of early Islamic art I tried to show the logical ambiguities and the contradictions involved in the prevalent discourse on these or similar forms. Whatever thoughts and explanations are spun around words like "abstract" or "ornament" seem inadequate to handle the variety of experiences found in decoration. All that is reasonable to conclude so far is that decorative forms can sometimes be identified or described in terms of qualifying attributes like symmetry or simplification independent of their motifs, that more complex meanings may or may not be found in them, but that they definitely do (or at least are meant to) carry beauty and provide pleasure. To say this, however, is hardly helpful without knowing what beauty or pleasure is. Although there are difficulties in the theoretical presumptions and assumptions of the subject, the preceding remarks are not entirely useless as, in a more practical way, they suggest the presence of four levels or layers of interpretation in handling ornament.

One level is that of the motifs, life-size statues or vegetal scrolls, put on the surfaces of buildings and objects. These motifs appear to have, at least within the traditions of Western art, a set of hierarchies. One set has, at this stage, been defined through the existence or absence of an outside referent, of an external statement, which, in most cases, is something represented (a bird, a house, a circle) but need not be that. To the topical hierarchy assumed for motifs I have added a hierarchy of design or a musculature that, through relationships of size, location, and so forth, favors one motif over the other. Whereas the first hierarchy is independent of any one object or building, the second one is on the contrary only apparent in an artifact. Further reflection is likely to bring additional hierarchies to light.

This leads me to the second layer of suggestions emerging from my examples. Even if they can be made to coincide, it is essential to separate, at least analytically, the making of an object or a motif from its perception. In Gombrich's great and wonderful game of "making" and "matching,"[52] the issues are not as clear and simple as finding the "correct" meaning for a given form. For the historian, the critic, and the viewer have a degree of right to their own interpretation of someone else's work, and this interpretation need not be the same as the maker's or patron's. The very fact, for instance, of putting icons or other religious and liturgical objects in museums diminishes, perhaps even removes entirely, their original pious meaning, but maintains and even enhances their calliphoric and terpnopoietic values. And it is certainly possible, as has often been done, to appreciate profoundly and thoughtfully an image from a religious setting of which one is unaware or which one even abhors.

The example of icons is but one of many instances in which the discussion has constantly reached a third level of understanding the arts, a level in which ethical and esthetic values and purposes are involved. How they operate and whether it is indeed true that ornament highlights the morality of artistic creativity and judgment are still matters to be examined.

Finally, a preliminary sketch of the concerns raised by just trying to find out about decoration led me to dismiss traditional terms like "abstraction," or even "decoration" itself, as confusing and imprecise. Neologisms like "calliphoric" or "terpnopoietic" stress the importance of attributes (beauty and pleasure in this instance, but these need not be the only ones) of works of art that are not so much the property of the object as something—an emotion, perhaps, a momentary involvement, or a passion—given to the object by its user or viewer and then, almost by necessity, attached to it. Following Bakhtin in a visual sense, then, I would argue that a progressive dialogue is established between viewer/user and artifact that feeds on itself and changes both viewer and object as it goes on.[53] It is easiest to see in architecture, where the continuous dialogue between a building and society leads to constant redecorating, additions, and other modifications that reflect the wealth and depth of a relationship between a built space and a surrounding society. Even in the academically and visually stable field of Western painting since the Renaissance of the sixteenth and seventeenth centuries, what we feel today about a Raphael or a Rembrandt is hardly what the artist or his contemporaries experienced.[54]

Why is it that even a cursory consideration of the nature of certain designs that are neither entirely mimetic nor nonmimetic and of theories of ornament and decoration could lead us to consider such weighty issues of esthetic and moral philosophy? It is perhaps true, as Ruskin or Le Corbusier's anonymous teacher, among others, would have suggested, that to deal with whatever ornament may be strikes at the very core of the visual experience, where that experience is not skewed by taste, snobbery, ideology, social convention, ecclesiastical or political restrictions, stylistic salesmanship, and all sorts of other refinements that limit the emotional and sensory freedom of each viewer. If so, artistic traditions, like the one issued from the unique conditions of medieval Islamic history, like the worlds from which come the Irish manuscripts of the sixth century (see fig. 30), Inca sculpture, or ancient Chinese bronzes (see fig. 94), are all traditions that avoid the straitjacket of copying nature or else transfigure visual and imaginary experience into other types of forms. By doing so, they lead most powerfully and most directly to the very root of our need for pleasure through the eyes. Clearly there is a process of ordering visual experience, as was indeed well seen by Gombrich, that is independent from the cultural forms it has taken. To call this process ornament or decoration is not appropriate, for ornament itself can be the message that is communicated. What then is this process?

The answer to be elaborated in these essays derives from the remarks made earlier that to study and to understand an object, an artifact, or a building is to establish a relationship with it and that these relationships are practical, physical, sensory, and psychological, but in large part emotional. They are or can be relationships of love, as when the French architect Claude Perrault compared his feelings for a building with the emotions aroused by "passionately . . . lov[ing] a face."[55] And, indeed, reading one of the most celebrated philosophical discussions of love yields a possible cue to guide thought and reasoning in dealing with ornament.

The text is found in Plato's *Symposium.* The assembled companions of Socrates, as is their habit, fail to find a reasonable definition of love and bog down in a series of logical contradictions between what they think is love and the effects or aims of that love. Socrates intervenes by relating the disquisition made to him by a woman of Mantinea called Diotima. The premise of her argument is the existence of a unique and eternal pure form whose absolute beauty is the object of man's contemplation and the source of his action. But that ideal is a theoretical one that does not allow for enactment in time and therefore for its own continuity through procreation. In practice there is a being, love, that "interprets and conveys messages to the gods from men and to men from the gods," which hovers somewhere "between wisdom and ignorance." Love is neither the lover nor the beloved, neither the possessor nor the object possessed, neither a man nor a god. "He is a great spirit; everything that is of the nature of a spirit is half-god and half-man." He is "of an intermediate nature." The word used by Plato for this "spirit" is *demon (daimon).*[56]

A similar reasoning can be developed around what has been called ornament, without necessarily agreeing to Plato's idealistic premise or with his intellectually and logically developed distrust of the arts in general and of the visual arts in particular.[57] Ornament is itself or exhibits most forcefully an intermediate order between viewers and users of art, perhaps even creators of art, and works of art. This intermediate spirit takes many forms, but all of them are characterized by one central feature: while necessary to the comprehension of a work of art, they are not, except in a few extreme cases, the work of art itself. Like Plato's demons they are what some literary critics have called the prisms mediating between the world and the text or the text and its readers.[58] In the words of a French poet and literateur well versed in the cultures of Asia, beauty itself is an intermediary,[59] suggesting by inference that it is not a property or an attribute of a work of art. And Sigmund Freud wrote in *Beyond the Pleasure Principle* that repetition, so common in ornament, "give(s) the appearance of some demonic force at work."[60]

It is clear indeed that the existence of demons and of intermediary zones of perception and understanding, perhaps even of creativity, have been suggested by many scholars and thinkers. In proposing that these terms are of particular, if not exclusive, importance in revealing what ornament is, I only mean to argue for terminological convenience. As I will try to show, to deal with these intermediaries is a different process from that of mimetism or of abstraction. It seems, therefore, important to argue for a differentiation of terminology according to the ways of understanding required by different kinds of visual experiences.

How many intermediaries are there? Probably a limited number of demons or spirits really exist, although the question may deserve further theoretical elaboration. Four of these demons will be presented here as intermediary veils through which works of art are perceived and ultimately reached and as examples of the kind of search that could be pursued with other motifs.

The four intermediaries with which I shall deal are writing, architecture, nature, and geometry. The first one is the most complex, but I shall begin with it because it is the one for which traditional Islamic art has provided the most numerous documents and because it can most easily allow for synchronic and diachronic arguments and conclusions. The other three intermediaries are more ubiquitous, although the monuments of Islamic art or within the traditions developed in Muslim lands exhibit many and unusually important examples within each group. Yet, as I shall indicate, with architecture and with nature, we also reach other, nonornamental features and it is to an elaboration of these murky boundaries between ornament and representation that the conclusion will be devoted.

CHAPTER II

The Intermediary of Writing

THE PREVIOUS chapter introduced a fascinating painting on paper from one of the albums in Istanbul (pl. 3). The painting is probably correctly dated to the fifteenth century and it is reasonable to assume that it was executed at or for one of the several Turcoman courts controlling Iraq, Iran, and much of central Asia under the general cultural umbrella of the Timurids.[1] Within the range of relatively small miniatures typical of the art of Persian painting, the dimensions of this particular painting, forty-five by fifty centimeters, are unusual in size and suggest some other function than that of illustrating a book. To my knowledge, there is no hint about the original purpose, context, or setting of the page.[2]

Its assemblage of lines and neat geometric figures in six colors over a red background can be interpreted at several different levels. These levels are usually perceived separately and exclusive of each other but they can be imagined in concurrent combinations. For instance, it is a static, fixed, combination of repeated shapes to be explained through an analysis of patterns of tiling. Any one of the shapes can easily be imagined as a piece from a jigsaw puzzle. The skillful observation of congruent possibilities for not more than a dozen pieces of different color *and* the eventual discovery of an overall design can presumably lead to the reconstruction of the image. At another level it is a completed composition that lends itself to analysis and explanation through its several symmetries, through its rotation around a central square fulcrum, or through the effectiveness and operation of its different colors. At this particular level this painting, relatively unusual within Islamic art, seems so closely related to Mondrian's experiments (pl. 4) and to other paintings from the twentieth century.[3]

But there is a third level of meaning to this peculiar composition. It contains the name of Ali rotated in four quadrants and depicted in every one of the colors used in the painting except for the red of the background. This sort of rotation is not original except for its complex elaboration in our example, as fifteenth-century and probably already earlier architectural works are often provided with stucco motifs or with colored tiles and glazed bricks repeating the name of Ali (or of God, or of the Prophet Muhammad, or else some other pious reference) around a central point.[4] The name Ali is a common one and it is theoretically possible that we are dealing with a sort of personal logo identifying and glorifying a patron. But it is much more likely that we are seeing a pious image commemorating the son-in-law of the Prophet. For all Shiʿites, he was, of course, the first *imam*. But it is not necessary to understand our painting automatically as a sectarian holy image. Shiʿite allegiance was not common among fifteenth-century rulers and the love and admiration for Ali were not restricted to Shiʿites. Mystical orders as well as literary or artistic circles saw in Ali a moral model as well as the first artist in Islam.[5] In other words, even as one recognizes the meaning of the written letters, the specific contextual and synchronic significance of the image eludes us.

I will return to yet another way of looking at this painting in the following chapter. Even preliminary observations about it suggest three, perhaps even four, approaches to it. One is to analyze it as the result of a process of creation and to concentrate on whatever preceded its completion, the genetic condition and the pedigree of a work of art, which so preoccupy art historians. At another extreme, it can be seen as a completed set of forms open to the nearly free inquiries of criticism and to far-flung comparisons from the whole spectrum of visual experience regardless of time and place. And, then, it can be simply the apparent carrier of a specific time- or culture-bound message through the medium of writing, and what it says becomes more important than how it says it. There is, of course, a fourth level of analysis, the level of esthetic judgment at which we transfer our own reaction of pleasure or distaste at seeing it into an attribute of the object or argue that some combination of attributes, a predetermined canon, makes this a work of beauty or, contrariwise, one to be condemned.

All these approaches must eventually be argued out and weighed in order to understand this unusual painting. I shall, in this chapter, concentrate on only one of them. That our image deals with writing cannot be contested, since its main subject is a combination of three Arabic letters that spell out a name. But the written message is not immediately clear. It is not clear in the way in which a page from a fourteenth-century Koran from Egypt (fig. 29) is immediately and correctly read by nearly anyone knowing not even the language but only the script, while even those who do not practice either script or language still know that it is probably writing.[6] It is also unclear in a different

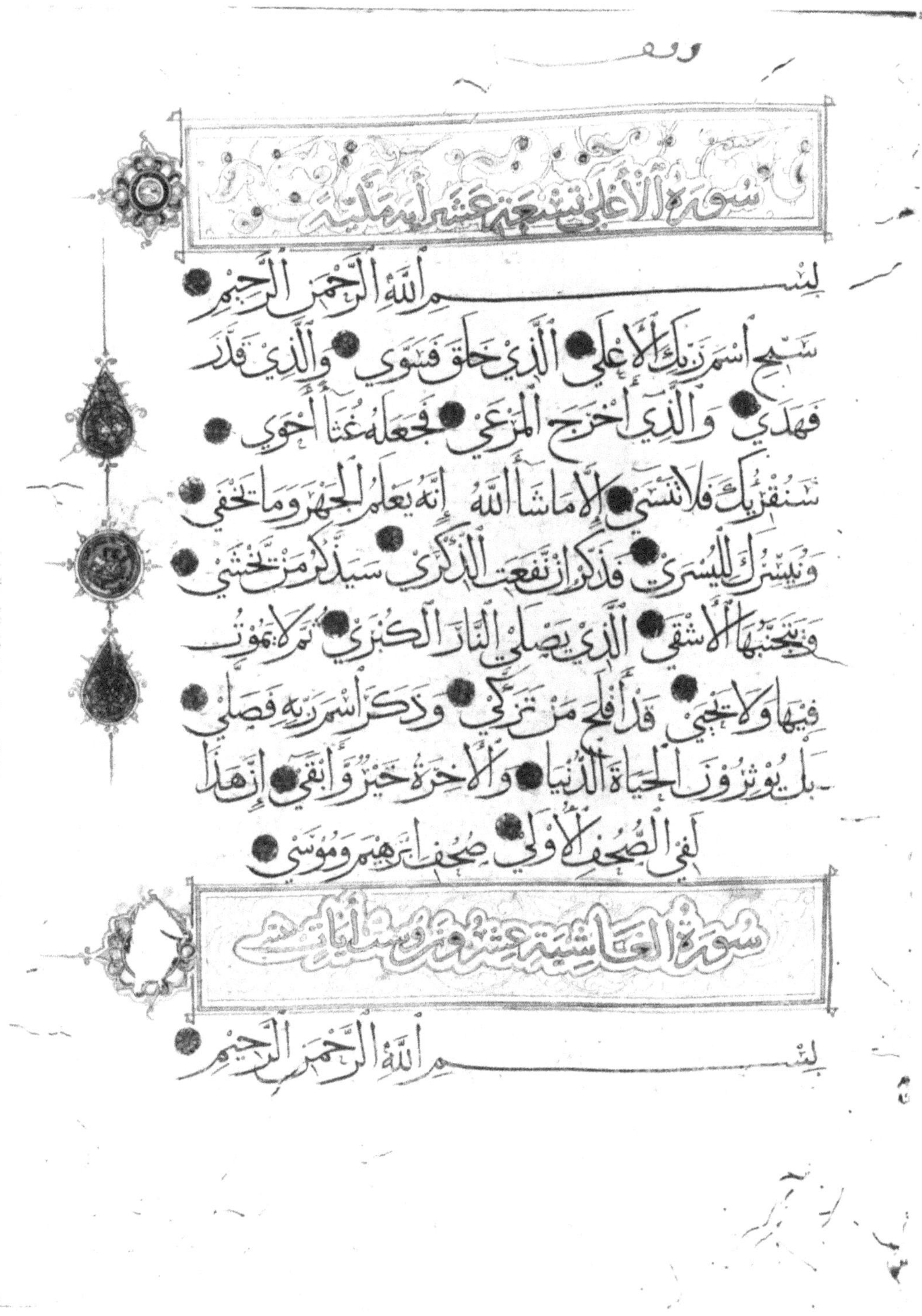

Fig. 29. Manuscript of the Koran, Egypt, 1320, *surah* 88 (end). Dublin, Chester Beatty Library, 1481, fol. 301v.

way from the written motif on the tenth-century ceramics discussed in the previous chapter (figs. 5–8). There is no doubt that something is written on the latter and that it is, in all likelihood, meaningful, but the reading of it is difficult, even for scholars or viewers fluent in Arabic, not to speak of simple speakers of Arabic. On another tenth-century ceramic (fig. 12), yet another distinction is introduced: letters are without doubt depicted, but no meaning can legitimately or, at least, securely be provided.[7] In the instance of our page, it is difficult to figure out that it is writing and it was probably not immediately understood in the fifteenth century either, although certainly more easily understood then than now. Once one has figured it out, the meaning of the writing is relatively simple to understand, but that meaning provides no clue as to purpose, function, or use, unless some association is already made with the shape of the design, with its colors, or with some other attribute we no longer identify, such as its initial purpose or location.

THESE FEW examples of writing with a range of possible or actual meanings show that what is known as calligraphy or, in a more general way, the uses of writing in art are not simple issues as is asserted in the many books and catalogues dealing with the calligraphy of the Islamic world, and in fact with calligraphy in general. The popularity of the subject is unfortunately hardly matched by the intelligence of what has been written about it, a very few exceptions notwithstanding.[8] What is perhaps even more important and interesting is that the initial epistemological problems posed by the Istanbul painting—What has made me, an observer of today, see writing? Why does it matter? Does the reading of the writing help or hinder my pleasure at looking at the painting?—emerge in every one of the major artistic traditions that involved themselves with writing before the sixteenth century, in the West and elsewhere.

Many pages have been written on the Book of Kells (fig. 30) and it is difficult not to be excited by the vibrant magic of its cell-like composition with swirling atoms transfiguring and engulfing the first three letters of the name of Christ in Greek. The transformation of initials will become a major activity of Western, Slavonic, and, perhaps to a smaller degree, Byzantine Greek monastic copyists and it is true that, just as with the Iranian Ali page, letters are illuminated and sometimes changed beyond recognition, as in celebrated Carolingian manuscripts like the Sacramentarium Gelasianum or the one from Gellone (fig. 31).[9] But that tradition which will spout the wonderful initials of the Romanesque and Gothic periods is only partly congruent with the Arabic or Persian ways with which I began. For the Western transforma-

Fig. 30. Incarnation Initial (Chi-Rho), Book of Kells, ninth century, fol. 34. Dublin, Trinity College Lib. 58.

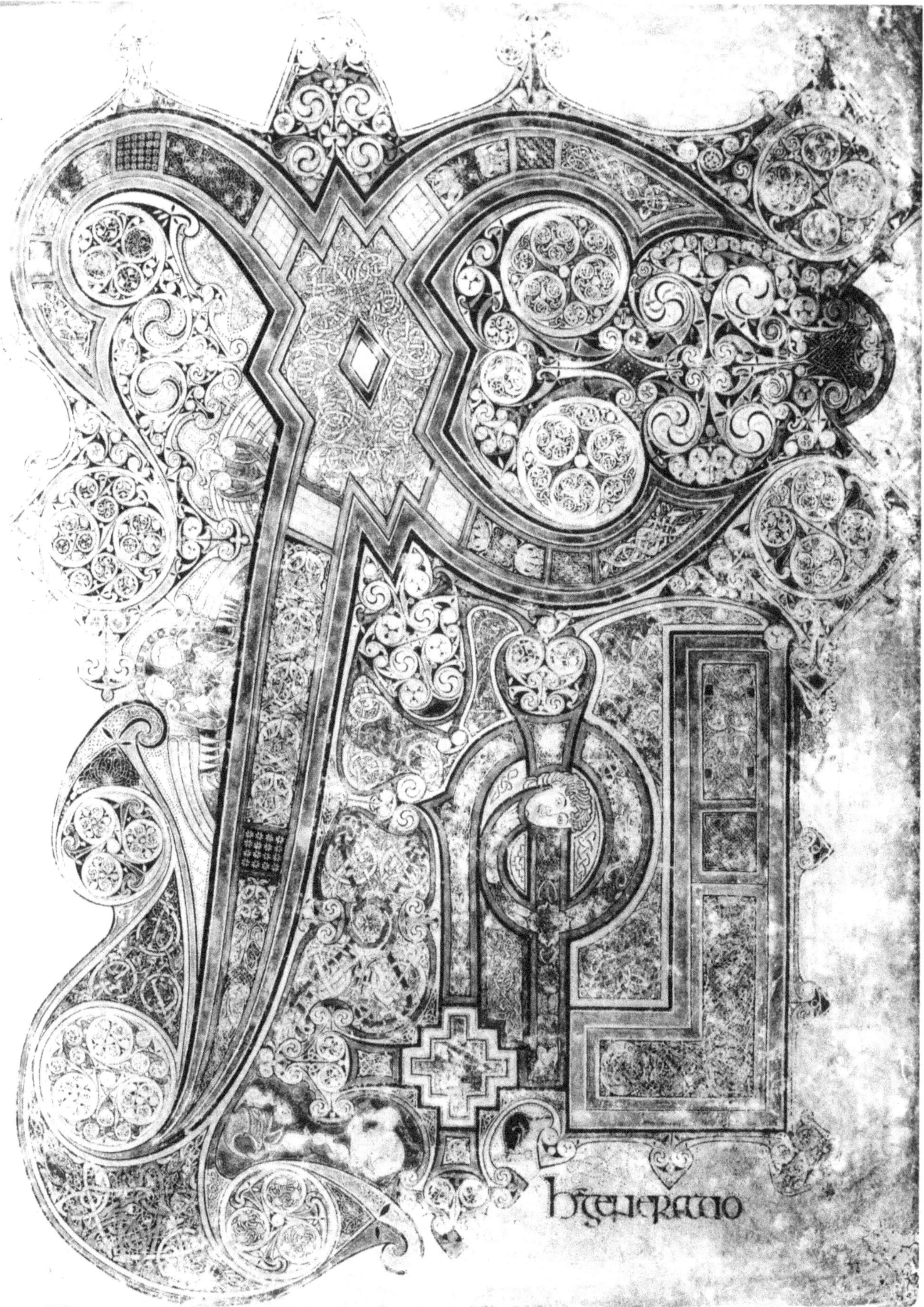
h generatio

Fig. 32. Lectionary from Luxeuil. Paris, Bibliothèque Nationale, Lat. 9427, fol. 144.

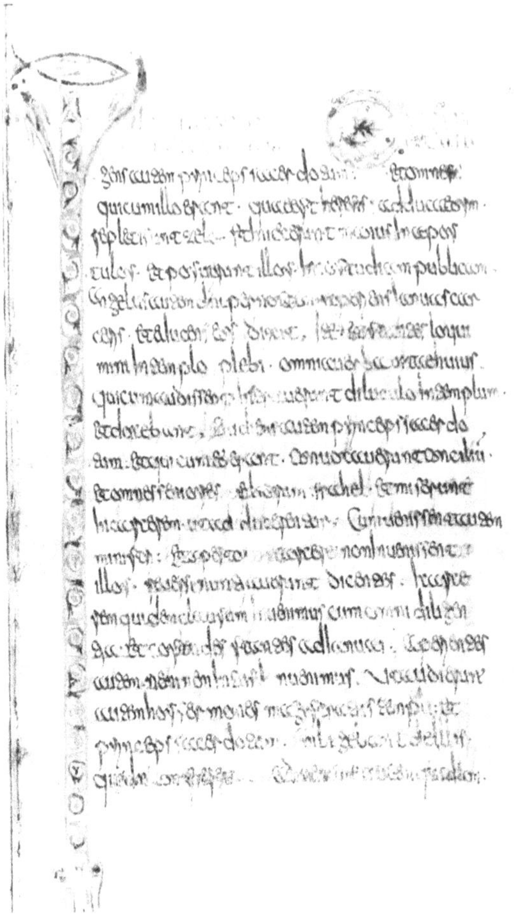

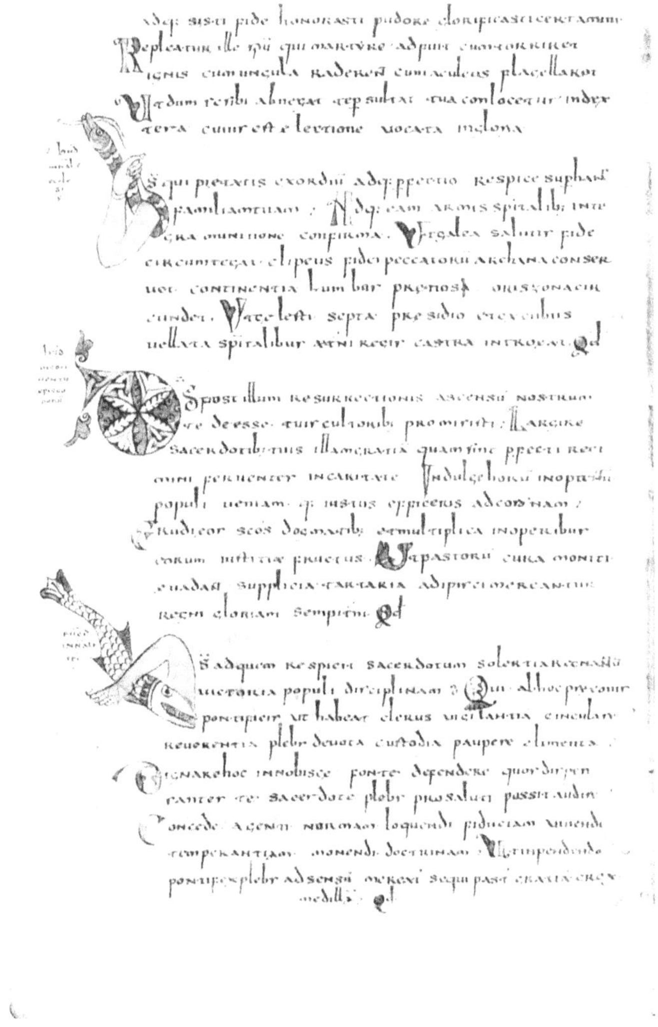

Fig. 31. Sacramentary from Gellone. Paris, Bibliothèque Nationale, Lat. 12048, fol. 164v.

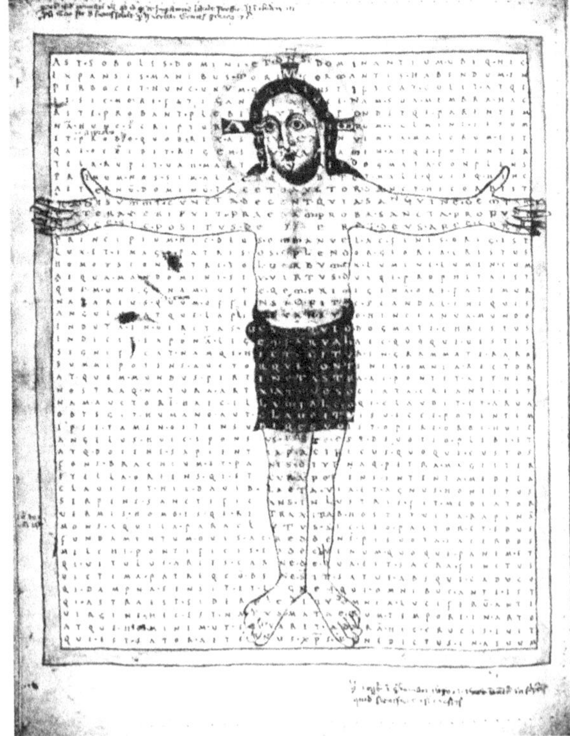

Fig. 33. Hrabanus Maurus, poems. Vienna, Österreiche Nationalbibliothek 652, fol. 6v.

tions of letters at the beginning of a Biblical, patristic, or liturgical fragment do not affect completed words. They are signals of some sort for the reader or user of the book; they are not logical or imaginary identification tags for a meaningful unit of writing. Furthermore, the internal visual unity of most of the full-page images with letters or of the initials does not compel one to read the texts before or after them.[10] The transformation of letters almost removed them from being part of the written text.

It is in fact difficult to assess the nature, in reality even the existence, of artistic writing in Western medieval art. Scholarly wisdom has identified from the end of the seventh century—with examples like the lectionary from Luxeuil (fig. 32)—a modification of writing in Latin through the consistent care given to each letter, the exaggeration of slants, and a number of other features that tend to make letters more similar to than different from each other. As a result, pages of manuscripts become settings for more or less pleasing formal compositions rather than invitations to read. From the time of the first Carolingian uncials of the eighth century to the computer designed or painted advertisements of today, hundreds, possibly thousands of different models exist of a Latin alphabet made to please or to attract attention through the consistency of a style of writing.[11] There have remained in public and private collections millions of examples, from rare books to personal love notes, of a practice—the utilization or invention of consistent means for distinguishing the ways in which words and letters are presented—that is neither the making of unique works of art nor the direct and immediate expression of a text but which affects the simple act of writing.

Within these often published, if rarely discussed, sets of examples of different styles of writing, more complex transformations also exist. I shall only illustrate one of them through a striking, if not particularly beautiful, page from an eleventh-century manuscript of poems and prayers about the Holy Cross written by Hrabanus Maurus (fig. 33). There the letters, which are part of a poem, have been spread like a repeated pattern of dots almost indistinguishable from each other over the powerful, if awkward, representation of an emperor in one example and of a crucified Christ without a cross in another.[12] As often in Western art, a mimetic representation has overwhelmed writing and almost downgraded it to the role of a background. Writing is more easily definable by its formal role in the making of a page than by its content. Many other examples can be found in Western medieval art of the upstaging of writing by representation, a phenomenon that played its part in later Islamic art but not, insofar as I have been able to figure out, in the Far East.

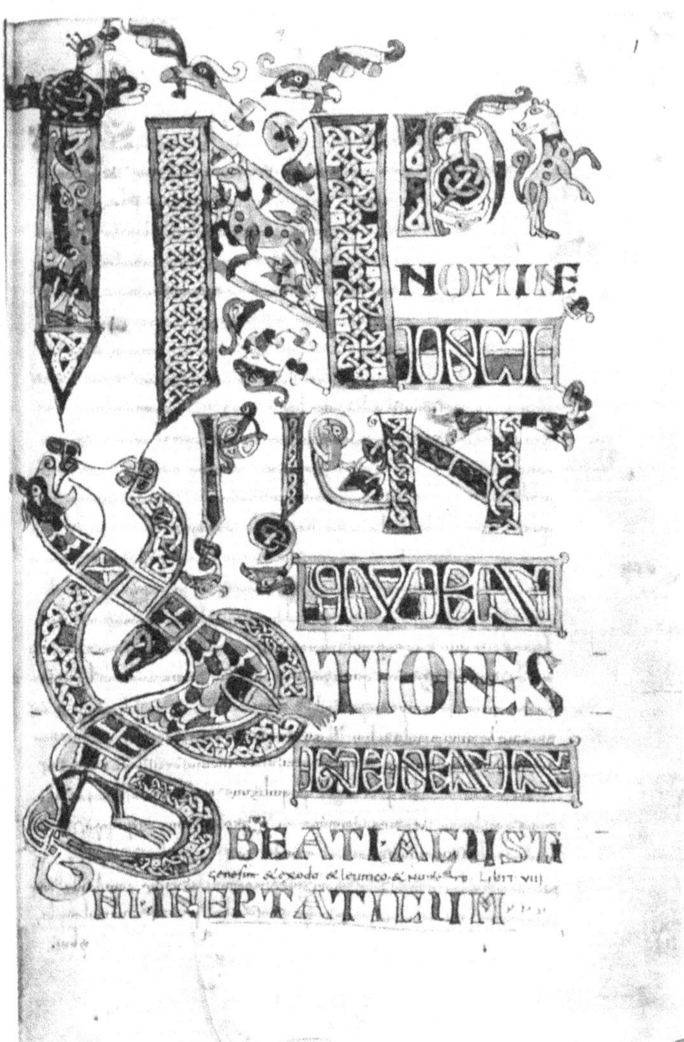

Fig. 34. St. Augustine, title page. Paris, Bibliothèque Nationale, Lat. 12.168, fol. 1.

The masses of examples of willful modifications introduced into the writing of Latin letters are almost exclusively on manuscripts and they are all later than classical Roman times, whose majestic inscriptions remain by the thousands with hardly a playful scratch to alter the limpidity of letters. The modifications within the Greek, Latin, and Cyrillic alphabets can be categorized as sets of more or less standardized but differentiated types, like the special treatment given to initial letters, and occasionally some curious and, at first glance, idiosyncratic and unique rather than typical alterations in the use of letters within legible sequences (fig. 34). To my knowledge, purposefully illegible or meaningless sequences of Latin, Greek, or Cyrillic letters do not exist until the twentieth century. Contemporary infatuation with the senseless and with the absurd, however, has led to such uses in the arts of the past century, both in painting and in graphic art or in publicity and propaganda.[13]

The third great tradition that has been called "calligraphic" is the Chinese and its Korean and Japanese derivations and complements. Here again let us begin with immediate and primarily visual observations of what is identified as calligraphy.[14]

First, unlike what happens in the West, elaborate and complex writing appears on many different materials: bone, wood, bronze, ceramic, artificial means of construction like bricks, silk, and, of course, paper. Second, as in all traditions, writing appears alone or in combination with other artistic endeavors. The latter are most frequently mimetic representations of all sorts of things, as is exemplified by the paintings in which a landscape acquires a piece of writing as a counterweight (fig. 35). But they may also be the simplified shapes usually known as ornament, as in the justly celebrated early bronzes (fig. 36). When in combination with something else, writing is composed with, but physically apart from, whatever is the other part of the combination, a landscape, a flower, or an animal. It is haughtily separated from its visually perceived companions. Also clear, even to the untutored eye, is that writing comes in several manners, at times squeezed in the straitjacket of a square or of an oblong (fig. 37), at other times flowing downward like water over rocks (fig. 38), most often as a sequence of apparently independently composed units (fig. 35). A further peculiarity of Far Eastern writing is that its basic unit, the polysemic character, is much more complex in structure than the Arabic

Fig. 35. Wu Chen, *Poetic Feeling in a Thatched Pavilion*, 1347. Cleveland Museum of Art, Leonard C. Hanna, Jr. Fund, 63.259.

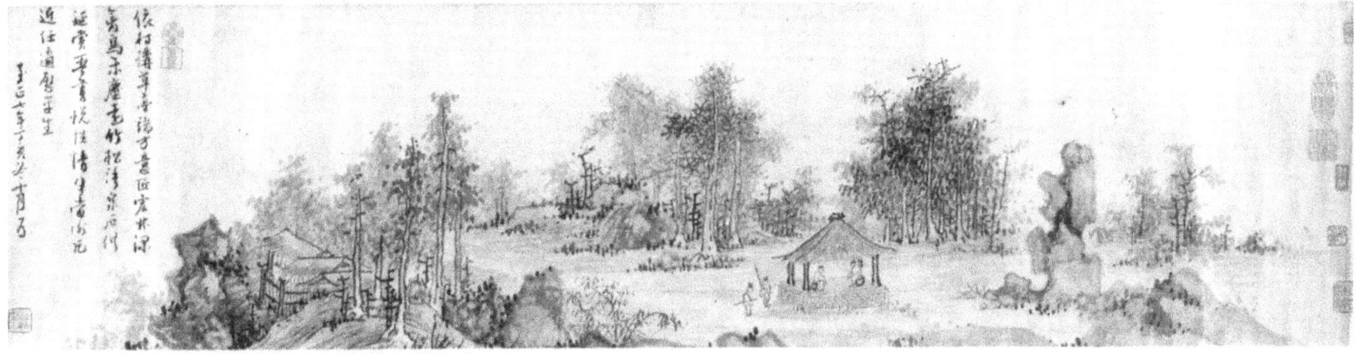

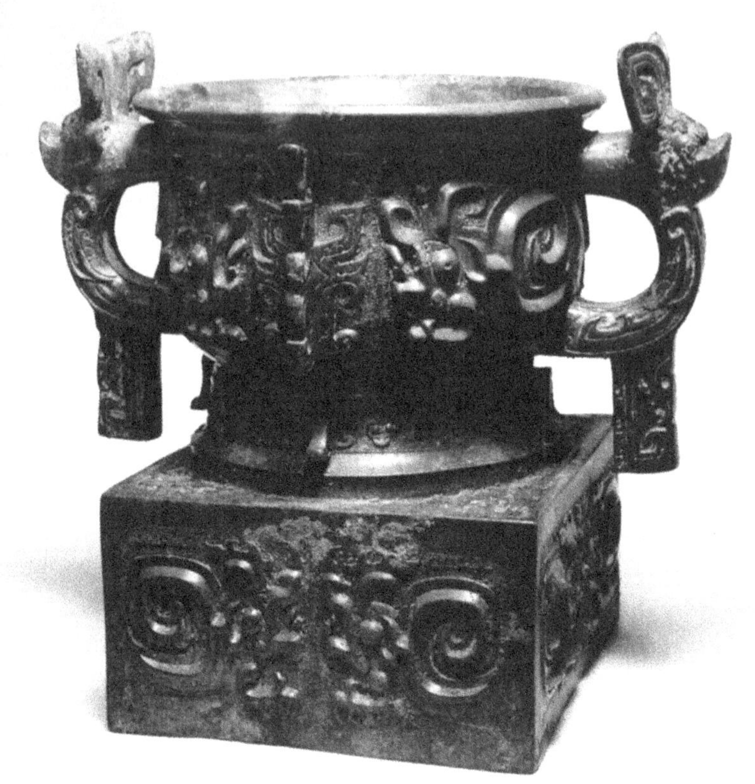

36

Fig. 36. Kuei type vessel, China, Early Western Chou, eleventh or tenth century B.C. Cambridge, Harvard University Art Museums, 1944, 57.1.

Fig. 37. Kuei type vessel, China, Early Western Chou, eleventh or tenth century B.C., detail of inscription. Cambridge, Harvard University Art Museums, 1944, 57.1.

Fig. 38. Liu Shih-ju, "Branch of Blossoming Plum," sixteenth century. Cambridge, Harvard University Art Museums, 1923, 191.

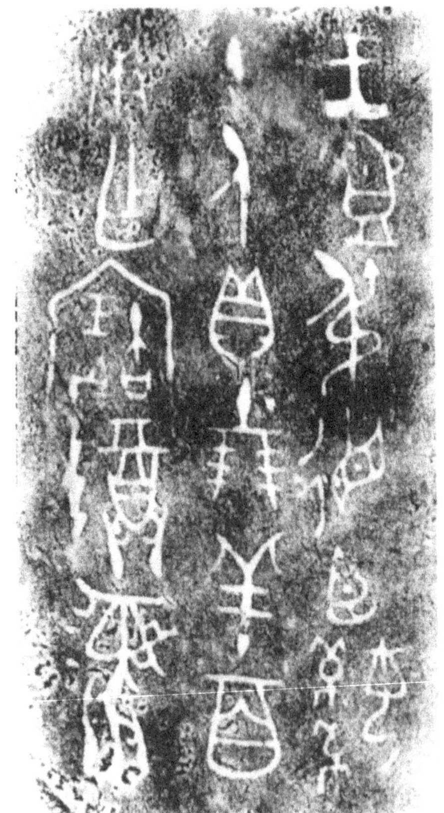

37

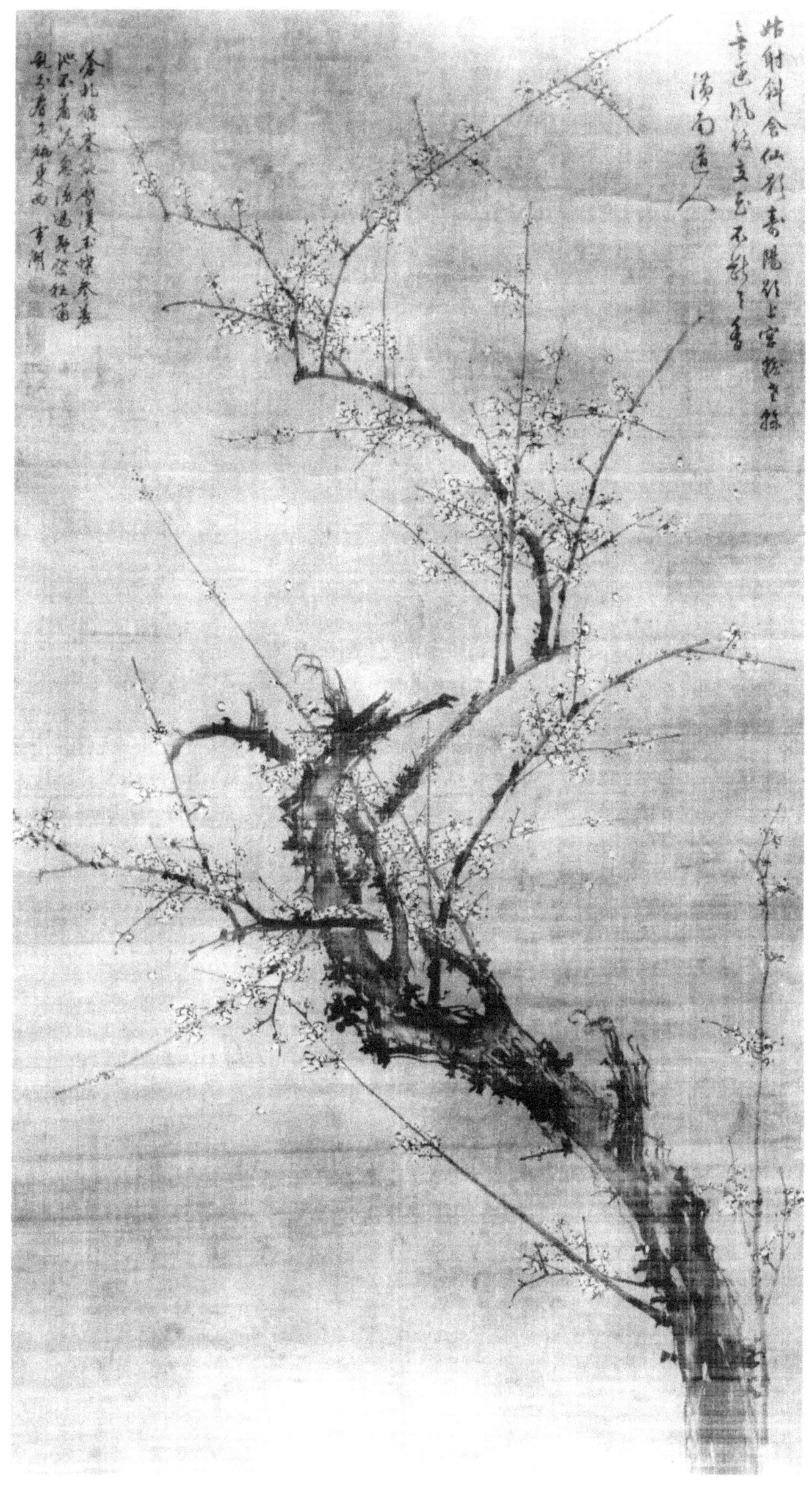

or Latin letter. Its complexity can easily be seen, even by those unfamiliar with the language, as the result of a multiplicity of arrangements of strokes, and it can reasonably be assumed that a meaning is attached to each combination. But, beyond their complexity, Chinese and Japanese characters assembled into written texts elicit a very special response from viewers; they attract even when they are incomprehensible.

One reason for this attraction is the perception by any visually trained or sensitive observer of a function that has been well put by a contemporary Chinese writer: "The essence of beauty in [Chinese] writing is not found in the written word, but lies in response to unlimited change; line after line should have a way of giving life, character after character should seek for life movement." And the authors of a classic book on Chinese calligraphy add: "A well-written character . . . to the perceiving mind it is a dynamic experience."[15] At the end of this chapter, I shall have more to say about the idea of life's physical presence in the appearance of Chinese characters, but in the meantime a second feature of Chinese writing is equally striking. It is the presence, almost palpable, of the brush in painted texts and of the chisel in examples engraved on stone, in molds, or on bronze. Although we shall see later how important the pen was to the writing of Arabic characters, the physicality of the instrument is far less obvious in Arabic or Latin writing and, for instance, the attention paid to the sharpness and precision of edges and outlines, even in the monumental and, at first glance, free-wheeling Ottoman religious inscriptions from the nineteenth century (fig. 39), freezes the design into a highly controlled, perhaps even arbitrary and scholastic, straitjacket.

The contrast with the treatment of the Arabic alphabet explains the third reason for the esthetic appeal of Chinese writing. It seems accessible and available to all. Nearly everyone who has encountered the Chinese language, especially in China itself, finds himself doodling pseudo-Chinese characters, fully enjoying pressing pen or pencil on paper and creating combinations of strokes that seem to relate to the experience of being surrounded by these lively designs. At a more interesting level, French and American painters of the 1950s consciously drew their inspiration from Far Eastern calligraphy and made all sorts of pronouncements like "[calligraphy has] not metaphysics, but a direct manner, an acute, meditative power which speaks without word" (about Hans Hartung) or "multiple space bounded by involved white lines symbolizes higher states of consciousness" (this was written by Mark Tobey, who studied Chinese calligraphy, but not the Chinese language).[16] These statements, if not paintings, are indeed examples of what the French painter George Mathieu must have meant when he talked of a "délire calligraphique."

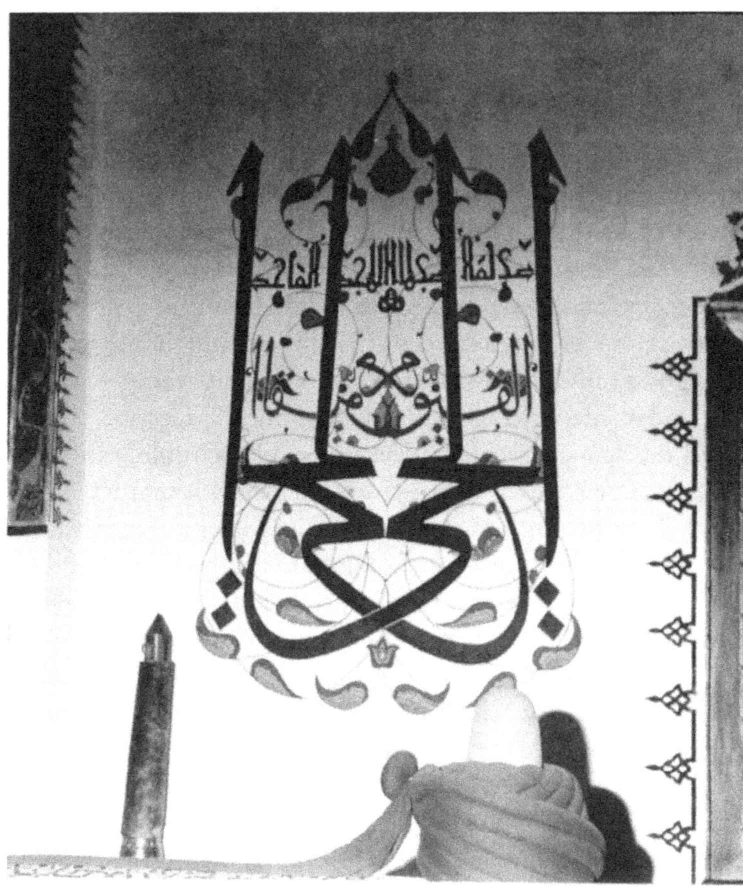

Fig. 39. Turkey, Edirne, Eski Cami, inscription on wall, nineteenth century.

Their importance for our purposes is that they exemplify for Far Eastern writing a quality of universal esthetic appeal independent of its meaning.

We shall see shortly that these interpretations are not entirely inappropriate and not as superficial as they seem to be. We shall also see that they elucidate something of major importance for my purpose of understanding the esthetics of writing. In the meantime, however, the Far Eastern examples, like the ones in Latin or Arabic characters, share a number of rather peculiar characteristics. In all cases there are two obvious efforts. One is the transformation of the simple action of communicating in writing through a series of devices; at times this transformation ends up by making the communication difficult to receive or even meaningless. The other effort is to provoke on the part of the viewer an esthetic reaction, which would be a reaction of pleasure. Writing is calliphoric, that is to say a carrier of beauty, and it becomes terpnopoietic by bringing pleasure. Whatever the sequence of the emotional or psychological reaction, beauty becomes pleasure. Alternately, pleasure at seeing leads to labeling the seen as beautiful. At least, so it seems from reading the literature on calligraphy.

Difficulties arise, however, as soon as one tries to understand what actually is beauty or even artistic quality in writing. The cause for this difficulty is a simple one: the absence of a proper distinction between writing in a variety of scripts meant exclusively to be read and writing in order to create additional and at times alternate effects. Because nearly all publications on "calligraphy" are either catalogues or technical manuals on "how to" do beautiful writing, they rarely, I would even say never, question the artistic merit and the esthetic quality of the works they discuss, almost assuming—or so it seems—that every item of ancient hand-made writing is an example of calligraphy.

When more or less mechanical reproduction was made possible, essentially with the availability of printing in China from the eleventh century on and in the West since the late fifteenth,[17] the mere antiquity of a fragment, until then sufficient to call it precious, lost some of its value in the West. It did not in China, where the availability of mechanical reproduction did not eliminate individual efforts in writing and almost fostered an intellectually and socially elitist view of the activity of writing enhanced by the availability of examples from the past. In the Latin world individual efforts were replaced by a formal typology of letters promoted (or demoted, depending on one's taste) to the level of one of the decorative arts with properly identified and individually named styles described in manuals and engraved on copper plates.[18] In the late sixteenth century a French penman, Jean de Beaugrand, invented the word "panchrestographie" for model books of one's abilities and versatility in writing,[19] something akin to the portfolio of today's aspiring artists.

All these examples are hardly works of art, nor do they claim to be. They are works of calligraphy for the very specific reason that it is for or around them that the word itself was developed. True, the word does exist in Plutarch, but it is rarely used by him and hardly at all in the Middle Ages; in medieval Greek, *kalligraphos* appears rather than *kalligraphia* and it always simply means a "scribe." The word reappears late in the sixteenth century and in the early seventeenth more or less simultaneously in Italy, France, and England and refers to something much less exalted than its contemporary use. The French humanist Etienne defines it in 1569 to mean "art de bien former les caractères" (the way to form letters well) and in a play of Ben Jonson quoted by the *Oxford English Dictionary*, a young man says: "I have to commend me . . . my kalligraphy, a fair hand, fit for a secretary." Milton in 1645 echoes wonderfully the sort of written pages common at the time when he writes that "a divine of note had . . . stuck it [a text] here and there with a clove of his own calligraphy, to keep it from tainting."[20] The culinary imagery of a well-spiced piece of writing is not peculiar to the seventeenth century in the West, as a ninth-century governor of eastern Iran is said to have referred to the decoration of a page of penmanship as "seeds of coriander."[21] It is a most appropriate image to anyone looking at the often pleasing and amusing designs created over the past hundred years by Western printers, whether for governmental or private purposes, as with university diplomas. All these are examples of calligraphy in the sense given to the word when it was reinstated or, more precisely, provided with a new charge during the Renaissance. Whether they are instances of an elaborate style of writing affecting all letters, whether they choose a few letters for particular emphasis, whether they are marginal elaborations issued from letters, or any combination of these models, works of calligraphy all share one feature—namely, that the specific content (as distinguished from message) of the text itself is either obfuscated and made difficult to read or even immaterial. There are many examples of pseudo-esthetic obfuscation, including the letters of many of our own friends (especially if trained in a design or architecture school) who have developed stylistically consistent scripts irritating to all their readers. And all of us have observed the second kind or synechdochal type of writing while waiting in the offices of professionals, as the quality of the decoration around fancy letters, especially in Latin, is supposed to reassure us about the abilities of our physician or lawyer.

Is it proper to transfer these uses, meanings, and associations to the three older traditions with which I began? Should one use the word calligraphy for all of them? Or does it confuse the issue to do so, because the use of a single word hides too many distinctions, often, as I shall try to show, precisely those distinctions that provide the main values to our uses of writing?

I shall try to argue that we are indeed dealing with different issues. I shall first present the case at a very theoretical level, then deal at some depth with the phenomenon of writing in the Islamic world, concentrating primarily on the medieval period between the ninth and the thirteenth centuries. And I shall conclude by returning to all the major traditions of writing in trying to draw up a broader hypothesis on the uses of writing in the visual arts.

THE MOST brilliant recent statements on writing have been made by Jacques Derrida in his *Grammatologie*.[22] From his rambling, at times irritating, but usually quite scholarly text, I would like to pick up four threads for our purposes. One, implied by the neologism "grammatology," is the existence of a science of writing.[23] What I understand by this is that the various processes that lead to the making and then the reading of something written possess principles and attitudes shared by all literate cultures, even if the specific manner in which these principles and attitudes appear may well vary to the point of incompatibility. The second thread is that writing is not simply, within semiotic theory, the signifier of something signified, the expression of an object or of a thought. It is in fact twice removed from its subject matter, as the word, spoken or recalled, comes between the object and its written form. As Derrida put it, writing is the signifier of the signifier. I shall argue later that the idea of beautiful writing allows us to get around this particular difficulty, but, as it is logical to assume that the reading of a meaning is the primary expectation of something written, the property of writing that is by definition twice removed from its subject has several consequences. One is a greater freedom of expression as well as greater opportunities to communicate. For instance, on a simple level of direct messages, abbreviations or mistakes can be handled in writing more easily than in speaking. Abbreviations do not need to subscribe to a requirement like that of vowels, and mistakes are avoided through an automatic system of correctives, as in the case of the plural, which is usually written more often than it is uttered. Another consequence is a potential for permanence and, therefore, for diachrony. The possibilities of remaining and of being used and reused were unavailable to a speaker of words until the invention of recording machines.

One implication of these properties of writing is that writing more than speaking is or can be a game. I use the term in the technical sense of an activity obeying a set of rules whose outcome is not predictable from the nature and identity of those involved in the activity. To use or write profanities in a sacred place is blasphemous, but it is not blasphemous to use the same script or the same letters for sacred or profane words. The act of writing is independent of the letters, words, or characters it uses and, with early pictographic exceptions notwithstanding, different from the meanings of letters, words, and characters. And another implication is my fourth and last thread derived from Derrida. Writing, he argues, is "une trace instituée" (built-in [or institutionalized] remains). I understand this to mean that time is always an acknowledged part of writing. It can be the short time it takes for a note to go from one desk to another or the eternal message of a divine revelation. Writing does not possess the immediacy of sound, but it can be made eternal.[24]

The point of these remarks inspired by the leading deconstructionist of today is that the act of writing lends itself to a specific and finite range of manipulations by virtue of a number of inherent properties of that act. Without even trying to be complete, one can say that writing, being movable, is a way to bridge space as well as time; it can proclaim the most vulgar thoughts and the most inspired ones; it can be beautiful or ugly; it can communicate openly or secretly; it can be majestic and visible from afar or fill the head of a pin. To subsume all these different actions of writing under the single term of calligraphy only confuses the meanings of writing. In order to identify alternate terms, the experience of a concrete tradition of writing is the guide I propose to follow.

FROM THE dizzying heights of theoretical abstraction let us then turn to the specific instance of writing in the Islamic world. Many details are far from worked out and thousands of visual or interpretative sources are yet to be discovered, but a certain number of facts are either known to be true or sufficiently likely to have been accepted by most scholars and a lot of amateurs. My initial approach to the question will be historical. I shall first sketch out an evolutionary process, one that has appeared to me to be reasonable from such information as is available and from an acceptable logic of development and growth.

By the end of the seventh century, the establishment of the Muslim empire from the Atlantic to Siberia required a common means to transmit both the prescripts of the faith and the needs of government and of control. The requirement was initially met, among other ways, by the Arabic language and, in a more permanent way, by the Arabic script, which, at various points in time, became the only script or one of the scripts for Persian, Turkish, Urdu, Malay, Swahili, and nearly every language practiced by Muslims.

Two other cultural features of the first Islamic centuries are pertinent to our purposes. One is the rejection of mimetic representation in anything official or formal. The concomitant result of the rejection was the elevation of writing into the main vehicle for signs of belief, power, legitimacy, and any one of the functions for which images were used elsewhere. The best-known early examples of these "images of the word," as they have been called,[25] are the coins of late seventh-century caliphs with ideologically loaded statements about the faith and the long inscription on the Dome of the Rock in Jerusalem with its proclamation of Islam's doctrines on Christ and Christology and with a statement of the new faith's ultimate victory.[26] But it would not be right to restrict to religious or political spheres examples of writing used instead of images, symbolic or representational. A tenth-century manual on the proper behavior of elegant people in Baghdad has several chapters on the poems, usually of mediocre quality, that adorned objects of daily use, such as bottles, cups, goblets, curtains, garments, kerchiefs, veils, and turbans.[27] They were also found on gates and in special types of salons known as *majalis*.[28] And a celebrated passage in Mas'udi's *Golden Meadows* identifies the writing of poetry on objects as an artistic innovation of the middle of the ninth century.[29]

Because of the paucity of remains, it is difficult to associate existing secular objects or monuments of architecture with what was clearly a major characteristic of the art of the ninth and tenth centuries. The earliest preserved use of poetry in architecture is found in the eleventh-century palace at Ghazni in Afghanistan, with Persian verses as long bands of stucco applied to walls and framing ornament. Objects with poetry became common from the twelfth century on, primarily in Iran, but they occur sporadically among Spanish and Sicilian ivories, Persian silks, and metalwork everywhere.[30] Except for Iranian ceramics and later Iranian bronzes, most of these examples are either unique instances of their kind or of uncertain provenance. It is, therefore, difficult to decide on their real value as types, and we are left, in fact, with the numerous formal and very repetitive formulas on official textiles[31] or with the far richer inscriptions, mostly of proverbs and of good wishes, found on ceramics from northeastern Iran (fig. 6, for instance).[32] It is actually tempting to interpret these ceramics as reflections, in a different area than Baghdad and at a more popular social level of the elegant taste (*zaraf* is the Arabic term for it) found among the snobs of the capital. But such a hypothesis is impossible to verify. What is clear is that the vast majority of written sources talks about the written word as a key sign of high taste.[33] Thus social elegance and ideological purpose turn during the first centuries of Muslim rule to the same means of expression, the written word.

The second cultural factor of early Islamic times that explains the growth of writing is the one most consistently mentioned by all writers on the subject. "Proclaim," says the Holy Book in the first statement to have been revealed to the Prophet, "and thy Lord is most Bountiful, Who taught by the pen [*bi-l-qalam*], taught man that which he knew not" (94:3–4). Or, elsewhere, "By the Pen, and what they [men] inscribe, thou art not, by the blessing of the Lord, a man possessed" (68:1). And a third passage from the divine message is more poetic and equally powerful (31:27): "And if all the trees on earth were pens and the sea—seven seas after it to replenish it [in a striking image of the sea as ink]—, yet would the Words of God not be spent." The point is simple. God has sent His message through writing and yet no writing will ever express the plenitude of the divine message. From the very beginning, the act of writing is at the same time a means of transmission and the only way one can even attempt to become aware of the limitations of man's perception of the divine. Practical and mystical themes will play their role in the interpretation of writing in Muslim lands and even more in contemporary interpretations of that writing, but the more important point is that, as writing was the vehicle of God's message, so God's message became a hallowed piece of writing and many an early (and late) manuscript of the Koran contains the information that it consisted of 114 *surahs*, or chapters; 6,236 *ayas*, or verses; 77,460 words; 321,250 letters; and 156,051 diacritical marks. From this sort of knowledge pertaining to the text of the Revelation itself, it was easy to imagine or assume that every letter or word had in it a particle of the divine, and thus that writing itself was holy. Later sects like the *hurufiyah* assigned a particular and unique significance to each letter, simply numerical at times but also characteriological or mystical.

Whether it is warranted to explain the transformation of writing in Islam through the nature of the Revelation remains to be seen. From the evidence it is difficult not to consider such a conclusion as anachronistic when applied to the early centuries of Islamic history. More practical issues dominated in the process of transforming the Revelation *and* government into written documents. The exact ways in which this was accomplished are still being investigated and the fabulous recent discoveries of thousands of early Korans in Yemen as well as ongoing painstaking analyses of early manuscripts in Paris and Istanbul have not yet been made entirely available and therefore not fully digested by scholarship.[34] The following scheme or scenario seems reasonable to propose on the basis of earlier scholarly studies (especially Nabia Abbott's), a small number of written sources, and a considerable number of available fragments on papyrus, parchment, metal, ceramic, and architecture, including some preliminary impressions garnered from the Yemeni finds available to me. This scenario varies in part from the one found in most books, because of my initial concern, which is not to understand *how* the writing of Arabic developed, but *what*, if anything, in it justifies calling it art.

Between the middle of the seventh century and the early tenth, a variety of scripts came into being with standardized general shapes of letters easily defined in formal terms like vertical or horizontal, rounded or angular, above or below a basic line, alone or attached to other letters (pls. 5, 6; fig. 40). A

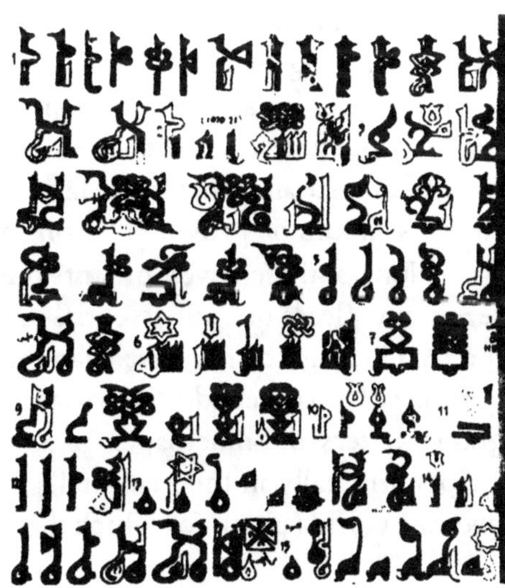

Fig. 40. A typical list of proportional letters.

typology of Arabic writing was established and it acquired a series of complements, dots for the most part, serving to clarify distinctions between sounds that are not expressed by the shape of the letter alone. Because it is not known how systematic and consistent the dots were, the number and variants of these scripts are also unknown. What is, on the other hand, certain is that a new verb was introduced, which is absent from the Koran and which may or may not have a pre-Islamic past.[35] The verb is *khatta*, whose verbal noun *khatt* is frequently translated as "calligraphy." At this stage, I am most hesitant to do so for early uses of the root in Arabic, as the root has no implication of qualitative judgment, nor does it always imply writing. What it does mean is "to mark out," "to outline," as in its well-known use for urban planning, where it refers to the fixing of boundaries between plots to be settled or built upon. In this last sense it comes up in the descriptions of the earliest new Muslim settlements in Iraq. The root *khatta* introduced into the action of writing, which was normally expressed by the much more common root *kataba*, something new that can perhaps best be imagined as an attribute of order and of reasonable consistency—in short, as a typology, a set of more or less consistent ways of doing things.

The need for such a typology for the transmission of writing was obvious enough if one considers the enormous spread of the Muslim world so soon after its creation, but what is even more remarkable is that it worked. It became operational, as we know from coins, for instance, which form our largest, most consistent, and best-dated source of written statements, albeit conventional ones. Minted in Spain or central Asia, they could be read by anyone who had learned the standard Arabic script, as they can be today.[36] Similarly in the scripts of early Koranic fragments, there is a typological consistency but variations in all sorts of details like proportions, thickness of strokes, spacing of letters, and so forth. The matching of most of the numerous names for scripts found in sources with any one specific type has not yet been possible. Whether these variations reflect regional, chronological, topical, or taste and patronage distinctions is impossible to say at this time, but answers should be provided by ongoing research.

None of these developments can be identified as esthetic, that is to say as seeking to please but not essential to the transmission of a text. Esthetic or, in the terminology of my first chapter, terpnopoietic intent appears, however, quite clearly in other additions made to writing. It can be the contrast between golden letters and blue paper on a celebrated manuscript or group of manuscripts originally in the National Library in Tunis but presently scattered all over the world (pl. 5), for which the imitation of Byzantine purple codices and

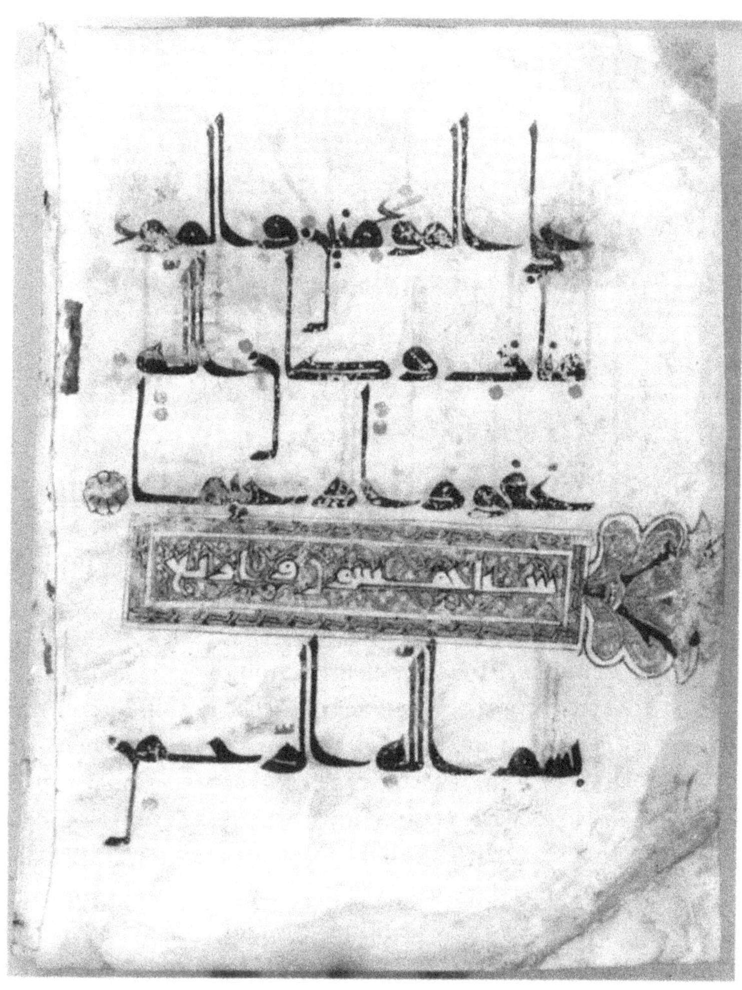

Fig. 41. Page from an early Koran, parchment, tenth century (?). New York, Metropolitan Museum of Art, Rogers Fund, 1937 (37.30).

therefore an ideological charge has recently been proposed as an explanation.[37] It can be a whole set of gilt or otherwise colored dots, flowers, or geometric and other designs (pl. 6, fig. 41). Their location often has the value of a sign indicating the beginning of a new *surah* or a necessary pause in the reading of the Holy Text; or else they are seemingly arbitrary, unrelated to the writing, but making it pleasant to look at a page.[38] All these signs, however, on Koranic pages are independent of letters and it is only on tombstones, best known in Egypt, that letters occasionally acquired a fleuron or some other extraneous feature as early as in the ninth century (fig. 42).[39] They do not create calligraphy—that is to say, writing with the intent of being beautiful. They *do*, however, create pages of books that are visually alive, even if sometimes disorderly or purposeless in the apparent randomness of their occurrence on any one page. They are neither sequences of visual elements indepen-

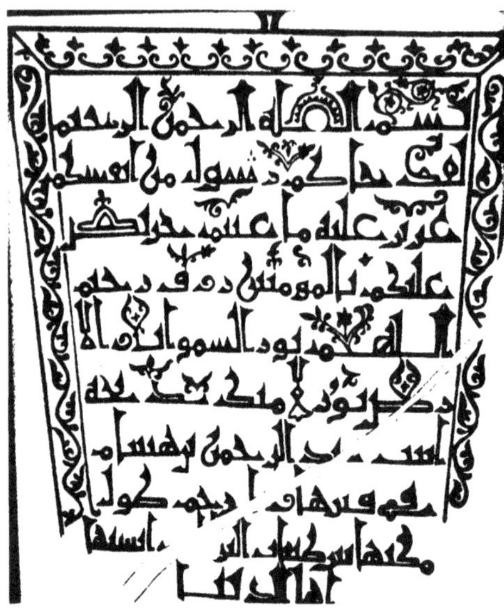

Fig. 42. Tombstone from Egypt with floral writing.

dent of writing nor clearly enough associated with specific places, like a given letter or a space between words, within a text, or within a page.

In short, during these first centuries there would have occurred a standardization of script types and an occasional concern for making a page, and by extension a book, attractive in the etymological sense of having something that draws attention to it. In Koranic examples, these additions may well have had practical aims like easier legibility and identification of canonical breaks or else pious ones of honoring and enhancing the Holy Text. Elsewhere they could simply have been proclamations or advertisements for a person or a thing, but, on the whole, I prefer to argue that, pending needed studies, their purpose is unknown.

The first four centuries of Muslim rule thus established several needs or modes of behavior that created a new setting for writing. There were rare and expensive books. There was the rich page with all sorts of signs for many different purposes. Expensive bindings transformed pages into single sets of attractive objects as early as the ninth century.[40] Gold or little bunches of leaves and flowers have landed on individual letters or are strewn amid letters and lines (pl. 6, fig. 41). There is in short a whole craftsmanship of illuminating a page or a text. At the very same time, from the early ninth century on, writing meant to be read and appreciated for the witticism, eroticism, or piety of its content made its appearance on items of conspicuous consumption among the sophisticated elites around the Abbasid court in Iraq, the urban rich of Iraqi cities, and perhaps their equivalents in a few provincial cities, Merv, Rayy, and Nishapur in the East, Fustat, Qayrawan, and Cordova in the West.

But none of these features are *calligraphic*, as they are not modifications of letters as much as additions to pages or even to lines. It seems more reasonable to understand these first Islamic centuries as centuries of many scripts during which two notions began to emerge. One is the notion of a beautiful or at least expensive-looking book and the other one is that writing carries information no doubt but also identifies categories of taste (and therefore of patronage) and can be used on all sorts of objects other than books.

Something changed in the tenth century. To put it more accurately, later times attributed to the early tenth century and to the vizier Ibn Muqlah, who died in 939 under tragic circumstances,[41] a series of changes whose existence and effects can be visually demonstrated in manuscripts and other written sources from the eleventh century onward. The invention was a new method, a new approach, a new way (the Arabic word used in the sources is *tariqah*, which means "path") for *khatt*, the orderly typology of ways to write. It was known as *khatt al-mansub*, a "proportioned script." In it the module for constructing letters was the dot, or rather the square or rhomb, produced by a pen put on paper and pushed open, then closed (fig. 43). A key, in the musical

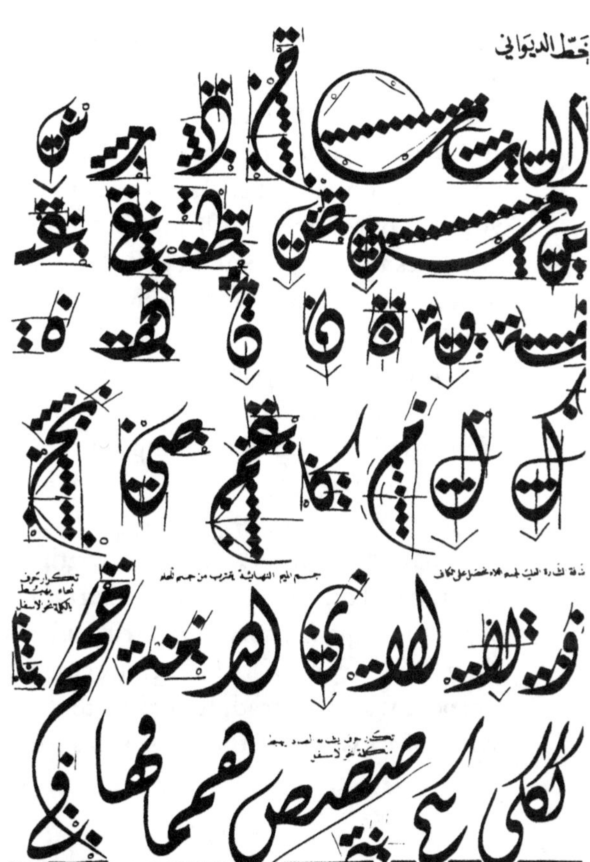

Fig. 43. Drawing of technique for proportioned script.

sense, to any piece of writing was given by the number of dots (three, five, or more) in the single vertical letter *alif*, and all other letters followed suit, thereby creating what was presumably lacking until then, a rationally thought out system of composing letters, words, pages, and, by extension, whole books. The method could also be repeated because an abstractly definable mechanism or canon existed for writing and for the evaluation of the writing of others. Like nearly all celebrated scribes after him, Ibn al-Bawwab, the next in line after Ibn Muqlah of a succession of celebrated and inventive scribes, is supposed to have been able to imitate any type of writing without being recognized as original. His own manner was also frequently imitated and even his signature was forged in a manuscript now in Istanbul.[42] He died in Baghdad in 1022.

The recognition of the hand of any one scribe has remained a difficult task even in much better documented later centuries, but the same difficulty no longer applied to scripts, since from circa 1000, if not as early as Ibn Muqlah himself, a succession of clearly identified and individually named scripts appears. These scripts almost never replaced each other but remained part of a cumulative written legacy of Islamic culture. Individual times, areas, artists, patrons, and perhaps even topics could choose their manner of expression from a variety of types and that legacy was still powerfully effective in the nineteenth century. The components of that legacy—the many ways of writing in Arabic characters texts composed in Arabic, Persian, Turkish, Urdu, and Malay—have often been listed, illustrated, and discussed.[43] Their majestic clarity limpidly proclaims the divine message of the Koran in the large volumes of the fourteenth and fifteenth centuries from Egypt (fig. 29) or Iran, or recites in perfect legibility the Iranian epic of the *Shahnama* (fig. 44).[44] The delicate and curvaceous stringing of letters and words in Iranian scripts from the early fifteenth century onward[45] creates subtler and more intimate settings for the reading of lyrical works or else, like the miniatures of the same time, lyricizes the epic (fig. 45). At times several scripts are used together and some ideological or cultural meaning is probably to be discovered in these recalls of past scripts (fig. 46).[46]

Most current scholarly writing identifies all these pages as examples of Arabic, Turkish, or Persian calligraphy. I prefer to consider them as various types of scripts, whose very strict rules of composition and proportion gave them consistency of formal arrangement and easy replicability. Their primary purpose was to be read, to make a text available. As in early Islamic times, the work of art was in all these instances something else than writing. Nowhere is

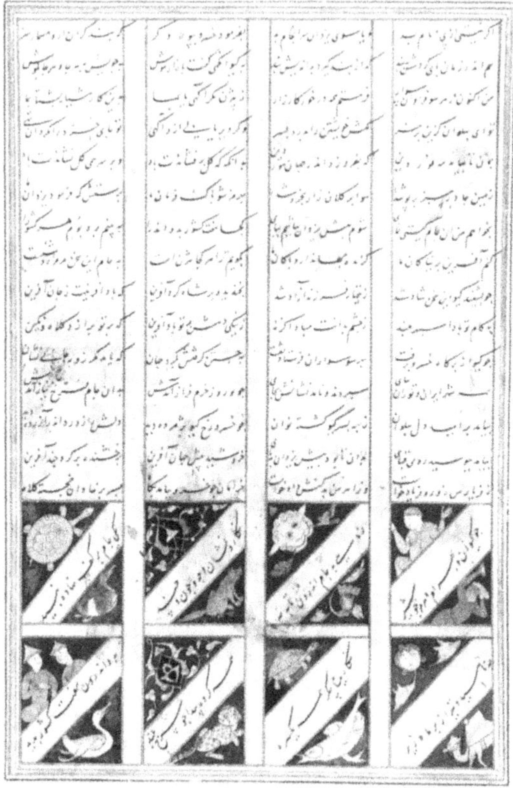

44

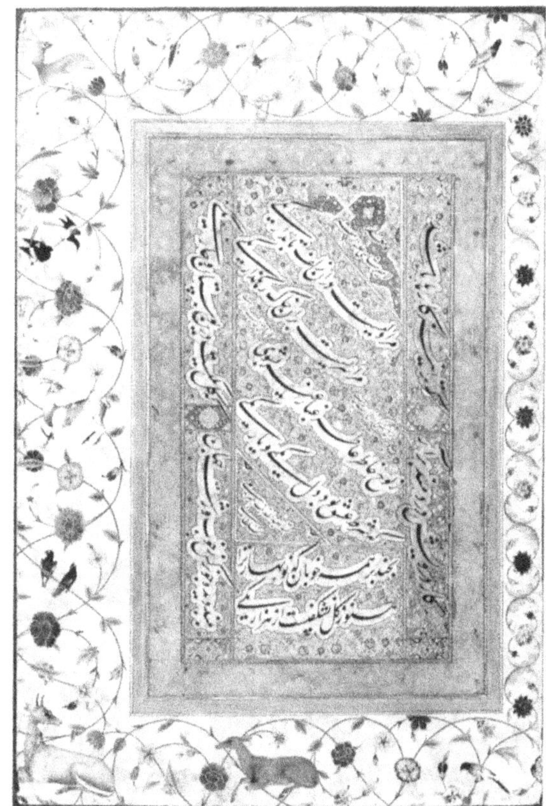

45

Fig. 44. Typical page in *nastaliq*, from a *Shahnama*, Story of Gurgin before Kay Khusraw, 1493–1494. Washington, D.C., the Arthur M. Sackler Gallery, Smithsonian Institution.

Fig. 45. Poem by Amir Shahi, Shahjehan album, sixteenth century. Washington, D.C., the Arthur M. Sackler Gallery S86.0090, Smithsonian Institution.

Fig. 46. Central Asia, Samarqand, madrasah of Ulugh Beg, 1417–1421; scripts in several different styles in entrance portal.

46

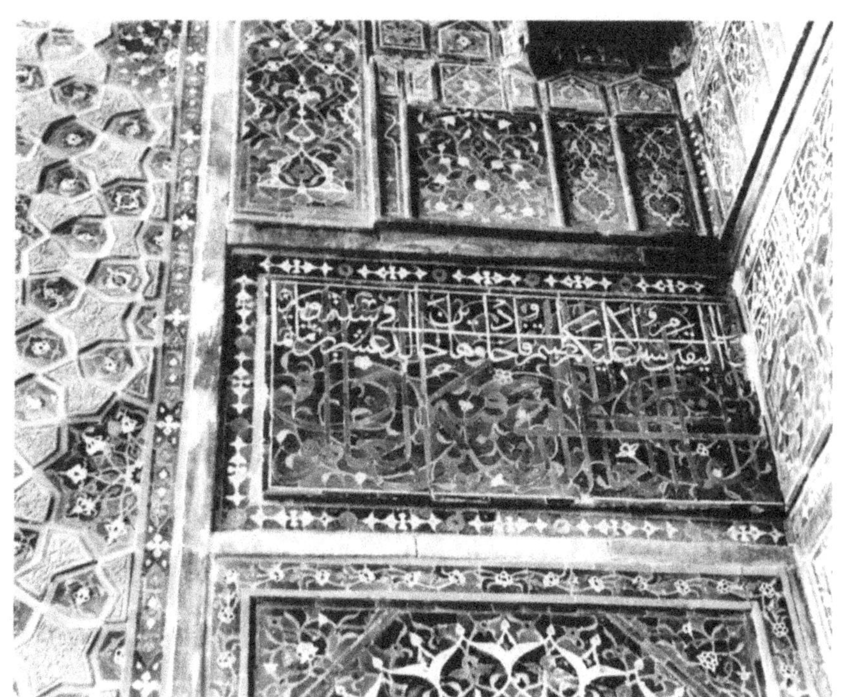

this more apparent than in manuscripts of the Koran. Three very different examples, which are just a century or so later than Ibn Muqlah's innovation, will illustrate my point and elaborate its implications.

Ibn al-Bawwab's Koran, dated to 1000–1001 and presently in the Chester Beatty Library in Dublin, is indeed written in a consistent and well-proportioned script, which makes every verse easily understood and every grammatical or semantic pause immediately visible (figs. 47, 48). It is a writing that almost disappears once it has carried its message. Bands of vegetal scrolls and numerous medallions point to the beginnings and ends of various canonical sections of the Holy Book (fig. 48); its vital statistics and tables of contents are set on cartouches of vegetal designs (fig. 49); at the beginning and at the end of the book handsome pages of colorful ornament face each other

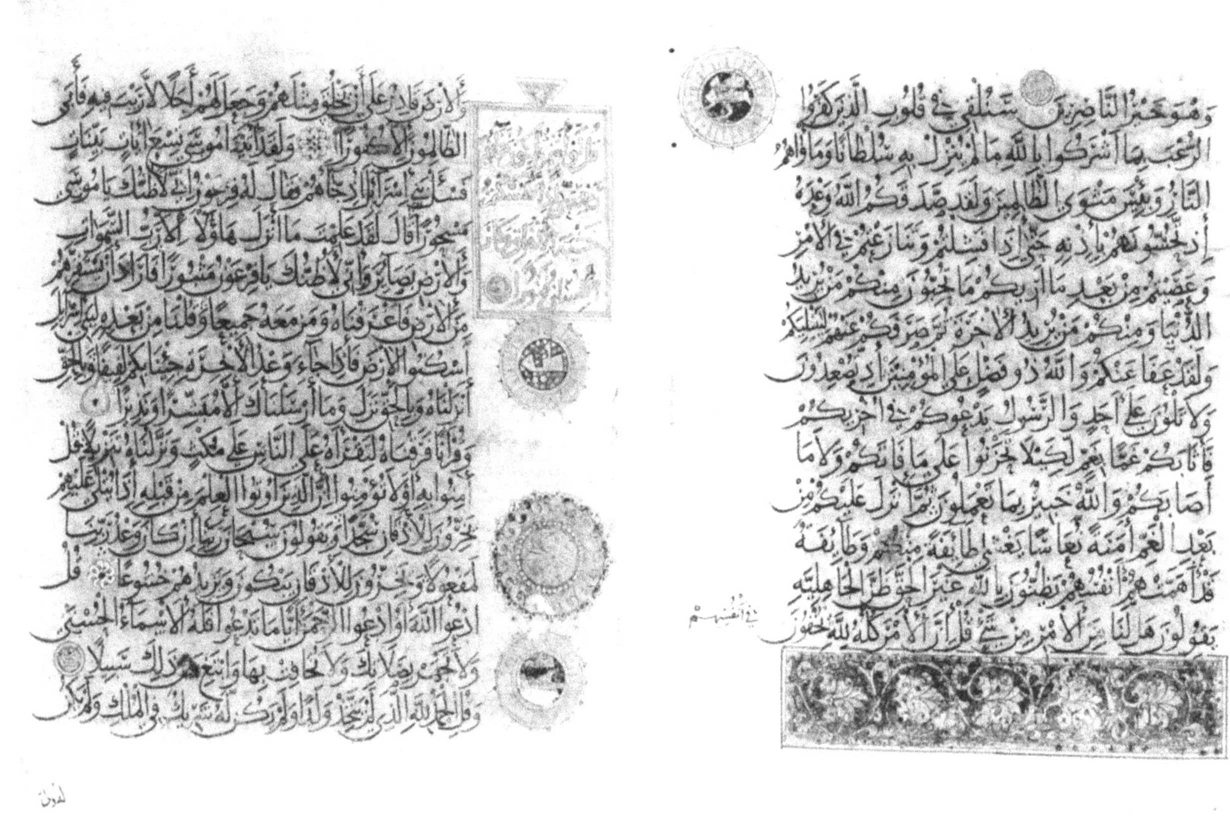

47 48

Fig. 47. Ibn al-Bawwab, manuscript of the Koran, 1000–1001, typical text page: fol. 138v. Dublin, Chester Beatty Library K.16.

Fig. 48. Ibn al-Bawwab, manuscript of the Koran, 1000–1001, text page: fol. 40r. Dublin, Chester Beatty Library K.16.

(pls. 7, 8; fig. 50). It is obvious, in this instance, that the work of art is the book. Additions were made to a straightforward written statement that enhance the pleasure, the sensuous attraction, of handling the book with a text of the Revelation, but these additions frame the written text, they are not *in* the written text. In fact, the small size of this codex gives it the quality of a personal object whose handling is as much a sensory experience as viewing it.

My second example is usually dated in the latter part of the eleventh century and consists of the pages, scattered over the world, of a Koran whose original volumes (it had been bound, probably from the very beginning, into several separate ones) are still in Istanbul.[47] Individual pages vary in many details, but the examination of two pages (pls. 9, 10) will suffice for our purposes.

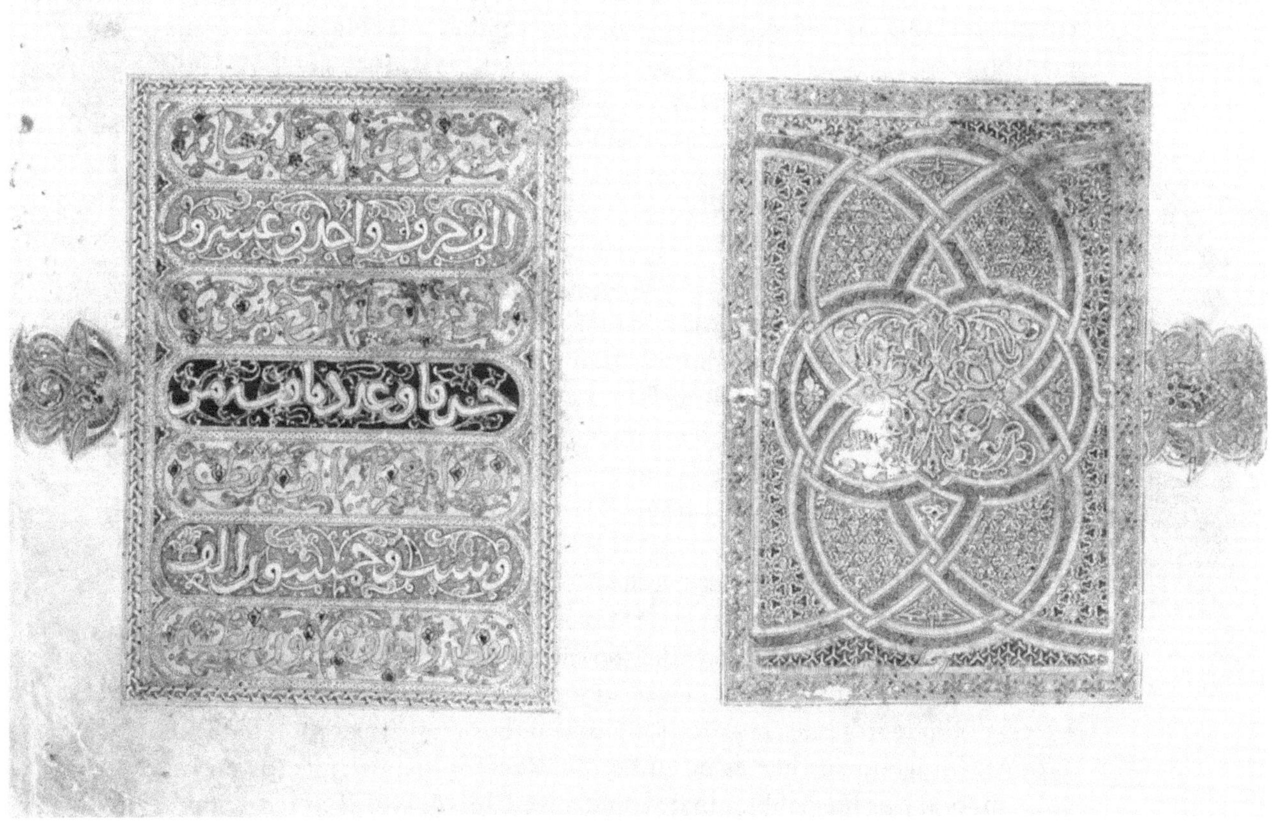

49 50

Fig. 49. Ibn al-Bawwab, manuscript of the Koran, 1000–1001, introductory page: fol. 7r. Dublin, Chester Beatty Library K.16.

Fig. 50. Ibn al-Bawwab, manuscript of the Koran, 1000–1001, introductory page: fol. 9r. Dublin, Chester Beatty Library K.16.

The writing itself is less clear than in the case of Ibn al-Bawwab's manuscript. The letters vary a lot in thickness, as hastae or rounded letters have been elongated or flattened out respectively, and as the diacritical marks are in colors that do not always make them immediately accessible, and as even "Allah," the word God, itself is depicted through the contrast between a very long first letter and a small square with indentations (pl. 10, line 3). Furthermore, even though there is no doubt about the visual primacy of the written text, the spaces between lines and letters have been completely covered with a vegetal rinceau of endless curlicues in every empty space. It is almost as though the writing is set on a rich background of vegetal designs, even though the design itself is carefully separated from the writing. Finally each page is carefully framed by a simplified form of ropelike motifs. In short, each page was seen as a separate object to be treated according to a single basic model thought up by a master scribe or by a patron. The differences between pages should probably be explained through classical art historical techniques of connoisseurship as reflections of different abilities or concern in craftsmanship.

It is impossible to know why the decision was made to create a fancy set of codices like this one, but it is possible to argue that the transformations effected here were not made in order to facilitate access to the text, but in order to provide a different sensation, perhaps the pleasure of contemplating successive smoothly and consistently designed pages and occasionally recognizing a passage or else stopping at a given passage and meditating on it, as every page I have been able to study consists of an excerpt that makes sense by and for itself. But there surely is a contradiction between the page as a unit and a continuous narrative text. Ibn al-Bawwab's Koran can easily be imagined actually read, page after page, by someone pious or just curious about a text. The so-called Qarmatian manuscript, wherever and whenever it was made, provided various successive experiences, which *may* have included the experience of reading.

My third example is a page in the Metropolitan Museum said to belong to a manuscript dated 1050 (fig. 51).[48] On it two basically consistent and quite readable scripts are used on several different scales in what is definitely a book and not a selection of pages. The variations interpret the text. Thus the large letters of the fourth line are part of the continuous Holy Text but refer to the Prophet Muhammad. Just as in numerous Western manuscripts (or even in contemporary printed Bibles that would have Christ's words in red within a text of the Gospels printed in black), the scribe modified his writing, in this case through magnification, in order to highlight a holy name. Variation in color and the curious incorporation of an elongated and leafy marginal med-

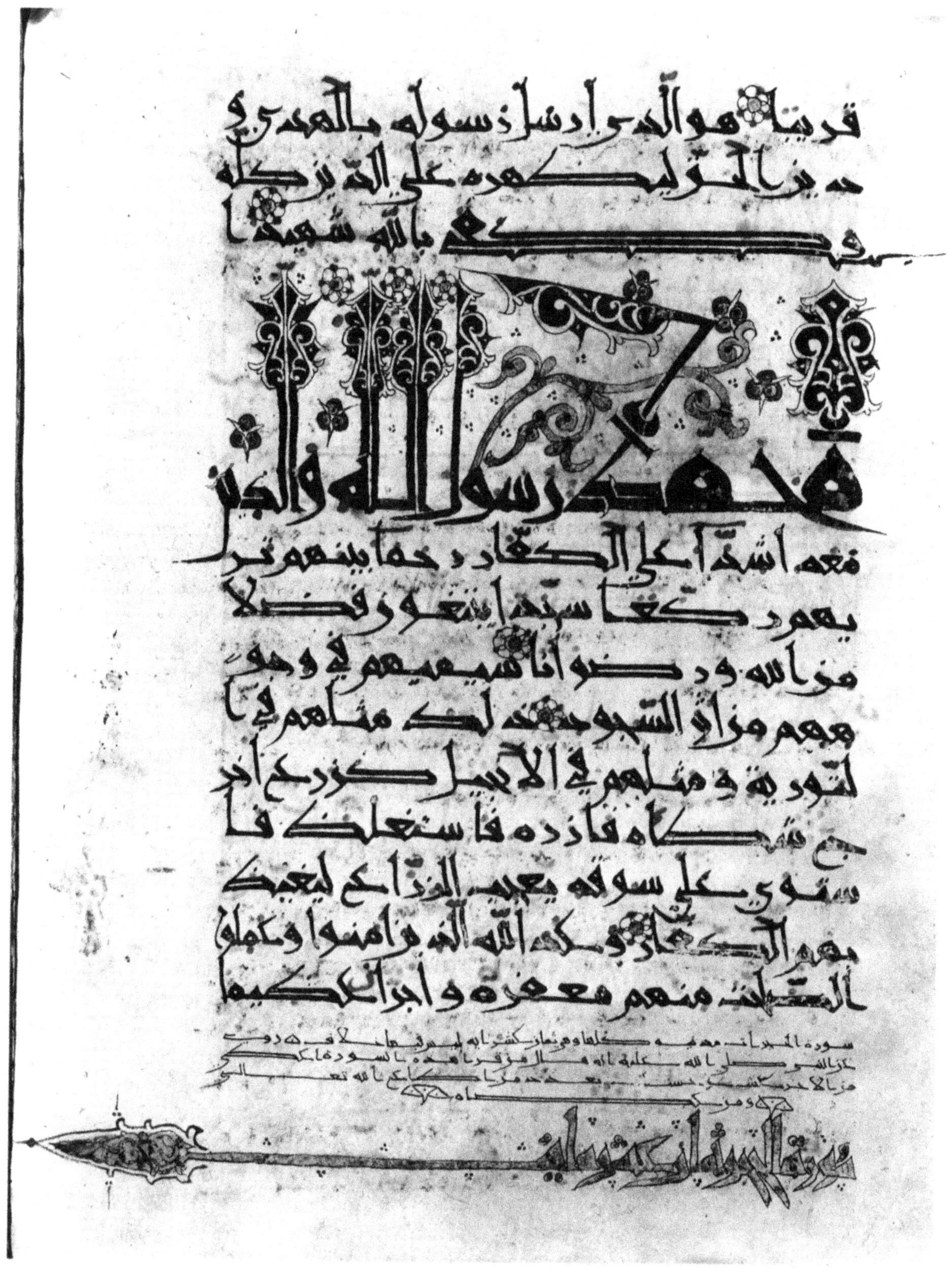

Fig. 51. Leaf from a manuscript of the Koran, eleventh century, *surah* 48:27 and following. New York, Metropolitan Museum of Art, Rogers Fund, 1940 (40.164.2a).

allion identify the title of a new *surah* or chapter, while the small characters above the title are factual data about the coming *surah* that are not part of the revealed text.

In this example, a script is simply modulated to meet a number of practical purposes, one of which is the celebration of the Prophet's name. At this stage of understanding medieval Islamic culture, there is no way to explain a choice that was probably connected to some expression of piety.[49] My first example was also that of script incorporated into a more fully thought out precious object, a book, and to excerpt its writing for special consideration and appreciation is to misunderstand its subordinate position in the visual compendium formed by a codex. It is only in the pages from the so-called Qarmatian book of the Koran that writing dominates visually but loses in legibility and in booklike continuity. Here, when we seem legitimately to talk of a work of art with each page, the mediacy of writing is no longer to the text it reproduces but to something else. It is possible, once again, that a cultural explanation should be provided for these differences. Some sort of hitherto unidentified pious or liturgical practice would have required a different approach to each page and the manuscript was meant to be read in one of several ways. It could have consisted of a succession of "holy" images. Or else one can imagine a pause as one moved from one page to the next one. But, on balance, the assumption of a terpnopoietic expectation seems easier to make in the absence of appropriate evidence about religious behavior in medieval Islam.

I SHALL RETURN later to a more general hypothesis with which to understand examples of writing after the eleventh century. In the meantime, my argument is that there was indeed a revolution in the ways of writing attributable to or later associated with Ibn Muqlah. That revolution took place during the tenth century, although no dated fragment can be associated with it before the following century. It did not consist in the establishment of what has come to be called calligraphy, of writing for its own sake and for a primarily esthetic purpose. Possibly much more like the typographic inventions of the sixteenth and seventeenth centuries in western Europe, what was created is a series of "types," both in the scientific and in the printing senses of the word. A new standard was elaborated that allowed for variations, as any type would, and the proportions defining each letter gave to the process of writing a mechanical side, which, as in printing, guaranteed quality and consistency. This conclusion is not simply a possibly arbitrary judgment pronounced on a few examples. It is also based on four additional arguments whose elaboration will permit us to delve more deeply both into the meaning of writing within Muslim culture and into the broader issues of writing as an art. These four arguments are the historical and cultural context for the innovations attributed to Ibn Muqlah and Ibn al-Bawwab; the peculiar developments of writing after 1000 in other media than the book; the elements of visual criticism that emerge here and there around writing; and the characteristics of collecting in traditional Islamic culture.

The Setting of Ibn Muqlah's Reforms

The specific context for the innovations of the tenth century is not known, but its broad setting is clear from the functions occupied by the innovators. They were all members of the administrative bureaucracy that ran the Abbasid government, viziers like Ibn Muqlah himself or functionaries known as the *ahl al-qalam*, "people of the pen" (as opposed to the military or "people of the sword," *ahl al-sayf*), or the *kuttab*, the scribes in chancery departments. A statement in one of the earliest books on penmanship, by al-Tawhidi, datable around 1010, emphasizes the importance of writing for government. "The written word," it argues, "can be read in any place and at any time. . . . It is only through written communication that a king who resides in the middle of his country knows about the welfare of the outlying districts, the safety of the frontier zones, and the stability of his realm. Without writing no administration could go on, and affairs could not be properly managed."[50]

The natural requirements of clarity and efficiency in administrative communications were given in the tenth century an additional impulse from two other sources. One is the spread and availability of paper, a cheaper material than the earlier parchment and papyrus, but one that, precisely because of its relatively low cost, transferred differentiations in value from the medium itself to what is put on it. Distinctiveness in writing became one of the criteria for social distinction, as literacy increased and materials on which writing occurred became more common and less expensive. The contrast is quite striking with the Christian West or Byzantium, where costly parchment made almost any book an item to be treasured. The second feature of this time is the existence, already mentioned, of a well-developed and sophisticated intellectual and social elite for whom elegance (exemplified by the *zurafa'*, the "elegant ones" of the texts[51]) was a major characteristic of writing as it was of clothes.[52]

Within this configuration of practical and fashionable causes, religious or even pious inspiration played a minimal role, if any. But the transmission and awareness of the faith was affected. It is sufficient to compare the absolute clarity and legibility of a page from Ibn al-Bawwab's Koran in the Chester

Beatty Library (fig. 47) with the visual brilliance but comparative senselessness of a page from a "blue" Koran (pl. 5) datable to one or two generations earlier or attributable to a different patronage. This contrast can be provided with an ideological significance, although not necessarily cause. It is in the realm of the minority and esoterically inclined world of the Fatimids and of Shiʿism in general that the blue Korans were executed, whereas the centers of the Sunni revival with its emphasis on the literalness and clarity of the divine message were the ones that fostered the new kind of precise writing.[53] The changes introduced by the bureaucrats could be used and perhaps interpreted in the religious terms of the cultural and political conflicts of the tenth century, but it is not the faith that compelled the changes. And the continuity of a relationship between writing and the formal expression of government and of power is demonstrated by such facts, among many others, as that the most complete manual of writing to have been preserved in Arabic is Qalqashandi's book of administrative procedures written in Egypt in the fourteenth century,[54] and that one of the most original and spectacular transformations of writing in later times was the very official signature of Ottoman sultans (fig. 52).[55]

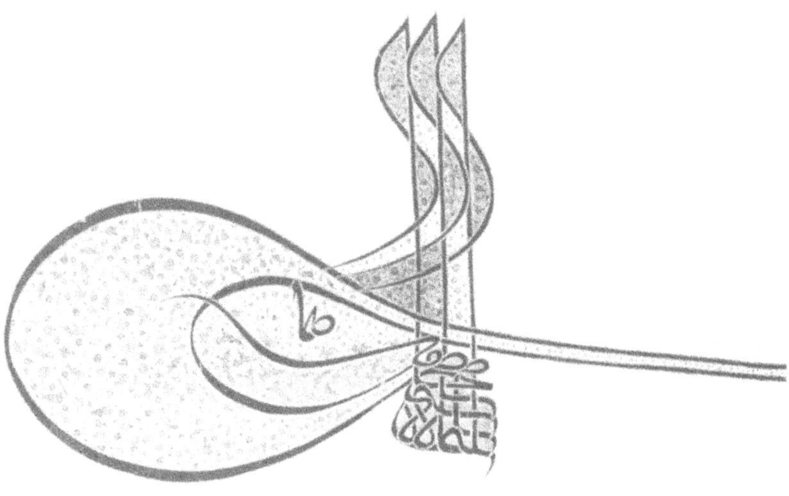

Fig. 52. *Tughra* of Suleyman the Magnificent, 1520–1566. New York, Metropolitan Museum of Art, Rogers Fund, 1938 (38.149.2).

Fig. 53. Iran, Mil-i Radkan, mausoleum, circa 1000. Washington, D.C., the Ernst Herzfeld archives.

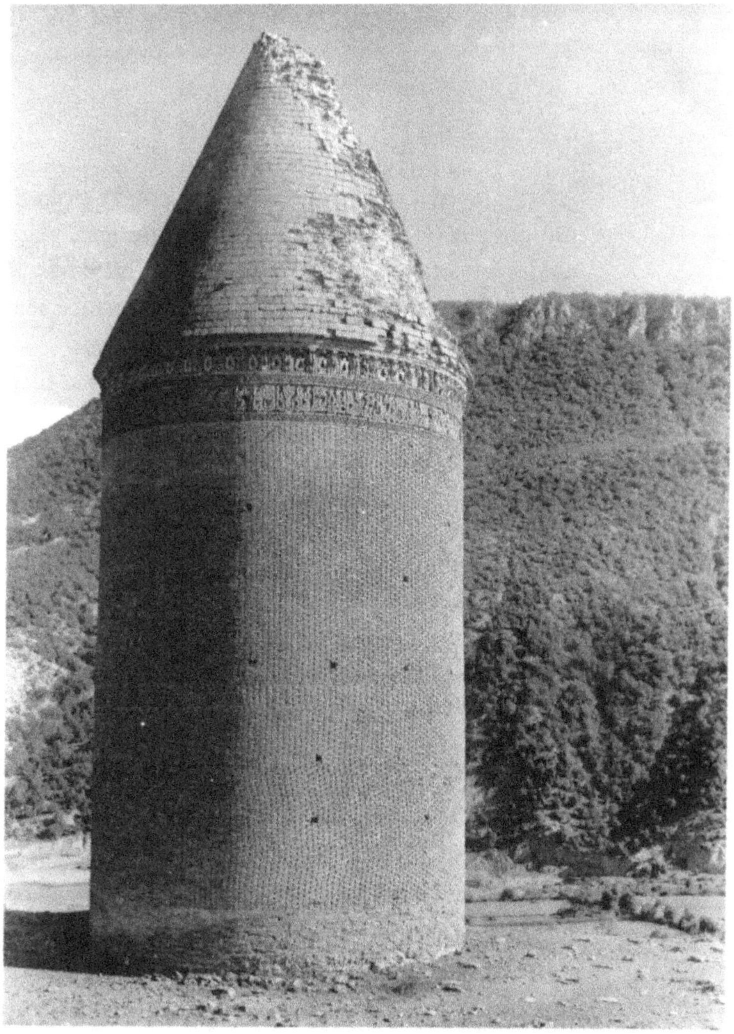

Explosion of Writing

Most of my examples so far and most of the discussion of the tenth-century changes in classical texts and in contemporary scholarship have dealt with writing in books. This particular form of writing must, however, be seen in the context of a true explosion of writing in all media. A few examples, more or less contemporary with the evidence from books, will suffice. In northeastern and central Iran a series of towers and mausoleums was built in the recently revitalized medium of baked brick. Nearly all of these buildings are provided with inscriptions for which individual bricks were baked or to which standard-size bricks were adapted. This is remarkable enough, but what makes this phenomenon even more striking is the suddenness with which a whole range of styles and techniques emerged within what has wrongly been called "brick style."[56] Mil-i Radkan (1020–1021) has complicated modifications of the upper parts of all letters (fig. 53). Gunbad-i Qabus

(1010–1011) is provided with strikingly bold and angular letters (fig. 54). At Gulpaygan (1104–1110) a geometric and vegetal band is introduced in the midst of letters (figs. 55, 56). The Nizamiyah of Khargird (middle of the eleventh century) has letters with carefully sculpted outlines, and each letter ending with a bouquet of leaves (fig. 57).

Roughly within the same period or a bit earlier, a similar variety overwhelms one group of underglaze slip-painted ceramics from northeastern Iran mentioned already more than once, on which the bold limpidity of letters and words (fig. 5) cohabits with wild or highly ordered combinations of letters (fig. 7), with other kinds of design, and even with demonstrably meaningless successions of letters (fig. 12).[57] Initially more subdued, transformations of the same sort occur in Egypt and in Iraq during the same period.[58] All these examples pave the way toward that passion for writing which characterizes Islamic art. Writing appears on all surfaces, whether buildings or objects, inside or outside. And the manners or modes of this writing are varied indeed. They can be haughtily clear and precise, just like Koranic manuscripts in Mamluk Syria or Egypt (fig. 29). They can be brutally powerful in the straightforward words of piety ("the one who trusts in God has made the right decision") of a late twelfth-century mosque in Mardin (fig. 58). They are artfully puzzling in the names of all the direct descendants of the Prophet Muhammad and of his son-in-law Ali found in a sanctuary near Isfahan (fig. 59). They become inhabited and animated in many twelfth- and thirteenth-century metal objects (fig. 60) and it is as animated letters transformed into puppets that many learned doctors or their students appear in the pages of an early thirteenth-century medical manuscript (fig. 61).[59] On fifteenth-century Iranian buildings letters can be loudly proclamatory, as with the enormous inscriptions of the citadel at Herat. They can also be set according to a hierarchy of exquisitely designed long Koranic quotations or historical statements

Fig. 54. Iran, Gunbad-i Qabus, mausoleum, 1007, detail of outer wall.

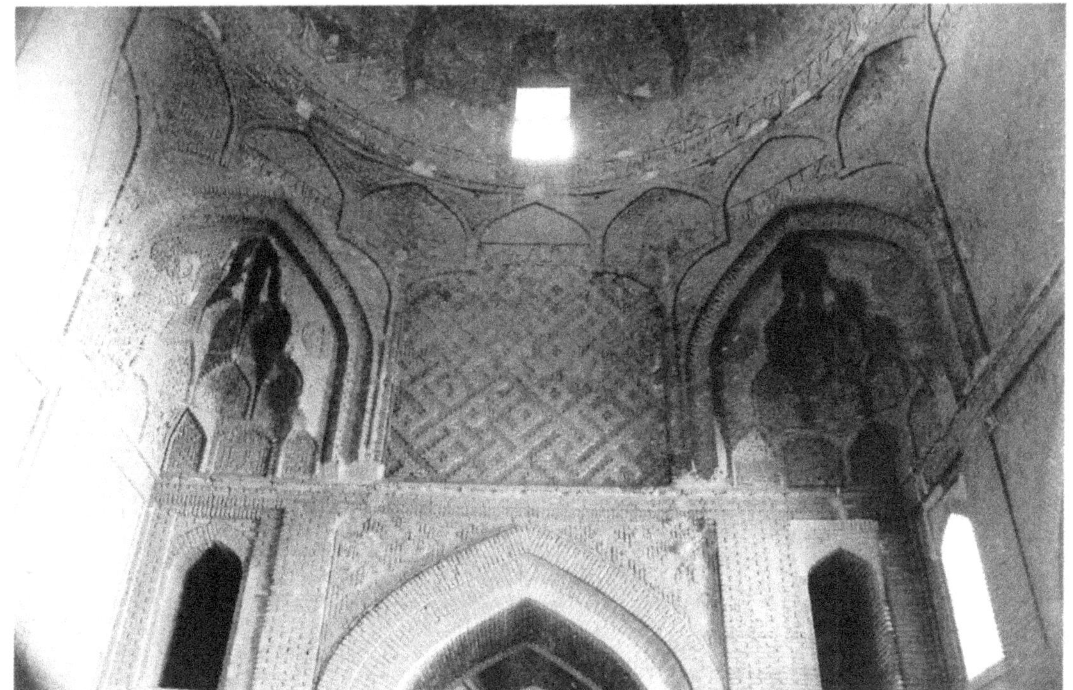

55

Fig. 55. Iran, Gulpaygan, mosque, early twelfth century, zone of transition.

Fig. 56. Detail of fig. 55.

Fig. 57. Iran, Khargird, stucco from Nizamiyah madrasah, late eleventh century.

Fig. 58. Mardin (Turkey), pious inscription in cut stone on wall of mosque, twelfth century.

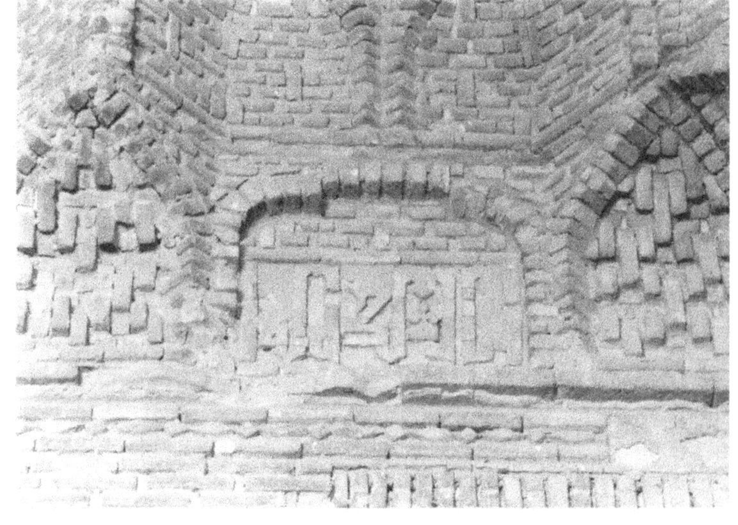

56

58

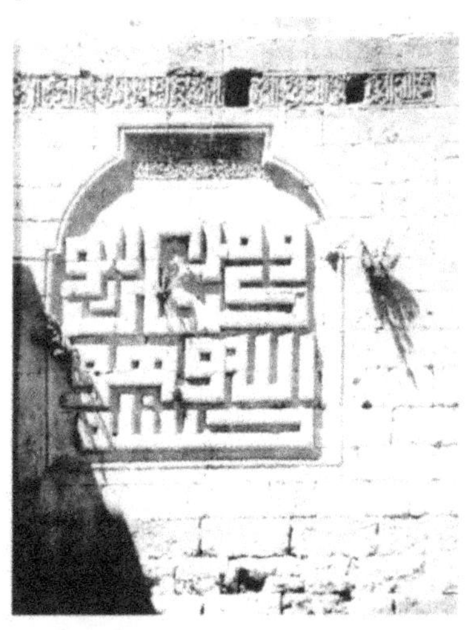

57

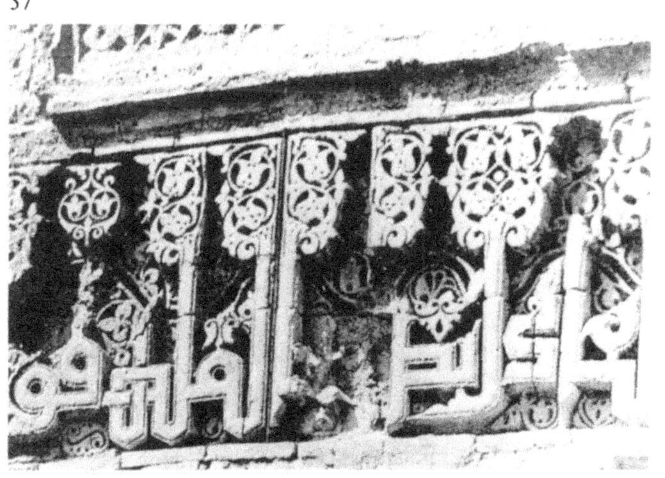

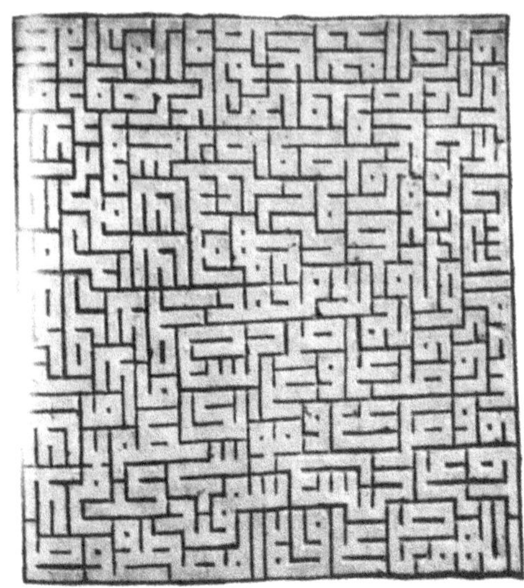

59

Fig. 59. Iran, mosque, Linjan (near Isfahan), twelfth century. Panel with the name of the descendant of the Prophet, cut or molded stucco, circa 1300.

Fig. 60. Metalwork with animated letters.

Fig. 61. Dioscordes, *De Materia Medica,* from a dispersed manuscript dated 1222. St. Louis, City Art Museum, no. 179.55.

Fig. 62. Central Asia, Samarqand, madrasah of Ulugh Beg, 1417–1421, writing in tiles.

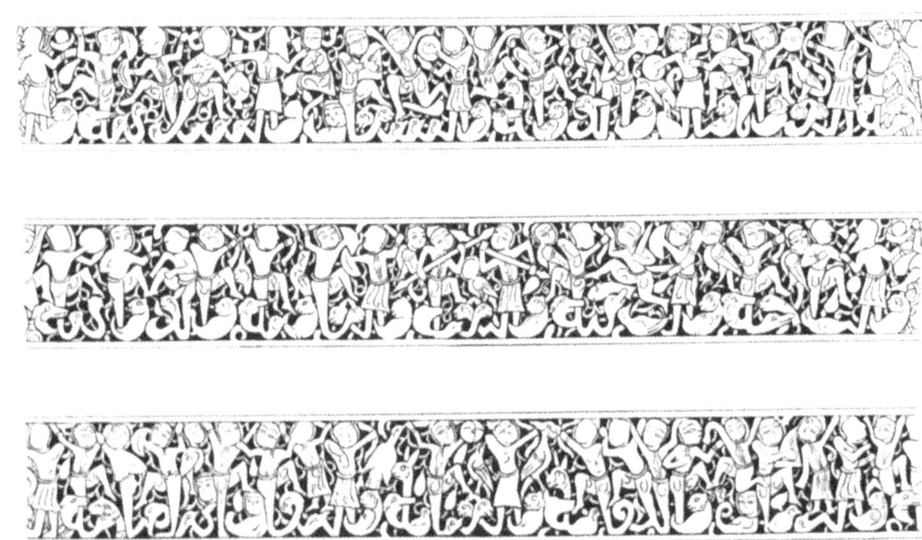

60

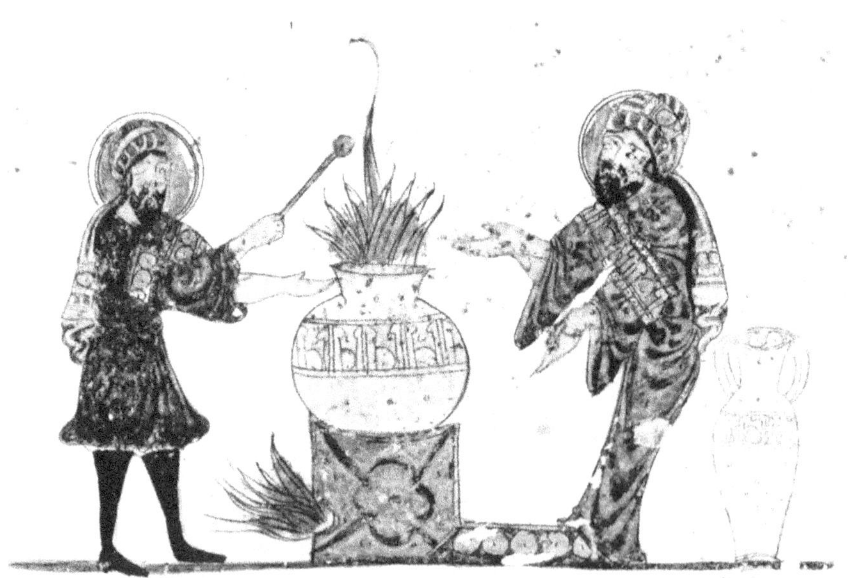

61

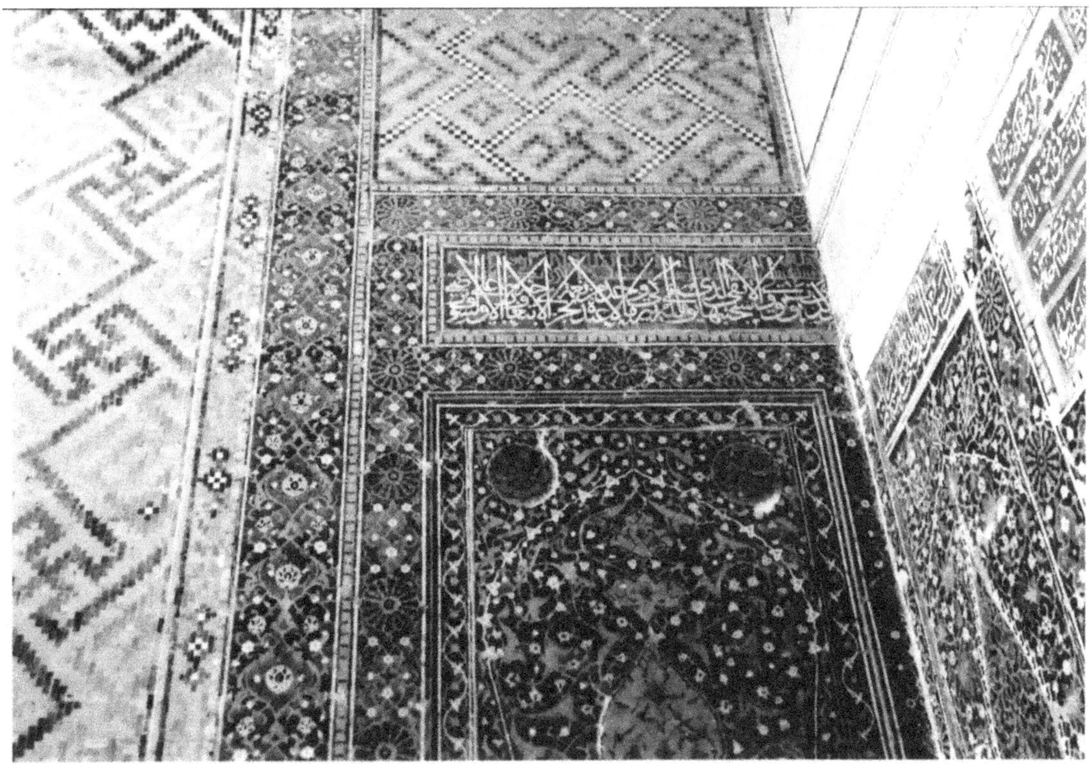

62

punctuated by the repetitive litany of blessings in a different color (fig. 62).[60] There are also totally meaningless inscriptions on objects and, as was indicated earlier, there are lengthy debates as to whether certain combinations of letters do or do not stand for whole words.

In part, of course, these examples of writing outside of the official tradition described in books on scripts and illustrated by manuscripts overlap with the latter and, especially from the fifteenth-century onward, well-known transcribers of books were commissioned to design inscriptions for buildings and probably objects.[61] This is a later phenomenon. My main point is that, initially, simultaneously with the appearance of formalized and orderly scripts in books and on official documents like coins, writing emerged on all media and with a variety of shapes and forms that defies a single explanation. The examples I have given are not only too numerous and too varied to allow for a single cause; they even include the very denial of writing—that is to say, letters that have apparently no verbal meaning associated with them.

Criticism of Writing

The third of my arguments about the meaning of writing in Islamic culture derives from written sources, from the numerous and very different statements made specifically or incidentally about writing. There is something arbitrary in my (or, for that matter, anyone else's) awareness of these sources. "How to" manuals or literary essays have never been culled systematically; many are unpublished and possibly even undiscovered. Exercise books that exist in many collections of manuscripts have never been analyzed and stories or remarks incidental but pertinent to writing are never rounded up in their entirety.[62] Yet enough examples of writing on writing have been made available that it is possible to propose the existence of a number of criteria that may outline an internal, cultural, traditional criticism of writing.[63] Just like our own contemporary criticisms of art or their Chinese equivalents, these criteria hover between the meaninglessly obvious, the obscurely esoteric, and the technically practical. But all together they provide a curious glimpse into the attitudes of Muslim tradition toward writing. These attitudes must, at this stage of research and knowledge, be considered achronically, if not really diachronically. In reality they no doubt have a history, and the differences between Tawhidi's eleventh-century essay on penmanship and Qadi Ahmad's sixteenth-century book on calligraphers reflect the almost insuperable distance between the caliphal world of Baghdad at a time of political decadence but cultural effervescence and the restricted Iranian world of the Safavids. On the other hand, Mustafa Ali's sixteenth-century book, the *Menaqib-i Hunerverai*, reflects the imperial power of the Ottomans, which guarded a Sunni orthodoxy as defined in high Abbasid times and which ruled over very diverse lands requiring direct and accessible messages. Granting, then, the likelihood of considerable differences in attitudes, expectations, and tastes between such diverse periods, I will still propose five themes of criticism about writing during the centuries of classical Islam.[64]

The technical area of criticism is the easiest one to define. At its simplest, it is an endless series of descriptions of pens and of ways to cut or handle them, of inks and of ways to store them, of paper and how to make it smooth. It includes also a level of mechanical composition, because a single mark of the pen, after Ibn Muqlah's reforms, became the module for the composition of letters and of the spaces between letters. These mechanistic evaluations are rarely used as critiques of specific examples of writing or of individual penmen, largely because the mastery of techniques was a prerequisite for acceptance as a professional. Only in the observations of seventeenth-century Iranian writers are individual idiosyncracies identified and explained, although rarely praised, and it is interesting that the only contemporary scholarly attempt to match written pages and critical judgments found it almost impossible to make the reader incorporate within his or her optic field the distinctions that were apparently made by sixteenth-century writers.[65]

A somewhat more fruitful criterion derives from the traditional literary habit of praising and even of explaining through comparisons. By listing a series of functions, purposes, or items *like which* a given object is, the man of elegant learning circumscribed the qualities of the object without ever saying what they are. We are given in this fashion a set of vestments through which we must feel or understand the technique of writing. Out of literally thousands of examples, let me pick four. "The heart is a mine, the intellect a precious metal, the tongue a miner, the pen a goldsmith, and the handwritten piece a finished piece of jewelry."[66] "Vowel signs have the same significance for a manuscript that white spots on the feet have for horses."[67] "The pen is a cypress in the garden of knowledge, the shadow of its order is spread over the dust."[68] The great Persian lyrical poet Saʿdi wrote: "If Ibn Muqla would come once more to this world, claiming to perform miracles in clear magic, he could not draw with golden ink an *alif* like you nor could he write with dissolved silver a *sin* like your mouth."[69]

What emerges from these selections is that writing is a specific moment in a series of closed processes of interpreting the world, a set of formulas through which life or the surrounding worlds are expressed; the paraphernalia of the experience of writing are means by which one describes and, therefore, feels secure with the world. In addition writing contains a potentially technical perfection that can only be explained by comparing it to horses, nature, or love. Many of these texts are, of course, poetic and use the natural device of similes, yet even the most prosaic sources imply that writing is judged properly if its technical proficiency leads one to see in it something other than itself.

Another area of criticism dovetails with an expectation of artistic creativity much broader than writing: writing must do something original and amazing; it must surprise, and it is the Arabic root *ʿajaba*, meaning "to wonder, to marvel," and from which derives the adjective *ʿajib*, "wonderful," the most common term even today in Arabic to express approval of a work of art. The point of this attitude can be illustrated by the master Umar Aqtaʿ, a one-handed penman of the late fourteenth century in Iran. He is said to have written for Tamerlane a Koran "so small that it could be fitted under the socket of a signet ring." But Timur thought it too small and did not reward Umar Aqtaʿ, who then wrote another copy where every line was one cubit long. It is impossible to know whether this was the traditional cubit, which hovered between fifty and sixty centimeters, because the Persian term used (*dharʿ*) is a rare one, but there is no doubt that the book was large, as Aqtaʿ tied it to a wheelbarrow in order to bring it to the world conqueror. Timur was duly impressed and rewarded the penman.[70] We may wince at this glorification of the monstrously large, but elephantiasis in art is a disease of rulers, and the

Mongol rulers of Iran, their Mamluk contemporaries in Egypt, and their successors in India more than once thought that bigger is better. Occasionally they were even right.[71] In fact, a whole script, *ghubar*, was created exclusively for unexpected combinations and it is a frequently recorded story that one scribe was so remarkable that he wrote only with his left hand, as though overcoming a handicap was a quality in writing. The point of unusual transformations of writing remained, however, and became in particular one of the glories of Ottoman penmanship (fig. 63). Its possibility of transcending writing and even manipulating it into mimetic representations (fig. 64) is still practiced today.[72] Already in the fifteenth century one ʿAbd al-Karim signed his name in the shape of a giraffe; but then he also thought that he was an emperor and there may have been something unhinged about his mind.[73]

I shall only mention the third criterion very briefly, not because it is not important, but because it is an area so totally unstudied that there is relatively little that one can actually say. Furthermore, this area requires philosophical and philological investigations beyond my competence. The criterion is beauty. Qalqashandi, our Egyptian bureaucrat of the late fourteenth century, has a whole section dealing with the *tahsin*, "esthetic enhancement," of writing.[74] The chosen passages are not very enlightening, either platitudes or redundancies, often related to the more technical aspects of writing like layout

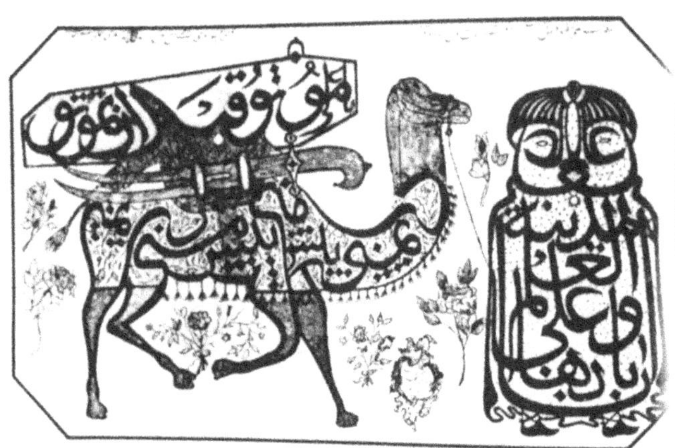

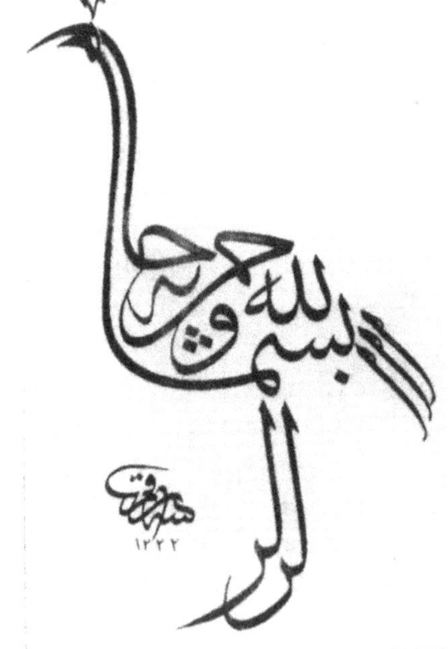

Fig. 63. Funerary procession of letters, Ottoman, nineteenth century.

Fig. 64. Bird in the shape of a *basmalah*, Ottoman, nineteenth century.

or shape of letters. A more systematic and relatively early statement on beauty occurs in Ibn al-Haytham's *Book of Optics* written in the eleventh century in Egypt and recently published and translated in exemplary fashion by A. I. Sabra.[75] Ibn al-Haytham is more concrete than Qalqashandi and I shall return in conclusion to some of his categories, but his specific references to writing are restricted to broad notions like "composition" and "order," in addition to the shape of individual letters.

Altogether there are in these few pages and in other related ones tentative suggestions for a broader theory of esthetics. Enhancement, for instance, by whatever means, increases the power or value of the scribe's work among people. It is compared with what eloquence does to speech. Beautiful writing as an attribute of the powerful ruler is claimed to have been required by the caliph al-Ma'mun,[76] but the more striking feature of all these texts is the presence of a vocabulary of esthetic appreciation, whose specifics can sometimes be guessed (as with *tartib*, some sort of proportion) but most of the time are still obscure or not concrete enough for the historian of art.[77] Something was meant by Qadi Ahmad when he says that a certain Maulana Mir Muhammad Qumi "wrote with extreme lusciousness, with much movement and maturity,"[78] but what it meant I cannot say. Similarly, the consistent use of the word *ṣūrah*, "picture, image," for the work of calligraphers in Ottoman sources may have interesting esthetic implications. On the whole, however, I feel more confident in arguing that there probably was a terminology for esthetic sensibility and judgment, but that these terms have not yet been properly fleshed out and identified.

Quite the opposite obtains when dealing with a fourth criterion, the connotative functions of writing ranging from identified symbolic values to looser associations with personal or cultural activities and beliefs. Much has been written about it and often, as in the several studies by Annemarie Schimmel, in ways that match beautifully eloquence and learning.[79] For our purpose of ultimately learning how to sketch out an appropriate esthetic response to writing, two themes seem to me to be of particular interest. One is a mass of associations made with individual letters, as with the *lam-alif* in amorous embrace (fig. 65), an image used quite concretely in one illustration of the *Maqamat* in the early thirteenth century showing two heroes literally embracing like the two letters (fig. 66).[80] Or, in another example, the association is developed between the *nun* of the eyebrows, the *ʿayn* of the eyelids, and the *mim* of the mouth; all together these letters say "yes" (*naʿam*). In mystical poetry, especially in Iran and Ottoman Turkey, such images played a major role and probably affected the visual arts, inasmuch as some scribes had con-

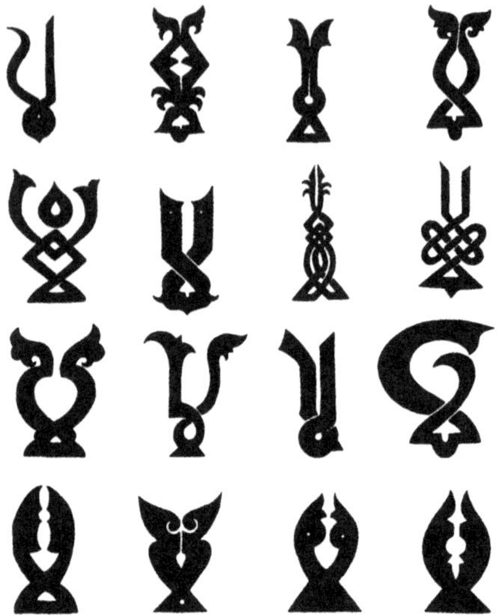

Fig. 65. Example of *lam-alif.*

nections with mystical groups. It is easy enough to provide an esoteric meaning to prayers or pious formulas transformed into birds (fig. 64) or into boats (fig. 67).[81] But on this score one wishes that the accumulated data were more accurate and more persuasive, as equally strong evidence exists to show that scribes were mostly bureaucrats belonging to the ruling elite rather than mystics outside of society's mainstream.[82] But then there was an accepted range of mystical practices that could well be expected of scribes to know.

Even though often entertaining and at times witty, these stories do not have much to do with an appreciation of writing; they are in fact verbal interpretations of letters, at best suggestions for the transformation of letters into something other than words, closer in fact to the transformations of letters in Western art than those of classical Islamic art or of China. They are a rupture in a traditional sequence from thought to writing, at best a source for eventual iconographic developments.

The other connotative theme lies in esoteric interpretations. Such are series of numeral equivalents to letters, which do everything from hiding secrets to predicting the future. Alternately the twenty-eight letters are seen as the equivalents of the days of the month and each one carries astrological meanings. In a world of constant astrological concerns, there is nothing surprising in this. More original is the transformation of letters and of their messages into statements of love and of holiness. These *hurufi* or "letter-centered" theories led in 1398 to the execution of their first proponent, one Fadlullah from Astarabad in Iran, but his ideas were maintained. A Bektashi

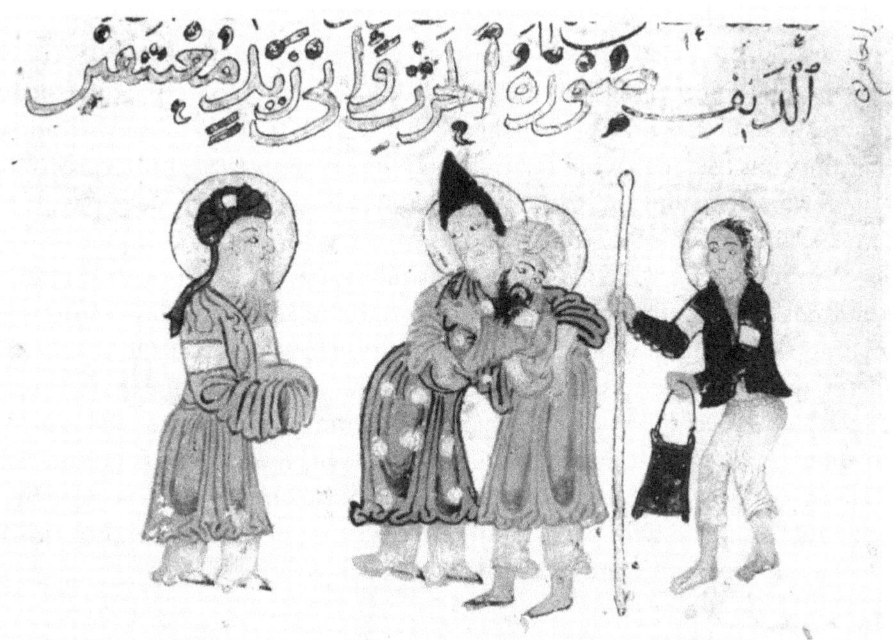

Fig. 66. Hariri, *Maqamat*. Paris, Bibliothèque Nationale, *arabe* 3926, fol. 68v.

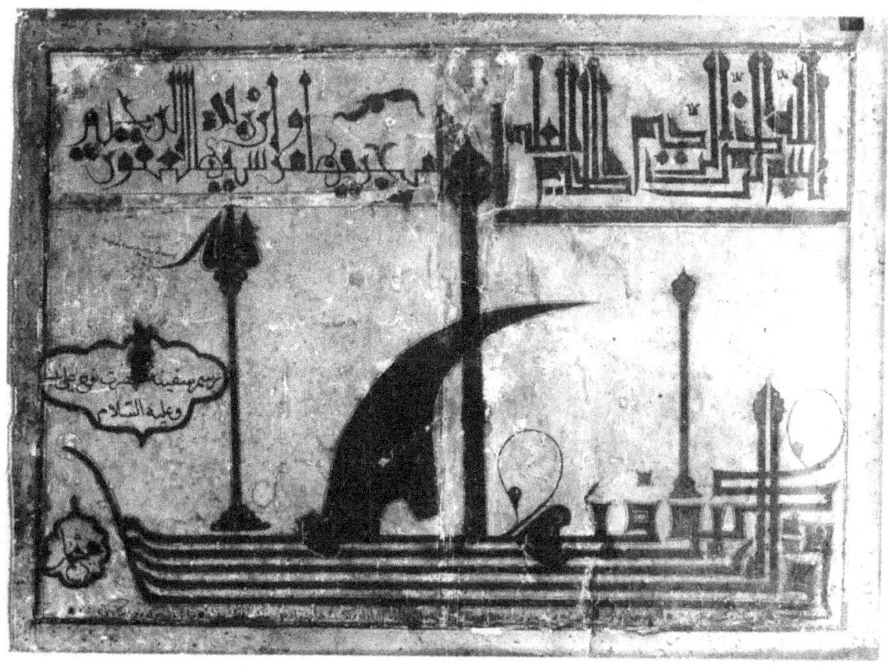

Fig. 67. Writing in the shape of a boat, Turkish, seventeenth century. Ross Collection, Boston, Museum of Fine Arts, 15.125.

poet wrote: "O you, whose sign [*ayat*, which also means the Koran] is the title page of the primordial *diwan*, the *tughra* [decorated imperial signature] of your eyebrows is the *bismillah al-rahmani al-rahim*."[83] Blasphemy to the orthodox in this amorous use of a sacred formula may also be seen as the full expression of love for another one and for God. And, when the Turkish poet Fuzuli says "my eternal prayer is the Koranic verse of thy face," he transforms writing into the symbol of that which is most beautiful, but neither he nor Rumi nor the hundreds of poets from Ottoman Turkey to Bangladesh who have proclaimed writing as the paragon of all beauty and virtue have helped us in transferring their sensuous awareness into an understanding of a written line. In fact, in one of those wonderful paradoxes that make medieval theology so exciting, according to the tenth-century writer al-Thaʿalibi, the worst of writing is the writing of angels because it must be illegible to humans. It is possible to imagine that some wild pages of illegible writing done in the eighteenth and nineteenth centuries were examples of angelic writing (fig. 68).[84]

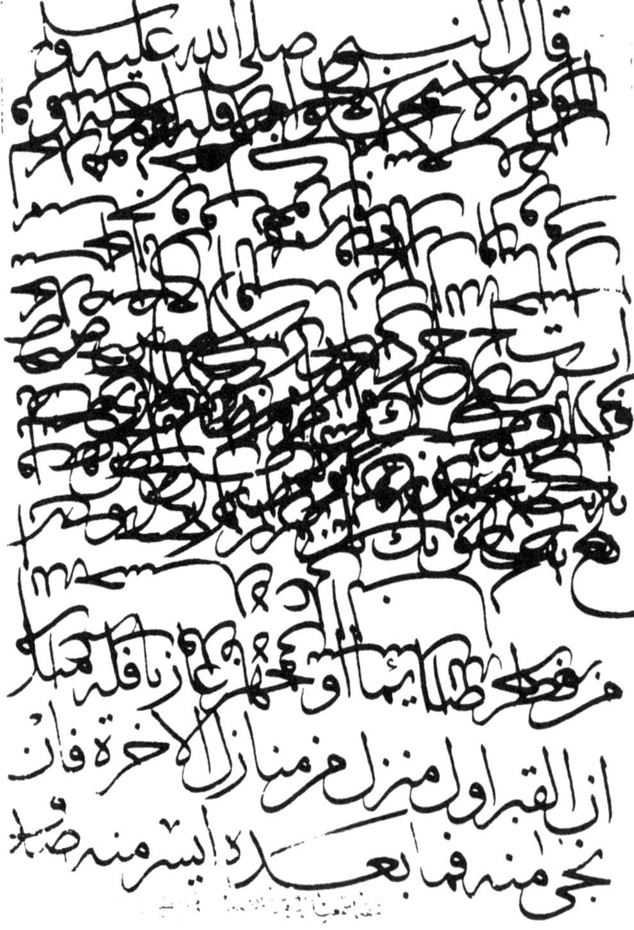

Fig. 68. Wild writing, Ottoman, nineteenth century.

My last example of traditional criticism is not directly helpful to understanding specific fragments, but it will lead to a possibly fruitful approach to the ways of writing in the Muslim world. Already Tawhidi in the eleventh century quoted someone as saying that "writing is the tongue of the hand. The intellect is the tongue of good actions and qualities. And good actions and qualities are the perfection of man." It is "the necklace of wisdom," just as pens are "the pack animals of the minds, the couriers of the natural facilities, the vanguards of intellects."[85] Six centuries later a Persian poet wrote that "The world found name and fame from the Pen; / If the Pen were not there, there would not be the world."[86] Penmen would be forgiven for having written so well the *basmalah* (the traditional statement *bism Allah al-Rahman al-Rahim* "In the name of God, the Compassionate, the Merciful," with which Muslims begin every chapter of the Koran as well as nearly all their accomplishments), while others would escape eternal punishment by sinning so much that the book of their evil deeds would become black and could not be read.[87] The critical interpretation that can be given to these and many comparable stories or images is that writing is seen and evaluated as a means of transmission. At times it merely passes on a statement, it allows a narrative to be fixed. At other times it proclaims, directly or indirectly, by the very fact of its existence, the power of a ruler or of God. At other times yet it is an act of piety that purifies both maker and beholder. Writing is indeed an intermediary, which is judged by how well it expresses the quality of its maker and affects the sensitivity of its user. Writing has an ethical component in the very special way of medieval Islamic ethics, whereby the intent behind the act is what validates that act.[88] But, since intent is not available to anyone but God, the viewer acknowledges the intent by providing his own interpretation of the writing and thereby enters into an ongoing dialectic relationship with the created object, which never stops at the object and yet cannot exist without the object.

I shall return to the way in which this conclusion can be translated into the understanding and enjoyment of Arabic characters within the Muslim tradition. In the meantime and before turning to the last argument for a definition of the meaning of writing in Islamic art, a sketch of a theory of visual criticism in the writing of classical times can be proposed. It includes technical requirements on the one hand and a series of factors affecting both the viewer-user and the maker. The requirements *and* the effects can, in preliminary fashion, be called esthetic, ethic, and marvel-making, but in all cases, at least in the classical tradition, the written part was but a vehicle, it was not the end of the experiment.

One last point needs to be recalled. Although Qadi-Ahmad does occasionally refer to the work of the scribe on stone or in colorful ceramics and later Ottoman sources talk about wall paintings, the literature on writing is almost entirely restricted to what was written on paper. The point will have its importance at the end of this chapter.

Collecting in Medieval Islamic Culture

My last argument for an eventual explanation of the tenth-century revolution in the writing of Arabic and of its subsequent avatars lies in the nature of collecting in medieval and immediately postmedieval Islamic society. The word "collecting" is used in a slightly different and broader sense from the usual one of acquiring and keeping works of art or series of artifacts. For instance, I am including patronage in my view of collecting, for what I am really trying to define is the social and cultural matrix that was able, by its position, wealth, or prestige, to sponsor, commission, acquire, and especially keep and maintain writing or whatever objects or monuments of architecture used writing. For practical purposes, the locus of collecting in this broader sense was the treasury, *khizanah*, or the *kitab-* (or *naqqash*) *khaneh*, the atelier for manufacturing and storing books or objects attached to courts.[89] But, ideally at least, the specific practice of collecting makes better sense if seen within the much wider context of the attention given to the arts in general, sponsoring new works or reusing old ones.

An understanding of collecting in the Islamic world could be done thematically, that is to say in terms of specific objects whose gathering one seeks to pinpoint or of works of architecture seen or admired by a given individual. It could also be imagined chronologically, since a major break occurred in its practice during and after the fourteenth century, in the sense that it becomes difficult to generalize for the whole Islamic world. Whatever may be true and valid in the heavily urbanized Arab North Africa, in Egypt, and in the Levant no longer obtains for the Ottoman, Safavid, and Mughal imperial courts. Both Ottomans and Mughals, much more than the Safavids, inherited practices from older non-Islamic cultures, which gave a special tenor to their collecting.[90] Such a study could also be based both on actual physical remains like the existing collections of Istanbul and on texts, either incidental stories or recorded lists, like the celebrated one of the eleventh-century Fatimid treasures in Cairo.[91] An attempt to correlate remaining objects and recorded data would be a truly fascinating endeavor requiring teams of researchers. And it should be possible to add architecture to the study, as the choice of buildings to be repaired and restored can often be construed, psychologically and ideologically, as an aspect of collecting the past. However, as none of the preliminary research has been done, I will hypothetically argue only two points pertinent to my purpose of understanding writing.

Written information dealing with treasures only mentions writing when it occurs in books and, more rarely, when it involves identifying something on a collected object, like the great silks kept in the Fatimid treasures, which had the names of countries or of rulers whenever lands or princes were represented.[92] Actually, to argue that writing was only significant because it appears in books is not entirely accurate. It is true that books were collected, at times for the sheer value of their numbers, as one can hardly imagine what was so great about having, as one of our sources asserts, twelve hundred copies of Tabari's important but ultimately not particularly exciting history of the Muslim world;[93] its educational usefulness could be achieved with fewer copies. Far more significant is the fact that, most of the time, a few pages from a book were sufficient to a collector, if the original book had been written by (or attributed to) Ibn Muqlah, Ibn al-Bawwab, or later Mir Ali Tabrizi, the alleged inventor of the elegant Persian script known as *nastaʿliq*. Although there were exceptions involving painters of pictures in the late Persian cultures of Iran and India, only copyists of texts succeeded in having their creations bought like real works of art—that is to say, recognized as such by the name of their maker and by their intrinsic quality. Following the practice of collecting everywhere, as it has been defined by Joseph Alsop, collecting led to forgeries.[94] Some of the latter were, quite naturally, attributed to well-known historical scribes, but there were also pious forgeries, for instance of Kufic Korans attributed to Ali, the paragon of so much that is esthetically good within the Muslim tradition, or historical frauds with national or other implications.[95]

It is difficult to know when an interest in collecting writing came into being and how widely it spread. The earliest clear textual information suggests Cairo and the eleventh century; historical logic would prefer Baghdad and the tenth. But these are secondary considerations, for in point of fact we do not possess more than a handful of examples matching textual references with actual objects, like the Koran copied and decorated by Ibn al-Bawwab (pls. 7, 8; figs. 47–50), which has been discussed earlier.

From the fifteenth century onward, however, a new vehicle appears for the collection of fancy writing and of paintings. The vehicle is the album, the *muraqqaʿ*, a miniaturized museum or an elaborate scrapbook. It gathered in a fancy binding all sorts of pages with writing and images, with several different motivations or justifications for the choices made.[96] We do not know when albums began to be popular, but they are attested in the early fifteenth century in several Turkic and Mongol courts of Iranian culture. Hundreds of images and thousands of pages or fragments of writing have remained, which had apparently been collected for the prestige or financial value of whatever was put on them. And the great scribes of these later centuries thus became true artists, because their work was acquired by the wealthy and kept, more or less carefully, in the pages of albums, which had become obligatory possessions at every court. At worst (or best), these scribes were employed by rulers to produce a constant stream of books and written pages. The Timurid prince Baysungur Mirza is alleged to have had forty scribes working at his court.[97] Under Suleyman the Magnificent, collections of writings by celebrated calligraphers were illuminated when added to albums, obtaining thereby an additional sign of honor.[98] These developments were probably restricted to the imperial courts and to a few dynastic courts following imperial models. How far they extended socially is in fact impossible to say, and my suspicion that they did not spread very far is largely based on the absence of a significant urban patronage of other than religious books, books on *adab* or belles lettres, or purely educational manuals.[99]

It is restrictive to limit the patronage of writing to the elitist collection of things, books or objects, with writing by great scribes. Fortunately, in one area the patronage of princes *was* destined to masses. It is the level of the public monument, in which, almost from the beginning of Islam and certainly from the ninth century onward, information about the building and all sorts of other messages, local and limited or universal and general, have covered and adorned walls of citadels or mosques. The writing on these artifacts other than books and especially in architecture is so original to Islamic culture, as writing is made to escape the rarified realm of the connoisseur—an experience unavailable in either the Far East or the West. The relationship between interiorized, private collecting and the public expression of writing is, however, a strange one.[100]

Original written sources have usually only recorded the purely informational data found in inscriptions on buildings, but there is a peculiarity about this written record I cannot at this stage explain. As we saw earlier, references to the artifacts used by the ninth-century Baghdad elite specifically mention writing as a novel adornment on monuments of architecture or on objects for conspicuous consumption, whereas the existing written records of monumental inscriptions, as found in chronicles or geographical texts, are limited to practical information like dates or names of rulers; texts by medieval literati rarely mention Koranic inscriptions or other information on which scholarship thrives and which do exist in remaining and still-standing inscriptions. It would almost appear, then, that the public message of writing failed to become part of the written record of later Muslim cultures. On the other hand, Qadi Ahmad in the early seventeenth century mentions quite frequently that great calligraphers worked on buildings, but he almost never quotes what texts they put up for view. In Meshhed, Isfahan, or Sinan's great mosques, and most spectacularly in the Taj Mahal, the major scribes of the time were responsible for the layout of writing, if not the choice of whatever was written.[101] None of the sources I have seen mention practical objects similarly decorated by major scribes, even though many were endowed with writing.

The peculiarity of this public writing, especially on buildings, is that its chances of preservation beyond a generation or so or, to put it more precisely, the rate of its semantic charge, varied enormously. In the mosque of Isfahan, dozens of inscriptions with very different purposes, ranging from grand pious proclamations to legal documents, cut into each other, at times even amputate Koranic quotations and render them meaningless, but one strikingly designed panel has remained untouched (fig. 69). It contains a fourth-rate poem, emphasizing the signature of the artisan responsible for most of the work in the sixteenth century.[102] In Jerusalem, inside the Dome of the Rock and the Aqsa mosque, successive restorations, especially relatively recent Ottoman ones, rewrote and summarized earlier inscriptions in order to keep the chronological record of the building, even if in very sketchy form, but destroyed the old inscriptions.[103] Mausoleums and madrasahs, on the other hand, as in Samarqand or Damghan, were rarely repaired and the writing on them has usually been preserved either, as in Cairo, because of the indestructible quality of the stone in which they are carved or, as with the Taj Mahal, because the writing is so fully part of the building. In general we are dealing with an as yet unstudied equilibrium between needed repairs and changing tastes or needs, whereby powerful statements of Islam are introduced in Hagia Sophia when fear for the superiority and safety of the Ottoman system had emerged,[104] while in Bursa's or Edirne's fifteenth-century monuments new requirements of taste introduce a powerful script (fig. 39), which is echoed in the Le Corbusier–like mosque of Serajevo in Yugoslavia (fig. 70), where once again writing is a means for a community of Muslims to assert its continuing existence.[105]

As to objects of industrial arts, whose early, pre–fourteenth century, examples have been better studied than the later ones, a valid generalization is equally difficult to attain, but a clear differentiation must be made between

Fig. 69. Isfahan, *masjid-e jomeh,* tile panel, seventeenth century.

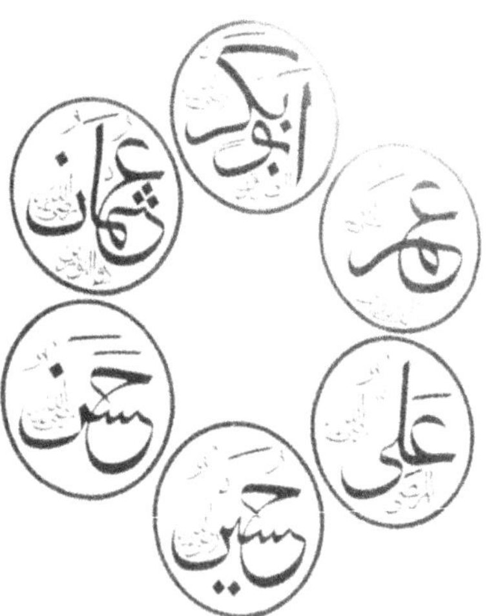

Fig. 70. Yugoslavia, Visoko, mosque of Sherafudin, completed 1980.

statements that are informative, as they provide a date or the name of an artisan, and a variety of generalities of good wishes or of possession. The former are object-specific and usually quite clear, the latter range from perfectly clear to ludicrously obscure, as, for instance, when animals or playful personages animate an inscription but make it almost illegible (fig. 60).[106]

In short, the collection of and caring for its works of art that the Muslim world developed over the centuries can be seen from two points of view. One is focused on the artifacts themselves. From that particular point of view a perfectly unoriginal hierarchy appears in which works of art—books or mosques—are preserved because of a continuous involvement with them of patrons and society and because of a consistent need for their preservation. But, then, below this relatively rare level of consciously maintaining the past, changes, abandonment, and adaptive reuses of all sorts are the norm. This again is not particularly unique, except that the renovation of surfaces and the rejection of permanent and, so to speak, nonnegotiable appearances are, to some, a cultural imperative of Islam. It is, after all, every year that the Kaʿbah is covered with a new cloth embroidered with a holy inscription, and the old covers are stashed away as having fulfilled their function and occasionally sold for profit or cut up and given as gifts or holy souvenirs, at least from the Ottoman court.[107] The object expects in short to change its skin and change its age, while writing was one of the signs that preserved history and identified the present.

The other point of view is that of the patron and maker. There, the practice of the traditional Muslim world nurtured and fostered a social institution that may also be universal, but whose Muslim form is unique: the institution of the "treasury," with its by-products like the court workshops and ateliers. Books, writing, objects were manufactured in order to be kept, most of the time, invisible, except on official occasions or as gifts to others. The peculiarity of the Muslim phenomenon is that the practice was not limited, at least not always limited, to princes alone. In 1148 a merchant from Herat, today in northwestern Afghanistan, made a pen case (fig. 71) for his brother

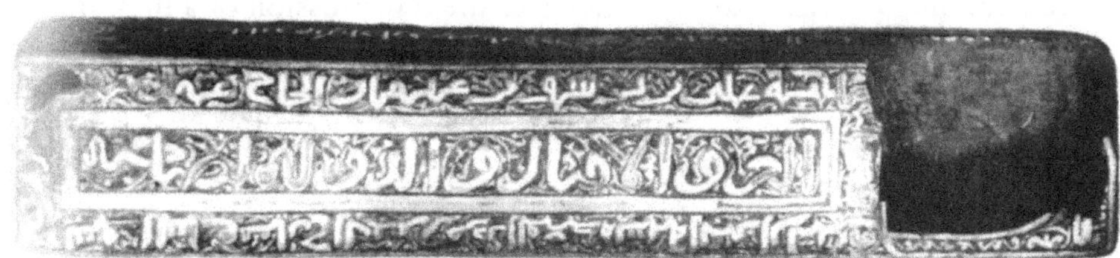

Fig. 71. Pen case, inlaid bronze, eastern Iran, 1148. Leningrad, Hermitage Museum.

who had gone to Mekka to accomplish the pilgrimage. It is a poignant object, now preserved in Leningrad, for a pilgrim from Afghanistan was probably gone for two or three years or more, without sending letters home. While working, the maker did not know whether the product of his hobby would ever be given to its destinatory, nor do *we* know whether it was or not. But he wrote on the object a statement about himself, his brother, and the object he made. This statement, a prosaic and factual one, became the message that allows modern scholarship to reconstitute a very specific and immanent object into a statement of brotherly affection.[108] The existence of this sort of social and personal depth to objects is a peculiarity of medieval Islamic art. It allows for a different discourse on these objects than the usual taxonomic one and the means to this difference lies in writing, not in the decorative forms, mimetic or not, that adorn the objects.[109]

It should be added that, while in the Middle Ages this sort of personal potential of the secular object seems unique to Islamic art, it reappears in Victorian times in the West, as constantly reengraved silverware or wedding rings are meant, once again through writing, to maintain family history.

We have wandered far and wide in developing a context within medieval and premodern Islamic culture that would have nurtured particularly original and varied uses of writing. It is appropriate now to pull these various considerations into a theory of writing in Islamic art before the momentous changes of the late nineteenth century. Historically, matters seem reasonably clear, as two impulses operated simultaneously within Muslim culture. One is, from the tenth century onward, the creation or invention of several types of consistent scripts, which became a typology of writing. Whether they were based on a rigid numerical system around individual letters as with Ibn Muqlah and Ibn al-Bawwab's inventions or on a more fluid flow as with several later Persian scripts, the purpose of these types was primarily to make a text available and to ensure its understandability among those who knew the language. Known primarily through books, these scripts were also used in monumental inscriptions, especially for dynastically sponsored buildings—that is to say, whenever the transmission of a message was essential. It is possible, as has been done for decades, to call this practice and the works that derive from it calligraphy, for indeed Islamic practices and the resulting creations relate to a Western practice of the sixteenth and seventeenth centuries that was called calligraphy. But, because the word eventually acquired an aura of esthetic content, I prefer to avoid it when describing or evaluating formalized scripts that differ in style, but in which order and legibility take precedence over beauty. I suggest calling them simply the *scripts* of high Muslim culture and, as already indicated by the title of the first book on the subject by B. Moritz, their investigation is correctly called "paleography," that is to say the study of ancient scripts.[110] The creation of scripts in this manner and for similar purposes of distributing information is a phenomenon also encountered in Western medieval society and probably elsewhere as well.

The second impulse is more original. Probably also in the tenth century, maybe as early as in the ninth, a popular urban Islamic culture of the big cities of Iraq, Iran, Turan, and later Egypt, Syria, and the Muslim West incorporated writing into the decoration of its objects. This phenomenon is known primarily through ceramics and metalwork, but it eventually extended to shrines and mausoleums, where it often encountered the royal or courtly patronage around which the first impulse of clear and orderly transmission predominated. The peculiarity of this second impulse is its exuberance. Be it on tombstones (fig. 41) and cenotaphs or on ceramic plates (figs. 9–12) and silver inlaid cups (figs. 60 and 72), on the walls of mausoleums like Kharraqan's (fig. 73) or sanctuaries like the Karatay madrasah in Konya (fig. 74), letters and words can be perfectly clear and meaningless as well. They can in

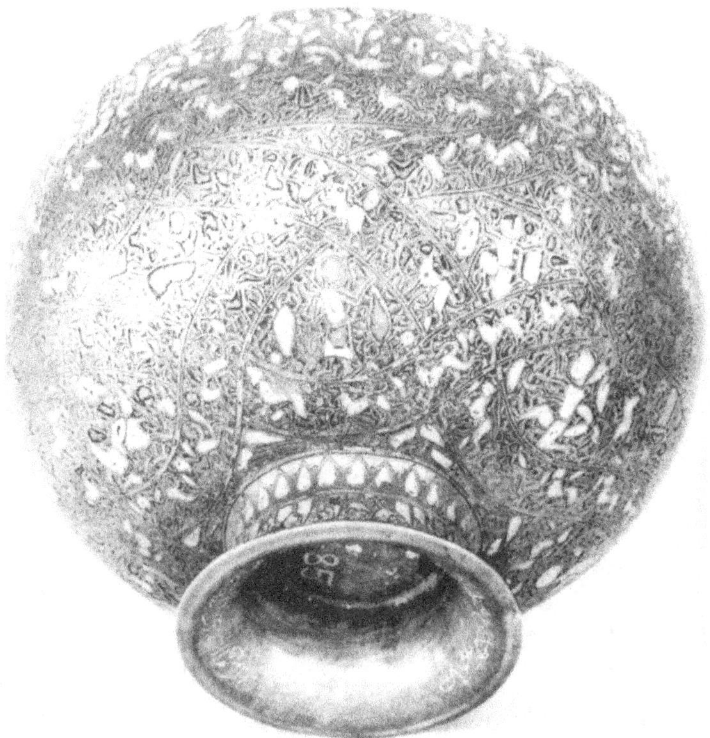

Fig. 72. Cup, inlaid bronze, early thirteenth century. Cleveland Museum of Art, Purchase from the J. H. Wade Fund, 44.485.

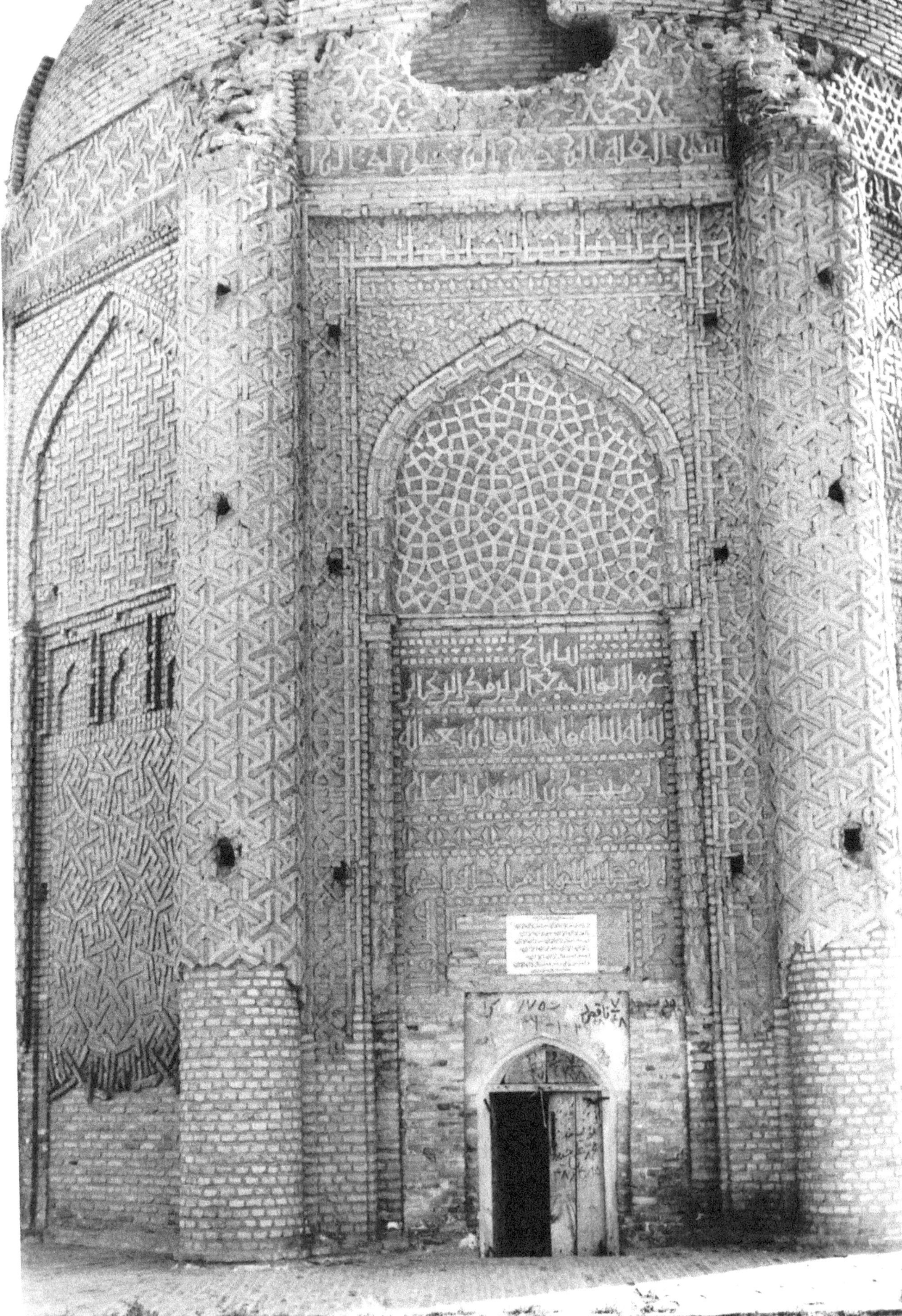

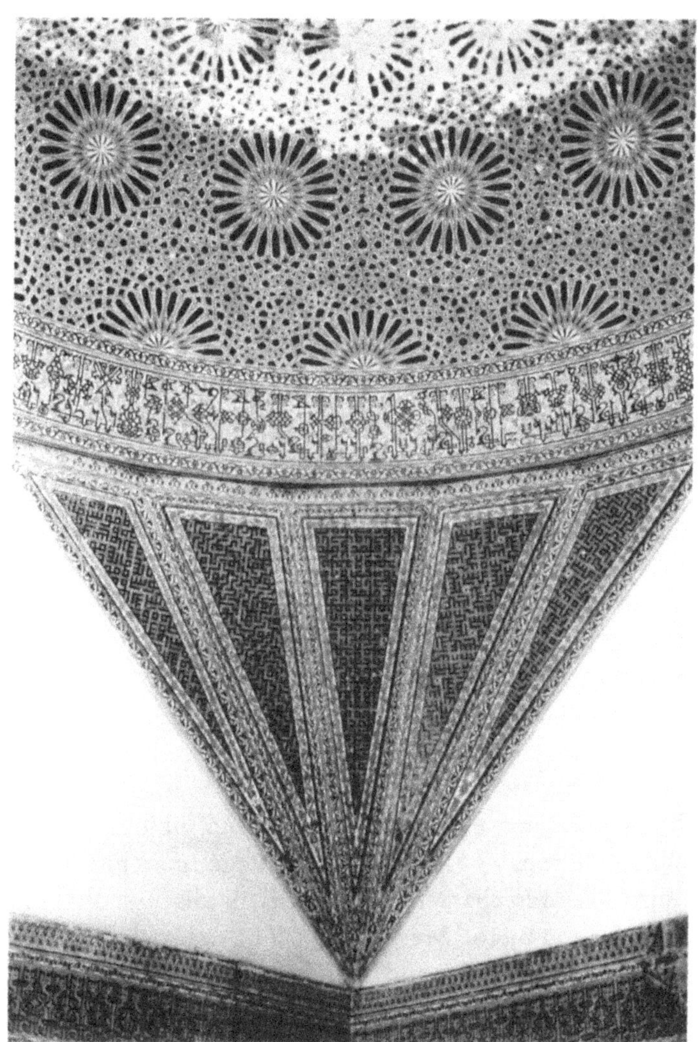

Fig. 74. Turkey, Konya, Karatay madrasah, 1251–1252, interior detail of dome.

general not be understood from the ground. It is as though the point of the writing is no longer the concrete message of its words, but something else. It is indeed possible, as has been propounded by a few scholars over the years, that specifically Islamic mystical or generally esoteric meanings can be given to these uses of writing.[111] Mysterious individual letters were indeed part of the Koranic message and all sorts of numerical and magical meanings were (and still are) given to letters. But, even if occasionally esoteric meanings are legitimate for this "nonword" writing or invisible messages, they do not explain the richness and variety of uses of writing. It is rather as though an unbridled energy transformed letters into floral designs, combating heroes, smiling faces, or severe linear compositions.

Fig. 73. Iran, Kharraqan, mausoleum, 1093.

So it was up to the thirteenth century. This energy is more difficult to trace during the domination of patronage by feudal or monarchial dynasties in Anatolia, Iran, and northern India, while the Arab Mediterranean, where these dynasties were less effective, loses some of its artistic inventiveness. But it may well be to the same currents, modified no doubt by all sorts of other impulses, that one owes the imaginative animals (fig. 64), boats (fig. 67), houses, or even landscapes done with letter and words, meaningful or not, from the Ottoman world to Mughal India and even beyond to Bengal.[112] It is perhaps when the literate population was smaller and Islam was newer that such transformations of letters were more common.

I shall return presently to an explanation of this peculiarly Islamic urban phenomenon, because its impact is related to yet another facet of classical Islamic civilization. Most of the scripts created over several centuries remained in the collective memory of the culture. At times they acquired concrete iconographic meanings as with archaic angular Kufic scripts used for titles in Korans (fig. 29) and also in secular books as well as for pious images. In these later uses the association of a script with a level of patronage becomes forgotten and all scripts participate in the rich vocabulary of artistic creation.[113] Few visual features of Islamic civilization exhibit an equally vital ubiquity or a similarly ubiquitous vitality. In today's rather loose language of architecture or painting, it is writing in Arabic characters alone that is discussed from Morocco to Malaysia, that is used by the Muslims of China to proclaim their difference from the prevalent Han culture, and especially that is argued to be *the* prototypically Muslim visual domain.[114]

How successful these modern experiments are remains to be seen and I shall return to a few examples shortly. In the meantime, I only want to point out that the sociohistorical context of a populist streak next to an imperial and bureaucratic one may well elucidate *how* a certain phenomenon—the ubiquity and variety of writing and the cultural concern for it—took place, maybe even *why* it took place *where* it did. It is hardly likely that administrative needs alone explain the rich phenomenon we have described. Although we can posit the populist streak, we cannot quite account for it. Neither the permanence of bureaucracies nor folk traditions fully explain the continuity of experiences with writing within the Muslim world. In order to find a possible explanation or at least a reasonable hypothesis, let us identify as carefully as possible what exactly it is that we seek to understand and to do so initially as an exercise of perception, more or less independent from whatever contextual knowledge one may have. What *is* our experience of writing in Arabic characters?

Three different experiences, I submit, must be carefully separated if we are to understand this writing. The first experience is that of reading a text. The great Mamluk or Ilkhanid Korans (fig. 29), the lengthy historical or religious inscriptions on buildings (fig. 62), the elegant pages of the *Shahnameh* (fig. 44) or of any Persian poet are all instances in which the piece of writing—on a wall, an object, or a book—transmits a message, a specific date, the Holy Text, or a beloved poetical fragment. The written part is, in the strictest possible sense, an intermediary that becomes almost unnecessary to the one who has learned its message. Its primary value is clarity for the widest possible audience and this value was expressed in a measured order, which can be coldly powerful in Mamluk Korans or Timurid facades or playfully coy in Safavid *Shahnamehs*, but in all instances effected by a hand drilled to perfection in the practice of a skill, of a competence. Its second value lies then in its formality. What I mean by that is a consistency of linear movements, which are nearly always horizontal, directional, and dynamic. They emphasize the right-to-left movement of the Arabic alphabet and their rhythm is compelled by the repeated beat of the vertical parts of letters known as hastae.[115] The writing is experienced like an official procession through a rigid and strict ceremonial order and, whether in a book as in many examples already seen (pls. 7–10; figs. 29, 43–45, 47–50), on the facade of a building like the stunning one in Konya's Ince mosque (fig. 75), in the stucco mihrab introduced on Mongol orders in the Great Mosque of Isfahan (fig. 76), or on hundreds of faience titles, the writing may be surrounded by all kinds of decorative motifs or even sit on top of a bed of floral or other designs, as well as appear starkly unadorned and alone on a bland background. In all cases, however, it leads to entry into a building or to a holy statement and a secular story; it is the means of access to a thing or to a space that exists independently of that particular piece of writing and it is that mediator which accompanies one's entry into the building and which seeks one's attention inside a building, just as it remains a constant companion of the user of a book or the drinker from a cup.

A second kind of experience is just about the opposite of the first one. I would like to call it "monoptic," giving to that new word the meaning of something, in this case writing, being perceived at one glance, even if it is not immediately legible. Let us just take the example of a plate in floriated Kufic from the David Collection in Copenhagen (fig. 11) and the early fourteenth century inscribed square from Linjan (fig. 59).[116] In both cases the fact of writing is immediately perceived but its reading is complex and time-consuming. In fact it requires rotating the object or being rotated around it. While it is possible to move a ceramic plate, the wall inscription at Linjan can be guessed at only because one knows the sequence of names of the Prophet's

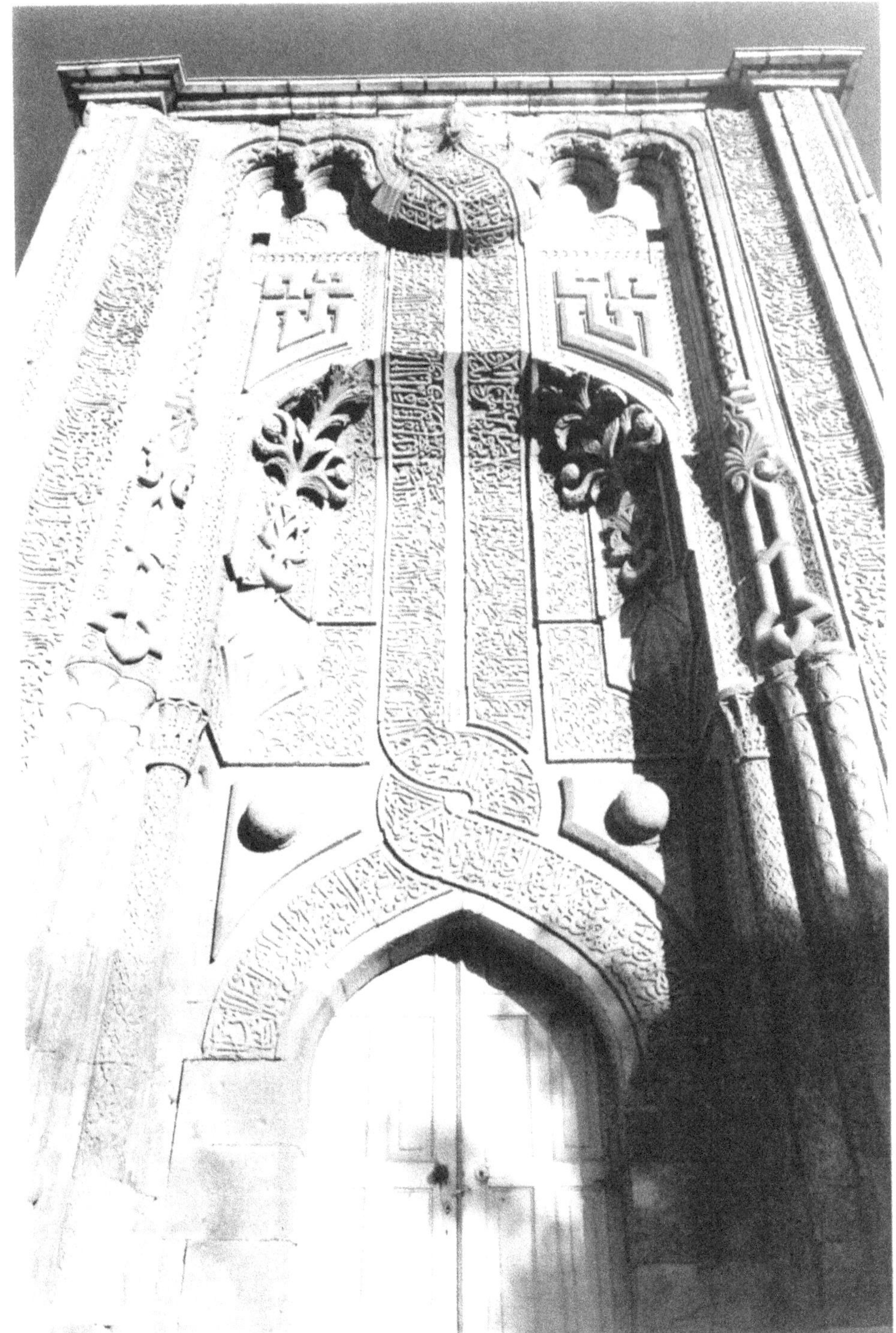

Fig. 75. Turkey, Konya, Ince Minareli madrasah, 1260–1265, facade.

Fig. 76. Iran, Isfahan, Great Mosque, mihrab of Oljaytu, 1310.

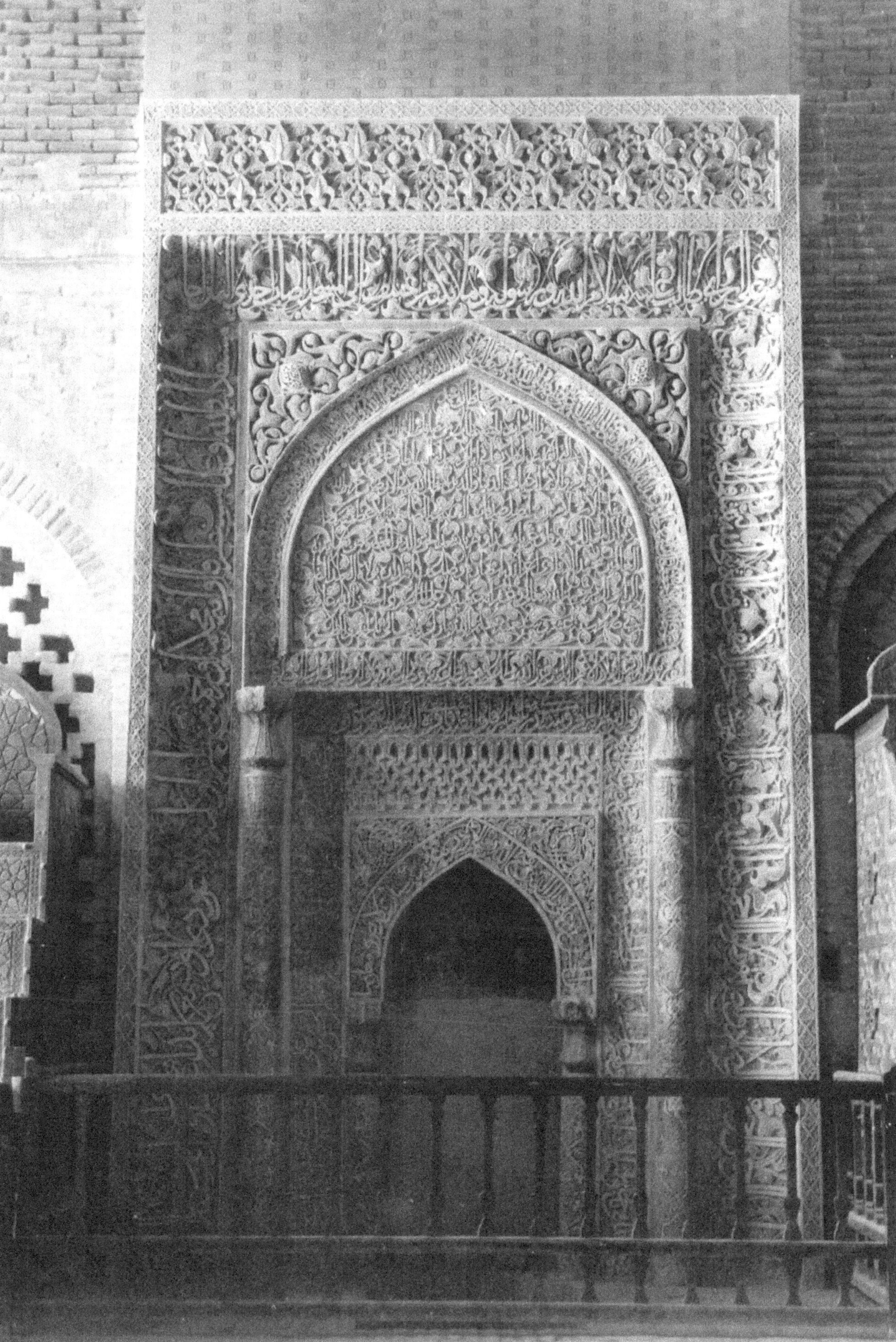

descendance, as one knows in advance the topic of hundreds of similar, although usually less complex, inscriptions all over Iran. Single leaves with a single poem found in many albums (fig. 45), the carefully crafted *basmalahs* of Karahisar (figs. 77–78), or the more playful inventions of later times (figs. 63 and 64) also lead to a monoptic experience. In all of them, the exact meaning of the words becomes, within limits yet to be determined,[117] secondary to the composition of parts. Letters can be modified, extended, looped, shortened, thickened; dots and diacritical marks float around letters rather than help fix their specificity; loops and hastae become flowers or leaves; poems are set obliquely on the page (fig. 45), as though denying the page itself, and the endless proverbs of Nishapur ceramics work their way uncomfortably around the rims of plates, while "correct" orthography is frequently violated for the sake of the composition.[118]

In most of these cases the experience of the written form is not the experience of a text; the eventual decipherment of the text hardly makes the effort worthwhile, as pedestrian aphorisms, repetitive good wishes, or simple praises of God or of the Prophet never contain anything unexpected. So often, especially after the fourteenth century, this type of monoptic writing is used

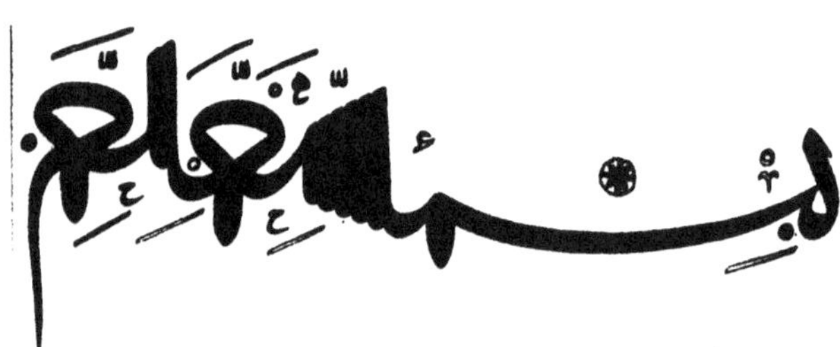

Fig. 77. Karahisar, *basmalah*, fourth version.

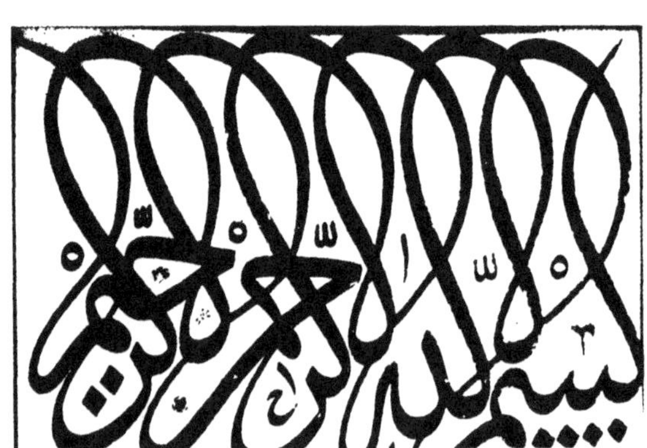

Fig. 78. Karahisar, *basmalah*, second version.

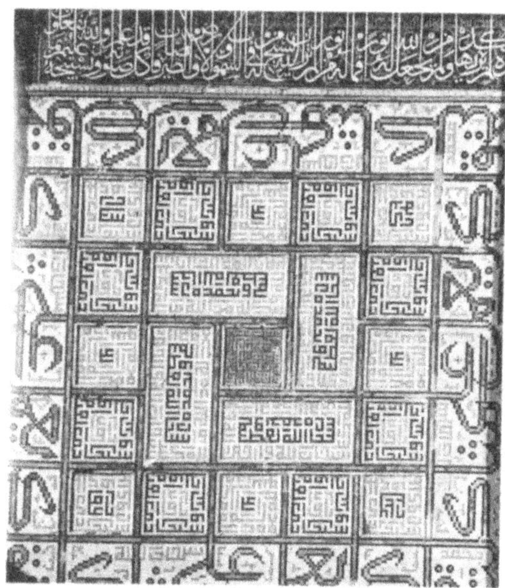

Fig. 79. Gazur Gah, wall of shrine.

for the simple statements of the faith ("Glory to God," "God," "Muhammad," "Ali," and many variants on such themes) that it becomes almost iconic. Walls, especially in Iranian sanctuaries, for instance the shrine at Gazur Gah (fig. 79),[119] come covered with a seemingly haphazard series of pious images in written form, in the way in which ex-votos, icons, or offerings (at times all three functions gathered in one object) adorn Christian Catholic and Orthodox or Hinduist shrines. The viewer, user, or observer is left wondering whether he should or should not seek the text in these examples. The answer is obviously yes, but to lead to a text is not, as with my first experience, the primary point of the writing.

There are, in fact, two sides of this second experience. One is to become attracted to the writing, that is to say, to have one's senses so affected by the arbitrariness of a line, the languid elongation of a loop, or the daggerlike precision of a hasta, that the pleasure of looking predominates and a terpnopoietic function takes over. The second side is the search for an explanation of the pleasure or the excitement, whether it is eventually to read a text or simply to enjoy the shape taken by a traditional formula. Both sides of this experience have transformed the object with writing into a mirror that projects itself back onto the viewer and forces his meditation or his involvement with the written statement. There is something narcissistic in this experience, but then the experiences of art and of mysticism include a great deal of self-love and once again writing is the intermediary that makes possible an experience not contained in what is written.

The third experience of writing can be dealt with more briefly, because writing in it is subordinated to other designs, to some of which I shall return in subsequent chapters. Iranian painters, for instance, composed their miniatures according to the rhythm created by the columns of text and often enough, especially in later times, a few verses hang in a landscape or adorn a building (fig. 80).[120] Carpets or silk coverings for tombs combine writing with other themes (fig. 81) and on the metalwork of Egypt or Iran, writing, specific or not, is constantly mixed with other motifs. The quality of these written fragments varies enormously, and it is difficult to assume a single experience

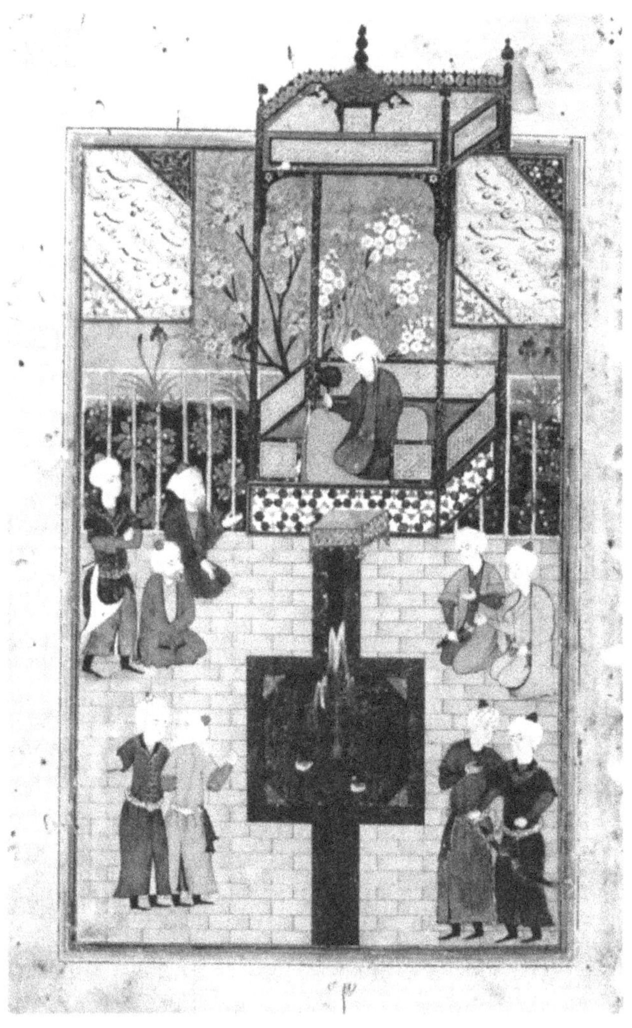

Fig. 80. "Yusef Presented with a Mirror," Jami, *Tufhat al-Ahrar*, Iran, ca. 1540. Washington, D.C., the Arthur M. Sackler Gallery, S86.0046.

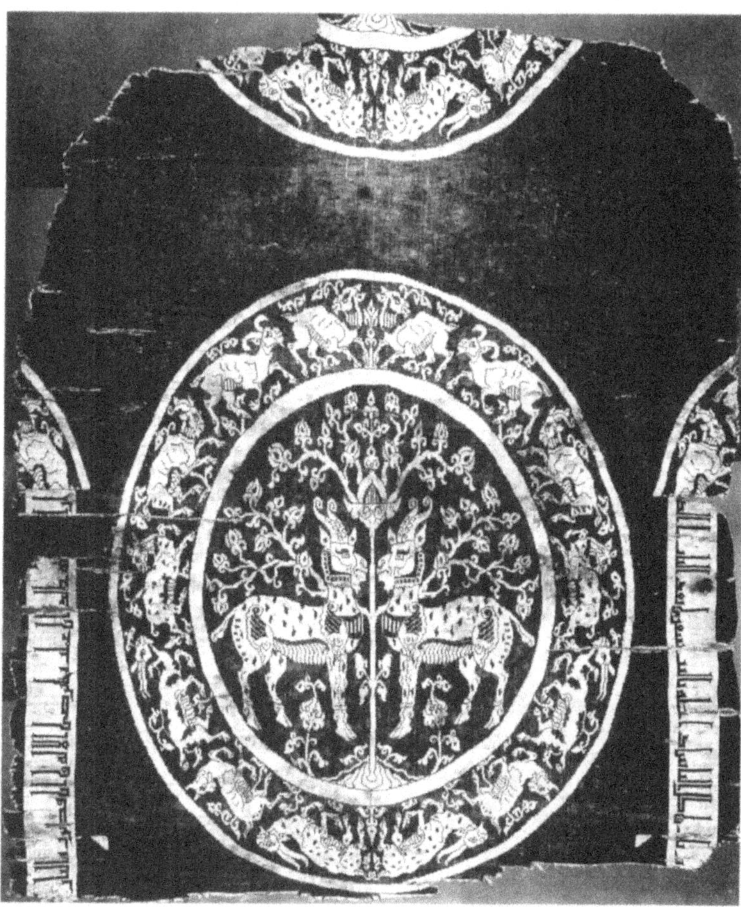

Fig. 81. Fragment of a tomb cover, Iran, 998 (388 A.H.). Cleveland Museum of Art, H. M. Wade Collection.

derived from their perception. I will limit myself to only one point: within the mass of perceptible categories available, the contemporary eye excerpts writing immediately after figural representations. It is as though, in the development of one's discourse of perception and thought about an object, writing is the next layer to be identified after mimetic themes. The reasons for this reaction are beyond the concern of these essays and my point is simply that, within this experience, writing becomes, in conjunction with other motifs, one of the means of access to the surface of an object, a way to understand it rather than to feel it.

There probably are other experiences of writing within the Islamic tradition. There is, for instance, an experience of power, as in the huge shields hung

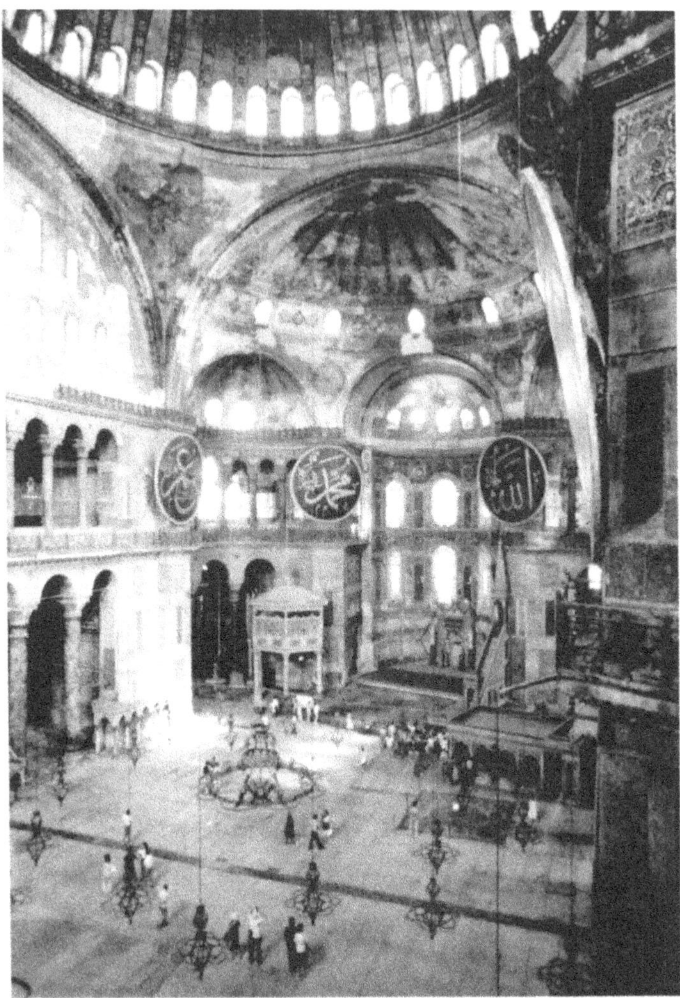

Fig. 82. Istanbul, Haghia Sophia, interior view.

inside Hagia Sophia (fig. 82) or the immense thirteenth-century Qutb Minar in Delhi (fig. 83) with its rings of writing. These are among many examples of works in which the size, the character, or the location of writing are indicative of authority and of sovereignty. At another extreme, several scripts from chanceries are so convoluted in their attempts to limit the number of their possible readers that one can imagine the experience of writing as the solution of an absurd puzzle.

The three main experiences I have discussed all show writing as an intermediary mode both in creation *and* for perception, a mode that directs intellect or emotions to a wide range of possible interpretations. Why did this take place within the culture of the Islamic world? Or rather, when there are concrete sociocultural reasons for this or that transformation of writing as a physical experience, why did the Muslim world maintain writing as its central intermediary function for so many centuries? The reasons are not as simple-minded as a Revelation through a book or the mysticism of the pen, although both were factors in certain areas or at certain times. The true reasons must be sought much more profoundly within the fabric of classical Muslim life than within the mechanisms of the Revelation or of esoteric interpretations.

The fundamental reason, it seems to me, is that the traditional Muslim ethos was based on the transient nature of life and on the mediating power of the community in making possible the preparation for another life, the true and only life. Words, spoken but especially written, held the whole community and later a number of independent communities together. They were the natural cement or glue of society. But their importance was not in themselves, it was rather in their mediation between several different lives or levels of living: this life and eternal life, the life of the simple man and the authority of the ruler, the life of toil and the desire for pleasure. Words helped the faithful in prayer and in fear. One of the most wonderful examples of both appears among the riches of Suleyman the Magnificent and his time. Next to severely ordered writings on boxes for books of the Koran (fig. 84) with their implication of a clear and limpid world, there are the nightshirts and undershirts of the rulers (fig. 85) with thousands of prayers and Koranic quotations embroidered on a vestment that is like a talisman protecting the body from death and sickness.[121] Words were everywhere and it may be just indeed to follow

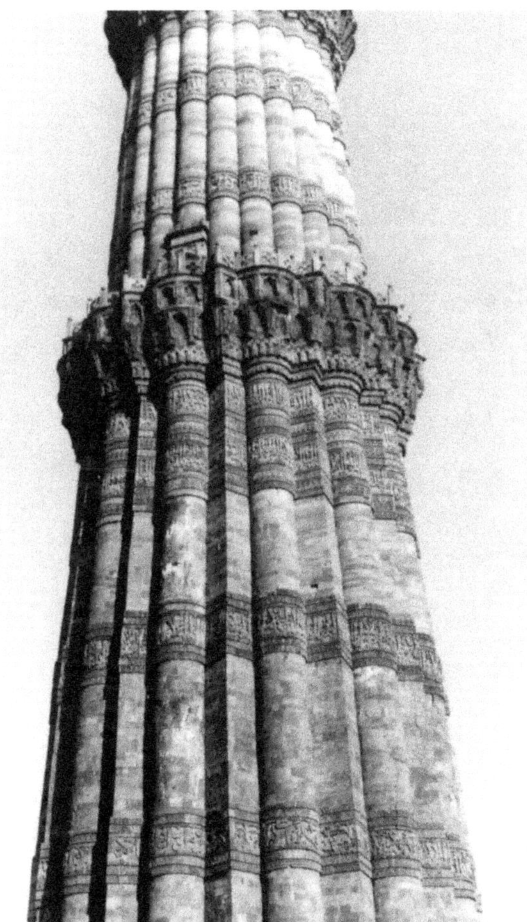

Fig. 83. Delhi, Qutb Minar, detail of inscription, 1211–1236.

Fig. 84. Wooden box for Koran, sixteenth century. Istanbul, Turkish and Islamic Arts Museum, no. 2.

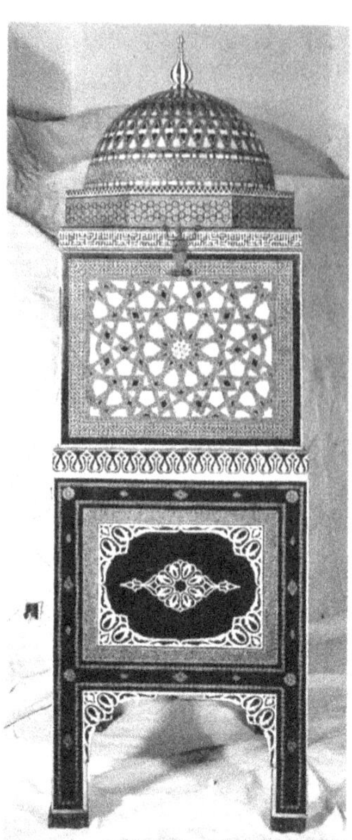

Fig. 85. Nightshirt of Suleyman the Magnificent. Istanbul, Top Kapi Seray Museum, no. 13/1150.

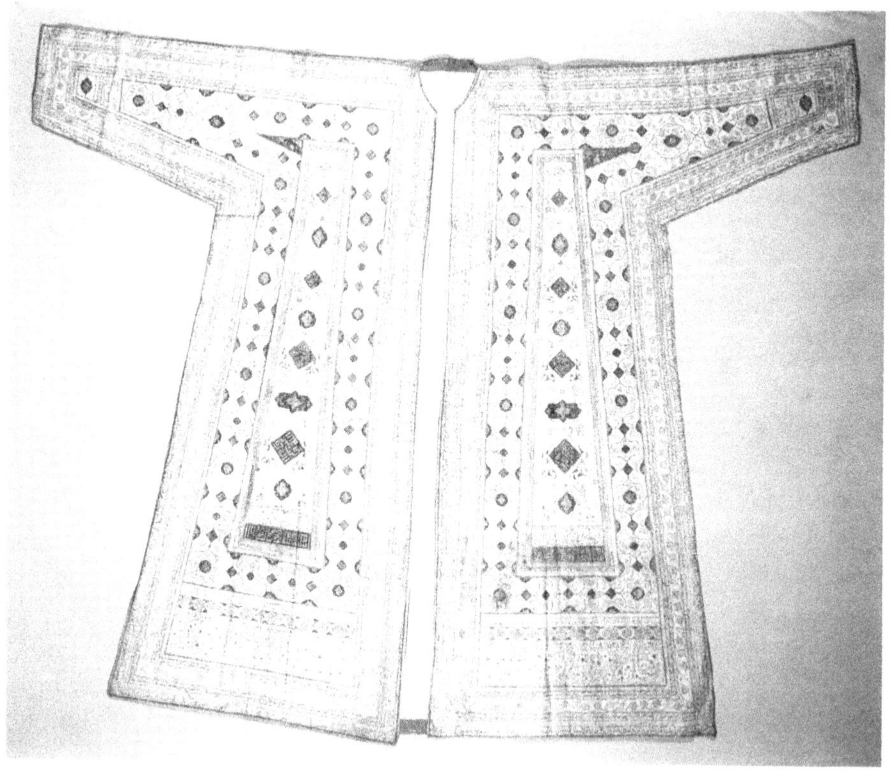

Derrida and argue that, on the sleepwear of Ottoman princes, these signifieds of signifieds are twice removed from the statements embroidered or painted on them.

But, in fact, writings also signified another reality than that of the words and thoughts they represent. They also signify sensory pleasure in the expression of everything. They argue that the perception of everything, even if twice removed from its source in the mind or in the collective memory and mode of action of a society—what Foucault called its *epistemé*—can be immediate, powerful, perhaps even pedagogic by being transformed for the pleasure of the senses. At this level, writing has become art. It may indeed be legitimate to talk about calligraphy, since the making of pleasure or beauty is an essential part of the experience I have sketched out. But calligraphy in this sense would be a quality we today or the viewer-user of the past bestows on certain instances of writing; it is not necessarily an innate property of each script or of each example of something written.

In discussing the operation of writing during the formative centuries of medieval Islamic culture, we dealt simultaneously with three orders of phenomena. One is historical and chronological, in which my emphasis was on the changes of the tenth and eleventh centuries with some of their implications for later centuries. The underlying assumption was that a push was given then, an invention made, that of a theoretically ordered writing, which then grew a variety of branches. Although a single chapter cannot do justice to a complex evolution, the point, I trust, was made that different periods require different interpretations and that the assumption of a single "Islamic" attitude to writing is a debatable and dangerous fiction. What did occur throughout Islamic history is the continuing transformation, the continuous life, of a phenomenon peculiar initially to the needs of Muslim politics and culture in the ninth and tenth centuries.

The second order is a sociocultural one. At least at the beginning, there were two simultaneous currents in the uses of writing in classical Islam. One was fostered by the courts and by central authorities and was practiced by highly skilled professionals for the uses of one or more social and intellectual elites. It was, in short, a means to control and to distinguish: to control, because its production required a specialized investment in training; to distinguish, because the ownership and appreciation of the products were restricted to a social or political elite of power, which justified its position through the expression of real or assumed learning.

The other current is a populist one. Clearly identifiable in northeastern Iran, Iraq, and Egypt, it may have existed wherever great urban centers were found. Writing within this current is exuberant, varied, often of dubious legibility, but it carries a huge range of messages, from highly religious to prosaically secular. The two currents mingled with each other at various times and especially in certain places, like the Islamic frontier cultures of Spain, central Asia, and eventually Anatolia.[122] How they interacted in later times is, at this stage of research, a little bit clearer in the Persian and Indian painting of the Timurid and later periods than it is for writing in any subsegment of Islamic culture.[123] Two matrices for the uses of writing—one centralized and elitist, the other one populist—seem to have been preserved and are still found in the contemporary world, as in the wild decoration of Afghan trucks with folk writing of pious terms (fig. 86) on the one hand and, on the other, the formal imitation of Ottoman courtly ways in a Kuwaiti wedding invitation (fig. 87).

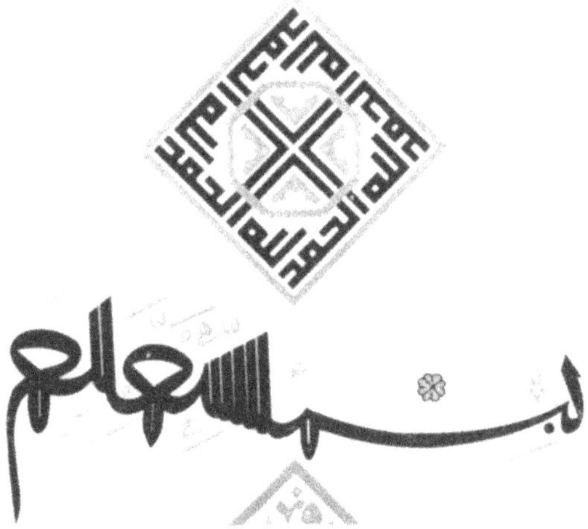

Fig. 87. Contemporary wedding invitation imitating Karahisar.

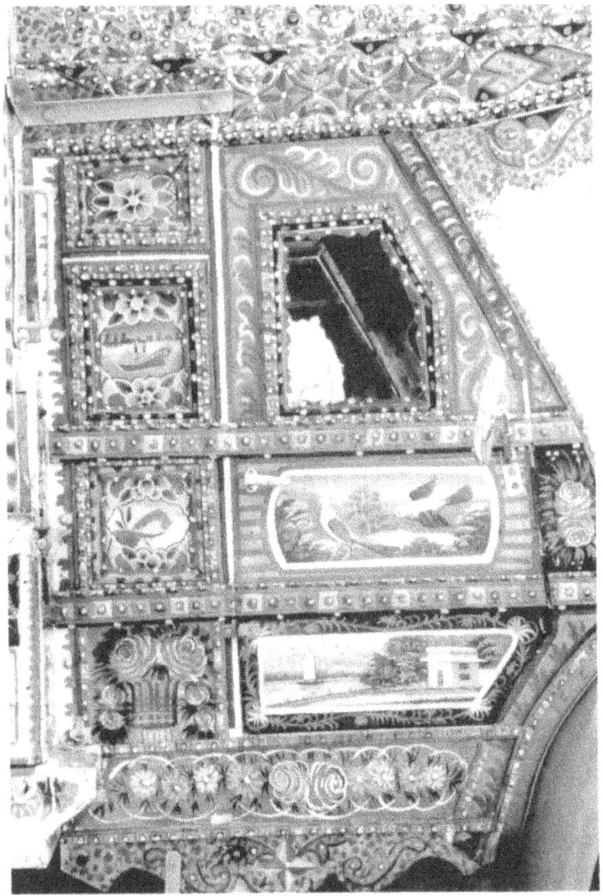

Fig. 86. Contemporary writing on a truck in Afghanistan.

The third order is an order of interpretation. On the one hand, a distinction was made between writing that, effortlessly and calmly, leads the reader to a text and such written artifacts as require efforts of perception for proper understanding; at times, I suggested, even signifying writing becomes meaningless as a signifier of words or thoughts and remains only as a signifier of some other signified, intent to please, amaze, or persuade. At this level we can modify Derrida's assumption of writing as a signifier of the signifier of the signified. In some written objects, like the Ali page (pl. 3), a *tughra* (fig. 52), or certain flowery inscriptions on Nishapur plates (fig. 7), the primary signified is not the word or combination of words that was written, but the artfulness of the craftsman, the imagination of the artist, or, in an inversion of esthetic behavior possible in a post-Bakhtian world, the pleasure of emotional, intellectual, sensuous reactions by today's viewer, regardless of the correctness or even appropriateness for the considered works of art, projected onto the object as examples of the pleasure or involvement of all viewers since the object's creation.

But another aspect of this order of interpretation has emerged. It is once again a contrast or a distinction to be made between a writing dominated by rules and a severe seriousness of purpose, on the one hand, and, on the other, one in which a degree of freedom and perhaps even of fun pierces through the restrictions of the Arabic alphabet and its diacritical paraphernalia, whatever language uses them. It is on purely visual grounds, almost without knowing the languages but with an awareness of many examples, that almost anyone can learn to distinguish the presence of formal canons and the liberties, at times mistakes, taken with canons or even examples of "countercultural" writing, as with some writing on ceramics or in later albums. The medieval writers from whose works I sketched out a sort of criticism of writing in medieval or premodern Islam acknowledge the existence of this counterculture by signaling the bizarre behavior of an occasional scribe, but, for the most part, they are committed to the values of order in the existing canons for writing.

It is difficult to decide, among all these activities, ways of writing or seeing writing, methods of doing and of appreciating, what, if anything, should be called calligraphy. My own preference would be to limit the specific word to the Western sets of types that developed the term in the sixteenth century. Only the formal statement of the major canons used for state documents or for majestic Korans may justify the maintenance of the term, as the order, consistency, and especially replicability implied by the term apply indeed. One or more standard orders did dominate the masses of remaining examples of writing in China or Japan as well. Writers on *shu fa*, the two characters usually translated as calligraphy, often talk of order and of method, and like their counterparts in Muslim lands, they constantly write about the almost magical technique of cutting and using brushes.[124] But in the Far East, perhaps more forcefully than in the Muslim world, a phenomenon appears that articulates quite strikingly the observations I have been developing so far. From the sixteenth century onward, numerous Chinese and Japanese artists transform a succession of characters into a free fall of brush strokes that visually outstrips any reading of a text (figs. 38 and 88).[125] When Chinese writers talk about writing, their imagery, admirably analyzed by John Hay,[126] does not dwell only on proportions and purity of line, but on life forces, on the storage of energy. It is as though both the making and, I presume, the viewing of "good" writing serve to release the living and active forces of nature that are good and noble and reward maker and viewer.

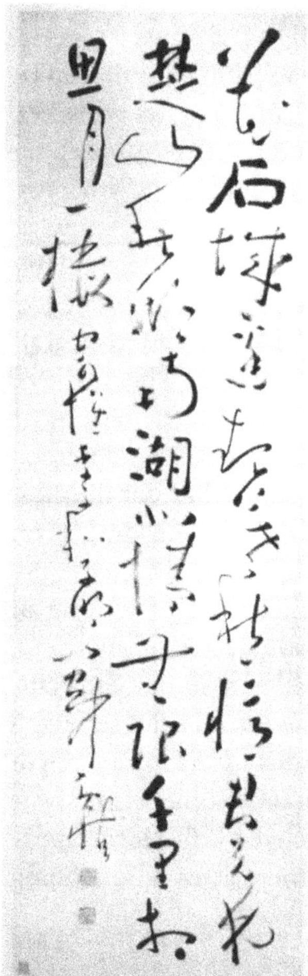

Fig. 88. Huang Shen (1687–1768), "Thoughts About Two Brothers." Washington, D.C., Freer Gallery of Art, 80.13.

A Muslim writer would not say such things, nor would an Irish monk or a Gothic illuminator. The reasons are that the Christian monk or the Taoist and Buddhist writers were affected by very different cultural pressures from those of bureaucrats and functionaries in Baghdad or Istanbul chanceries. But the differences are, I believe, more than social; nor are they induced by class distinctions. They reflect more fundamental positions of belief. To the Muslim, man's world is man's creation for God's sake and man is but the vice-regent for God of an independent and amoral nature. To the Irish monk, nature is evil and a tempter. And, even though the Gothic man may have enjoyed nature better than his Christian predecessors in the West, he was willing to be inspired by it, to represent it, not to judge himself through its presence in him.

Yet all these moments of time or areas of space—Far East Asian, West Asian, Mediterranean, European—picked up writing, a vehicle for the transmission of something else than itself, and transformed it into a neutral means to an end or into an end in itself in which meaning could become transfigured into free form.

Why did this happen to the written experience of speech and thought? Beyond ideological, political, economic, religious, or intellectual reasons, there was the recognition that the arbitrariness of the written sign can be harnessed for other purposes than that of copying something said or already written elsewhere. It can express visual or pious values that are not those of its literal meaning. It can be meaningful in a different way from the one in which it is legible. It is different enough from what it means that, just as an opera singer can charm and move while singing in a language unknown to her or to the listener, a viewer can be attracted and fascinated by ideograms or letters he does not "read," because their sensory or terpnopoietic quality has overwhelmed their meaning. This is why Italian painters of the Renaissance, Byzantine ornamentists of churches, and Romanesque sculptors picked Arabic letters to make pseudowords, occasionally and no doubt accidentally copying a pious Muslim phrase on the mandorla of the Virgin.[127] These Western artists and artisans did something that was impossible for their counterparts in traditional Muslim society: to pay no attention at all to possible legibility. Contemporary Western art has picked up Far Eastern calligraphy and transformed it into a pattern of design and into a technique for holding the brush or any other instrument of making. And contemporary art in Iran, Pakistan, or the Arab world has had a lot of difficulty in deciding how to make writing meaningful today. Should it be a form of antiquarian revival? Should it try to sell itself as a product? Should one try new formal transformations of letters or play with letters as befits the recreational expectations of today's art?[128] A striking example of contemporary confusion lies in a mosque recently completed in Tehran. Built in baked brick and occasionally glazed ones, the mosque is proudly presented in an article devoted to it as full of "calligraphy" (fig. 89). In fact, so much writing oozes out of its surface that hallowed formulas have become repetitive dots and the most obscure corners are covered with Koranic quotations or whatever, as though an empty space would be an embarrassment to obvious religiosity.[129]

In their different ways, all these examples, whatever their origins, contemporary or ancient, are parodies that did not realize or understand that writing on buildings, objects, or paper is either a means to something else and then shines by its clarity and transparency, or an end in itself and then it is a mirror of the charge the viewer or the maker puts into it. True intermediary in the first instance, it partakes, in the second one, of that meditation on one's self which has created so much of the art of mankind. It is no longer a mediation but a work of art.

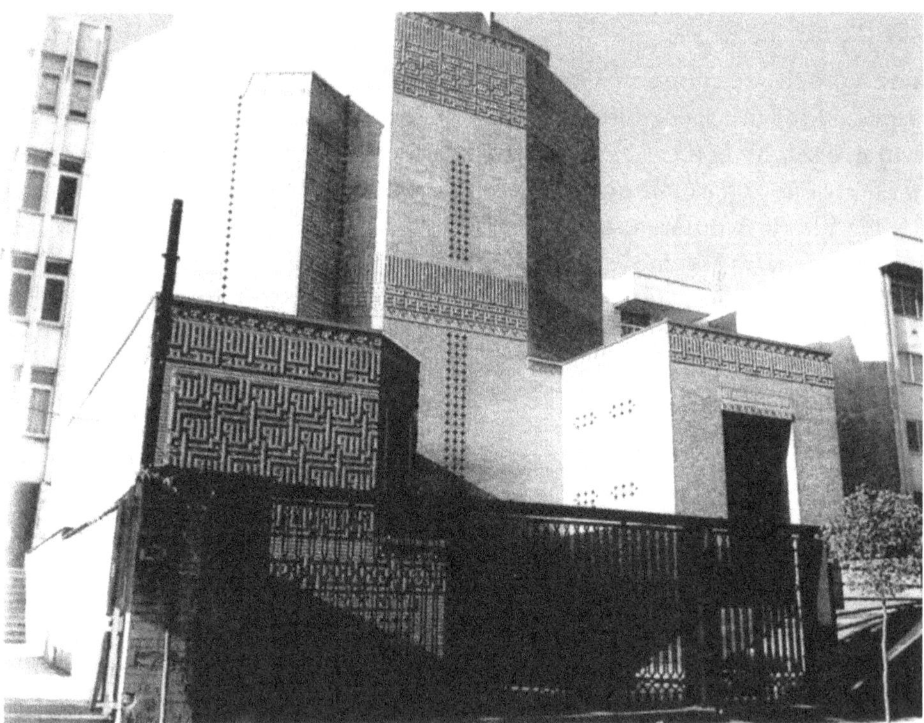

Fig. 89. Tehran, Al-Ghadir Mosque, built in 1985, walls with writing.

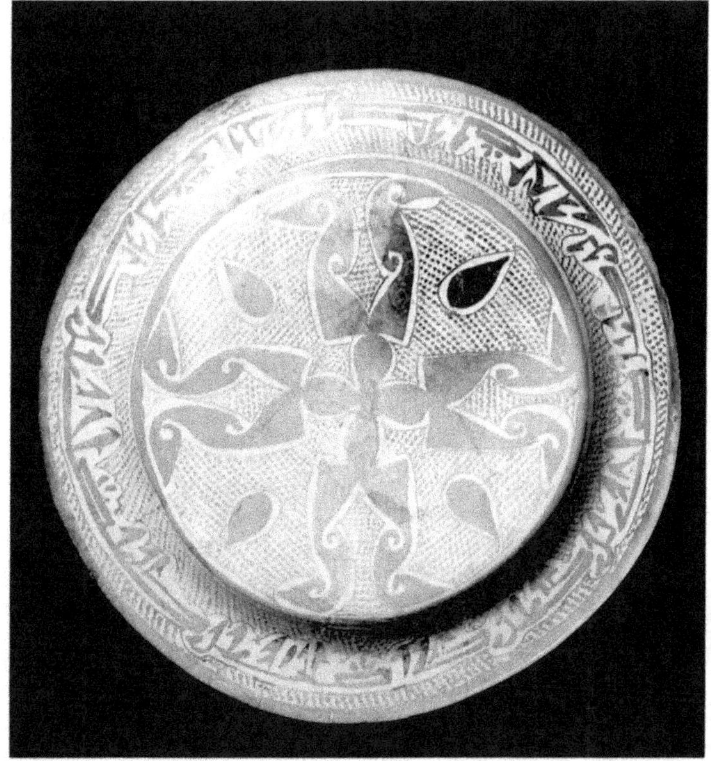

Plate 1. Ceramic bowl, luster painted, Iraq, ninth or tenth century. Copenhagen, David Collection, 26/1962.

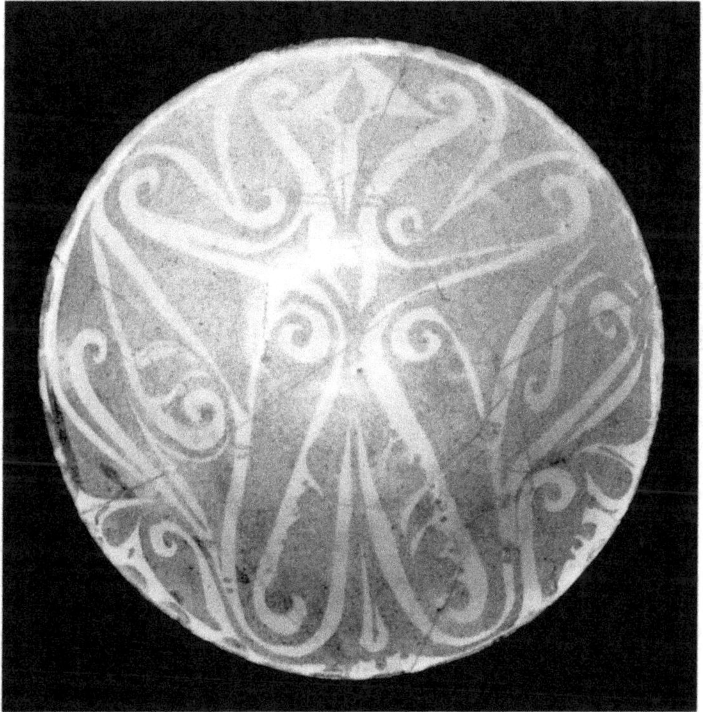

Plate 2. Ceramic bowl, luster painted, Iraq, ninth or tenth century. Copenhagen, David Collection, 14/1962.

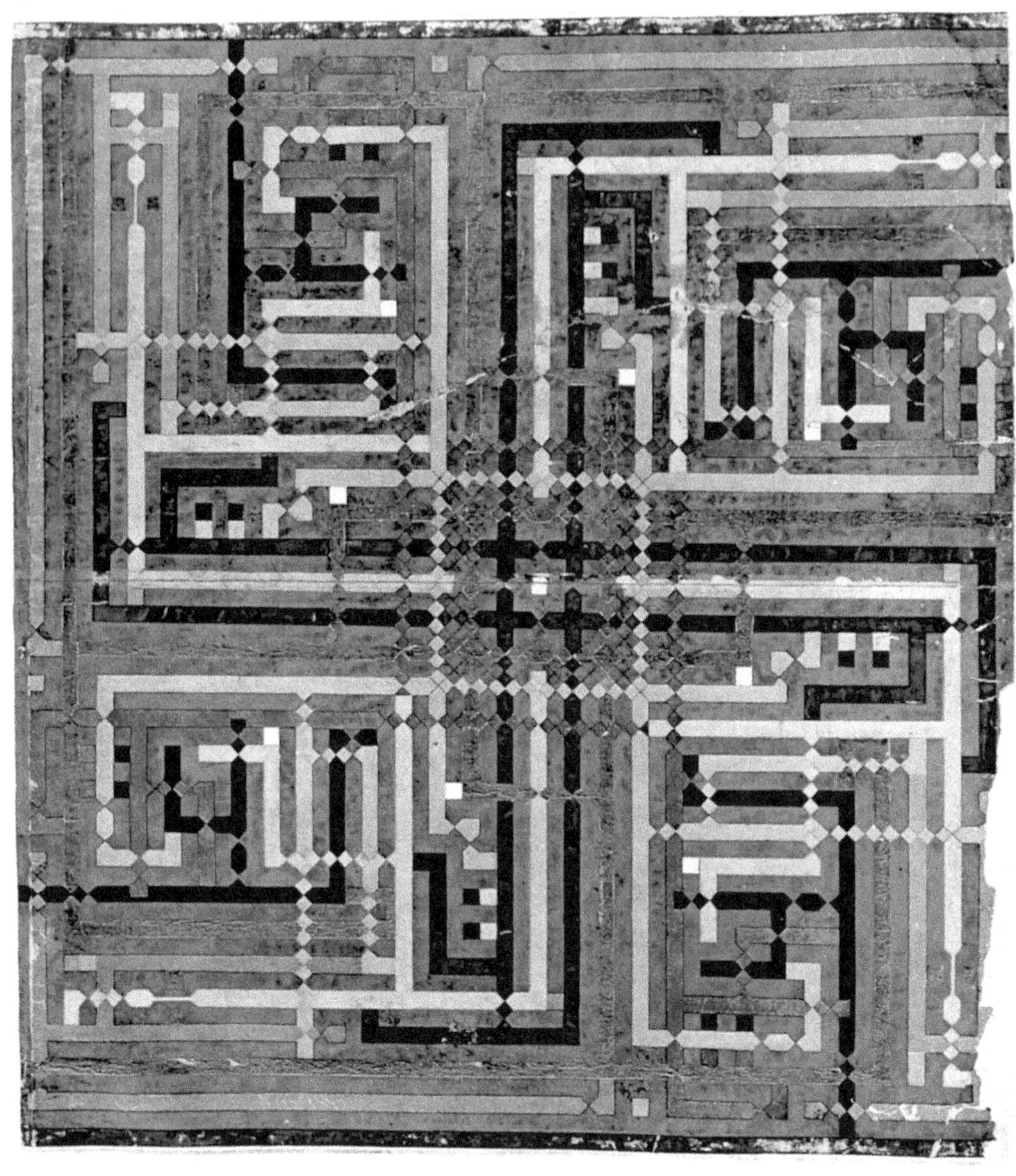

Plate 3. Painting, Iran, fifteenth century. Istanbul, Top Kapi Seray Museum, *Hazine* 2152, fol. 9v.

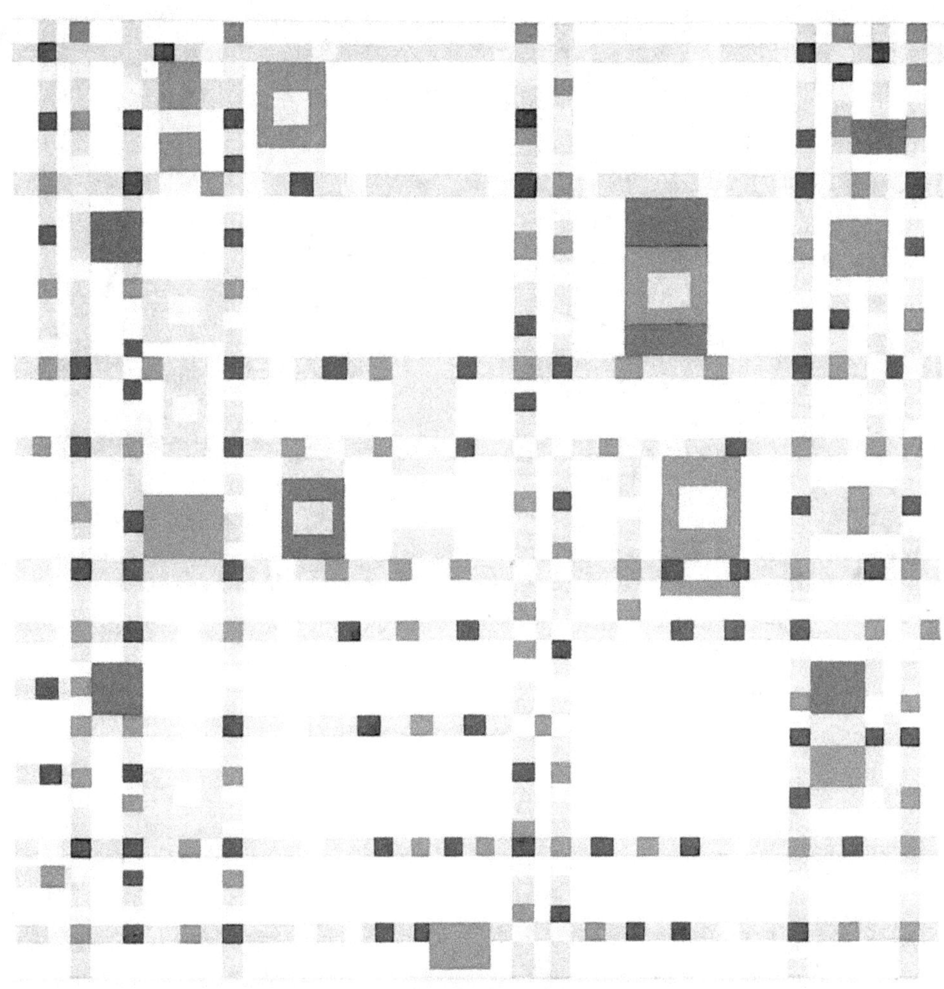

Plate 4. Piet Mondrian, *Broadway Boogie-Woogie,* 1942–1943. New York, Museum of Modern Art, cat. no. 422.

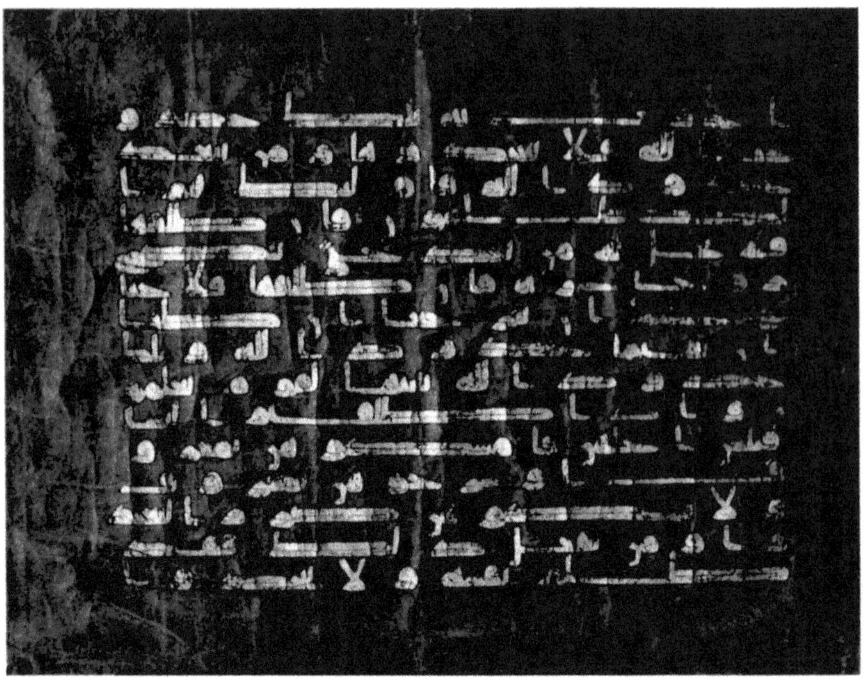

Plate 5. Example of "blue" Koran, probably Tunisia, tenth century. Cambridge, Harvard University Art Museums 1967.23.

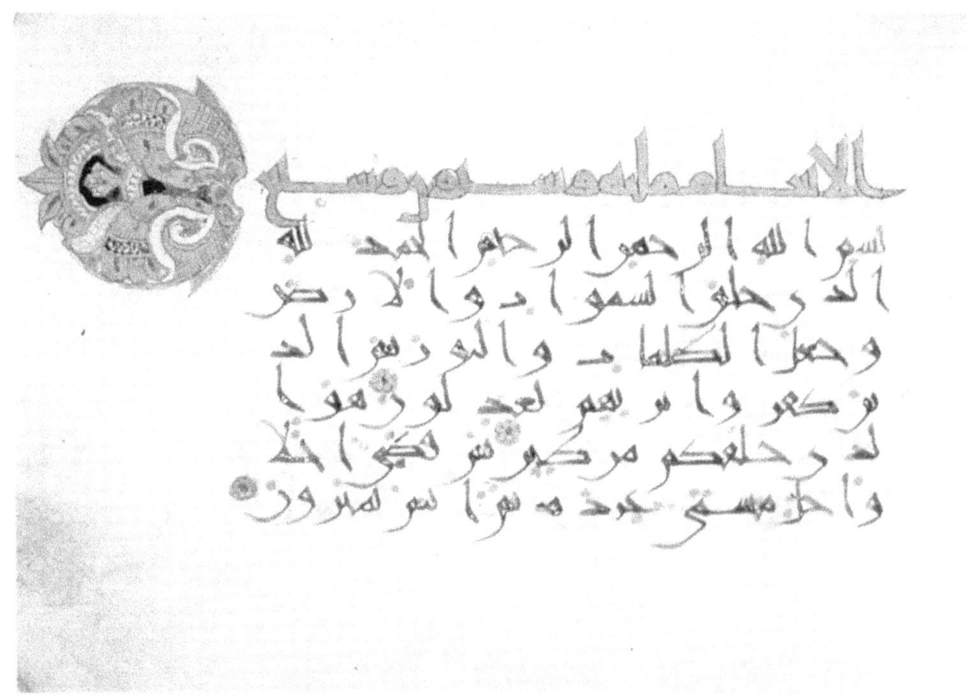

Plate 6. Page from an early Koran, parchment, ninth century (?). New York, Metropolitan Museum of Art, Rogers Fund, 1962 (62.152.2).

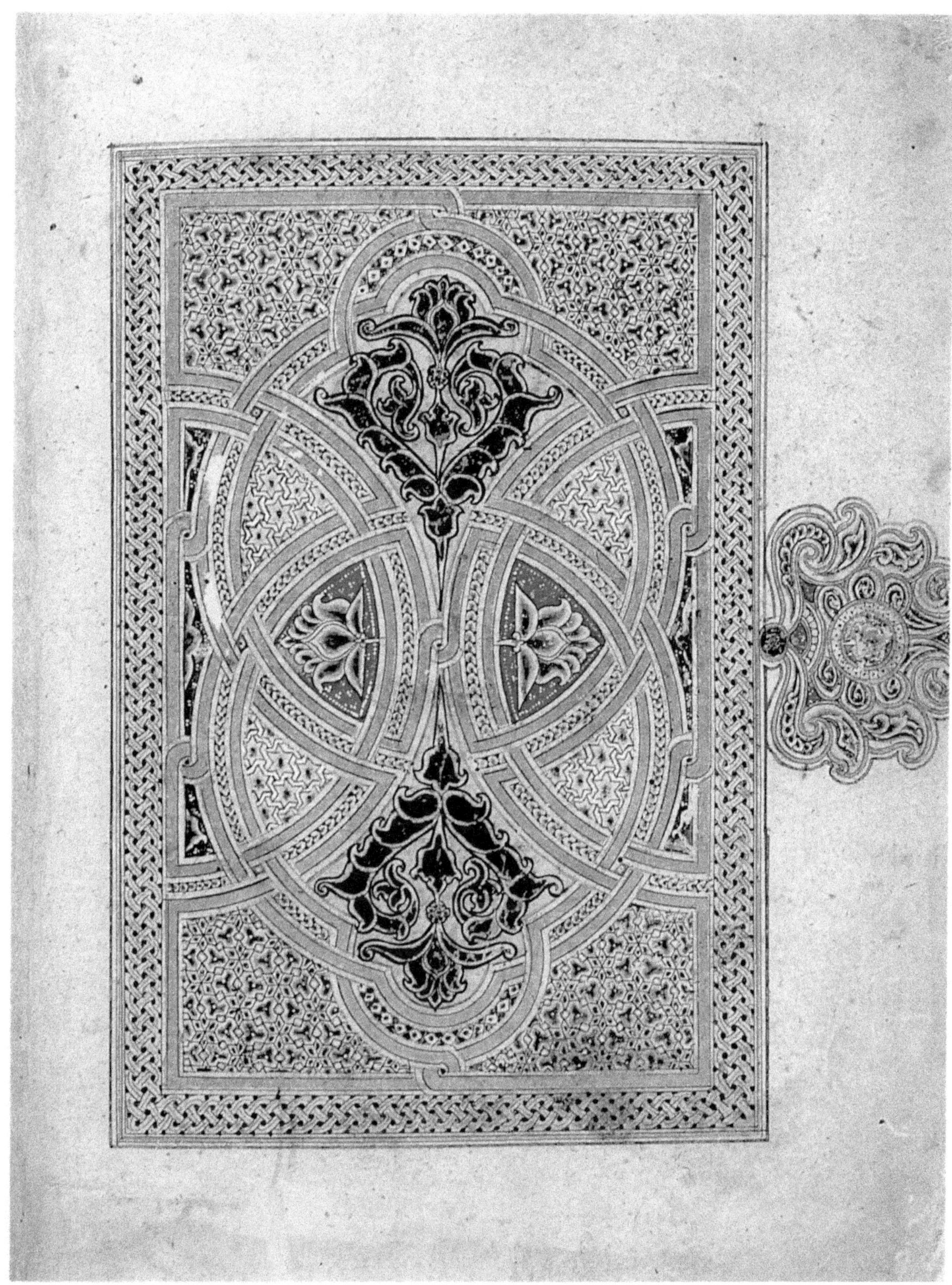

Plate 7. Ibn al-Bawwab, manuscript of the Koran, 1000–1001, end page: fol. 285r. Dublin, Chester Beatty Library K.16.

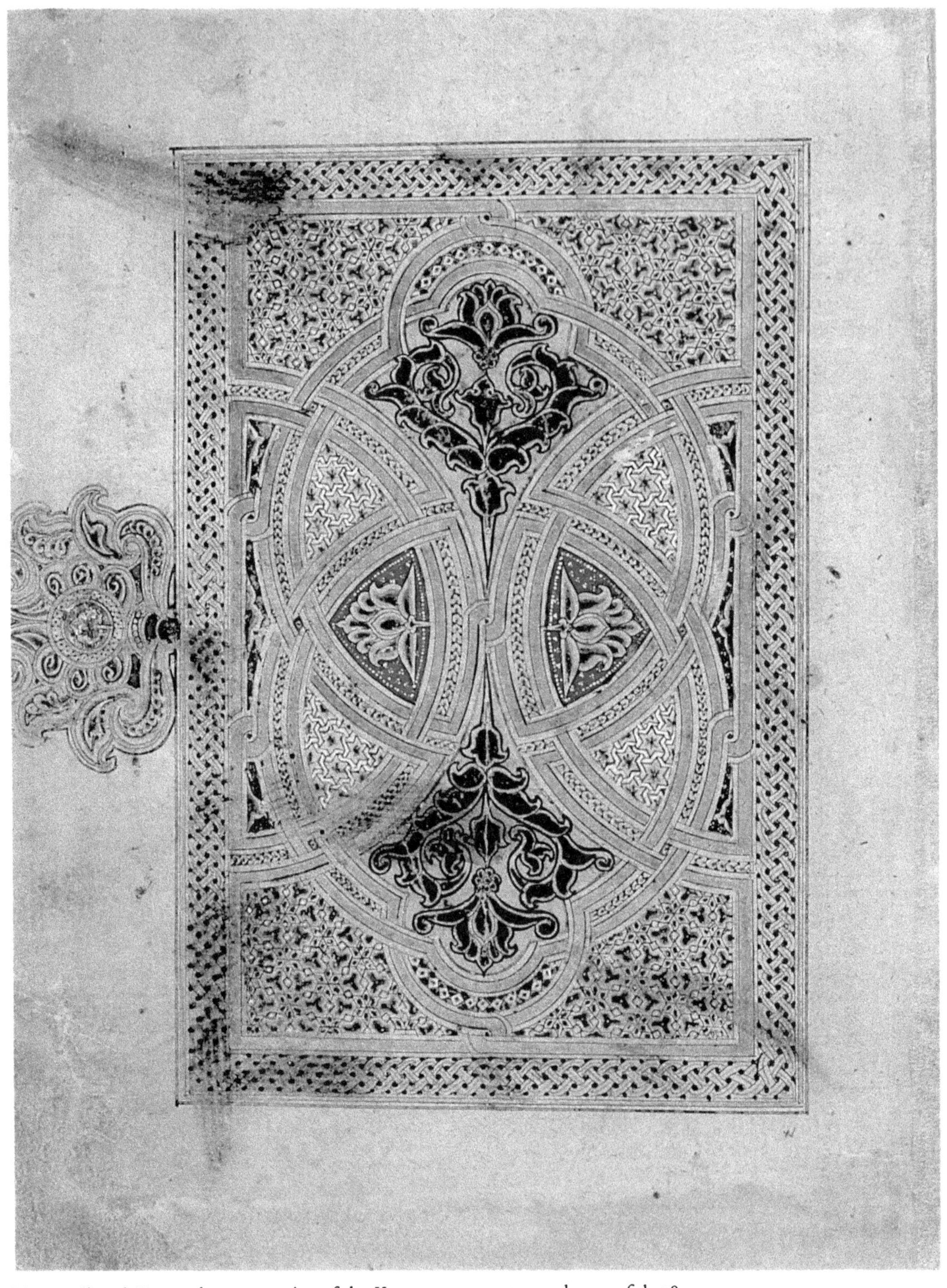

Plate 8. Ibn al-Bawwab, manuscript of the Koran, 1000–1001, end page: fol. 284v. Dublin, Chester Beatty Library K.16. EH.

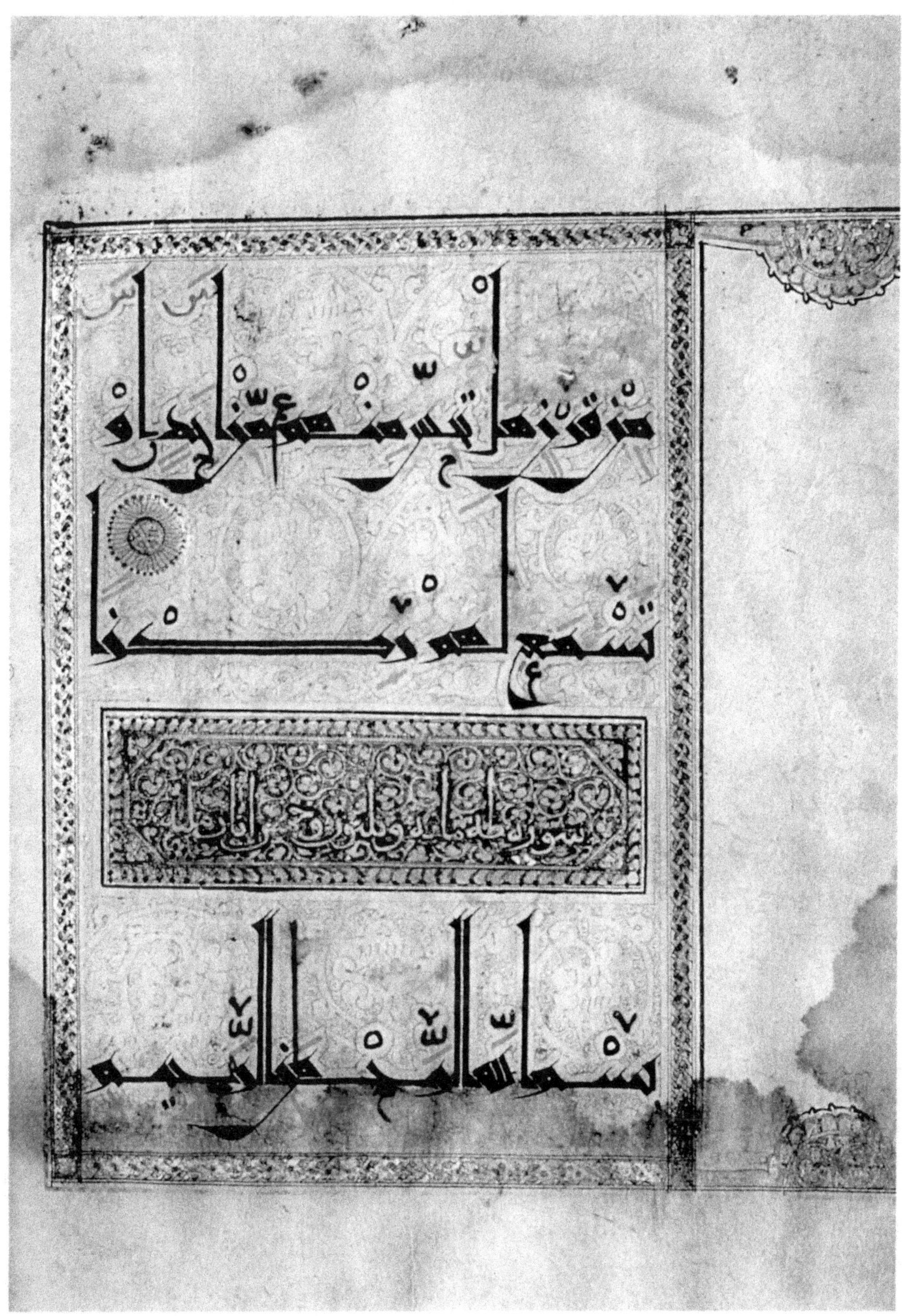

Plate 9. So-called Qarmatian Koran. Istanbul EH 12, fol. 38v.

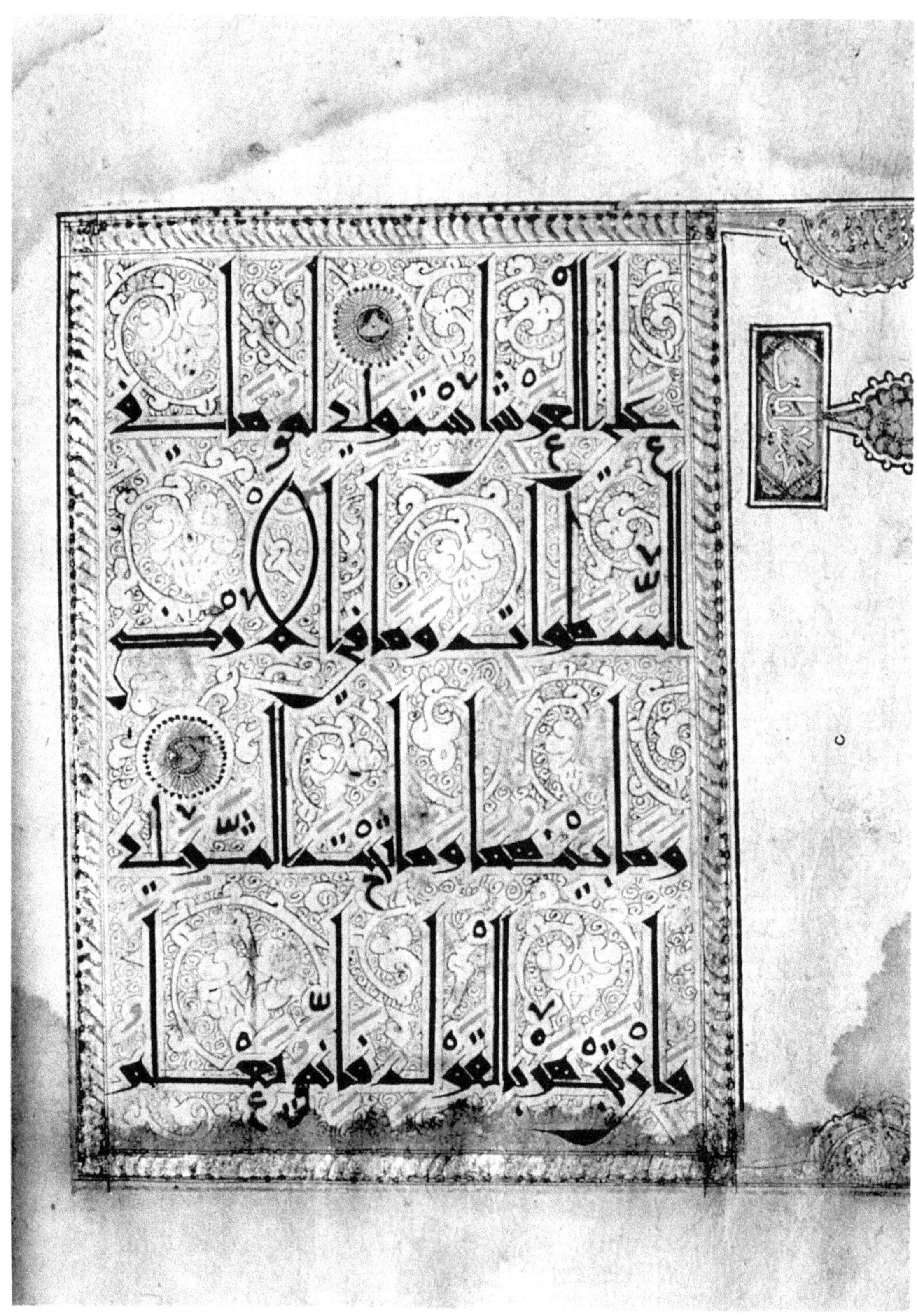

Plate 10. So-called Qarmatian Koran. Istanbul EH 12, fol. 39v.

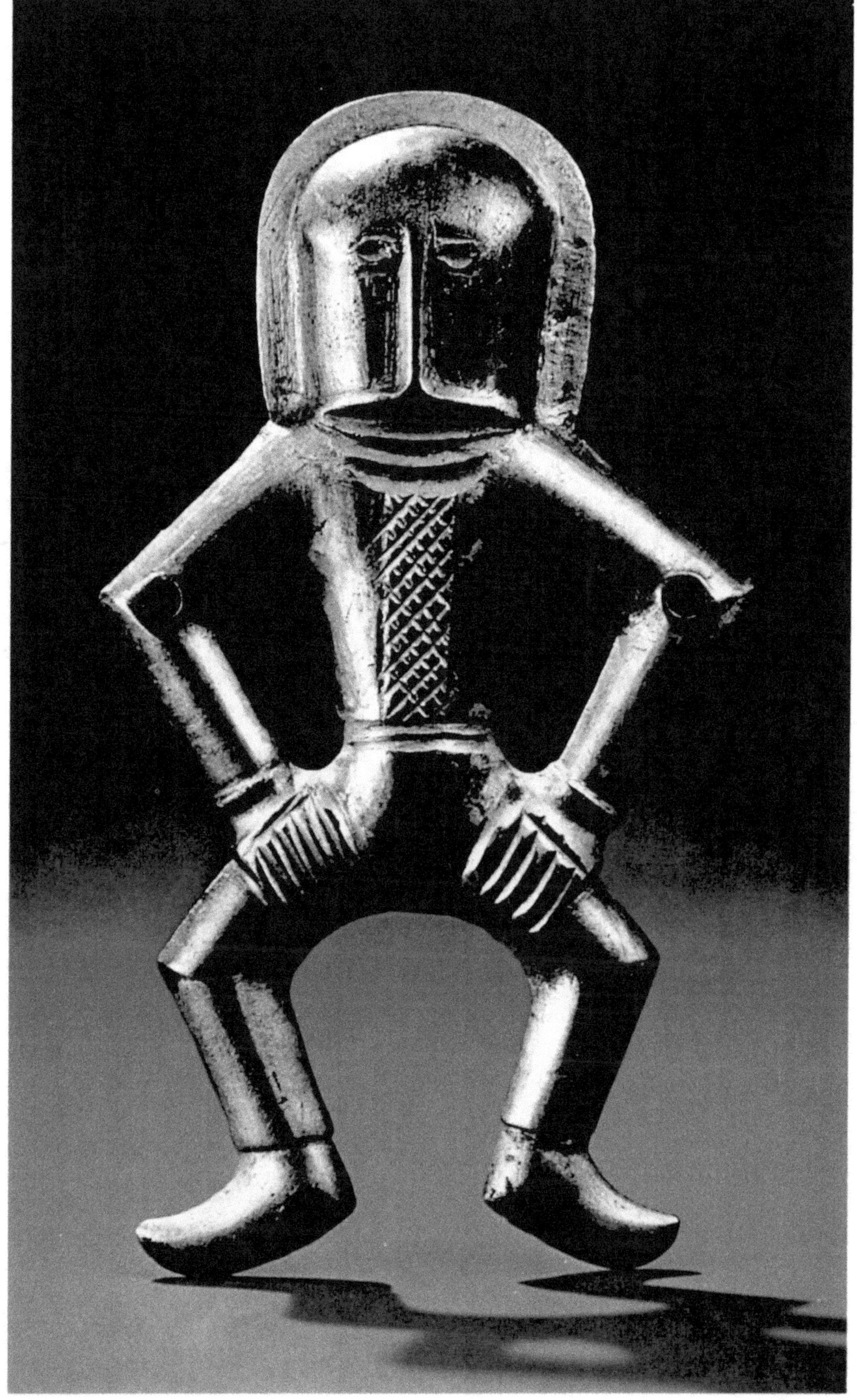

Plate 11. "Dancing Man," silver gilt, sixth or seventh century. Kiev Historical Museum, A2584.

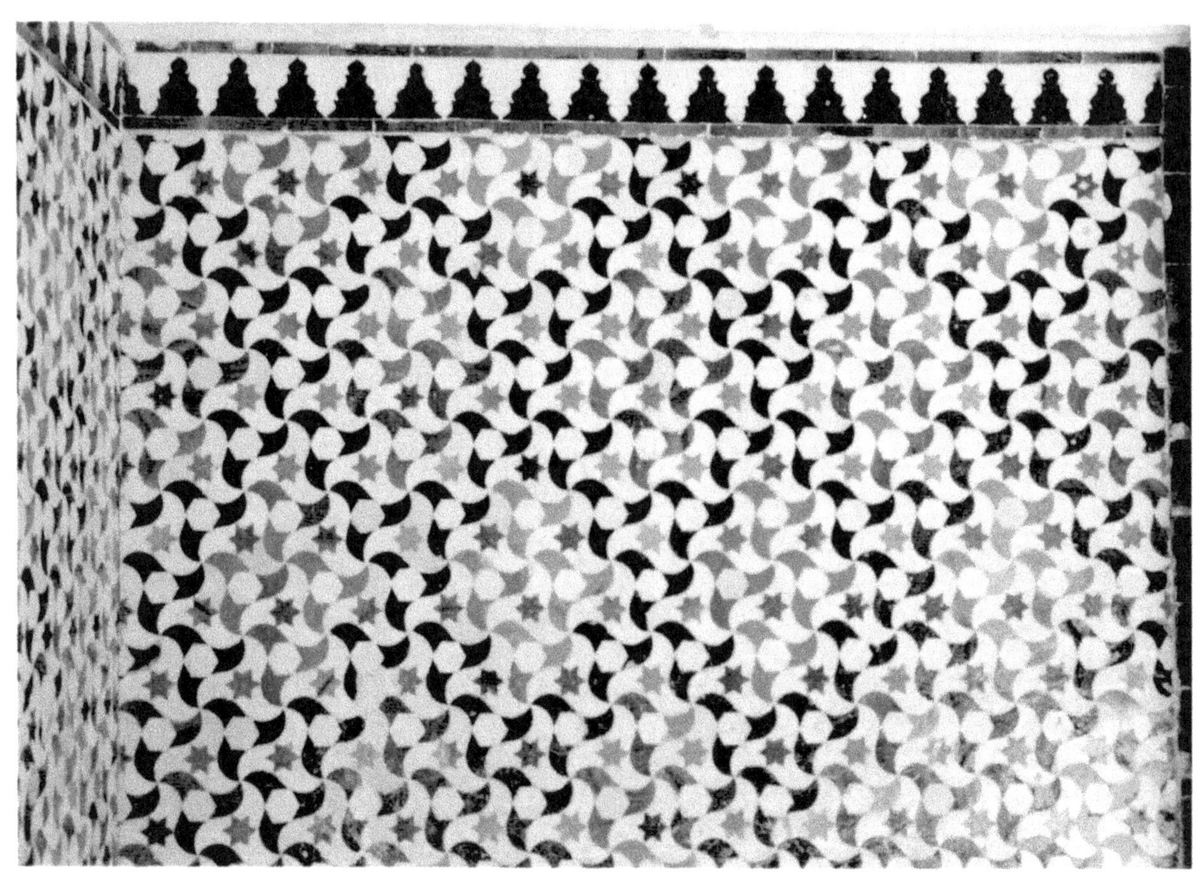

Plate 12. Granada, the Alhambra, Hall of the Ambassadors, fourteenth century, geometric pattern.

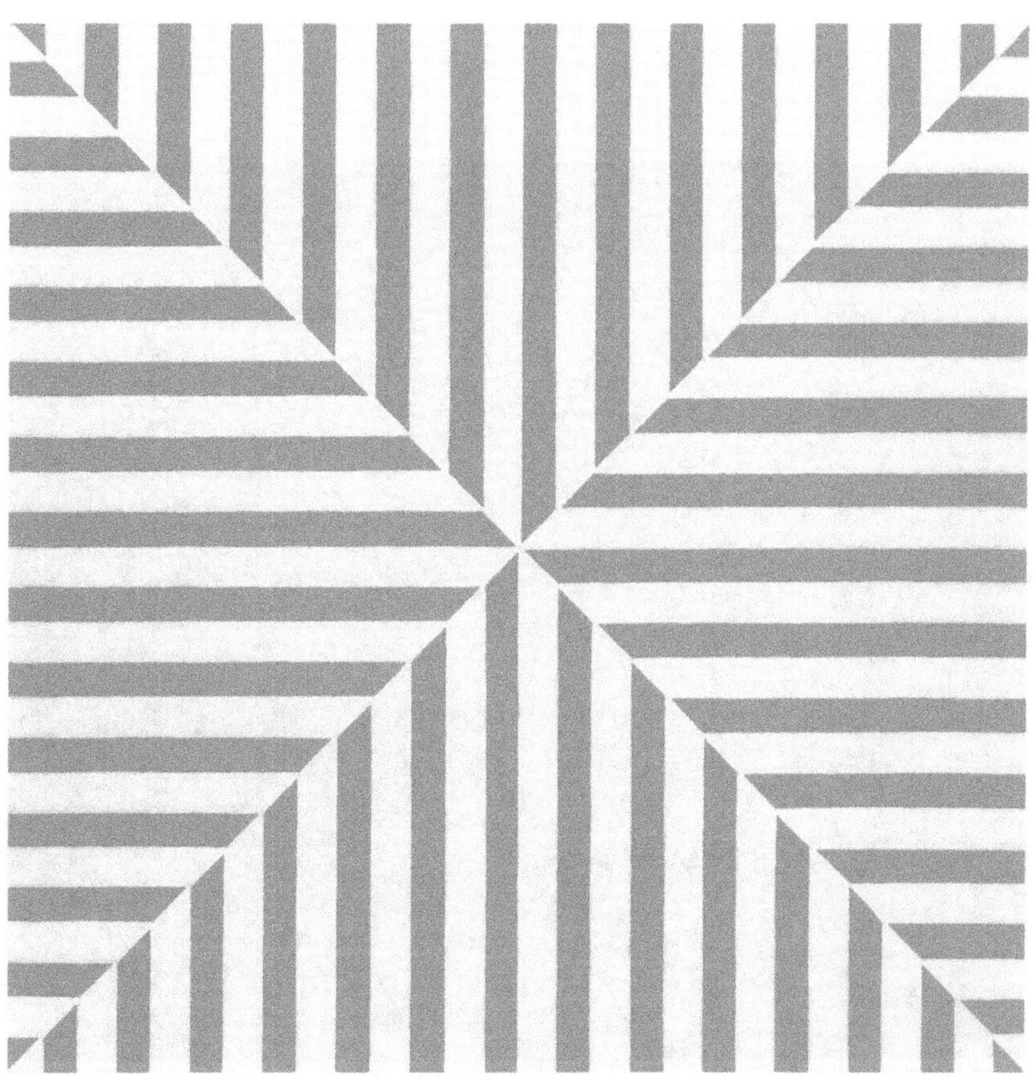

Plate 13. Frank Stella, *Marrakech,* 1964. New York, Metropolitan Museum of Art, cat. no. 422.

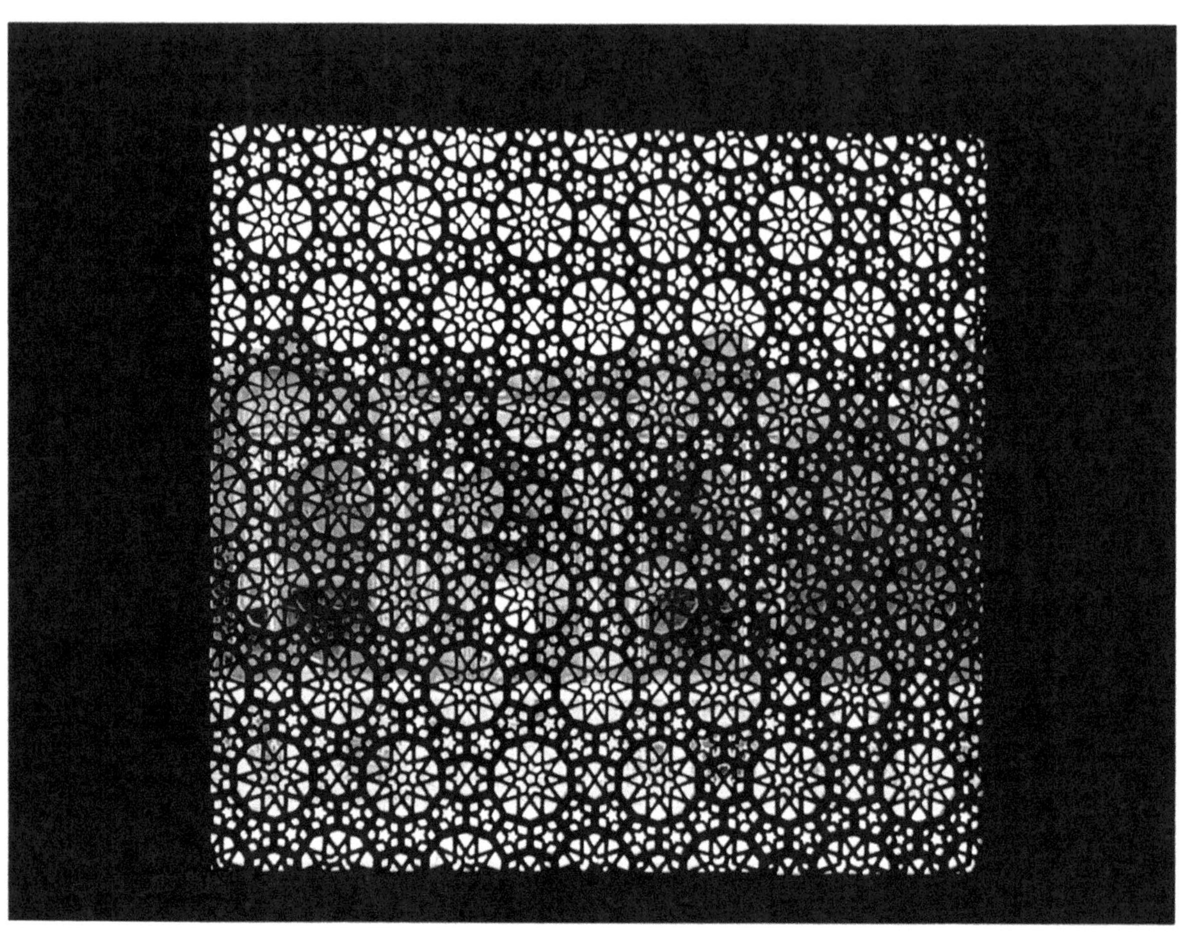

Plate 14. Agra, Tomb of I'timad al-Dawlah, 1628, window with geometric grillwork in marble.

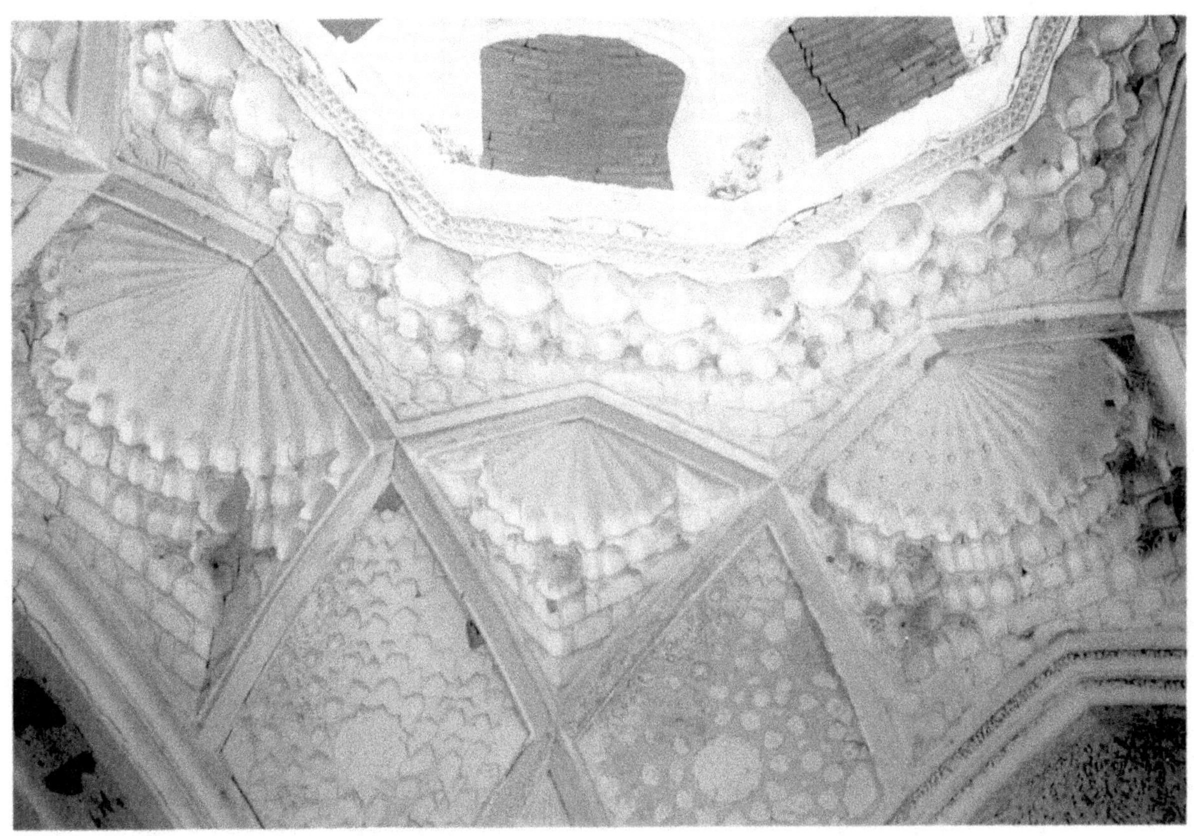

Plate 15. Iran, Khargird, madrasah, mid-fifteenth century, interior of dome with *muqarnas*.

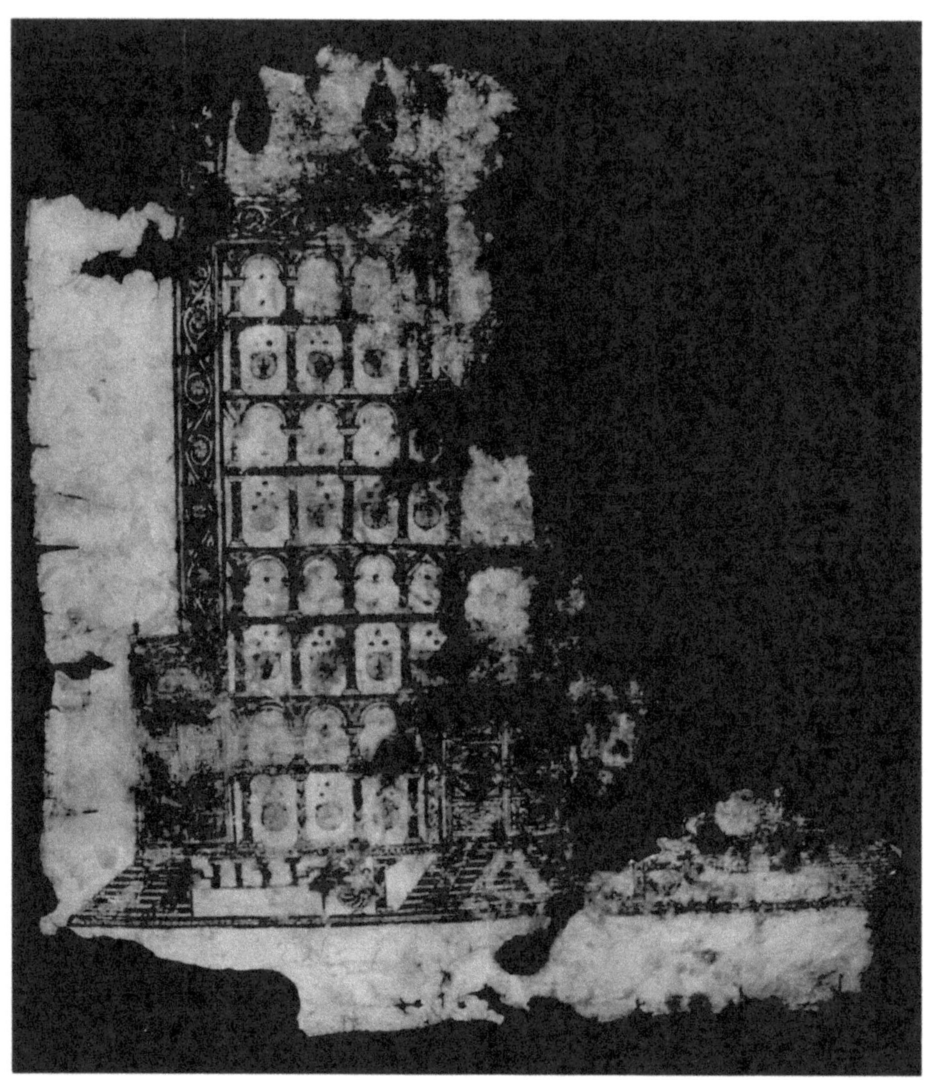

Plate 16. Frontispiece from a Koran, parchment, eighth century (?). San'a National Museum.

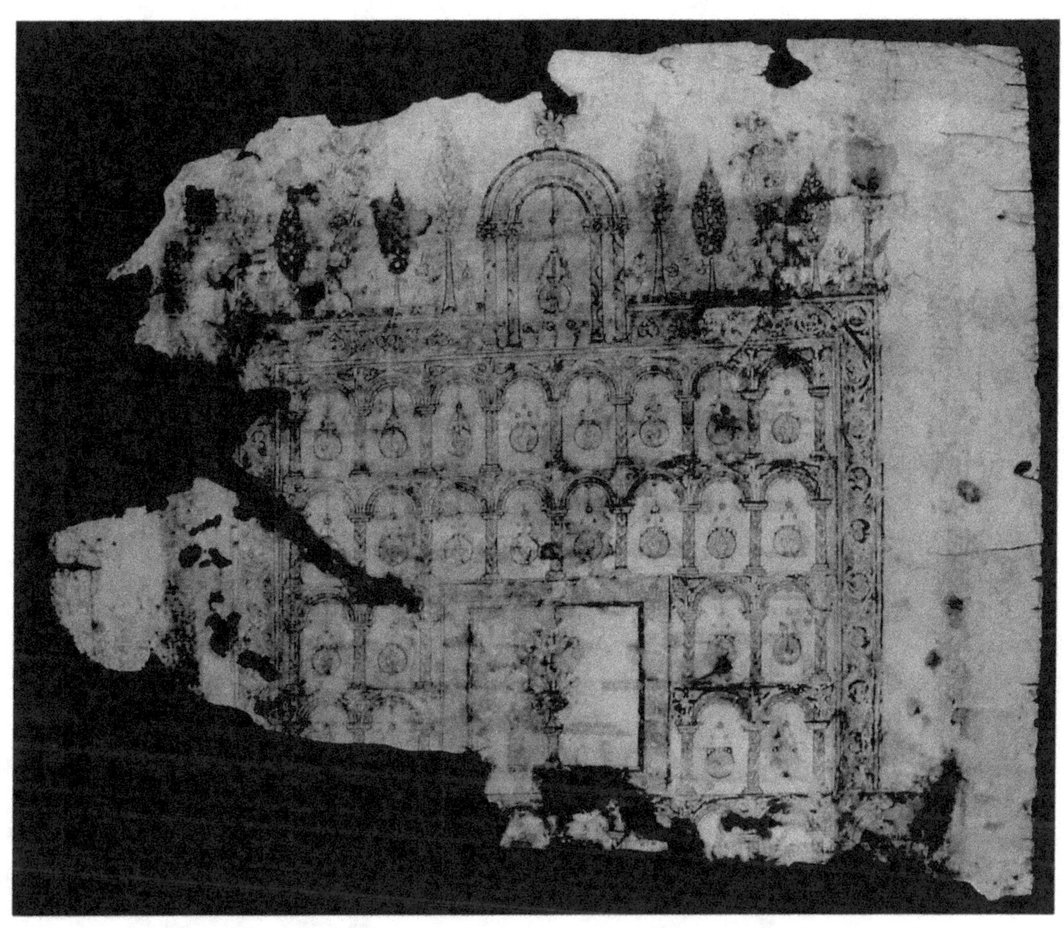

Plate 17. Frontispiece or finispiece from a Koran, parchment, eighth century (?).
San'a National Museum.

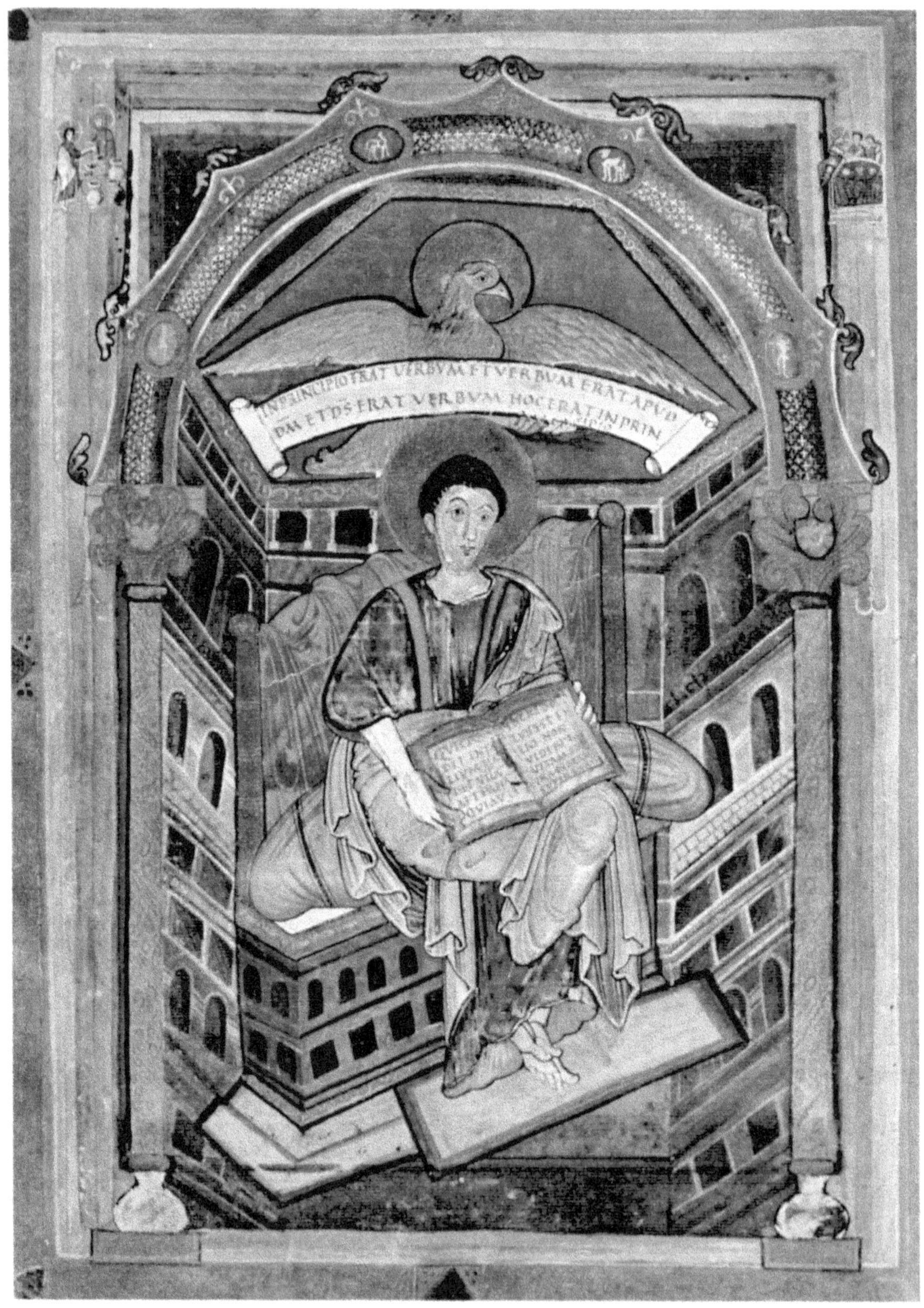

Plate 18. St. John, Gospel book of St. Médard. Paris, Bibliothèque Nationale, *lot.* 8850, fol. 18a.

Plate 19. Roman wall transformed by architectural painting.

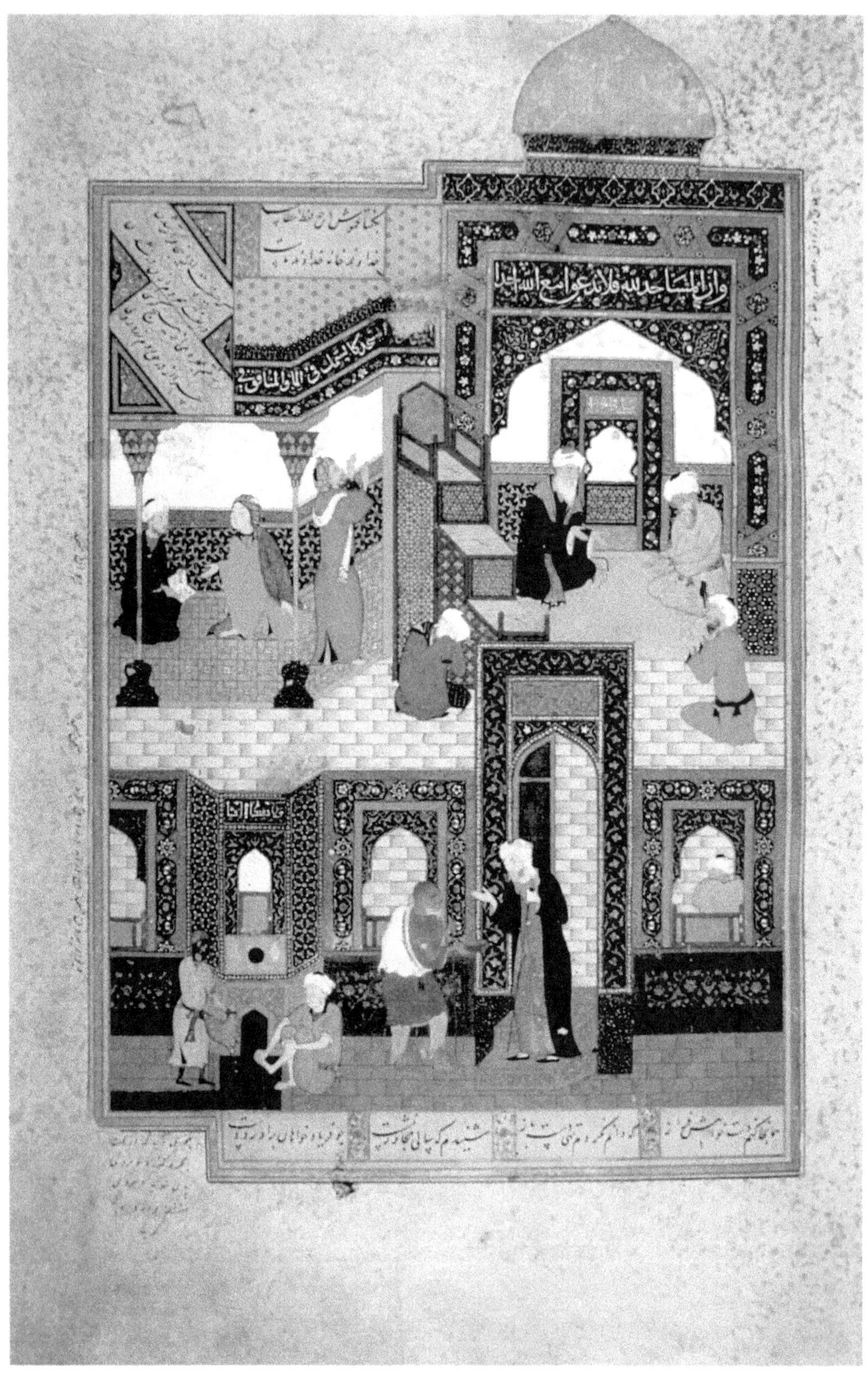

Plate 20. Saʿadi, *Bustan*, 1488, fol. 26. Cairo, National Library.

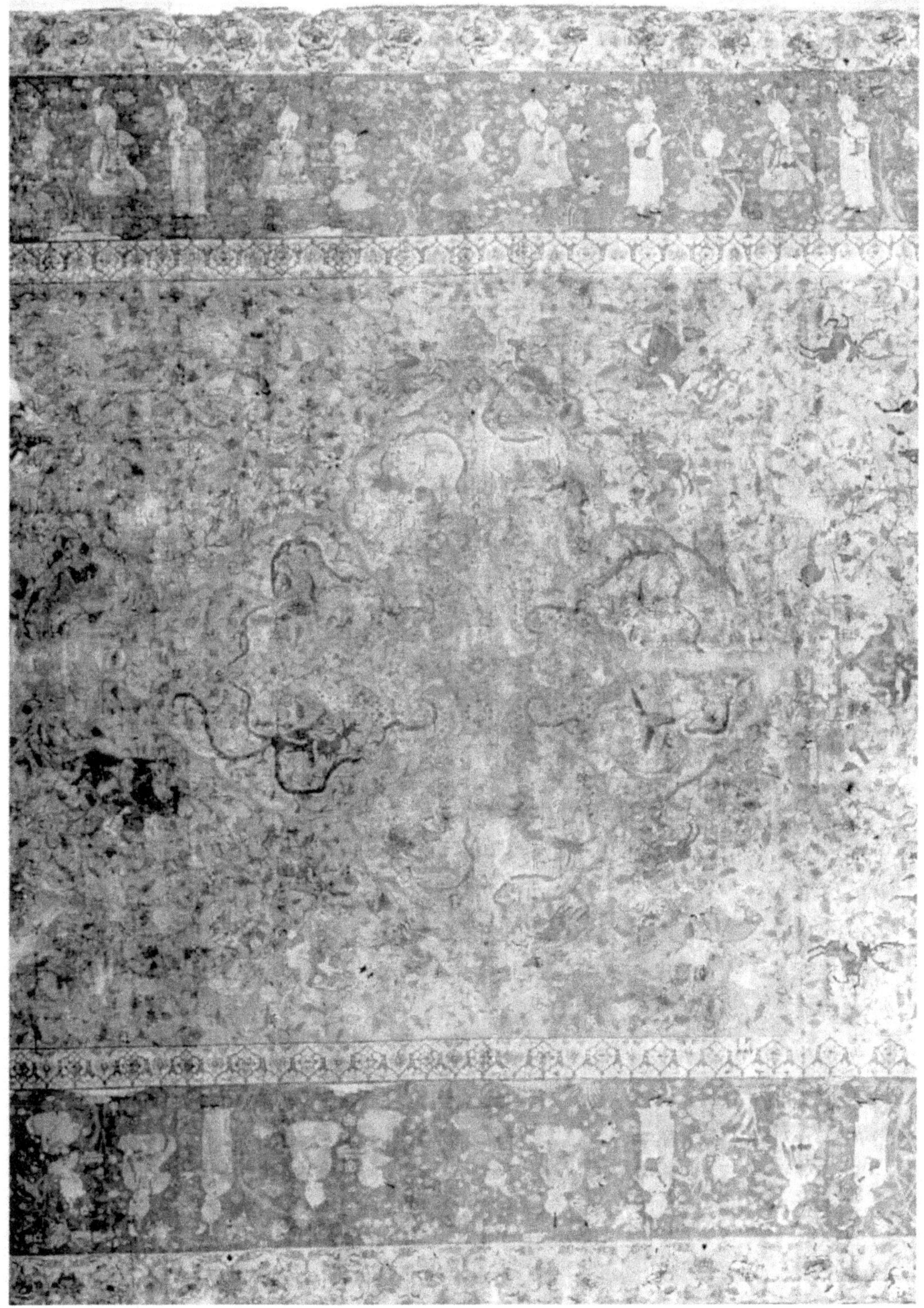

Plate 21. Silk "hunting" carpet, sixteenth century, detail. Boston, Museum of Fine Arts, 66.293.

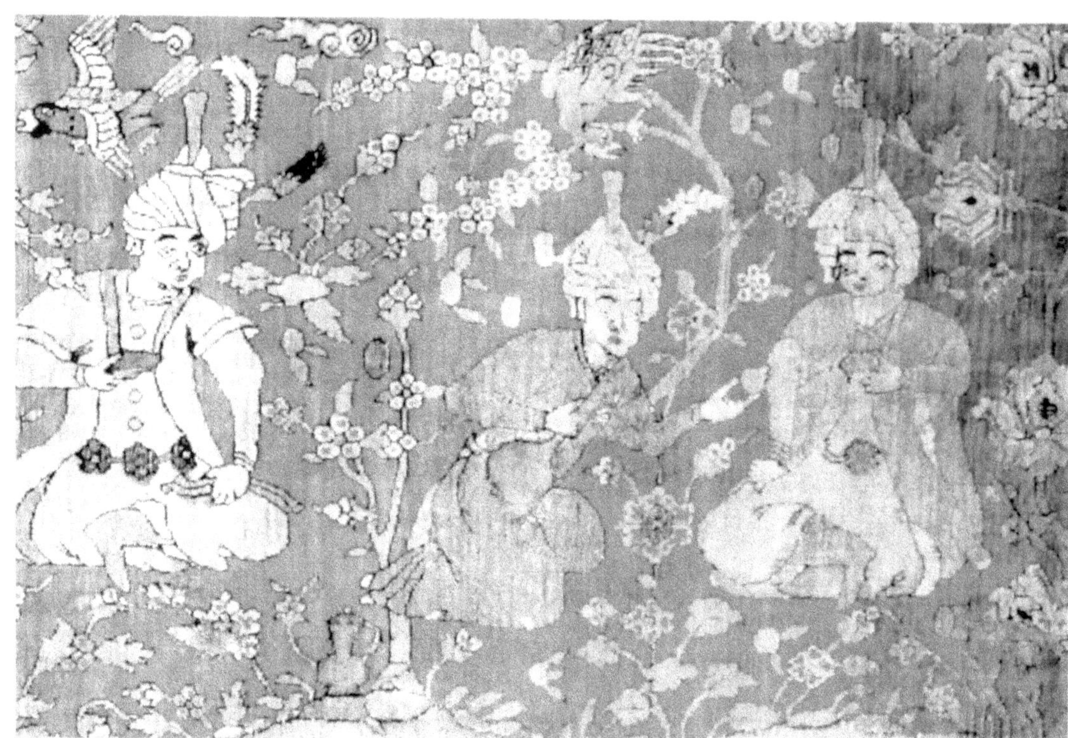

Plate 22. Detail of pl. 21.

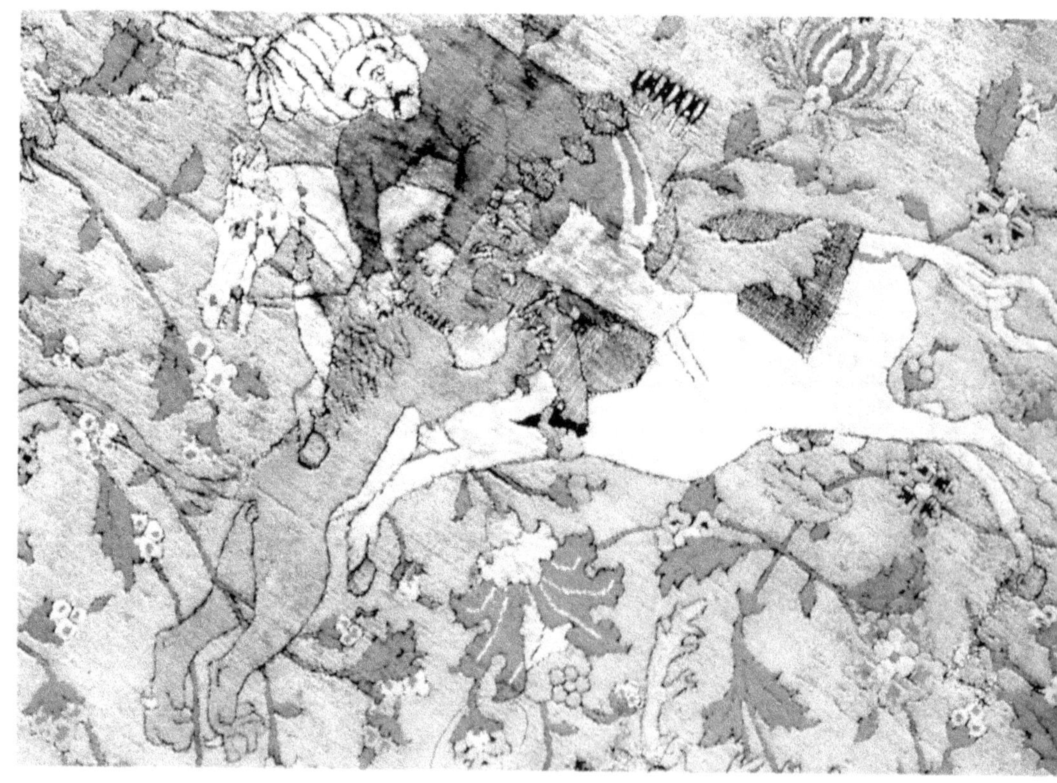

Plate 23. Detail of pl. 21.

CHAPTER III

The Intermediary of Geometry

More than once already the word "geometry" has cropped up in these pages and statements have been made or concepts introduced that have lent themselves to geometric formulation. The Timurid painting with the name of Ali (pl. 3) can easily be understood as a solution to a typical geometric problem of filling a square space with three kinds of polygonal pieces (a square, a rectangle, and a six-sided regular polygon) in several different colors according to a predetermined pattern or possibly as a free and arbitrary exercise. Cultural reasons required that the reading of the name of the Prophet's son-in-law be given, so to speak, top billing in the understanding of this particular image and in one sense it is right to do so on the principle that the most concrete and most specific explanation of a work of art always takes priority over all others. But it does not exclude other interpretations, and it is legitimate, even for those who are aware of the specific meaning of an image or of a building, to ponder its alternate values.[1] Furthermore, recent studies on patterns and tiling, on symmetry, and on color have dealt with another kind of issue this painting seems to have handled, the issue of filling space, known technically as "tessellation through isometry." Nearly all studies on this topic mention and, at times, analyze works of Islamic art.[2]

Two double pages at the beginning of Ibn al-Bawwab's unique Koran in the Chester Beatty Library (fig. 49) and its finispieces (pls. 7, 8) are composed into a geometric net, which appears at first glance as octagonal medallions or intertwined circles. In fact it consists of two intersecting nets, one of closed and clearly outlined forms and the other one of continuous frames. Regardless of the composition, however, the point of this ornamentation is a simple one: geometry, either alone or as the visually dominant theme on a page, was a significant part of the transformation of a text or a book into a work of higher or more expressive quality, at least in classical Islamic art. And the importance and prestige of geometry were acknowledged in written sources. One of the endlessly repeated praises for a good scribe is that he is the engineer (*muhandis*) of writing; the modifier *mansub*, which characterizes the reforms introduced into official Arabic writing during the tenth century and discussed in the previous chapter, means "proportioned" and implies the notion of ratio between parts so central to any geometric thinking.

These preliminary examples lead to three propositions. First, a type of design we call geometric was consistently present in much of the decoration of classical Islamic art; following Gombrich's formulation of the major functions of ornament as framing, filling, and linking, geometry was certainly used for framing and for filling, while linking, as illustrated by the examples already shown, used geometry as well, although less consistently. Second, the medieval Muslim world was conscious of a judgment based on measurement or on rational proportions and expressed this judgment through metaphors, similes, and other ways for critical thought in traditional culture. Third, even the few examples I have already shown illustrate (or suggest) that, in addition to terms like "filling," "linking," or "framing," which require a predicate (filling or framing something, in short a relationship to something else), descriptive terms are needed for a different kind of function, since a geometric design may simply be an end in itself and the exclusive object of delectation. Such is the case with the pages in Ibn al-Bawwab's Koran (pls. 7, 8; fig. 49), as well as of many other early copies of the Revelation, where it is true but probably incorrect to say that geometry "fills" a page. It is objectively true because a page is covered with geometric ornament, but it will only be correct once it has been demonstrated that enhancing a page was the exclusive objective of the geometric design. In the Ali page (fig. pl. 3) one *can* argue for a near equivalence between geometry and writing. Only our own automatic, probably strictly Western, and post-Renaissance assumption that writing is, like representations of living beings, more meaningful than other types of design makes us call this page the "Ali page" rather than "exercise in tiling."

These observations illustrate a typical art historical problem of an apparent conflict, or at least an unresolved relationship, between two categories of visual observation and reasoning. On the one hand lies a taxonomy of forms, a list of numerically and algebraically definable, achronic, and culturally independent items like circles, squares, rhombs, duodecagons, or stars. On the other hand, a cultural, synchronic, and unique moment of time chose to make, show, acquire, order, or use these forms in or on a single object. Each category leads to different methodological models. Taxonomy demands precision in description and leads to endless subtleties in understanding the shapes one sees, whereas any synchronic search demands the unraveling of a moment in time and space and requires other competences than those of articulating visual observation. The question is whether the two approaches can or even should be reconciled. More precisely, what criteria of judgment, analysis, or appreciation are appropriate when one considers geometry-related issues? Are they the criteria of the culture or of some abstract mathematical construction? What is the appropriate equilibrium between the two?

Before investigating these problems within the specific case of geometry in Islamic decoration, two preliminary questions must be dealt with. First, what is it that we mean by geometry when we talk about it as it appears on the surface of works of art? Are there perhaps other ways of defining it than through a study of surfaces? Second, are the uses of geometry peculiar to Islamic art or, as with writing, is the Muslim phenomenon a special and perhaps uniquely original exemplar of a practice found in many places?

To answer the second question first, we can begin with Owen Jones, the fascinating theoretician of ornament and student of the Alhambra from the first half of the nineteenth century, and two of the propositions he put forward as general principles for decoration. "All ornament should be based upon a geometrical construction," argues proposition eight. The ninth proposition is a bit longer: "As in every perfect work of Architecture, a true proportion will be found to reign between all the members which compose it, so throughout the Decorative Arts every assemblage of forms should be arranged on certain definite proportions; the whole and each particular member should be a multiple of some simple unit." And, as a sort of note to the proposition, he adds: "Those proportions will be the most beautiful which it will be most difficult for the eye to detect."[3] Jones's propositions are interesting for several reasons. First he sees comparable properties in decoration and in architecture, a point of view that will be elaborated in the following chapter, while his remark about a hidden value to geometry will be important for the concluding chapter of these essays.

But his more immediately important point is that all ornament is based on a geometric construction. If this is so, then geometric theories of ornament should apply to all artistic traditions. And indeed, a large group of early Greek vases with meanders (figs. 90 and 91) and other repeated motifs is known as the "geometric" group of ceramics.[4] Prehistoric and early historic ceramics from Iraq, Iran, or India (fig. 92) have striking geometric designs on their surfaces and some Iranian ones even acquired unusual shapes, which may occasionally be defined geometrically as well (fig. 93).[5] The religious buildings of Mitla in southern Mexico are covered with a mosaic decoration, most of whose shapes are clear geometric figures or derive from such figures.

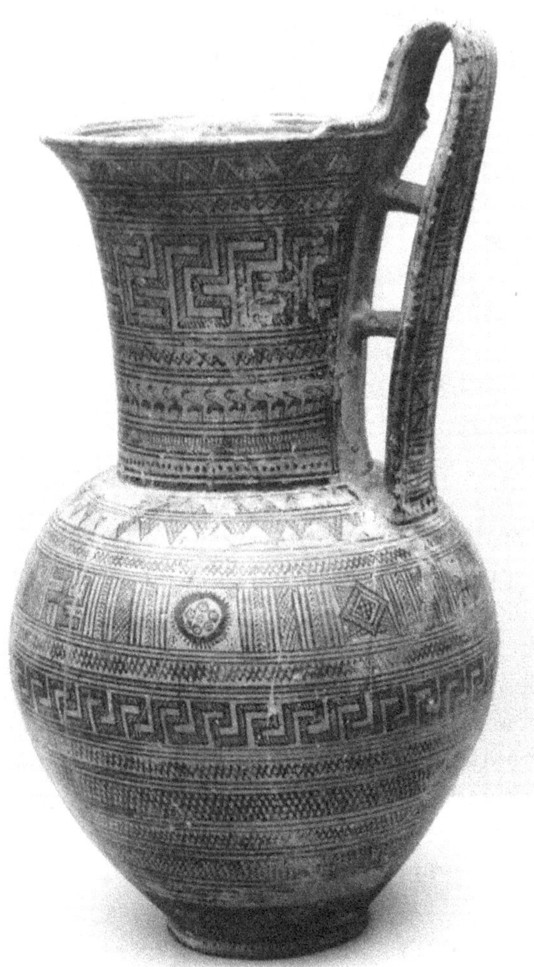

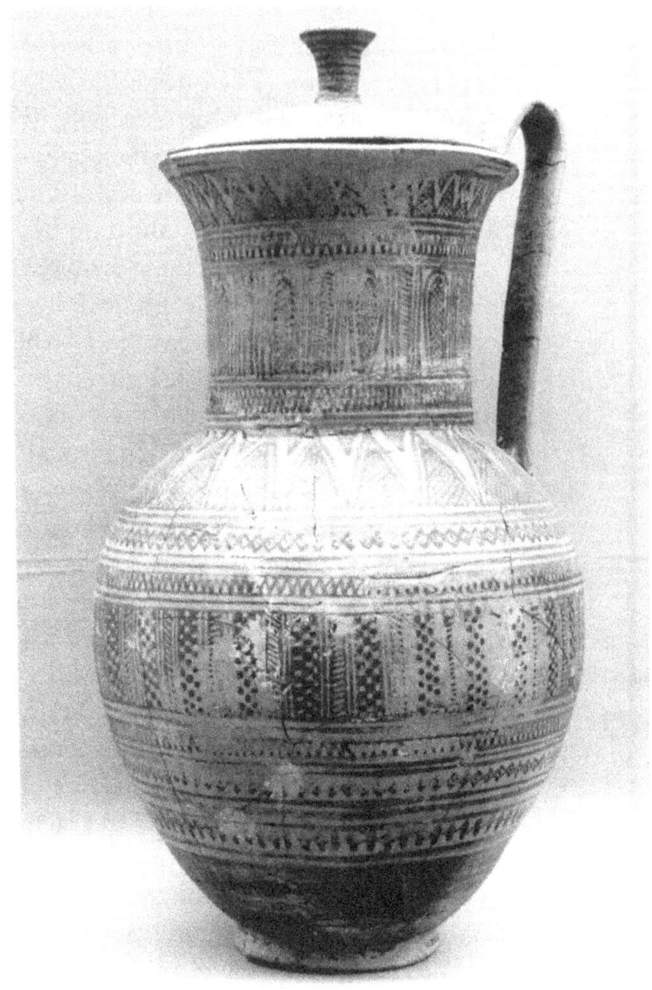

90 91

Fig. 90. Greek vase with geometric design, ninth or eighth century B.C. New York, Metropolitan Museum of Art, Fletcher Fund, 1941 (41.11.4).

Fig. 91. Greek vase with geometric designs, eighth century B.C. New York, Metropolitan Museum of Art, Rogers Fund, 1910 (10.210.6.AB).

Fig. 92. Iranian ceramic, early ninth century B.C. New York, Metropolitan Museum of Art, Rogers Fund, 1965 (65.61).

Fig. 93. Amlash pottery from Iran, eleventh or tenth century B.C. New York, Metropolitan Museum of Art, gift of the Teheran Museum, 1939 (39.60.9).

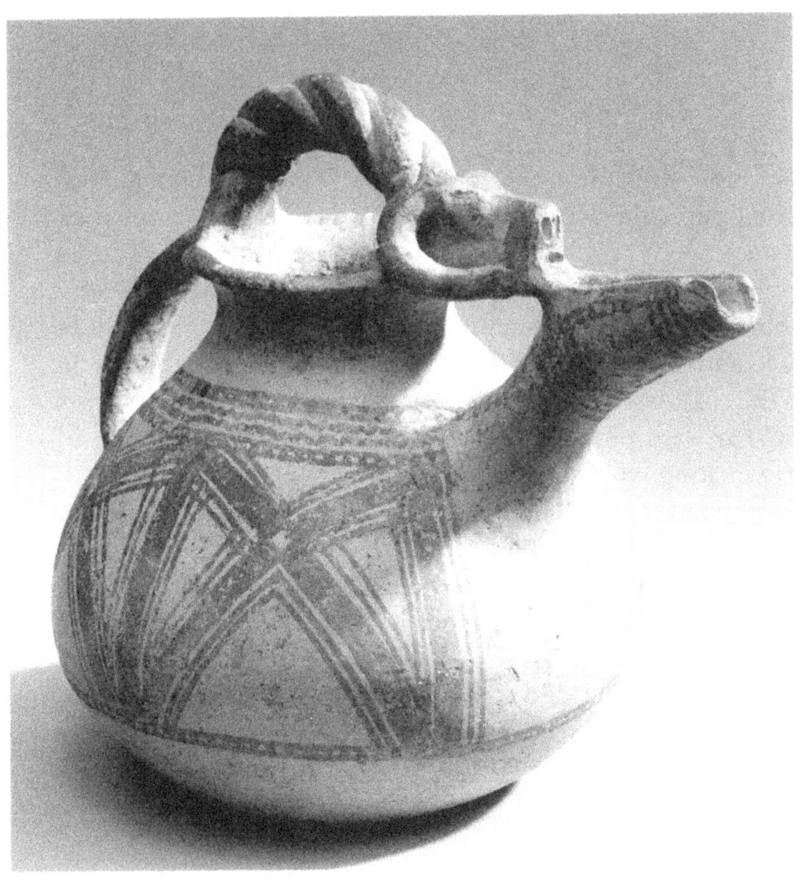

92

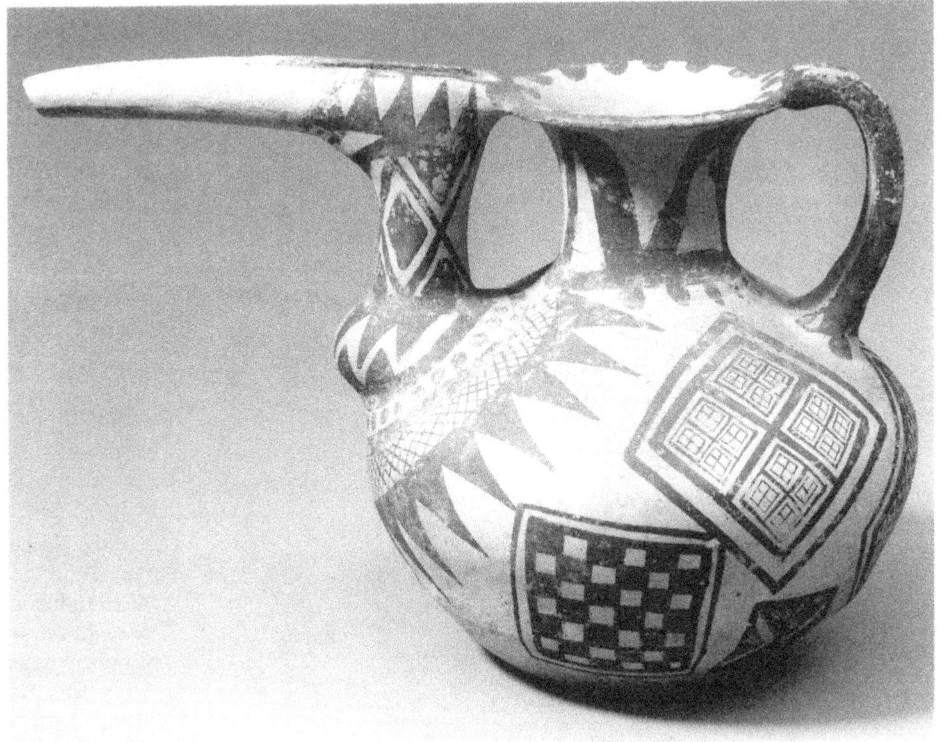

93

Mayan facades are more difficult to interpret, but at Tikal and Uxmal geometrically defined figures do occur mixed with other representational or clearly symbolic ones, while ceramic pieces or textiles are frequently adorned with patterns of diamonds, squares, or indeterminate shapes strewn regularly on a surface.[6] Chinese bronzes lead to a similar problem of interpretation. In some of them decorative designs and even shapes are clearly definable in geometric terms (fig. 94), but it is not always clear whether geometric shapes were meant by the artisans or whether they are our contemporary way of defining or approximating what we see.[7]

The issue becomes even more complex when one looks at the metalwork or textiles from the art of the northern steppes of Russia and Siberia, both ancient fragments retrieved archaeologically (figs. 95, and 96) and precontemporary documents of what is usually called folk art (pl. 11). It is often through

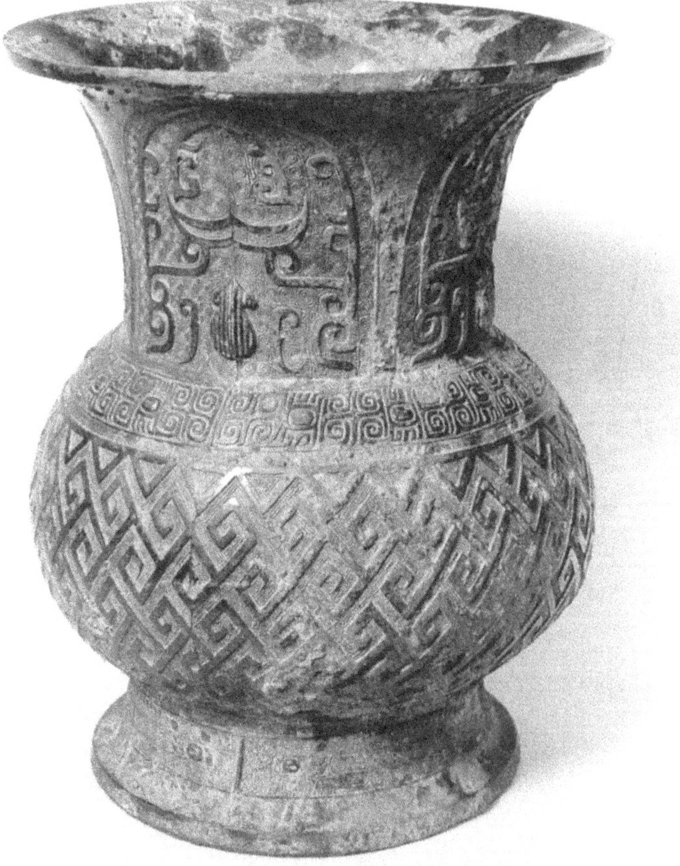

Fig. 94. Ritual vessel type Toun, China, Early Western Chou, eleventh or tenth century B.C. Cambridge, Harvard University Art Museums, 1943, 52.93.

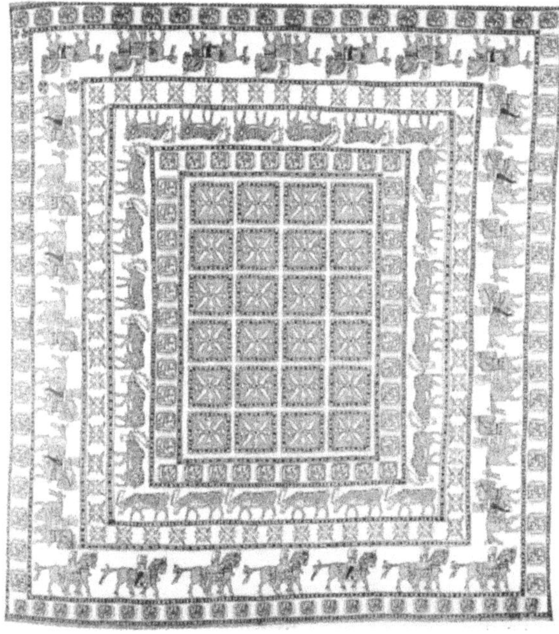

95

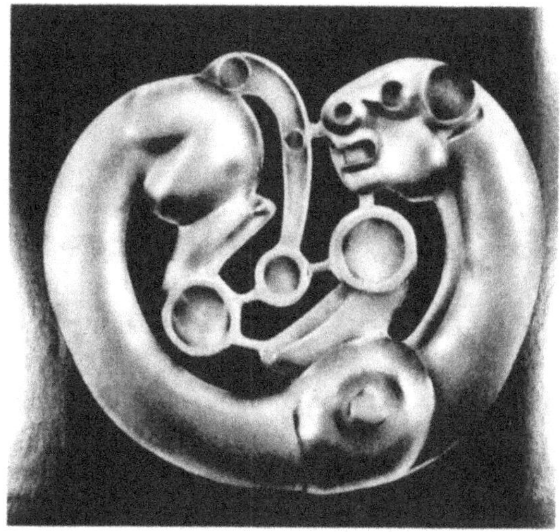

96

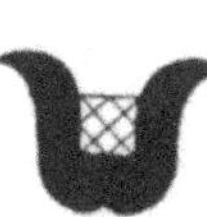

97

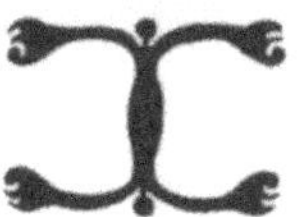

98

Fig. 95. Rug, Pazyryk, sixth century B.C.

Fig. 96. Gold lion, Scythian.

Fig. 97. Drawing after Central Asian design.

Fig. 98. Drawing after Central Asian design.

information available about the latter that the former is explained. Let us take, for example, the celebrated knotted carpet from Pazyryk (fig. 95), the oldest carpet in existence and one of the most stunning archaeological finds of the past half century.[8] Of its six zones of decoration, two are nonmimetic, representing figures without external referent, for which only geometry-derived descriptions are immediately reasonable, like squares, bordered or not, with designs arranged around two axes of symmetry. Further investigation may reveal that two spirals arranged like the graphs of economists mean "two dogs fighting for a bone" (fig. 97), and a symmetrically arranged concoction with two rectangles is "two tigers dragging a cow off into a thicket" (fig. 98). But these Rorschach-like interpretations, while delighting voyeurish instincts for hidden meanings in everything, are dubious without a kind of evidence that is almost impossible to find.[9] Initially it is only in geometric terms of curved or straight lines, of squares, circles, and triangles, and of proportions of size or volume between them that we can best describe an object like the central segment, perhaps the body, of a striking gold lion now in the Hermitage Museum and originally from Siberia (fig. 96).[10] The difficulty of distinguishing between animal and geometric forms in metalwork appears all the way across northern Asia to the frontier of China.

Northern Eurasian art is not unique in leading to geometric definitions. Symmetry or asymmetry in patterning or in hatching characterizes the stunning body painting among the disappearing tribesmen of the Nuba area in south central Sudan mentioned earlier in another context,[11] while in northern Nigeria, among the lively sedentary Hausa, the powerful decoration of facades (fig. 99) or of clothes (fig. 100) consists of motifs that again at first glance can be best described in geometrical terms.[12] In most immediately visible ways geometry was relegated to a relatively limited role in Western painting

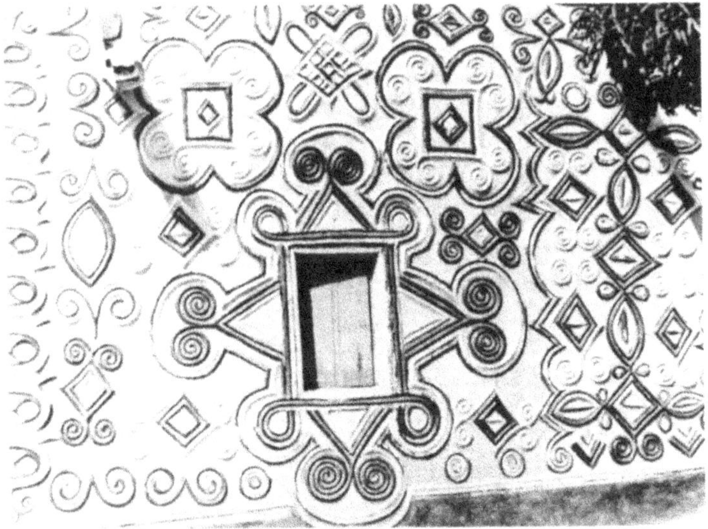

Fig. 99. House facade, Hausa area, modern.

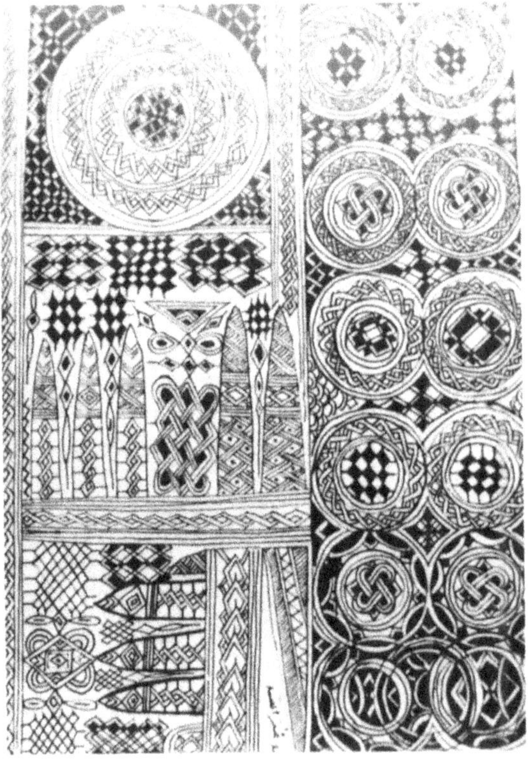

Fig. 100. Textile, Hausa area.

and sculpture from the Middle Ages onward, except for mosaic and other tesselated floors of southern Italy and for marquetry and other techniques of applied and industrial arts almost throughout. But it became strikingly powerful in our own post–cubist times. In the twentieth century, a very special position is occupied by two Dutchmen, Mondrian on the one hand with his powerfully evocative polychrome squares (pl. 4), and Escher on the other (figs. 101 and 102), whose articulated statements and images are striking and consciously elaborated instances of a specific order of mathematical problems. In truly contemporary art, several practitioners from the New York school and from elsewhere have experimented with stark geometry or with designs closely related to it.[13]

Hardly a systematic survey of all existing instances of geometry in ornament, the examples I have gathered are not quite random or accidental and

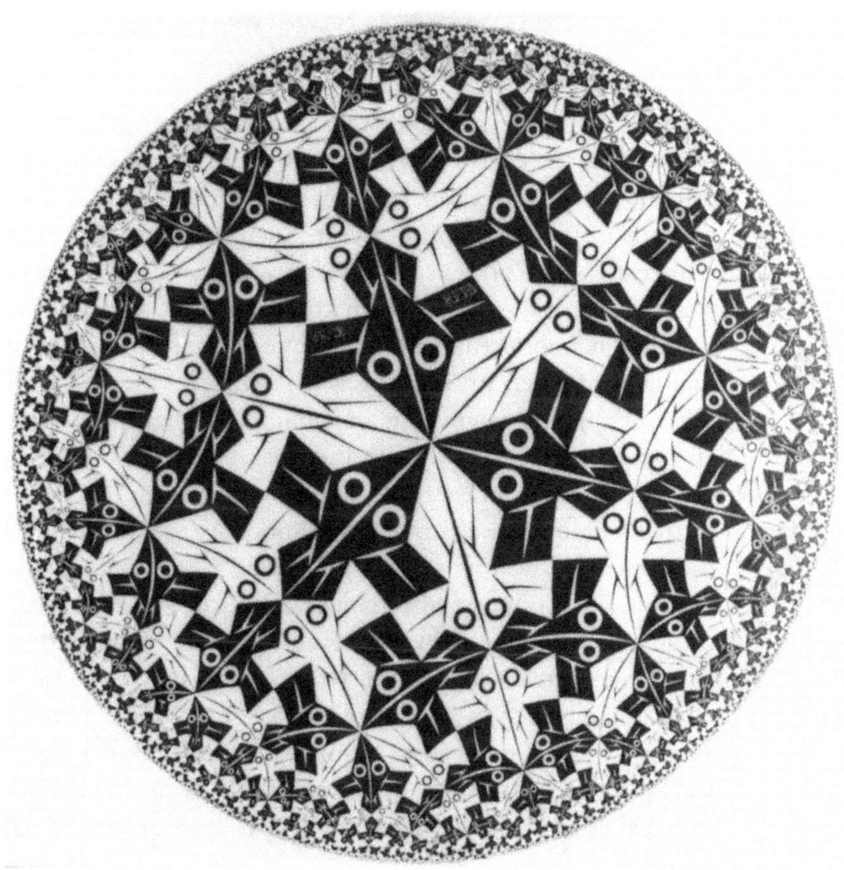

Fig. 101. Escher, *Circle Limits I.*

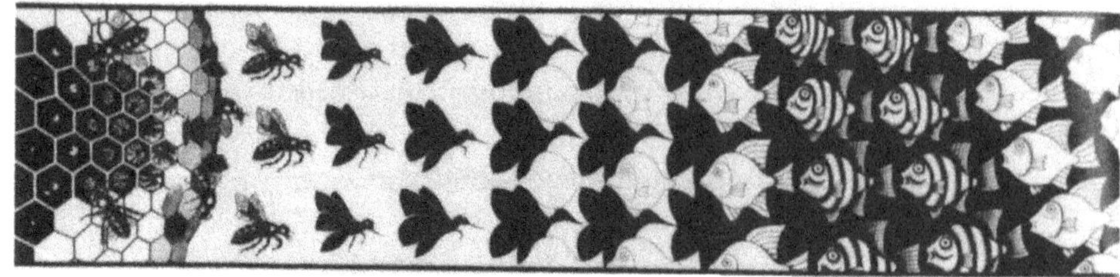

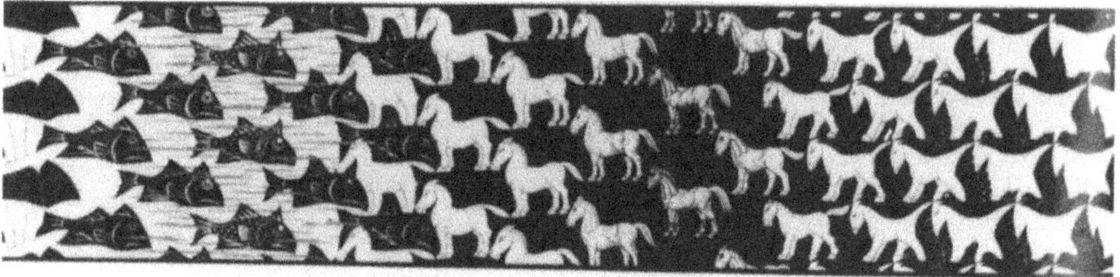

Fig. 102. Escher, *Metamorphoses*, detail.

illustrate two points. One is the ubiquity of geometry at any period of time and within any culture. But this ubiquity is not consistent. Geometry as a primary subject is almost absent from major cultures and techniques like western European painting before the twentieth century or Tang and post-Tang Far Eastern art (except for a few categories of mostly practical objects). It is sublimated into building in the formal art of India, as both traditional writing on architecture and contemporary interpretations of standing monuments have given much weight to complex systems of proportion with or without appended symbolic meanings. Geometry, however, shines in nearly all the industrial arts of India and with the *mandala* it becomes a particularly clear and pan-Asian example of a denotative sign that acts occasionally as the virtually ubiquitous connotative symbol of a vision of eternal truth and eternal movement as well as eternal quietude.[14] This peculiar fact, that geometry lends itself so often to alternate explanations, is, however, troubling, as it is frequently difficult to separate semiotic from symbolic meanings.[15] The wonderful geometric threshold drawings from Hyderabad in India, which have been studied recently as examples of folk art,[16] turn out to actually "represent" spaces for specific purposes, a marriage platform or a place of sacrifice, while the Nuba body paintings mentioned earlier (fig. 27) literally talk about being married or nonmarried, pure or impure, chief or subordinate, and so forth. In short, the formal ubiquity of geometry in so many places and times conceals variety in the density of its presence and especially in its meaning; geometry may well be more iconophoric than is first assumed.

The second point derived from my selection of examples is that the areas and times that most consistently exhibit geometric ornament are at the periphery of major cultural centers or at the edges of dominating social classes. Nearly all my illustrations are from the northern, "barbarian" areas, pre-Columbian or provincial South America, African villages, the coverings of floors, the techniques of ceramics and textiles, and an orphan within the pantheon of contemporary painters and draftsmen like Escher. It is as though geometry was the privilege of the illiterate, the remote, the popularly pious, the women using (and/or making) textiles and ceramics. For the dominant groups or classes, geometry may not have been necessary or else it was subsumed into secondary realms of their visual spaces, because whatever it accomplished was replaced or implied by alternate forms or signs. As we shall see presently, quite the opposite occurred in the Muslim world. The point remains, however, that, at least as an initial observation, geometry or a category of forms resembling geometry is most frequently associated with industrial arts like textiles or ceramics, that is to say with the areas of creativity in which functional purpose dominates the fashioning of the object, where craft predominates over art, as even Escher's fantasies (maybe even the contemporary paintings of a Frank Stella) appear more than once as art becoming craft. In most of them, the construction of the image is so clearly apparent that each image can (or seems to) be easily reproduced.

Yet we know, even from the examples I have given, that some geometric forms were given meaning and probably that none can be said to be without possible meaning. The question is how meanings—iconographic, semiotic, or symbolic—can be given or have in practice been given to geometric forms. The circle may well be granted a theoretical cosmic and metaphysical potential, but this does not mean that every circle represents or evokes the universe or the totality of life. It is not easy or abstractly logical to detect automatically matrimonial status or social position in a combination of triangles or in a set of straight lines. And, while it is legitimate enough at professional mathematical levels to see arbitrary signs and numbers as a language, that language is hardly accessible to most mortals. Therefore, the further analysis of the particularly rich trove of geometric forms that occurs in the Islamic world should help clarify, if not resolve, the more universal problem of how and why it is that meaning can be attributed to geometry.

THESE REMARKS on the presence of geometry in so many different places and at so many different times lead directly back to my other initial question: what is it that we are entitled to call geometric in decoration?

The word geometric has been used for three different kinds of forms. The first one, most strikingly illustrated by mosaic tiles and stuccos of the Alhambra (pl. 12), by wooden mihrabs (fig. 103) or doors in Egypt, by brick minarets of Iran (fig. 104), by certain Mondrians (pl. 4) or Stellas (pl. 13), is a form that *must* first be described as a geometric pattern in order to be understood. However devious and complex the means of making or reconstructing any one example may be and however deep the social and contextual meanings that can be eventually articulated for it, the object is, first of all, definable as a *regular* figure creating a "regular" pattern. Whole manuals have been written on how these patterns operate and how they create lattice nets that organize space for the possible but not necessary deployment of other motifs or else of congruent tiles that cover a whole area with carefully thought out separate pieces.[17] Although probably infinite in their variants, these regular figures are limited in the number of basic types that produce them. One knows, for instance, that, through the four operations that create repetition—translation (copying as on wallpaper), rotation, reflection, and glide reflection (moving a unit along a single track)—only seventeen planar and seven linear patterns can be formed.[18] In a sense, the intellectual problem posed by any one ornamental design of this type is relatively simple. It is to discover its theoretical type, either by measuring and drawing a given pattern or by finding it in books of models.[19] As we shall see, the more difficult question is *why* this type of regular geometry was used in ornament, not what it is.

The second kind of geometric form is much less rigid and, therefore, more difficult to define. In one of the sculpted panels of Mshatta (fig. 23), the predominating vegetal design occasionally contains totally independent circular units, which could be called rings, hoops, or circles. In other words it is a unit that, by the absolute regularity of its outline, can best be defined geometrically, but the fact that there are little "pearls" in the frame of the circles and that the surrounding vegetation is almost tropically dense transformed the circle into a concrete object. It is as though decorated rings were left in the midst of vegetation. On the same facade of Mshatta, it has been argued that the growth of the vine is sometimes arranged "geometrically," meaning that it forms very regular spirals and approximates adjoining or intersecting circles (fig. 24).

Nearly a thousand years later than Mshatta the surface of a magnificent Turkish ceramic is also divided by dozens of circles generated by a thin vine,

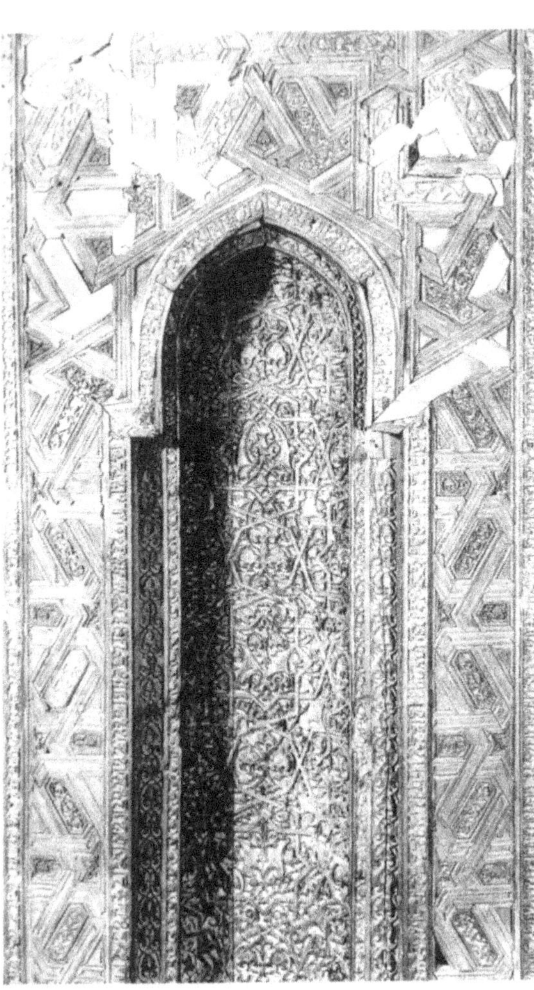

Fig. 103. Mihrab of Sayyidah Nafisah, wood, twelfth century. Cairo Museum of Islamic Art.

Fig. 104. Central Asia, Bukhara, brick minaret, Kalayan Mosque, 1127.

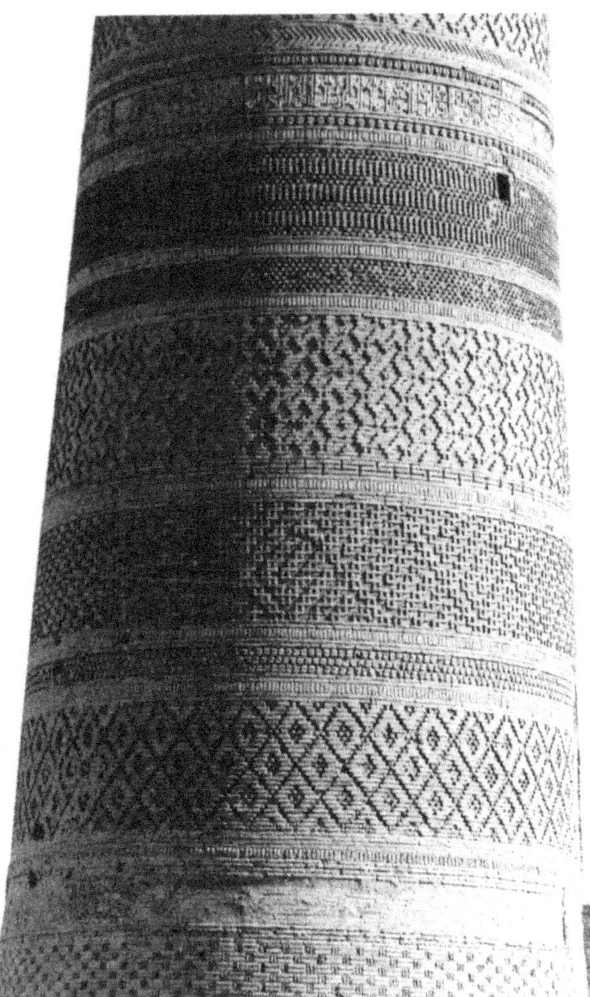

which has almost lost its vegetal sense (fig. 105).[20] In the centuries intervening between Mshatta and the Ottomans, it is by the thousands that we can count examples of an occluded geometry of regular motifs supporting writing, vegetation, animals, or even personages. In some instances, traditional and very obvious triangular models govern the composition of large illustrations of the Persian epic (fig. 106), and a scholar was able, some fifteen years ago, to suggest that *all* compositions in paintings from Muslim lands were based on the spiral.[21] This particular theory is dubious, if only because the absolute consistency claimed for it is not only unlikely but in fact absent or contrived. But the existence in Islamic art and probably in many other artistic traditions of what may be called an *implied* geometry seems clear. Less rigorous than the regular variety, its point is rarely itself, it is rather a convenient means with which to hang a narrative, ornamental or other. It is the trellis on which the vine or the ivy is grown or displayed. Its evaluation is less a matter of matching it with a mathematical formula than of deciding whether it served as a straight-jacket, almost drowning whatever it carried (fig. 103), or as a silent or, more exactly, invisible support for a statement that would collapse without implied geometry (fig. 24).

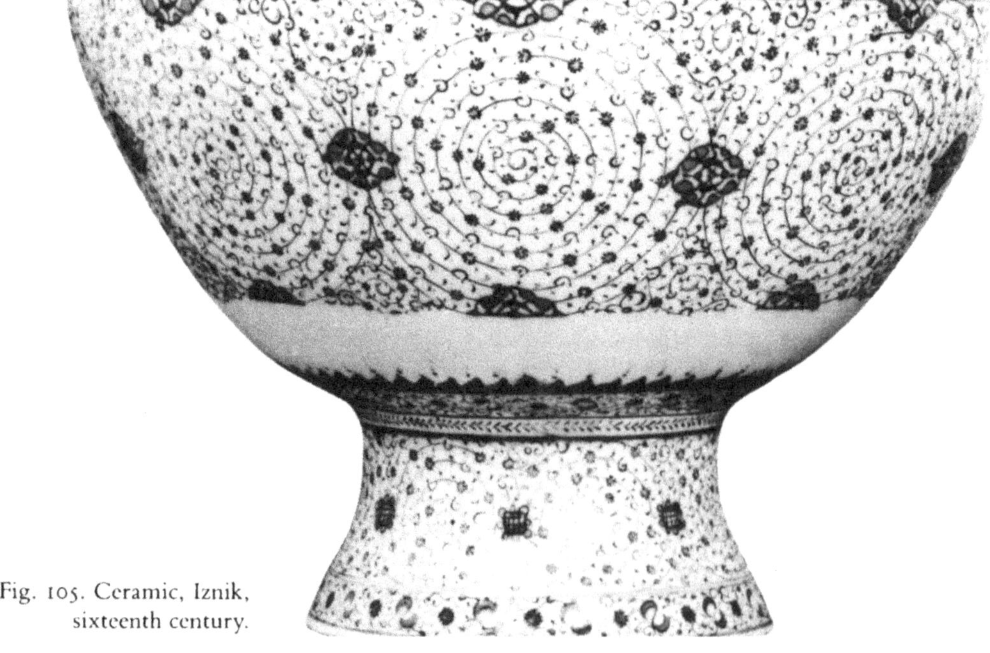

Fig. 105. Ceramic, Iznik, sixteenth century.

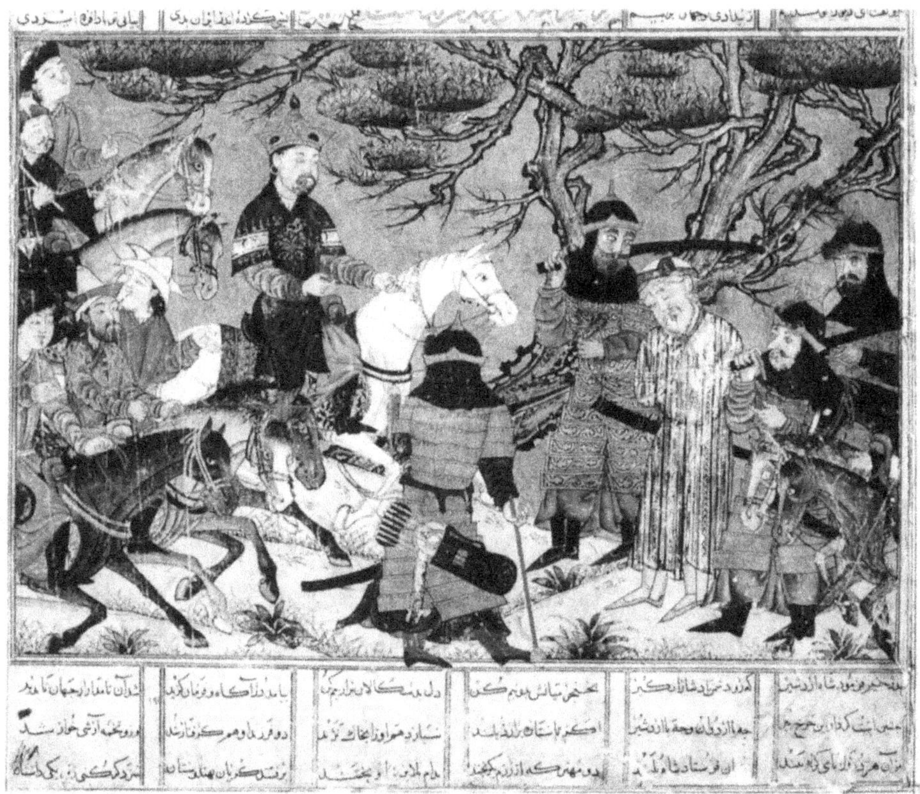

Fig. 106. *Ardashir takes Ardawan prisoner,* so-called Demotte *Shahnama,* probably Tabriz, circa 1336. Washington, D.C., the Arthur M. Sackler Gallery, Smithsonian Institution.

The third kind of geometry could be called *loose* geometry. On the one hand, it includes all repetitive motifs whose rhythm requires calculation; these occur in many border patterns on mosaic floors (fig. 107) and on objects and in allover designs common, for instance, in ceramics (fig. 108). For the most part, it consists of the mass of designs in which the eye sees a circle, a square, or a triangle, without being ever quite sure that the artist or craftsman wanted such figures to be seen or that he composed his design with them as supports. The technology of weaving and especially the drawloom made this loose geometry frequent in textiles, but I would also include in this category such peculiar compositions as a strange group of facades from Kazakhstan in Soviet central Asia. The most striking example is the eleventh- or twelfth-century mausoleum of Aisha-Bibi near modern Dzambul (fig. 109). The making of the terracotta plaques that adorn its facade required at least an approximate measurement of the surface of the facade. Each plaque has a shape that is geometrically defined, and the ornament in most of them is so far removed

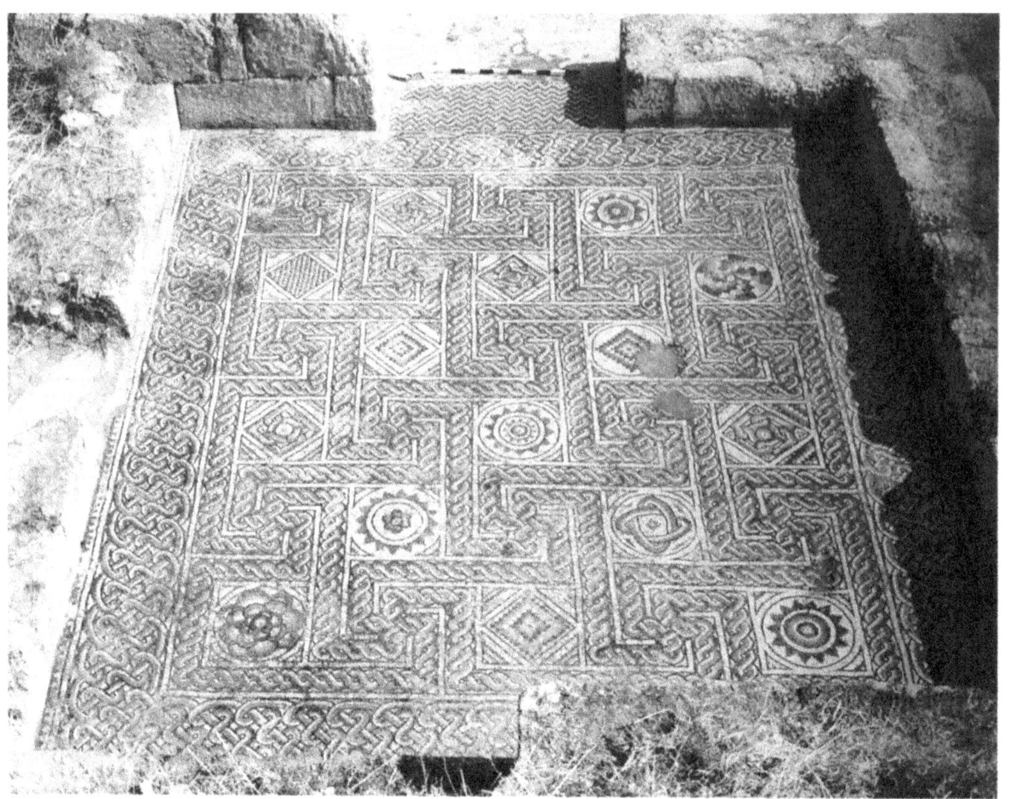

107

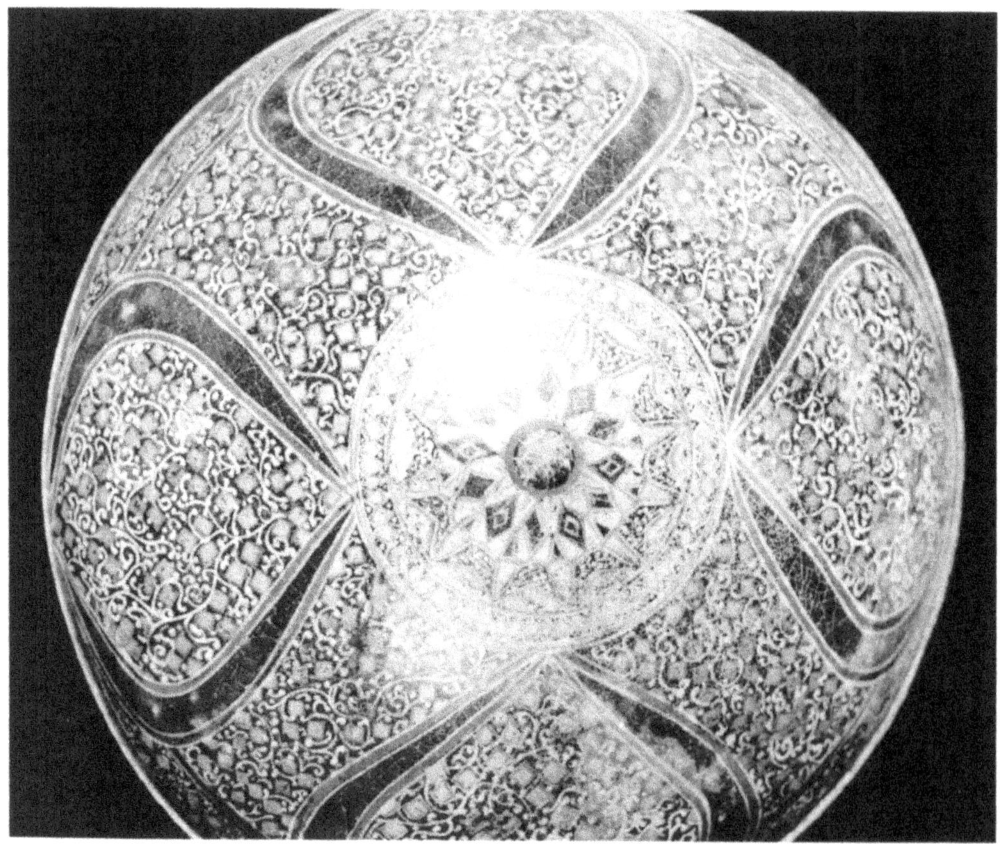

108

Fig. 107. Khirbat al-Minyah, mosaic floor, eighth century.

Fig. 108. Ceramic, Iran, thirteenth century. Paris, Louvre Museum, MA04501.

Fig. 109. Dzambul (Kazakhstan), facade of Aysha Bibi Mausoleum, twelfth century.

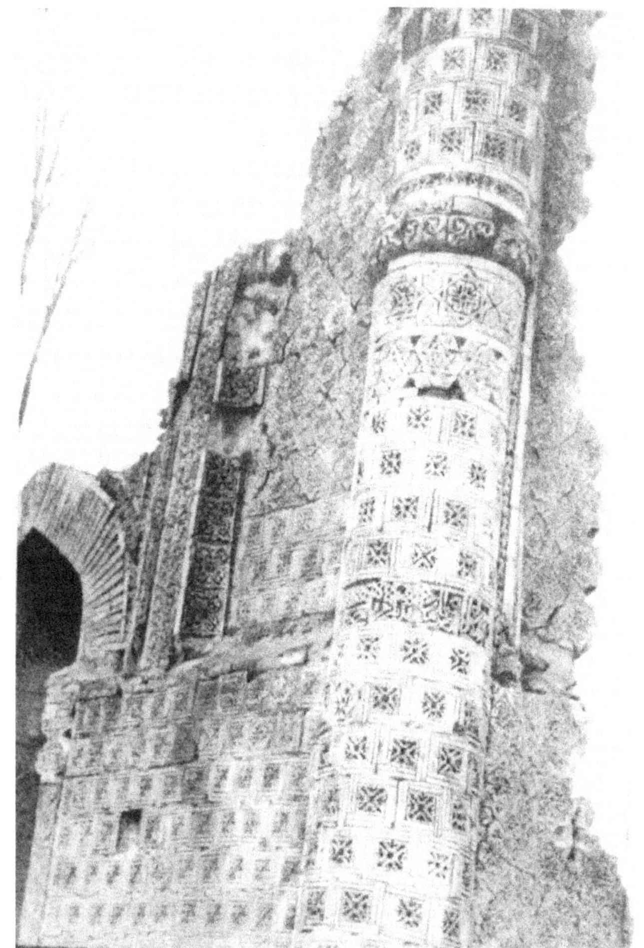

109

from its vegetal origins that a series of geometric terms like axes and symmetry describes these plaques best.[22]

Geometry appears, thus, as a frequent category to classify, describe, and comprehend the visual experience of many objects or monuments of architecture. It is also part of the process of creating things, most particularly works of architecture, where systems of proportions for the establishment of plans and elevations have been worked out in the practice of building or, especially in Renaissance Europe and later, through manuals like Alberti's or Serlio's. In the nineteenth century, Owen Jones, quoted earlier in this chapter, is only one of many writers on the geometry of decorating architectural surfaces.[23] As a mode of perception or as a process of creation, geometry is clearly a significant intermediary both for making and for seeing and thus legitimately belongs to the zones of understanding I am trying to investigate.

But what does it really do? How *does* it allow for perception? And what is it that one sees through it? These general questions can be put more forcefully and more concretely. The visible geometry on surfaces may be more or less what it is in architecture—that is to say, a means to compose that satisfies at the same time a great number of impulses and of practical and psychological needs. Being measurable in advance, it is a means to guarantee physical stability and to justify budgetary expenses. Being rational and rationable, it is also a way toward one or more harmonies of proportions and thus either the reflection or the illustration of some mathematical and philosophical ideal or the most attractive way to grasp a viewer's or user's attention because of the immediate recognition most of us have of geometric shapes. Within any one of these conceptual domains well studied in architecture, geometrical ornament or geometry in ornament would simply be either an organizing principle for something else or a convenient way toward perceiving something else, at times both. In other words, implied and loose geometry may vary in degree of looseness or of implication, but both are unavoidable mechanical or perceptual instruments for composing surfaces or for seeing and understanding them. To become aware of these instruments may have all sorts of practical values—to reconstruct an artisan's or an artist's procedure, to date and localize a work of art, to describe a painting or a vegetal scroll—but such an awareness is not more than recognizing a part of speech, it does not deal with the message transmitted by it.

On the other hand, what I called "regular" geometry, geometric ornaments that are ends in themselves, do pose additional questions. If it is not carrying additional visual statements, what *does* it mean? Is it correct to interpret it in geometric terms alone?

To propose an answer to these questions, I will turn to the tradition of Islamic art, which, I believe, was alone among the major traditions of the arts to use geometry, at least in many if not all places and at most times, as the central motif of its architectural decoration and to a smaller degree of the decoration of its objects.[24] I shall deal first with the geometry of decoration in one early Islamic example, Khirbat al-Mafjar. I will elaborate from it a hypothesis for a series of Iranian monuments of the eleventh and twelfth centuries, which are particularly unique and original, and, briefly, for the Alhambra. A set of broader considerations on geometry as an intermediary will close the chapter.

KHIRBAT AL-MAFJAR, located in the lush and hot valley of the Jordan, not far from Jericho and the Dead Sea, is the richest and best preserved of a series of monuments from the first half of the eighth century romantically known as the Umayyad desert palaces. Umayyad they are, as all of them, and especially the five or six excavated ones, were sponsored by princes of the first Islamic dynasty. None of them is, however, in the desert, as all are related to some form of agricultural, commercial, or even industrial exploitation of the land. The word palace may also be too fancy and too specific a name for a rather inchoate group of villas with a lot of urban amenities.[25] What many of them were, and Khirbat al-Mafjar most emphatically so, are fancy places for pleasure and enjoyment. Their walls, floors, and ceilings were covered with mosaics, paintings, and, most unusually for the area and the time, stone and stucco sculptures, at times of personages and animals, which are among the more surprising works of early Islamic art. For a variety of reasons, one can argue that the decoration of these establishments belongs to the wide category of late antique or early medieval Mediterranean secular art without significant cultural differentiations.[26] Among these monuments, Mafjar is the best published and the only one on which there is the beginning of a discussion, even of controversy.[27]

For our purpose, the extraordinary feature of Khirbat al-Mafjar, a feature shared in part but not quite as richly with Qasr al-Hayr West,[28] is the abundance of geometry in its decoration of plaster and of mosaics. The point is interesting historically, as there is no earlier example known to me of such wealth of geometric design, but in order to explain it, we must try to understand a little better what this geometry is.

There are three types of geometry at Khirbat al-Mafjar. There is the implied, at times even emphasized and articulated, geometry of organizing other, mostly vegetal but in one celebrated instance human, motifs (fig. 110). At times this geometry of frames is subdued and implicit, but, more often than not, circles, half-circles, or rounded polygons seem like straightjackets (fig. 111) forced on unsuspecting leaves or trees, as though the making or the

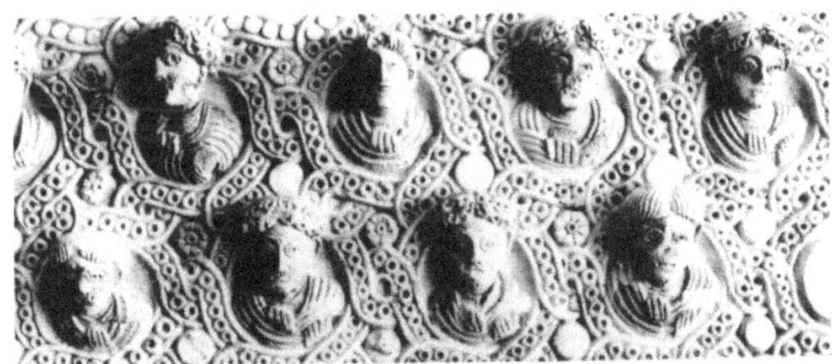

Fig. 110. Khirbat al-Mafjar, stucco panel at entrance of palace, eighth century.

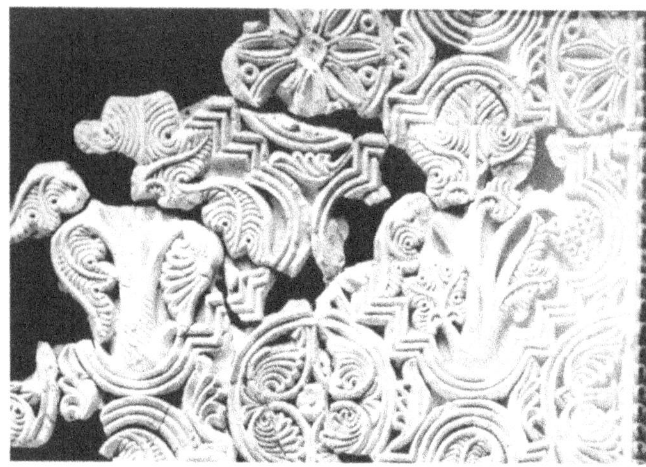

Fig. 111. Khirbat al-Mafjar, detail of vegetal ornament, eighth century.

perception of whatever covered the walls of the palace required an order of fixed contiguous space dividers.

A second type of geometry, with already many models in classical art, is particularly frequent in mosaics and consists of closed geometric units fitted into an available space (fig. 112). The patterns of these designs were usually first composed for one quarter of the area to be covered and then repeated four times; there are also several instances of a single motif repeated however many times may be necessary. At times some other nongeometric motifs fill intermediate spaces, but most of the time the geometric design is alone and, as can be seen on some mosaics, such as the illustrated one, the artisans had to develop awkward combinations in order to provide for the designs a fitting

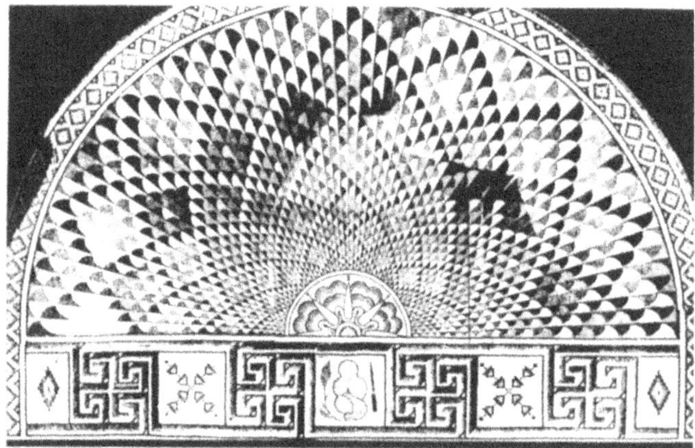

Fig. 112. Khirbat al-Mafjar, mosaic geometric design.

end or beginning within the space available. Furthermore, the complexity of these geometric designs is unusual for mosaics. On one panel (fig. 113) color variations provide two simultaneous impressions of a design. On another (fig. 114) circles diminish proportionately in size, as one moves from the periphery to the center. Yet another example transforms circles into four ovals or into rounded polygons. And, in a stunning display of all these ways of virtuosity, the central medallion of the bath floor is a dizzying pattern of movement that required considerable geometric knowledge (fig. 115). While mosaics exhibit these compositionally closed patterns in a most forceful and immediately accessible way, many of the patterns exist also in the large stucco panels covering the walls of the palace.

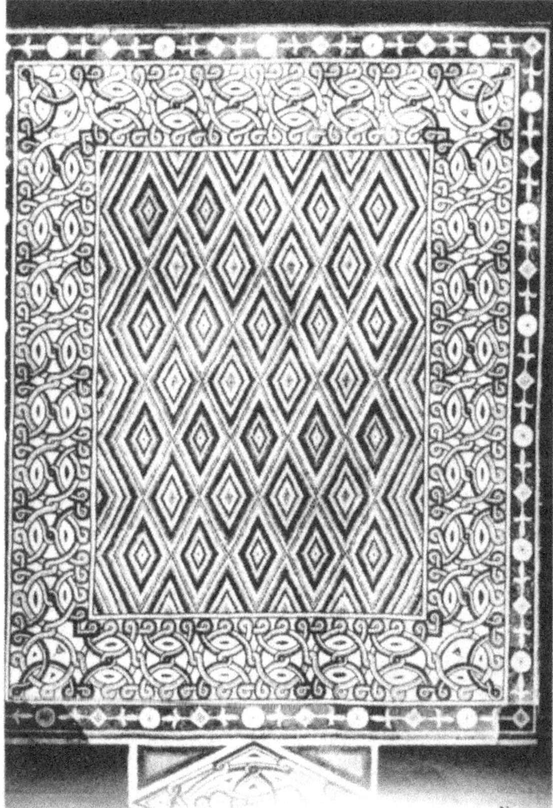

113

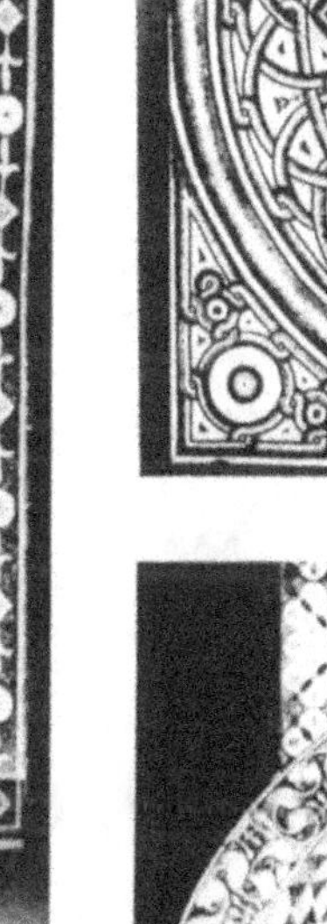

114

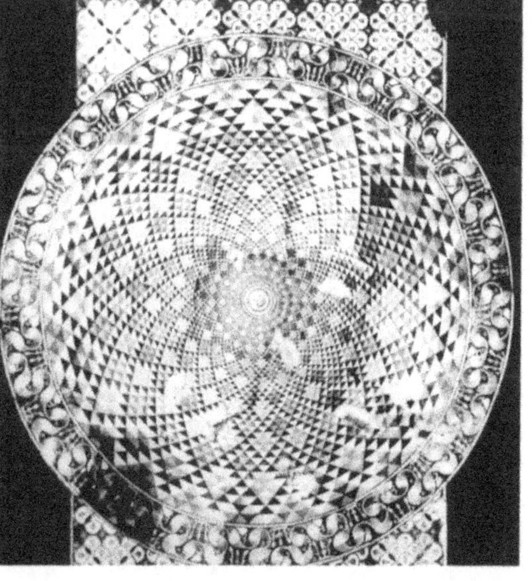

115

Fig. 113. Khirbat al-Mafjar, mosaic panel

Fig. 114. Khirbat al-Mafjar, mosaic panel.

Fig. 115. Khirbat al-Mafjar, mosaic floor, central panel.

The third type of geometry at Khirbat al-Mafjar is particularly frequent on stuccos and in window grilles, but occurs also on two unusual mosaic panels on the floor of the bath (fig. 113). The originality of this type has already been recognized by Robert Hamilton, who called it the "wallpaper method."[29] Its key feature is that it has no limit of growth and simply stops abruptly whenever a border, the wall, or the floor area stops. Most of its themes are more or less linear, with immediate vertical and horizontal repeats, but in a few panels partial rotations of the geometric design occur that elongate or otherwise deform a simple swastika (fig. 116), a bit in the manner in which concave or convex mirrors deform shapes in amusement parks. The central circular panel of the bath hall (fig. 115) with its stunning rational progressive decrease in the size of the units of design is not only a masterpiece of geometric design around a sort of linear fan, but it is also a pattern that has a source (the center of the circle) but no logical end.

A variety of more detailed investigations, which have not so far been carried out because they require tedious and time-consuming measurements, would bring out several additional variants of the same basic patterns or perhaps even an additional way of identifying a geometric design. But no new discovery will, I believe, challenge two conclusions about the stuccos and mosaics of Mafjar. One is their novelty within the art of decorating buildings in all the regions, from Spain or Scotland to India and central Asia, issued from

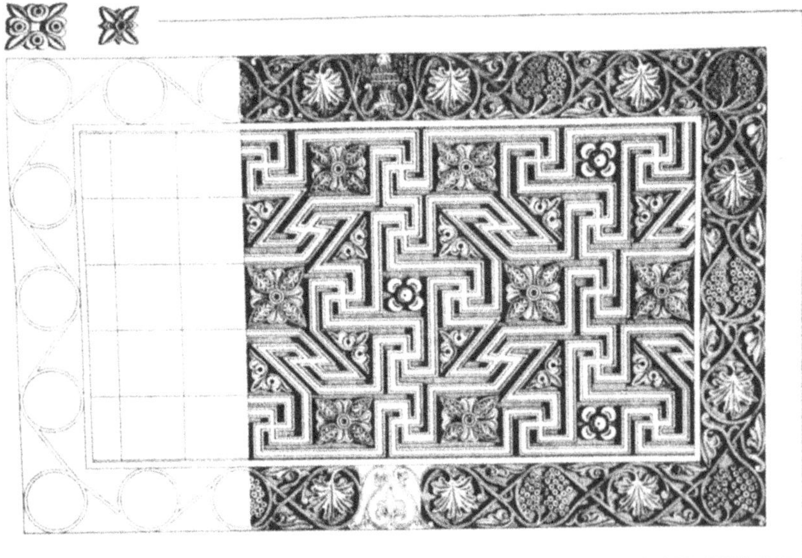

Fig. 116. Khirbat al-Mafjar, reconstruction of stucco panel.

the mixed inheritance of Iran and the Mediterranean. However fascinating and important, the historical and genetic dimensions of this ornament are not pertinent to my purpose in these essays.[30]

The second conclusion *is* pertinent indeed. It concerns the interpretation one can give to the geometric ways of Khirbat al-Mafjar's decoration. The first, or implied, geometry may have acquired its ubiquitous character through the process of rapidly decorating large spaces; geometric frames or medallions are an easy way of covering space and possibly a convenient way of organizing and controlling labor crews. Wallpaper effects or single geometric "images" are also easy to explain as ways for the rapid covering of floors or walls, as geometry has the advantage over vegetal or other ornament of being easy to repeat once the first module has been created. It is, however, hardly likely that the early Muslim princes who sponsored these palaces were held back by economic considerations and the quality of their mosaics in particular suggests that the best craftsmen of the Mediterranean were available to them who would not have been likely simply to fill spaces with ready-made patterns. It is reasonable, therefore, to wonder whether there may not have been some meaning attached to the geometrical patterns that were chosen and especially to the peculiar and imaginative variations given to them. Nothing in the cultural context of the time and especially of these palaces suggests a symbolic or otherwise thematic meaning for geometric forms[31] and it is, therefore, within some property of the geometric forms themselves or of the types they illustrate that we may find an explanation.

A clue may be derived from the variations given to a pattern based on a swastika (fig. 116) and from the peculiarity of large floor mosaics (fig. 115) that their motifs cannot be perceived at once, "monoptically" to use the special meaning of this word introduced previously. In these cases, and in many others, the main operative property of geometric patterns was repetition and repetition was meant to evoke the one technique that has repetition of motifs as its primary technical feature—that is textiles. It is only, I submit, because the new Umayyad patrons wanted to create the effect of textile covering, whether with rugs or silks, that they transformed so completely a Syro-Palestinian stone architecture characterized for many centuries by its decorative sobriety and preference for sturdy masonries.[32] The cultural reasons for their taste need not concern us at the moment, but it is possible to propose from a variety of sources that a textile effect was the primary sensory expectation of early Muslim taste makers from Arabia and that the spaces in which they lived were covered with silks, linens, and rugs.[33] What does matter is that geometry, in this interpretation, was a vehicle through which an effect was achieved that was not inherent to the nature of geometry. Geometry was manipulated not because it was an end in itself, but because it was an intermediary to some other effect. Only the importance of that other effect (the textile esthetic) to the patrons of the time explains why so much effort was spent on the geometry of two Umayyad palaces. Geometry is, in this hypothesis, an intermediary to another technique, not a representation of it, but an expression of its essence.

SEVERAL CENTURIES later, beginning, apparently, in eleventh-century northern and northeastern Iran, something quite different took place. A series of some forty remaining buildings or fragments of buildings were decorated in what is known as the "brick style." Their means of construction, brick, also became the means of their decoration.[34] Most of these buildings are towers dominating cities and landscape (fig. 104), at times attached to mosques and serving to call for prayer or else simply serving as beacons to travelers; mausoleums, for the most part for secular leaders (fig. 117), frequently individuals whose lives and activities were not recorded in chronicles; or mosques, like the celebrated Great Mosque of Isfahan (fig. 118). I am only aware of two extant purely secular monuments of the time to have used brick geometry in extensive fashion, the little-known twelfth-century palace in Tirmidh, at the frontier between Soviet Tajikistan and Afghanistan, and the twelfth-century caravanserai of Robat Sharaf on the road from Meshed in Iran to Sarakhs on the border of the Soviet Union.[35] The majority of the early examples of this style are within the Iranian and Turanian sphere, but in the thirteenth century it spread to the Mesopotamian valley and had an impact on the architecture of northern Iraq, Syria, and Anatolia.[36]

Some of the decoration consisted of inscriptions, already mentioned earlier (fig. 53), but the vast majority involves geometric patterns. Nearly all of them belong to the "wallpaper" or continuous type, in which a segment of an unlimited and repetitive sequence is put on the wall. All of them are composed according to one of the three types of basic designs that will dominate geometric patterns from the eleventh century onward and which are identified by the geometric figure that best characterizes its most visible panels and by the numerical module to its proportions. These shapes and the numerical keys attached to each one are, respectively, the square and root two, the hexagon and root three, and the pentagon and the Golden Mean.[37] All three are present in the late eleventh-century mausoleums at Kharraqan (fig. 117; also see fig. 53). These strange buildings in the middle of the landscape are at this juncture the best-preserved and earliest examples of a geometric system,

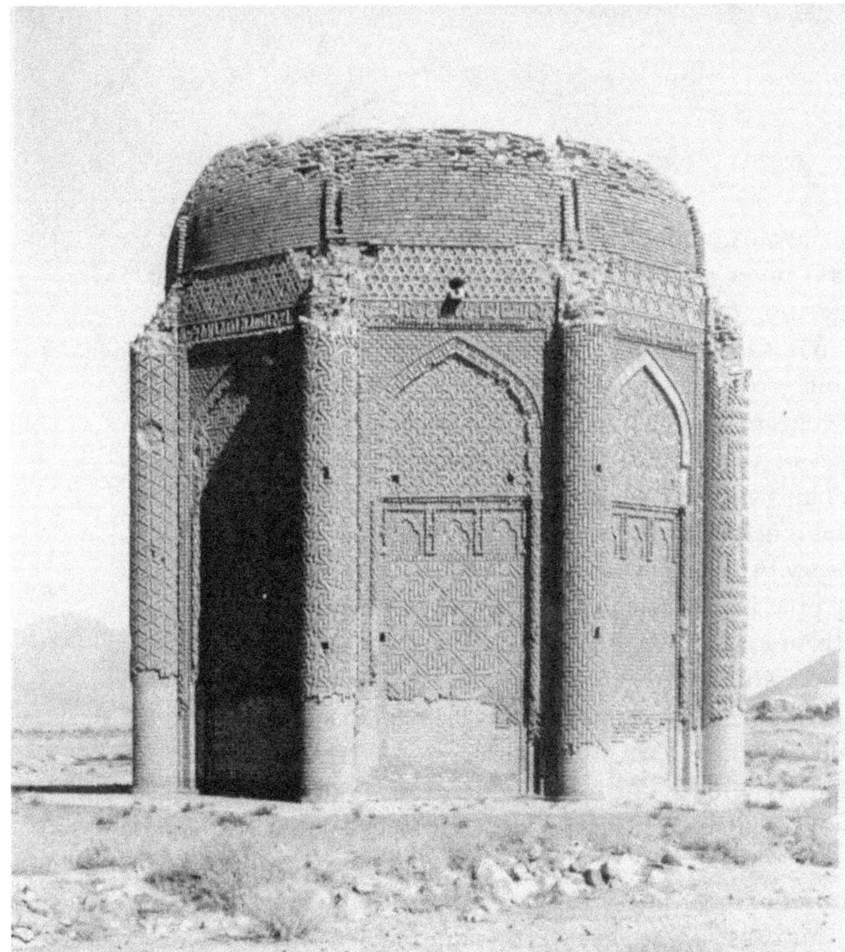

Fig. 117. Iran, Kharraqan, mausoleum, 1087, back.

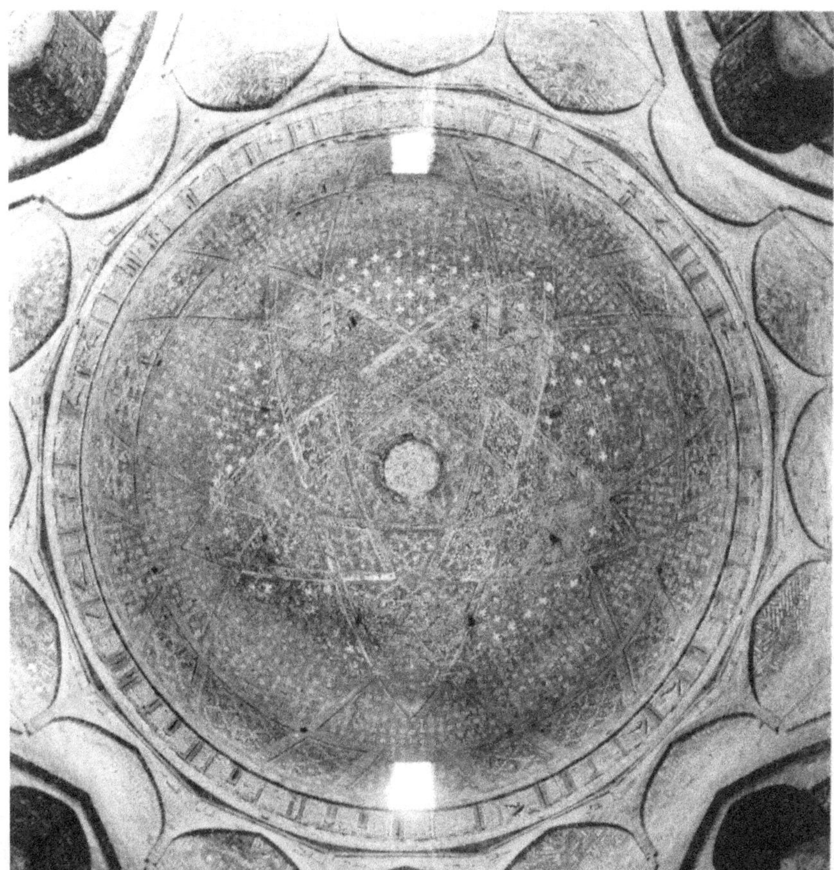

Fig. 118. Isfahan, Great Mosque, north dome, 1088, interior.

which, from then onward, embarked on a distinguished career carrying it through the brilliant outer walls of Timurid madrasahs to the spectacular geometric ornamentation of Mughal India (pl. 14).[38]

The time when this new geometric ornament appears, the eleventh century, and its organic growth over subsequent centuries are easy enough to demonstrate. My concern is not, however, with historical development or with another aspect of these motifs that has occupied many scholars and amateurs: the ways in which any one pattern has been composed. An understanding of the latter is helped by the existence of several manuals dating back to the eleventh century. All of them focus on problem solving and some of the early ones are very precisely directed to craftsmen. They are "how to" manuals reflecting the theoretical learning of mathematicians at the end of particularly fruitful and successful centuries of growth for Islamic science and technology.[39] These are important issues, just as it is interesting and important to understand how and why these manuals were preserved over the centuries and occasionally revived, as with the new Mongol patronage of the fourteenth century, which was emulating the by-then mythified rulers of Abbasid times.[40]

But these questions are outside of the purpose of these essays. What does concern me is why such abstract designs were put up and how one is or was to look at them, how they are (or were) meant to be perceived. Contemporary texts that provide answers about how to design have not suggested so far a clear direction for interpreting particular designs.[41] We are left with the monuments themselves and with more general assumptions and observations like the ones with which I began this chapter.

I shall limit myself to only two sets of remarks. One deals with the quality of the work done as measured by the variety and terpnopoietic effectiveness of the designs. On the Kharraqan mausoleum (fig. 117) or the Bukhara tower (fig. 104), the effort put into differentiating each side of the octagons or the several layers into which the towers were divided is quite striking. By contrast, however impressive, the Demavend mausoleum (fig. 119) is repetitive and many other towers, one in Kerat in northeastern Iran for example, exhibit only a minimal amount of modification in the layering of bricks. Because no functional or regional distinction can legitimately be made between buildings of different quality, the appropriate conclusion is that the differences must be read in social terms, as distinctions between different ranges of investment in creating and transmitting a visual message. At this stage of research, I hesitate to go much further or to propose concrete forms or modes of social patronage, but a hypothesis can be proposed by comparison

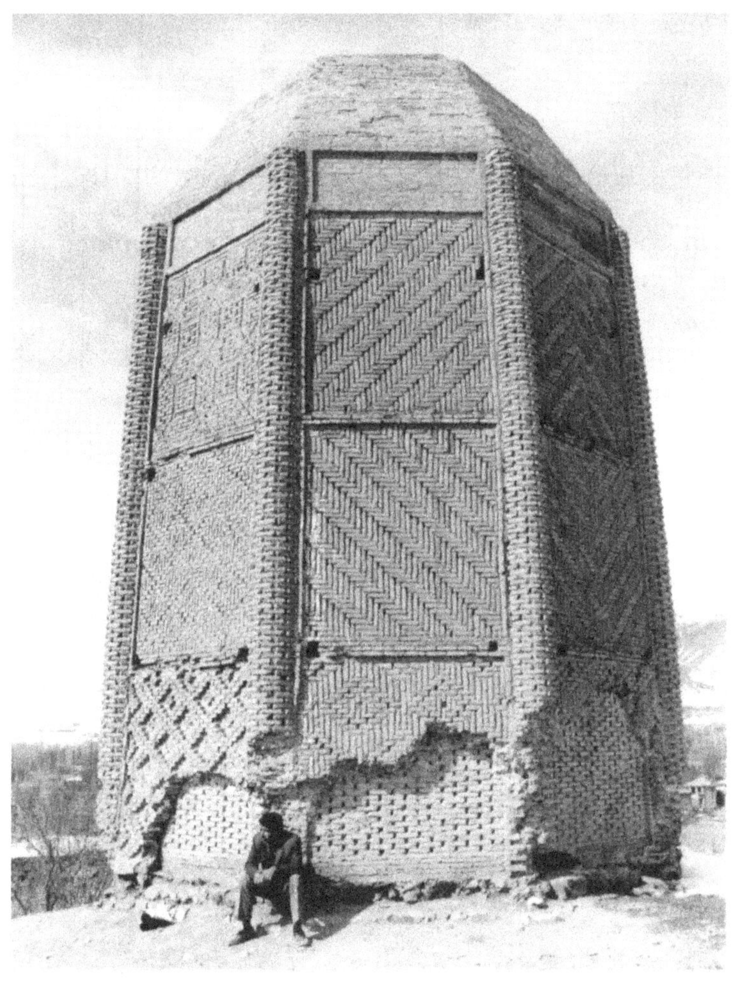

Fig. 119. Iran, Demavend, mausoleum, circa 1100.

with clothing rather than, as with Khirbat al-Mafjar, with textiles covering walls. Distinctions were always made consciously and deliberately, both by wearer and by viewer, about and through clothes and, even now, we deduce a great deal of correct or incorrect information about people from the clothes *they* choose to put on. Various social entities were communicating something about themselves through the wealth, luxury, and exuberance of the geometric designs of monuments, which were nearly always at the edge between public and private realms.[42] And it is probably simpler and safer to conclude that the message was not in the specifics of the geometric pattern, but in the *fact* of the richness and variety of the design and, presumably, of the texture of the materials used. What was being projected is an esthetic proposition for esthetic appreciation, not a specific iconographic message. This explanation would serve as an illustration of the Arabic root *fanna*, which in its second form *fannana* means to "modify," "to variegate," and which was at that time emerging as the root from which the word for "arts," *funun*, will eventually come.[43]

It is thus possible to argue that the new and sophisticated geometry of designs from the eleventh century onward was a means *through* whose manipulation some message independent of the means themselves was transmitted. Such would also be the point of the most uniquely Islamic invention of the very same centuries, the *muqarnas* (pl. 15, fig. 120). This extraordinary and immensely flexible combination of three-dimensional units revolutionized all transition zones inside buildings, on their facades and in their entrances, in all passages toward ceilings and especially cupolas, in capitals and cornices.[44] We would have in the geometry of the *muqarnas* an almost perfect instance of an intermediate domain in the visual arts, as the fact of its existence and the richness of its avatars take precedence over the specifics of its forms.

However simple and persuasive this conclusion may be, a second remark introduces some nuances to its simplicity. There are in fact examples where it is legitimate to provide a concrete meaning to elaborate geometric ornament or where concrete meanings must exist, even if we do not see them or know them.

The most celebrated example is the so-called north dome of the Great Mosque in Isfahan (fig. 118).[45] Its carefully designed decoration consists of

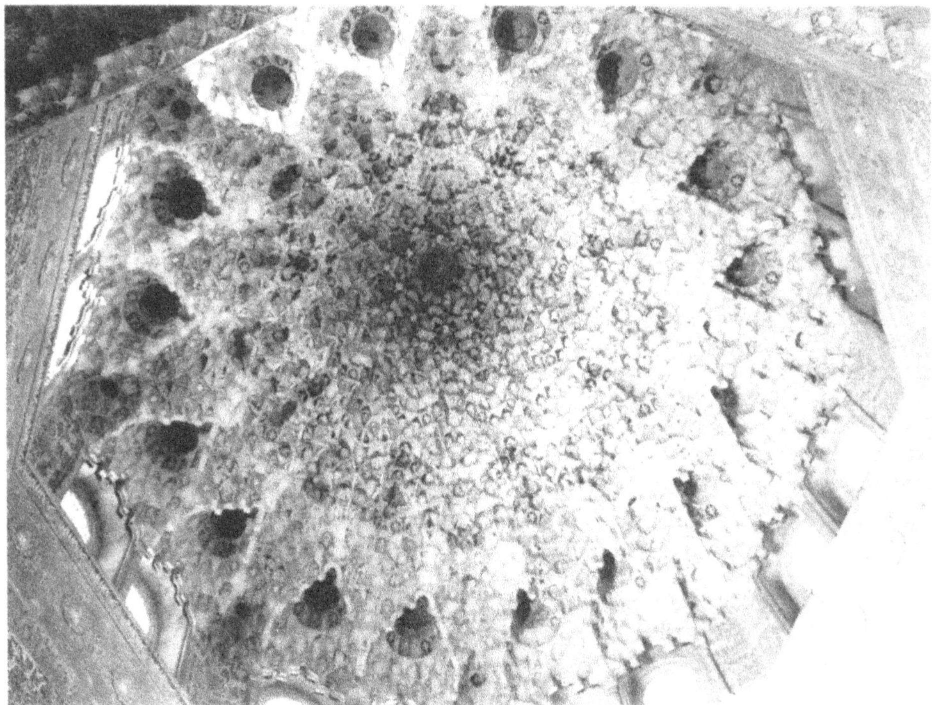

Fig. 120. Granada, Alhambra, Hall of the Two Sisters, muqarnas ceiling.

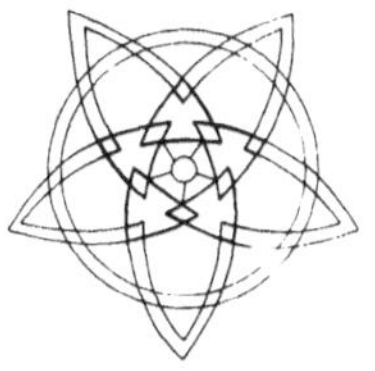

121

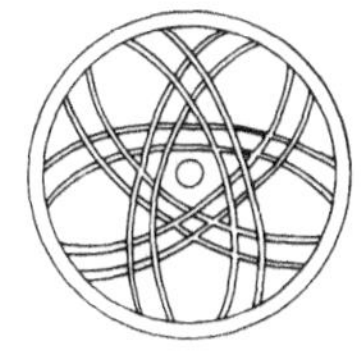

122

Fig. 121. Isfahan, north dome, first interpretation.

Fig. 122. Isfahan, north dome, second interpretation.

five pairs of curved ribs enclosed within the masonry of the vault and generating a carefully worked out succession of curved surfaces from a pentagon in the center. The visible design is only a segment of a much larger completed design. Furthermore, the opportunity of highlighting the interstices between bricks made it possible for the designer to propose different and alternate readings of the dome. The rhombs or triangles around the pentagon can be given prominence (fig. 121) or else the pentagon itself and the line of brick derived from it (fig. 122). And it is easy to multiply possible visual effects of this striking dome. None of them is necessarily the exclusively correct one, but the originality of the dome requires a specific rather than a general explanation for two reasons. One is that, in the elaborate richness of its design, the dome is unique within a fairly sizable set of comparable and more or less contemporary domes. The other reason is that the complexity of the dome's design subsumes a single purpose developed by a unique mental and/or esthetic purpose. If one agrees with the suggestion inspired by the inscriptions of the mosque that the north dome was a programmatic building, that is to say a building dedicated to and reflecting the ambitions or the vanity of a specific vizier,[46] the inventor of the design could be the patron or someone closely associated with him. It is more likely to have been someone with a geometric bent. The only plausible explanation was suggested to me nearly a generation ago by the late Eric Schoeder. It is to connect the dome with the work and personality of Omar Khayyam who, at that very time, lived in Isfahan and was developing theories on the properties of irrational numbers (the whole dome is composed on the irrational proportions of the Golden Mean) and on conic sections (the ribs of the dome can be imagined as planes cutting a sphere (fig. 121).[47] What the connection may have been is still moot and will probably remain hidden, but it is at least possible to relate in time and place originality in thought with originality in form. A geometric form would have acquired a concrete meaning and become iconophoric or commemorative rather than ornamental.

Another iconophoric use of geometry is less subtle and less dramatic. It occurs over the entrance of one of the Kharraqan towers. There the geometric pattern opens up into star-shaped polygons framing the word "Allah," God (fig. 117). In the spandrels of the upper arch, an eight-pointed star is set out from the brick background, as though some special connotation should be evoked in whoever sees it. Whereas the message expressed in words is easily understood, the one expressed in a geometric figure is not, or else it requires a special cultural context as with the star of David, the seal of Solomon, the swastika, or the peculiar combinations of some national flags. Among the latter, the Union Jack and the Palestine Liberation Organization flags have unusual geometrical pattern and color combinations and they can be recognized from far away in ways that are not available for combinations of three horizontal or vertical stripes,[48] but only if the connotation of the form is part of the viewer's mental makeup.

Both of these ways of using geometry—as the fancy frame for an identifiable message and as a possible specific message itself—continued over the centuries. They can be seen in the wall coverings of Timurid mosques and madrasahs. In Samarqand, Herat, Mashad, or Khargird, geometric nets (pl. 15), occasionally of some sophistication, more often rather simple ones, created spaces for pious statements and hierarchical proclamations of a divine order (fig. 123) or else they serve as a sort of arbitrary boundary between an outside world and the space sponsored by the ruler for the operation of the faith. Following fifteenth-century examples, both Safavid Iran and the Mughals in India continued to use geometry in these two ways and occasionally introduced variations with powerful visual impacts. The whole Muslim world, in fact, with only the partial exceptions of the Ottomans, picked up the innovations of the eleventh and twelfth centuries and routinized them into elegant but highly standardized patterns on mihrabs, minarets, domes, and rugs everywhere. The metalwork of the Mamluks in the Levant, and especially in Egypt, or the cascading *muqarnas* and tile or stucco panels of Spain, Iran, and Mughal India are typical examples of a conventionalized transformation of an original invention.[49]

Just as in Iran, but here in a secular mood, instances exist, as with the dome of the Hall of the Two Sisters in the Alhambra (fig. 120), where an external indicator, in this case the descriptive poetry written by Ibn Zamrak for the palace, explains the domes as rotating heavenly spheres with planets and constellations.[50] These meanings cannot, however, be extended to all examples of the same form. One explanation for this phenomenon is that Islamic culture sponsored through geometry a set of neutral forms whose only purpose was to please, to make agreeable, thus to beautify. These forms could be charged through external vectors like inscriptions into becoming icon-

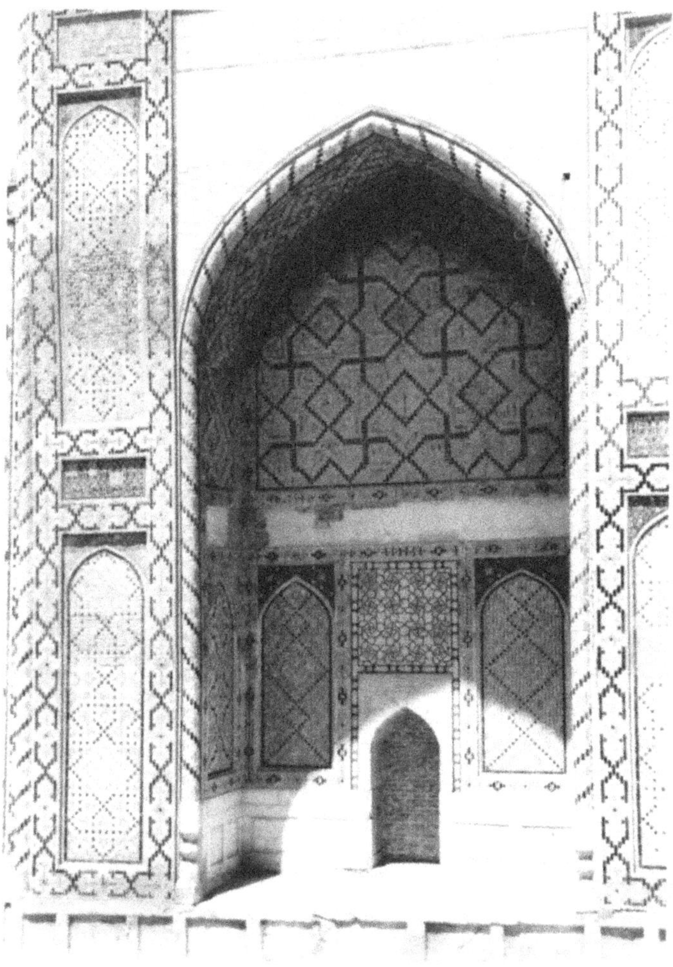

Fig. 123. Central Asia, Samarqand, madrasah of Ulugh Beg, 1417–1423, facade.

ophoric; they *could* become carriers of visual or other meanings, but such messages were not inherent to the forms.

Yet, to argue, as I did in the past, that the stupendous effort of carving out seven cubic meters of stones to make the muqarnas of the entrance to Sultan Hasan's madrasah in Cairo (figs. 124, 125), of ordering bricks glazed in many colors and all sorts of faience tiles in the madrasah at Khargird in eastern Iran, or of developing most of the seventeen possible transformations through symmetry as apparently happened in the Alhambra,[51] to argue that these investments of funds and energy were simply to create agreeable neutral forms seems dubious on two counts. It would be a misunderstanding of the position of visual experience within the Muslim culture, as it would, in fact, imply that visual experience is a very secondary part of the total esthetic experience of the culture. Such an alternative is unlikely because of the vastness and wealth of

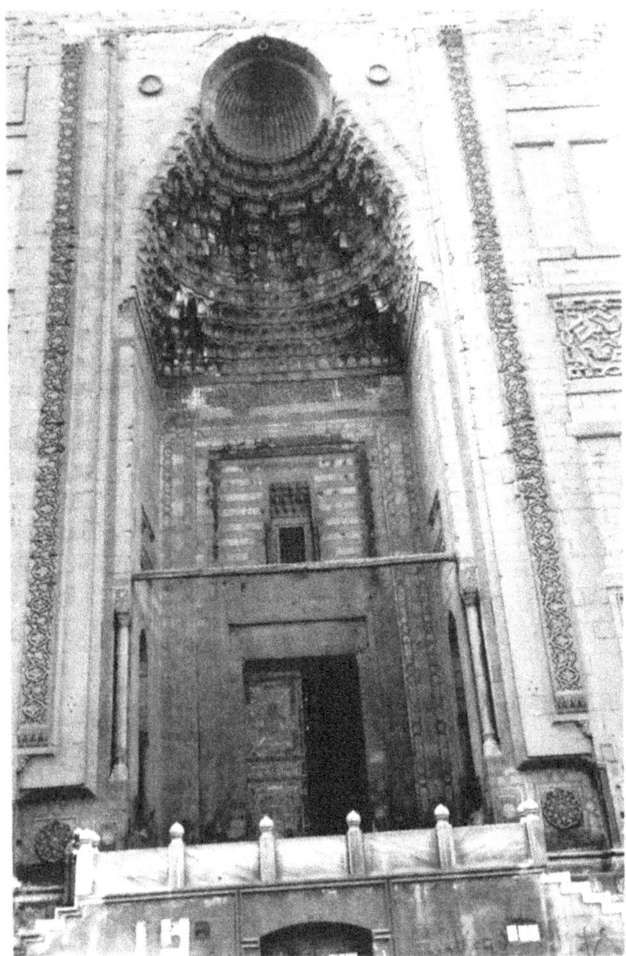

Fig. 124. Egypt, Cairo, madrasah of Sultan Hassan, 1354, entrance.

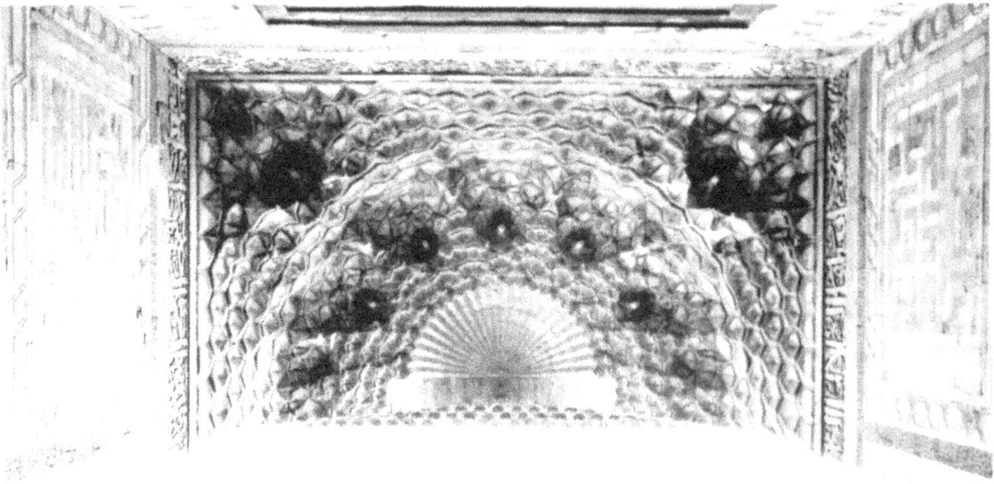

Fig. 125. Egypt, Cairo, madrasah of Sultan Hassan, 1354, entrance, detail.

the existing or remaining visual pool, which is a second reason to beware of too many "neutral" forms.[52] We are left then with a second objective, which is to find a different direction from the usual one for an explanation of geometry in Islamic art.

There can be a positive cultural explanation of geometry, as has been intimated by a number of writers over the past two or three decades.[53] In its simplest forms, it argues that geometry is the visual expression of a set of truths that dominated the traditional life of the Muslims until the appearance of contemporary disruptions. Thus astrological configurations, magical squares, cosmological considerations, and the central Muslim notion of Unity (*tawhid*) are all seen as numerical ideas for which a geometric formulation is not only possible, but even desirable. Many arguments of logic and of fact exist against this immediate interpretation of geometry, however appealing it is to a curious mixture of Western orientalists and Islamic fundamentalists.[54] The most important objections are several. There does not exist, to my knowledge, a single instance justifying the view that the Muslim community, the *ummah*, as opposed to individual thinkers, understood mathematical forms as symbolizing or illustrating a Muslim cosmology. Furthermore, we have no information to the effect that viewers of complex designs on walls, ceilings, or floors interpreted them in the abstract and schematic formulas of the orderly sketches needed by the artists or artisans to make their designs. Finally, although it has been shown that at least contemporary artisans are well aware of the complex technology of their designs, I do not know of many instances of a spectator or viewer being equally informed.

In short, at this stage of knowledge, it is only *our* evaluation of that geometry and of its cultural context that helps explain it. We can in fact propose, with only secondary modifications, that the paradigms sketched out about writing and script are applicable to geometry as well. Geometry is a perfect intermediary, for it attracts not to itself but to other places or to other functions than itself. The beautiful Timurid walls (fig. 123) circumscribe some other space than the observer's and make it desirable or admirable. The *muqarnas* of a Mamluk gate (fig. 125) is the threshold between two worlds. The multifaceted cup or ewer (fig. 126) adds to the pleasure of drinking from it. In all cases, the geometry is a passage, at best a magnet, to something else that it does not identify but which the culture deems desirable. Inside palaces or mausoleums, as in the royal tombs near Rabat or in the Alhambra with rich textures of geometric designs, it is a passage toward the functions of living or of awaiting eternal life that is expressed by geometric forms.

On the other hand, some geometric designs are an end in themselves,

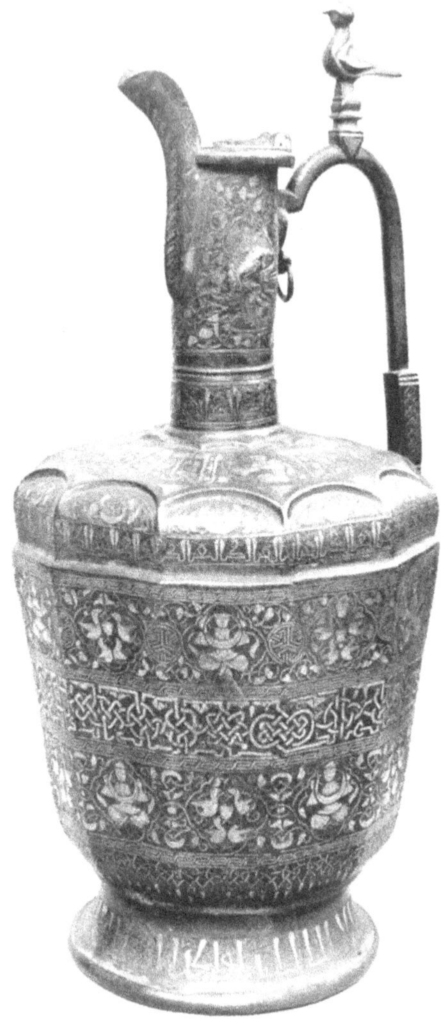

Fig. 126. Ewer, silver inlaid bronze, Iran, thirteenth century. London, Victoria and Albert Museum, 333–1892.

which, endowed or not with identifiable connotative meanings, become their own objects of contemplation. At times, as in the Alhambra, they even acquire signs, poems in this case, indicative of their specificity. At this, relatively rare, level, the intermediate geometry becomes the object of emotional or psychic involvement. Within this scheme, geometry is not different from writing. It too is a system of arbitrary rules manipulated for culturally significant purpose other than itself and ending up, because of this manipulation, by occasionally producing works of art.

But there is yet one last issue to deal with. Even though most cultures used geometry, Islamic art alone spread it so consistently throughout its creativity. Why? A partial answer is curiously provided by M. C. Escher. He argued that he had developed what he called "an affinity with the Moors . . . long before [he] discovered Alhambra [*sic*]." He found there (among the Moors) a similar fascination with "the *game* [my italics] of dividing the plane." In this game, writes Escher, "it is . . . unfortunate that the only people obviously intrigued by this possibility [filling of space]—the Moors—were not allowed to proceed beyond abstractions, quite apart from the question whether they would have wanted to."[55] Whether genuinely or *ex post facto* as a pose frequent among artists and all creators, Escher argues that there is a game of covering space, that is to say a desired activity with rules but without certainty about outcome. The geometry of what became known technically as "tesselation through isometry" (total covering with repeated motifs) is one way, perhaps the only one, of playing the game.

But, as his own words, and not only words, so eloquently show, ultimately "the silhouettes of birds and fish are the most gratifying shapes of all for use." Although he does not say so, the reason is simple enough. Even if the abstract rigor of science can be of use in the task of providing pleasure, it only does so when clothed with mimetic signs of recognition from the world of real or imaginary life. And, if the work of art does not lend itself to it, the artist, Rothko or Stella in our own times, will provide his geometric and abstract shapes with a mimetic title. The point emerged recently with the pyramid in the Louvre. I. M. Pei argued that he chose a pyramid so that it would neither imitate nor overwhelm the past, but "complement it by addressing the future." And, in discussing the same monument, President François Mitterand said, "I have rather classical tastes, and I am especially attracted to pure geometric form."[56] Both I. M. Pei and Mitterand transformed their esthetic decisions or pleasures into historical or social formulas. What matters is that a glass pyramid in the middle of Paris would have been silly without the Louvre around it, but the impact of the Louvre as a monument would have been destroyed by almost anything that was not a geometric shape.

Escher's point can be put in a different fashion with reference to two propositions that serve in part to answer the questions posed at the beginning of this essay. One is the historical judgment that the visual abstraction of geometry is an exciting but ascetic exercise, which rapidly reaches its limits or begins to repeat itself in contrived formulas. Such was the case with the ninth-century styles of Samarra (fig. 15), the geometric vases of Greece (figs. 88, 89), the post-twelfth-century geometry of Iran or of the Maghrib (fig. 104), many contemporary paintings (pl. 13), Chinese bronzes (fig. 94), and nearly all thoughtful experiments in geometry. In all these sets of creations, useless repetition or more or less sudden declines and returns to other forms become the rule. At least so it is in all the instances where learning or collecting transformed the geometric achievements into paradigms for cultural or esthetic values. But, and this is my second proposition, there always remains a geometric abstraction in folk art and in the arts traditionally associated with women, like weaving and certain types of architectural decoration.[57] The reason is not a poverty of imagery but a restriction of literacy. Geometry remains at its most powerfully creative when it is connected with the continuous life forces of society. Even if the language of available forms is at first glance limited, the vital virtuosity of the created object is much more powerful than the endlessly repeated sophistication of what was only effective when it was first created.

Geometry really works only as an intermediary. As an intermediary, it leaves to the viewer or user a freedom of choice no other intermediary seems to offer. In this respect, as a harbinger of free choice, geometry is a most dangerous mediator. It forces one to look and to decide what to think, what to feel, and even how to act. However, it rarely forces us to do anything precise and concrete like sleep or pray. The penalty of freedom in the arts is loss of meaning. Its reward is accessibility to all. Humble triangles on a dress or in the weaving of a basket or the very sophisticated brick walls of Iranian towers share an ability to make us wonder what they mean, because, like moths or butterflies, we are attracted to an abstraction that seems to be devoid of cultural specificity. It is only meant to be beautiful.

CHAPTER IV

The Intermediary of Architecture

SOME FIFTEEN years ago now the Great Mosque of Sana'a in Yemen was the site of a most extraordinary discovery. During cleaning and repairs to a building alleged to have been built in the early eighth century by order of the caliph al-Walid, the imperial sponsor of the first great mosques in Jerusalem, Damascus, and Medina, a cache or a repository was found of some forty thousand parchment pages with Arabic texts.[1] The state of these pages was deplorable, as whole codices seem to have been squeezed together for centuries and damaged by dampness, rats, and whatever else destroys parchment. The technical task of disentangling all these pages has only partly been accomplished so far and it will be decades before the full impact is felt of a documentation that will eventually revolutionize our knowledge of early Arabic scripts and of the ways in which the Revelation was written down.

According to preliminary information these pages came from about eight hundred copies of the Koran and, while there is, to my knowledge, no archaeological *ante quem* date for the trove as a whole, the fact that they are all on parchment guarantees an early date, probably before the eleventh century, when the manufacture of paper spread everywhere. The specific history of the mosque makes it possible to imagine that large numbers of Koranic manuscripts were hidden or discarded around 911–912, when the religiously heterodox and socially revolutionary Qarmatians deliberately flooded the mosque. An alternative date, 1130–1131, when a most extraordinary Muslim queen, al-Sayyida Arwa, ruled over Yemen and had the mosque rebuilt, is also a plausible time for the storing away of old books, but it would be of lesser usefulness for the dating of the manuscripts.[2] On the whole, there has been little disagreement about a fairly early date for the fragments. Perhaps the first trickle of scholarship on them has too easily pushed most of them back into the early eighth century without considering the following three centuries, which are still early enough by anyone's standards.[3] More disagreement has already emerged on the place of manufacture of these Korans. Local production in Yemen is slugging it out with importation from Damascus and imperial Syria on the assumption that the manuscripts are dated to Umayyad times. A remote third possibility is west-central Arabia, primarily Mekka and Medina; the two sites, but especially the latter, were significant centers of religious life in early Islamic time.[4]

However interesting and possibly important these classical art historical issues of dating and locating may be, I only mention them to set the context for two fragmentary folios with absolutely unique representations of architecture. Through a discussion of their peculiarities I will introduce the third of my intermediary themes in ornament, building and related man-made constructions.

The pages in question (pls. 16, 17) are the sides of two folios that, almost certainly, faced each other at the beginning of a volume or possibly several volumes, which harbored 520 folios containing the whole text of the Koran.[5] The first architectural page was preceded by a fancy but very badly damaged title page reminiscent of the title page of early Byzantine imperial manuscripts like the Vienna Dioscorides.[6] If the folios that have been associated with it turn out to be the right ones, the text of this particular codex was accompanied by an unusual complement of decorated frames around written sections and of vegetal ornament between *surahs* or chapters of the Holy Book.[7] Furthermore, the size of the book was quite extraordinary. Its folios measure fifty-one by forty-seven centimeters. Only one known parchment Koran is larger, although some stories, such as that of a celebrated manuscript allegedly going back to the caliphs Ali (ruled 656–661) or, more likely, Uthman (644–656) and kept in the Great Mosque of Cordova, imply that very large codices did exist. A few Western parchment manuscripts are roughly the same size.[8] It was, in short, a slightly megalomaniac luxury book, probably bound in several sections, and, for some reason or other, architectural representations served to open one or two volumes of a single complete Koran or to open and close one volume.

I shall return later on to why this may have been, but let us in the meantime try to understand what these paintings are. The two representations are sufficiently similar to each other to warrant that they were meant to represent or evoke (we shall see later the importance of the distinction between these two terms) the same function and that they utilized the same visual language. In addition, both are more or less symmetrical around a vertical axis and therefore the missing right side of the larger image can easily be reconstructed (fig. 127). Since they are not symmetrical around a horizontal axis, the lower part of the second image (fig. 128) and the top of the first cannot be reconstructed or imagined with the same degree of assurance, but the hypothetical reconstructions of the drawings are reasonable enough to serve my purpose of understanding, as clearly and as precisely as possible, how these images operate to make available and accessible whatever point they sought to carry.

A first set of features is shared by both images and suggests common characteristics for the representations, whether they are of two different buildings or two views of the same building. In these observations, the description of representations and the reconstructions (or construction) of the model(s) are constantly interchanged, because it is difficult for a visual analysis to separate, even in an attempt at a clinical experiment, model from image. Yet, for reasons that will emerge shortly, the description cum reconstruction that follows is affected by the previous knowledge of a viewer more familiar with Islamic than with other arts.

Both pictures suggest squarish buildings for which a plan and an elevation are proposed at the same time. In plan a fancy entrance facade (with three gates in one case, probably only two in the other one) opens into basically hypostyle spaces (that is, covered spaces with large numbers of repeated similar supports) probably composed along arcades; under each arch there hangs a lamp with a lit candle in a candleholder. At the opposite end from the entrance both buildings exhibit a large arched element, in one case fully embedded within the main building, in the other more modestly added to it, but in both cases projecting beyond the building. An orderly garden of vertical trees with flowing water at their base is depicted outside the building; it is shown above the representation of the building and is probably meant to be imagined along its back side. An unsettling feature is the artificial rinceau of palmettes that frames the buildings on three sides and which, for the sake of architectonic quality, has not been included in the drawings; it is not, apparently, a feature of construction, but it is visually striking in expressing the limits, the boundaries, of the buildings. It is unsettling because it introduces within the apparently coherent representation of something an incoherent feature that makes no sense from the point of view of the represented building nor from that of its picture. It only makes sense from the point of view of the relationship between the page and the image on the page.

Then there are differences between the two buildings. One (pl. 17) has simple arcades (probably six in number), a niche in the back which is clearly outside of the main composition, and a central court or at least an open space with a bouquet of flowers seemingly put on top of a column; its focal archway

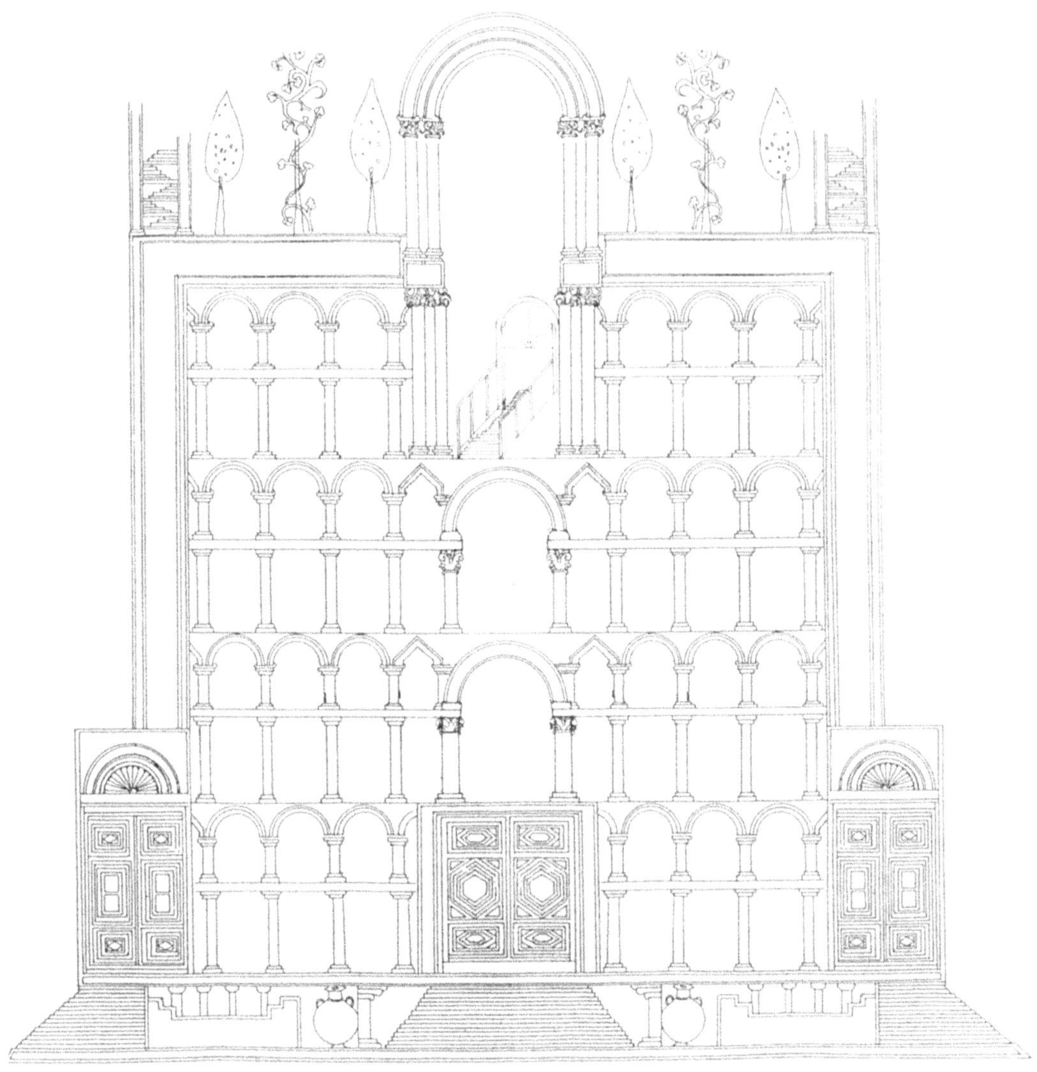

Fig. 127. Reconstruction of plate 16, frontispiece from a Koran, eighth century (?).

contains a hanging lamp, like every unit of the arcades. The other building (pl. 16) is set on a mound or on a height of some kind as it can only be reached through flights of stairs. Between the stairs are two curious constructions showing a low wall with four supports behind the wall and a large carefully drawn vase to the side. There is no way of knowing whether the second building had the same fixtures, but from the small bits remaining in its lower right corner it is certain that it had similarly shaped and similarly decorated double doors. The arcades of the first building were high and divided into two unequal sections by painted tie beams from which the lamps hung; four of these arcades are shown. Something special occurs on the central axis of the

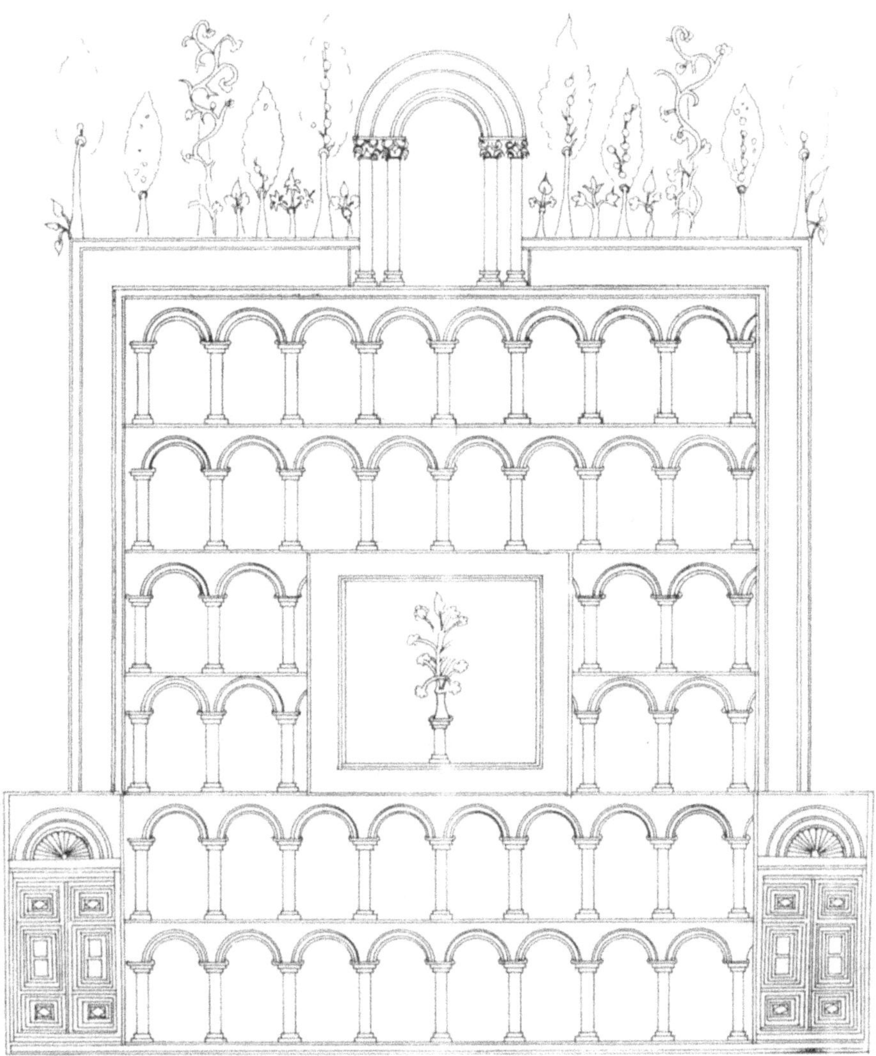

Fig. 128. Reconstruction of plate 17, frontispiece or finispiece from a Koran, eighth century (?).

building. It is simplest to understand it as a higher axial nave cutting through the arcades. The last arch abutting the central nave is pointed rather than semicircular and the extrados of the arch is decorated with what seem to be carved rather than painted braids. There are no lamps hanging in these axial spaces and the uppermost one with two sets of columns may well have been covered with a dome and certainly contained a major piece of furniture with a railing. On the upper left a more mysterious fragment has been interpreted by the first investigator of these pages as the beginning of a tower with a spiral staircase. Without excluding this explanation, which poses several visual and historical problems,[9] I prefer to argue at this stage that this detail does not seem understandable in the fragmentary state in which it is found. It is almost impossible to identify the elements that remain and nothing in medieval art, east or west, comes immediately to mind as one looks at it.

Once described and understood as visual experiences at the two more or less simultaneous levels of an image on parchment *and* of a built structure, these representations can be interpreted. Such interpretations can occur at three levels: cultural, codicological, and perceptual. Until now only the first one has attracted any attention from historians of art. The elaboration of these three levels and the extension of their implications and procedures to other works of mostly medieval art will occupy most of this chapter and I will, at the end, propose a more general explanation of the ways in which buildings or parts of buildings were used to transform the physical reality or the physical potential of architecture into a strikingly effective statement of something quite different from itself.

Cultural Level

The cultural or historical level is the one normally reached by those who, professionally or otherwise, have in their memory the experience of monuments of Islamic art as seen in books and pictures.[10] This group of individuals immediately sees the particular buildings of our pages as mosques, because of the hypostyle planning of space and, in one case, of an axial nave cutting through three arcades; because of a multiplicity of lamps known to have characterized mosques at some time or other; and because of a focus on a single arched space located in the center of the wall opposite the entrance. This back arch is easily interpreted as a mihrab, the traditional indicator of the direction for prayer or the symbol of the Prophet's presence. The piece of furniture in it becomes then a minbar, the high pulpit for the preacher. The peculiar constructions in front of the building can be understood as ablution areas and the landscape would be a garden surrounding the mosque. The scholar who interpreted the detail on the upper left as a tower understood it to be a minaret. Two closely related types of mosques would have been shown, one with a clearly defined court, the other one with emphasis on an axial nave, whether or not there was also an open space in it. One or both of these features are normally present in all early mosques, and especially in the large and official ones constructed after the Great Mosque of Damascus had been built between 705 and 715. Enough parallels exist between the terms of these images and mosques from the eighth to eleventh centuries to make the interpretation of the former as Muslim gathering places a reasonable one. Even the lamp shape

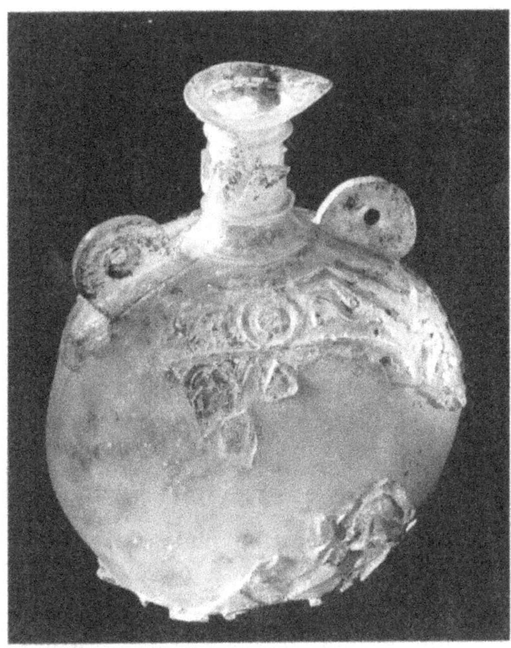

Fig. 129. Glass lamp, probably Iran or Iraq, ninth–eleventh centuries. Corning Museum of Glass L55.1.125.

is known through a small number of remaining early Islamic glass objects, which so far had never been identified as mosque lamps (fig. 129).[11]

A cultural interpretation of images such as these assumes that they represent something contemporary and in actual use, if not necessarily built at the time of the images. The latter, therefore, become archaeological and historical evidence, especially if the mosques involved can be identified. The cost of a large manuscript makes it unlikely that we are dealing with some provincial or secondary building. Damascus, the Umayyad capital with one of the most celebrated early mosques, Medina, the venerated city where the Prophet is buried, and Sanʿa, the capital of Yemen, have all been proposed. In all these cases, there are indeed features of the existing building that coincide with details on the images: for Damascus, the central axial nave, the three parallel aisles, the two tiers of the arcade; for Medina, the garden and the tower; for Sanʿa, generic features of hypostyle mosques rather than anything precise, unless one takes into consideration the decoration of buildings on the representations (painted columns, floral ornament on the sides), which *could* be related to the celebrated painted ceilings of Yemeni mosques. If, as I tend to believe, the images are later than the first or early second centuries of Islam, the nature of the evidence they provide is not altered, only its range, as it could serve to illustrate many more places than the three already mentioned. Cordova, for instance, did have fancy doorways and steps leading to the building as well as double arcades and a fancy mihrab. At this level, the possibly precise identification of the building transforms the image into a depiction, a sort of portrait. Once it is identified and some agreement is reached about the identification, conclusions are drawn around the subject matter of the image and no longer the image itself, whose details and idiosyncracies must be related to or explained by peculiarities of the represented building or of feelings contemporaries had developed about it. For instance, these images would indicate the presence in early mosques of triple-gated facades with fancy doors, of ablution areas outside of the walls of the mosque (as they will commonly be found in Ottoman times, but usually not in the Arab heartland of the Muslim world), and of minarets on the back wall of mosques. No evidence for some of these features exists elsewhere in written or archaeological data.[12]

The problem, then, with the two pictures from Yemen is that no known mosque is really recalled by them; for every detail that fits with one monument, a dozen do not. One is left, then, with four possibilities: it is not a mosque; it is an unknown mosque; it is the image of a mosque type rather than of a particular building; it is a mixed up representation of a particular mosque. Each one of these possibilities leads to all sorts of logical or factual difficulties and none seems, at first glance, reasonable, even though as we shall see, the first and the third one may be argued better than the other two possibilities.

The difficulty is, in my judgment, a methodological one. The classical historian of art jumped too early to a conclusion about the model behind the drawings. He did not consider two other levels of the drawing whose elucidation must precede precise identification. One is the context of the book as book and can be called "codicological"[13] and the second one is a more complex level of recognition of forms I would like to call "optisemic."

Codicological Level

The pictures are found in copies of the Koran and the question is why an examplar of the Holy Text would have been decorated with two architectural representations, presumably of mosques, or possibly two yolumes were illustrated with the same type of subject, apparently, but in different versions. The question is in part a taxonomic one, that is to say, one of identifying the order, within a book, to which these images belong. Are those images illustrations of specific passages in the Koran or of some other essentially narrative source? Illuminations or simply beautifully laid out pages serving to enhance the value, pious or other, of the book? Or else, dedications or remembrance signs, souvenirs, independent of the text but essential to the context, of the circumstances that created the book?

The Koranic text contains a considerable number of references to architecture. The most common and the best-known ones deal with Paradise, its mansions and pavilions surrounded by gardens. The believer, announces the Revelation, will be lodged "in lofty chambers of Paradise, underneath which rivers flow" (29:58). The same "lofty chambers" (*ghara'if*) are a recompense elsewhere (34:37) and appear as a sequence of constructions above each other in a third passage (39:30). There are also references to secular buildings, palaces or houses, and to parts of buildings, which can seldom be easily identified.[14] Only through great feats of imaginative contortion, however, could one see our paintings as "illustrations" of a specific passage from the Koran, although we shall see shortly that they may still be related to the Koranic text. Nor am I aware of any story or legend known in early Islamic times that could have been illustrated by our two pictures. Nothing would have brought an architectural vision into the Holy Book in the ways in which, for instance, a fantastic architecture was so important in the illustrations of the commentaries written by the monk Beatus to the Apocalypse (fig. 130). The context of these commentaries required images of celestial Jerusalem or of all sorts of imaginary buildings illustrating the Feast of Balthazar or many other topics, and these images are often more striking than the text itself.[15] Nor do we have anything comparable to the architectural setting of a common narrative text in

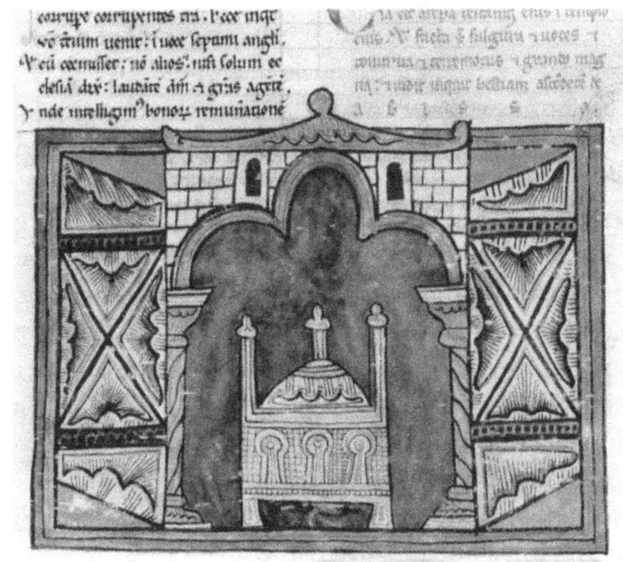

Fig. 130. Apocalyptic vision, Beatus Commentary. Paris, Bibliothèque Nationale, n.a. lat. 1366, fol. 101.

Arabic like the *Maqamat* of Hariri, where the presence or absence of buildings usually follows the requirements of the text but, in a few manuscripts, takes flights of inspired invention.[16] Our images are not translations into a visually perceived idiom of something *in* the book. They may, at best, be visual responses to some function of a text other than illustrative.

It is more difficult to eliminate outright the possibility of illuminations or of what can be called dedicatory signs. It is obvious that these folios enhance the book and it is interesting that such enhancements of Koranic texts through architectural features are not peculiar to the Yemeni manuscript. Long, band-like designs separate *surahs* from each other in parchment folios from several early Korans preserved in Cairo's National Library.[17] At times we simply see an endless arcade (fig. 131), which could possibly be considered as repetitive hatching on borders, but the floral motif that appears in the margin is standing on the same bizarre column as the bouquet in one of the architectural images from Yemen. On another folio (fig. 132), the medallion is replaced by a large arch decorated with flowers in an artificial composition. In a more vivid example (fig. 133), the whole band looks like two superimposed rows of columns, a type of motif found also among the stuccos from the eighth-century palace of Khirbat al-Mafjar.[18] But the most peculiar example occurs on a fourth folio (fig. 134), where the illuminator fulfilled a need often felt among decorators of early Korans: how to complete a line, when the text itself stopped halfway. The artist added what seems to be a section through a hypostyle mosque of nine or eleven bays, with a suggestion of receding pitched roofs, with a central axis emphasized through a large floral composition, and with the farthest nave to the right provided with curtains and seemingly separated from the main building.

At this stage, I do not have a concrete, contextual, and Islamic explanation for this phenomenon, nor can I point immediately to a possible non-Islamic source for it. What is clear is the fact that architectural forms were occasionally associated with the decoration of early codices of the Koran, even if not in the form of full page miniatures as in the San'a manuscript. Such specific associations of architecture with the ornamentation of actual books is not known to me for Korans in subsequent centuries, but it does appear quite forcibly in frontispieces of scientific and mostly pseudoscientific books in the thirteenth century (see fig. 166).[19] It is present, but in a more subdued fashion, among the enthronement scenes of later Iranian frontispieces. In the latter, however, the emphasis on architecture is much more strongly conditioned by the narrative content of storytelling.[20] Two rather unusual and little-known Arab Gospel books written in Kufic scripts, one dated in 859 and the other in

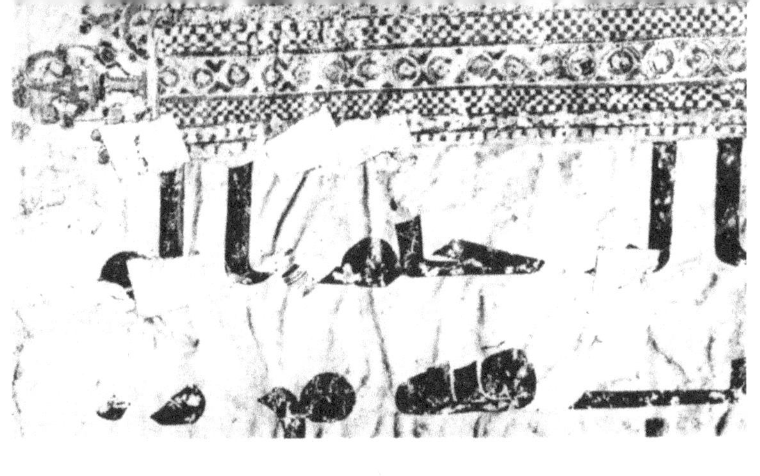

Fig. 131. Architectural motif, page from a Koran, parchment.

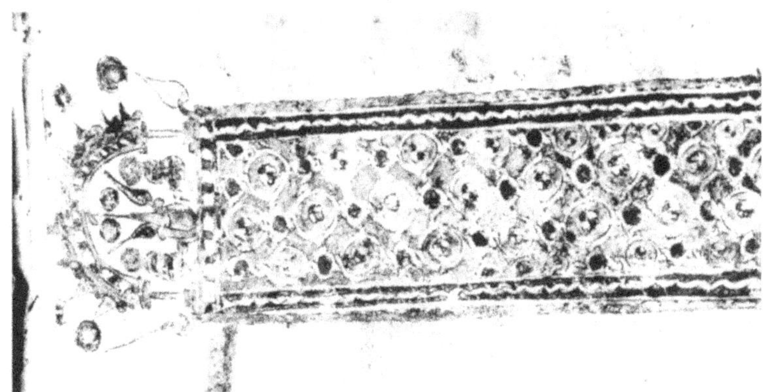

Fig. 132. Architectural motif, page from a Koran, parchment.

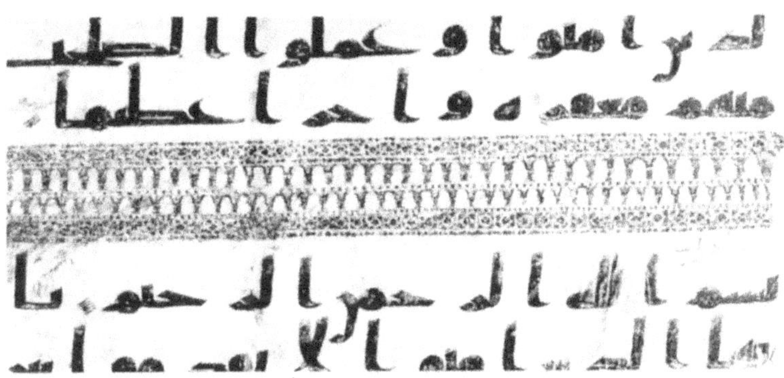

Fig. 133. Architectural motif, page from a Koran, parchment.

Fig. 134. Architectural motif, page from a Koran, parchment.

the tenth or eleventh century, are kept in the monastery of Mount Sinai. In them whole buildings—vaguely identifiable churches with hanging lamps and pavilions or ciboria in gardens—are found around Evangelists (Saint John in the later manuscript) (fig. 135) or as frontispieces (fig. 136).[21]

In the arts of late antique or of medieval Christendom, architecture is a constant structural but nonillustrative part of the decoration of manuscripts, relief sculpture, and wall paintings. Nearly all evangelists and many authors depicted on the first pages of eastern and western Christian books are set within the architectural setting of two columns and usually under an arch; canon tables were the occasion for a true festival of arches on slender columns (figs. 137, 138). Quite frequently plants, trees, flowers, even birds and other animals transform the sober arcades around relatively uninteresting but essential information into a rich whirlwind of activities (fig. 139).[22] Canon tables with colonnades are found in Syriac, Greek, Slavonic, and Latin books. Hebrew manuscripts contain spectacular buildings made out of letters.[23] In the Latin world both canon tables and portraits of Evangelists acquire a wonderful range of transformations. The Carolingian Vivian Bible has columns decorated with busts, vessels hanging like the lamps of our pages, a crown, span-

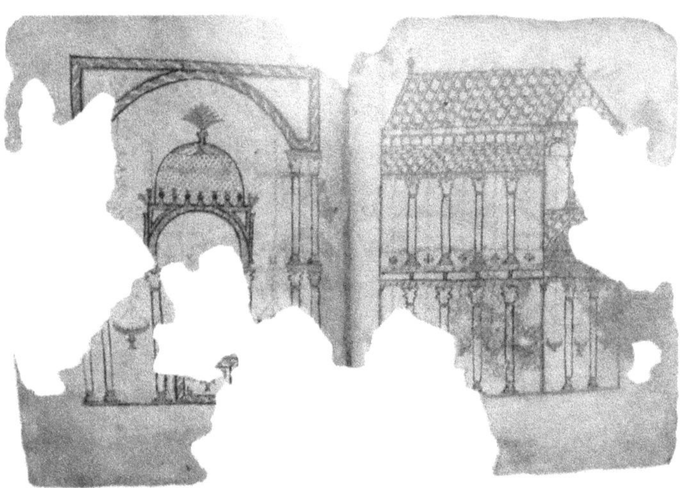

Fig. 135. St. John, Arabic Gospel book, Mt. Sinai, 854.

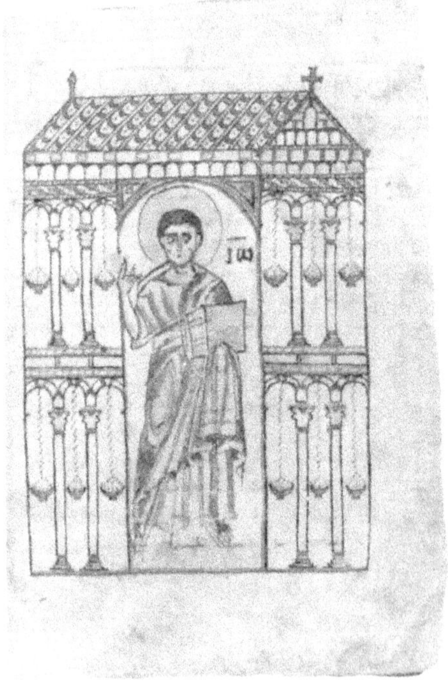

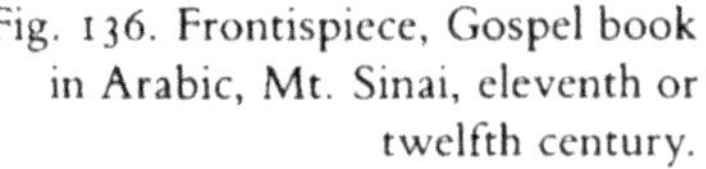

Fig. 136. Frontispiece, Gospel book in Arabic, Mt. Sinai, eleventh or twelfth century.

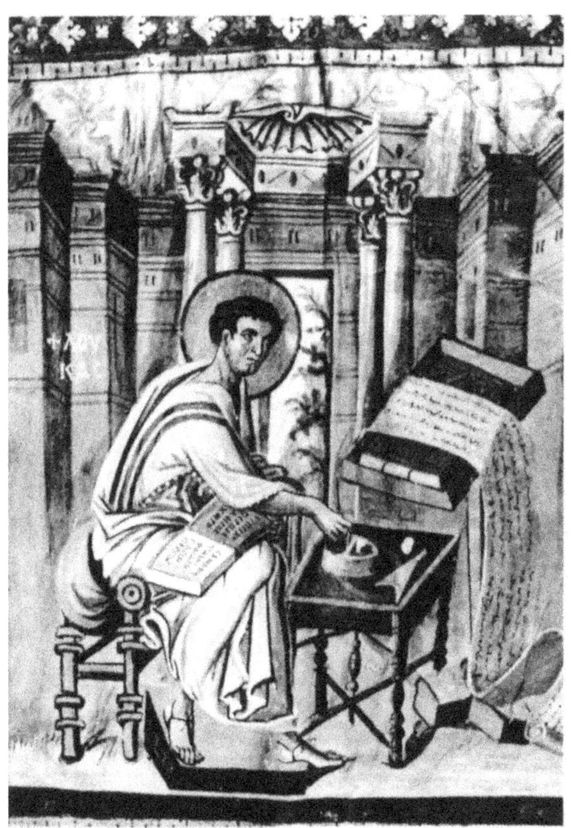

137

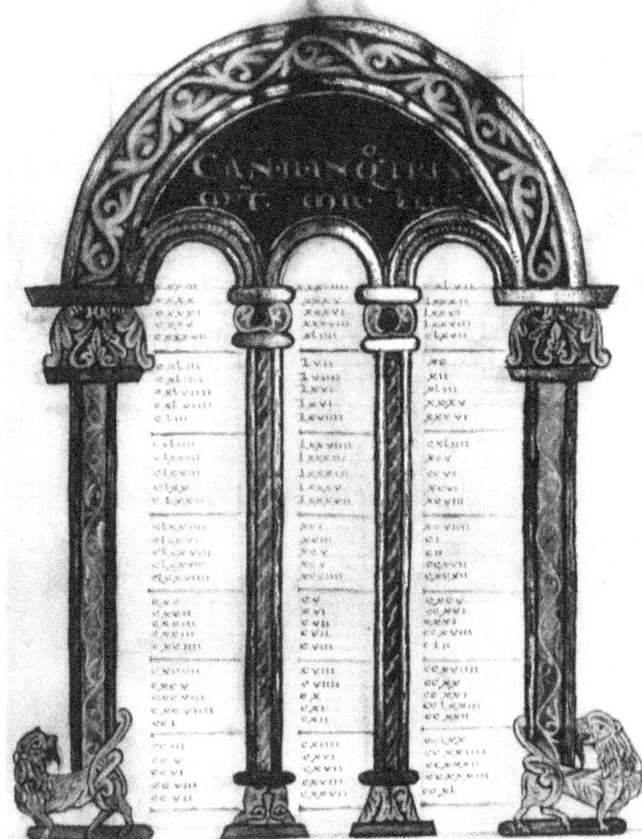

138

Fig. 137. The Evangelist St. Luke, Gospel book, Mt. Athos, tenth century.

Fig. 138. Canon table, Gospel book, tenth or eleventh century. Paris, Bibliothèque de l'Arsenal, ms. 592 fol. 14.

Fig. 139. Canon table, Armenian Gospel book, tenth–eleventh centuries. Venice, San Lazarro, 14001/108, fol. 8.

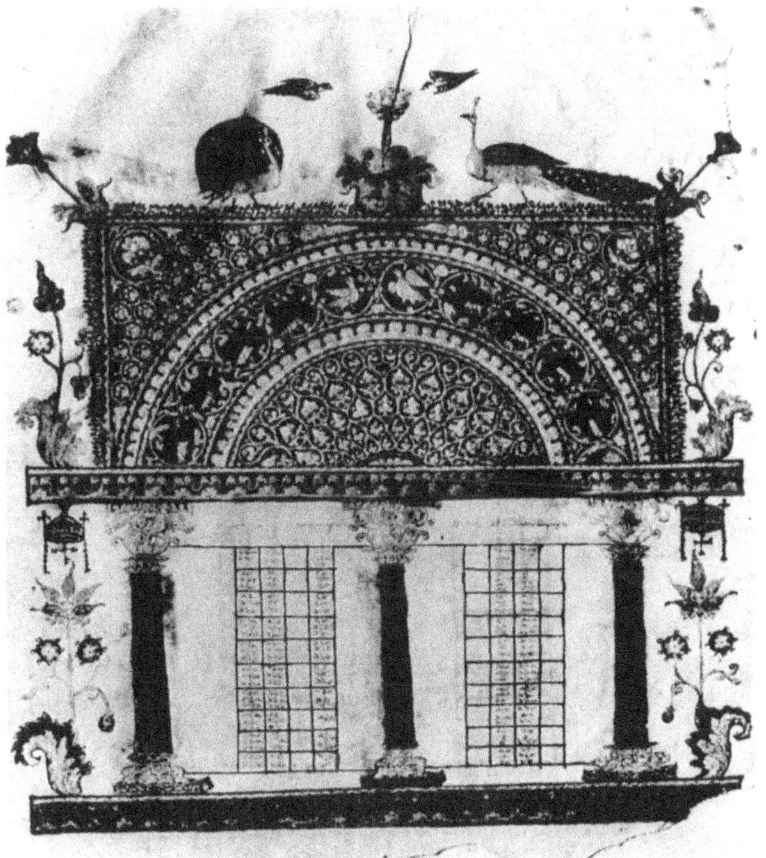

139

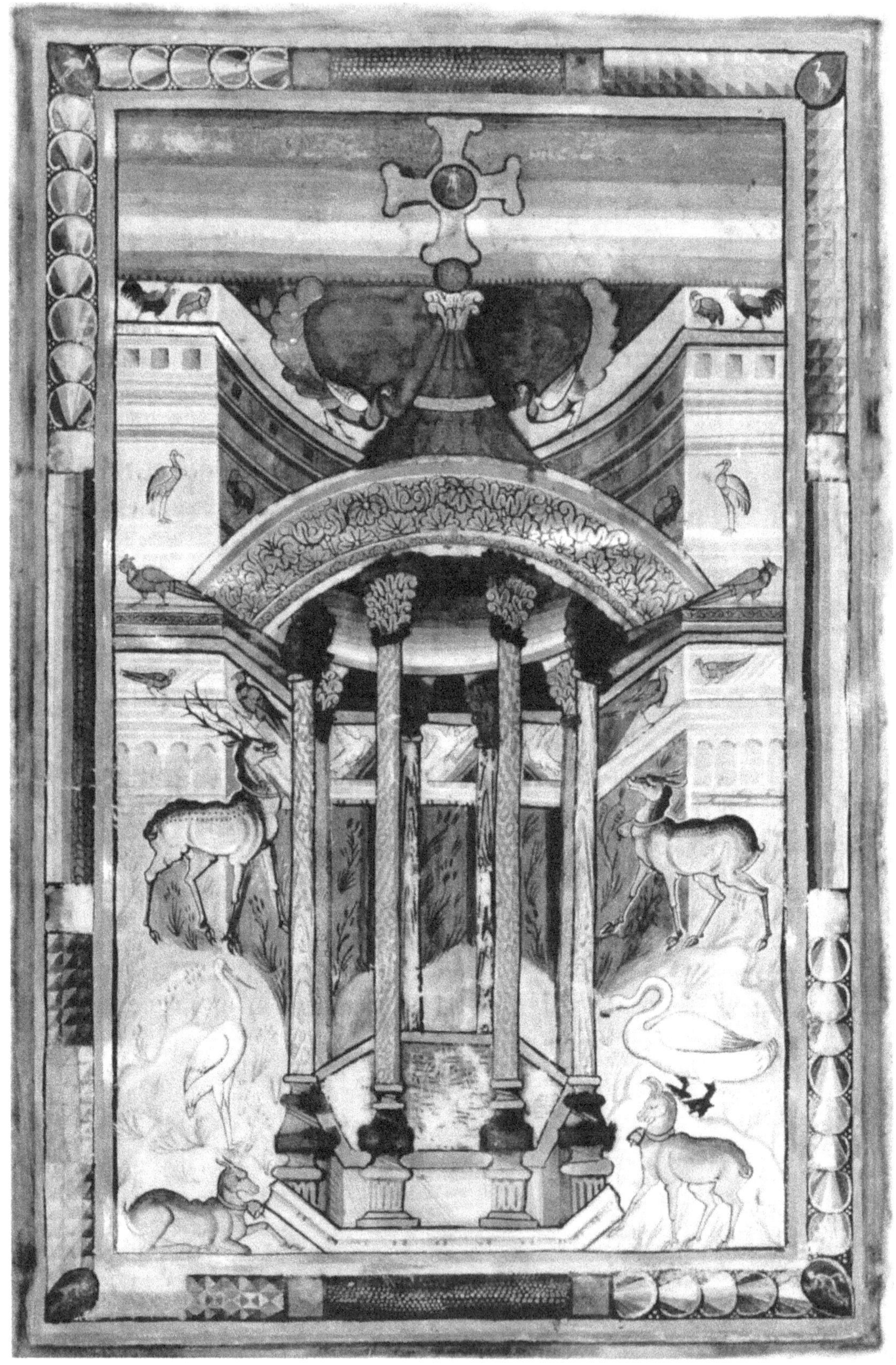

Fig. 140. "Fountain of Life," Saint Médard Gospel book, late ninth century. Bibliothèque Nationale, lat. 8850, fol. 6v.

drels with classical motifs turned into toys, and above it all bucolic scenes with animals. Other Carolingian Gospel books, like the Saint Médard one, have similar features (fig. 140). Animals would be forbidden in a Koran but a landscape set around a building is conceptually, if not typologically, related to the landscape represented with the same two dimensionality and spatial awkwardness in the Yemeni finds. As to the authors' portraits or those of Evangelists, the varieties of arcades are astounding within a small sample of early medieval examples from the Latin West: severe, accurate order with flowers and roosters in the corners, as in a Gospel book representation of Saint John, simplified in another Gospel book now at Soissons (pl. 18); almost completely transformed into geometric effects in a manuscript from Saint Gall, now in Vienna. An eleventh-century liturgical scroll from the Byzantine world begins with a stunning section through a church and little birds on plants on the sides of the building (fig. 141). From early Romanesque times, the scribe of a manuscript preserved at Cambridge (fig. 142) is shown with huge domical buildings in the ill-planned arch over him, while even more elaborate constructions appear in several Ottonian and later manuscripts.[24] The later Middle Ages continued in the same vein. In 1412 the magnificent dedicatory page of the Bible of Alba has the Virgin, the donor, and all sorts of events crowded in the midst of or in front of a stunning church unlike any Spanish church (fig. 143), and nearly every illustration of the *Grandes Chroniques de France* is surrounded by architectural elements.[25]

Sculpted examples are mostly on sarcophagi. There is a standard type of column with lintels, rounded arches, or triangular pediments. The celebrated sarcophagus of Junius Bassus (fig. 144) is a well-known example of the type, but the variants are equally fascinating: a variety of decoration, transformation of arches into trees (fig. 145), an arcade transformed into a house (fig. 146), and so on.[26] In the fourth-century ceiling of the Spanish church of Centcelles, the whole central part of the ceiling is organized by large painted columns,[27] whereas in the reconstructions of the Carolingian abbey at Lorsch and of the Benedictine church at Mals relief-sculpted columns and arches frame painted religious images.[28]

Other techniques were also affected by architecture—for instance, bookbinding and textiles. An extraordinary cover for the Epistles of Paul brought around 1147 to the famous abbey of Clairvaux is transformed into the elevation of a church facade with dozens of representations fitted into architecturally derived spaces (fig. 147).[29] The result is striking for not being a possible church facade, thus not a representation, but unmistakably evocative of one. And whatever the origins of the designs and the date of the fragments,

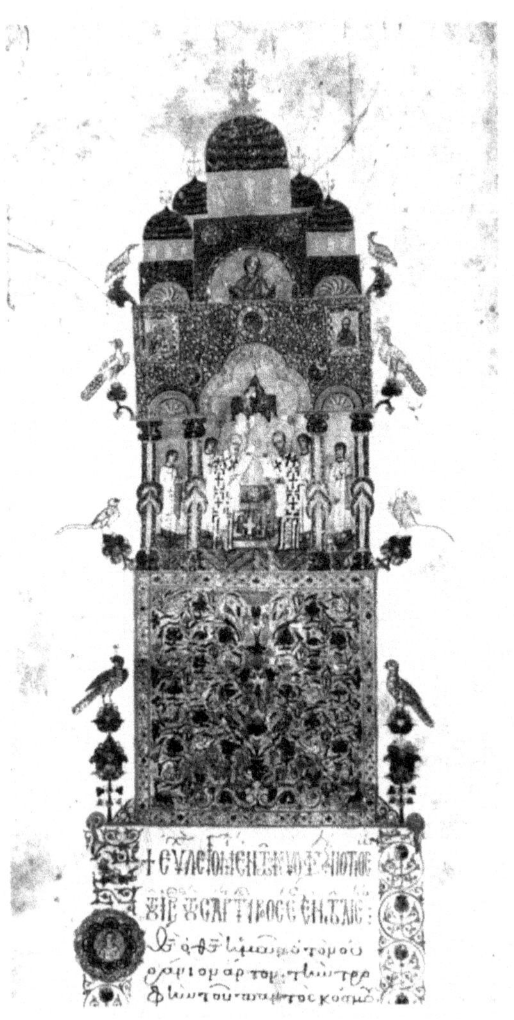

Fig. 141. Beginning of a liturgical scroll, eleventh century. Athens, National Library ms. 2759.

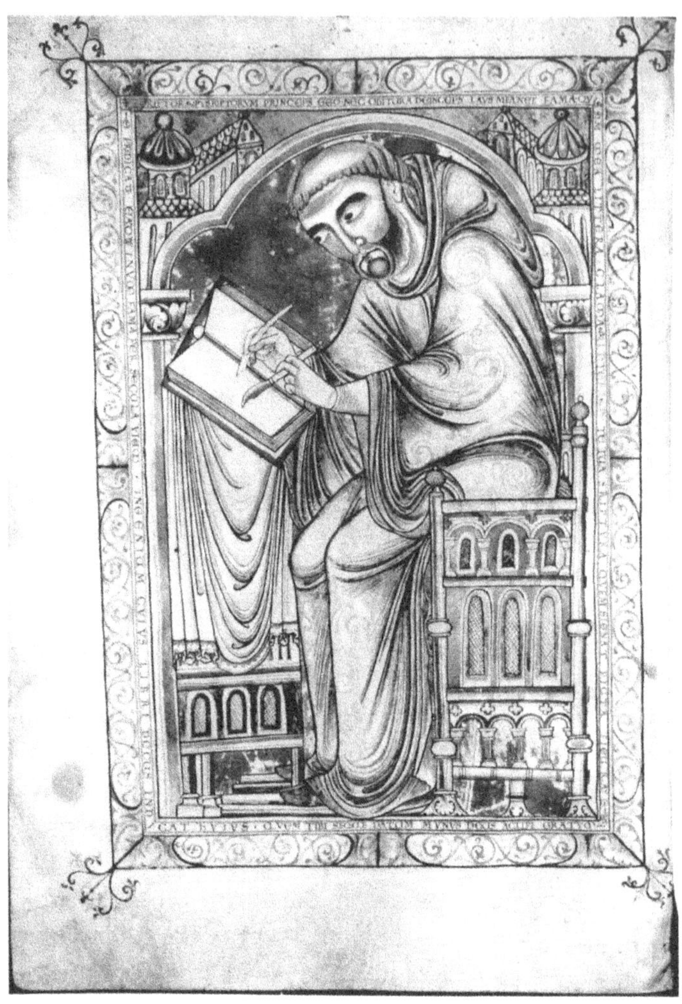

Fig. 142. Cambridge, Trinity College, Ms. R 17, fol. 1.

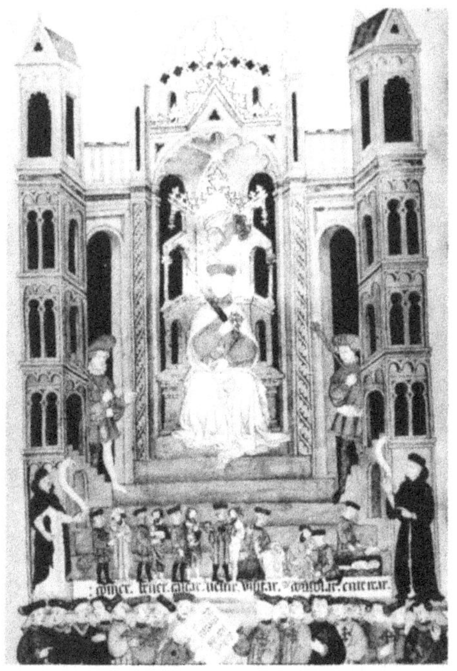

Fig. 143. Bible of Alba, 1412.

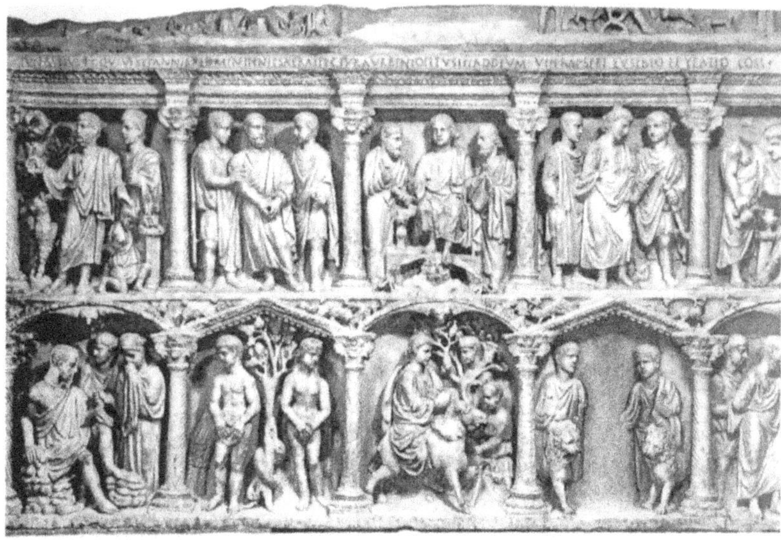

Fig. 144. Sarcophagus of Junius Bassus, fourth century. Rome, Vatican Museum.

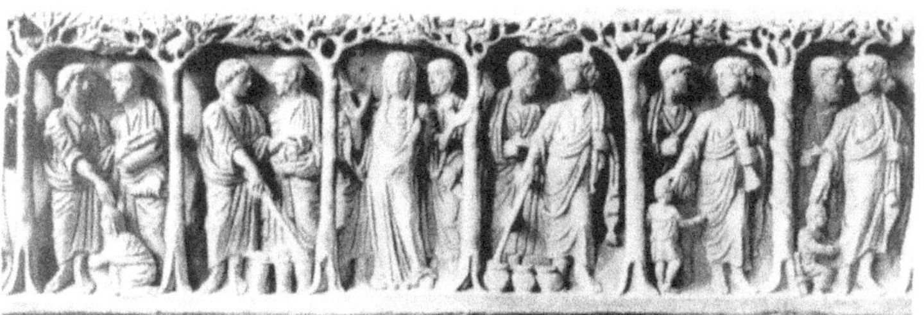

Fig. 145. Arches transformed into trees, sarcophagus. Rome, Vatican Museum.

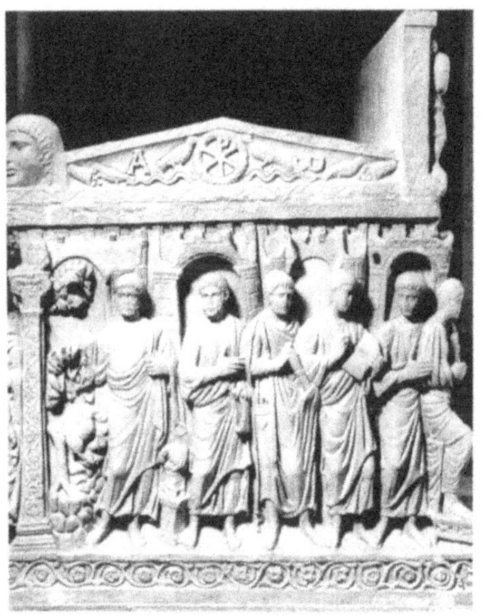

Fig. 146. Arcade transformed into house, sarcophagus. Rome, Vatican Museum.

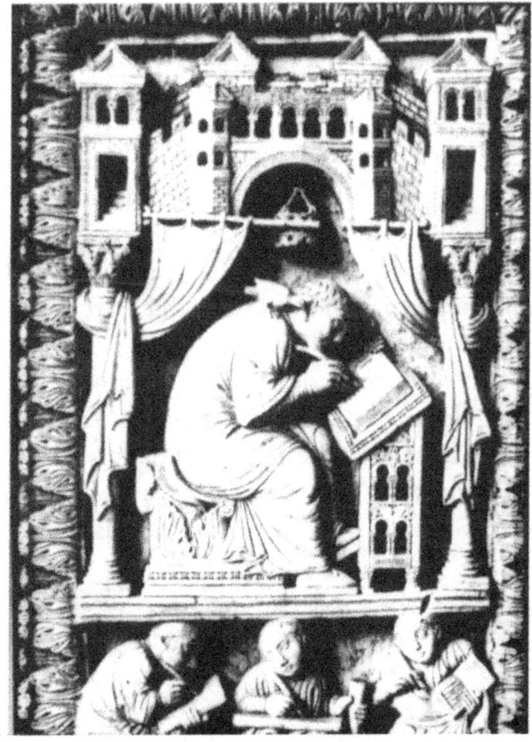

Fig. 147. Bookcover, Epistles of St. Paul, 1145–1147. Troyes, Bibliothèque Municipale, 2266.

thousands of Coptic textiles have riders running under arcades or personages standing in some form of architecture, while hundreds of ivory objects from late antiquity, Byzantium, or the medieval West have architectural frames for whatever is represented.[30]

In other words, at some level apparently connected neither with the text of a codex, nor the function of an object, nor with some obvious external illustrative source, architecture became in the Middle Ages one of the ways in which a topic is presented and, secondarily, a manner of organizing two-dimensional space. In none of the examples I have shown does the architectural setting play a precise iconographic role; it is quite unnecessary to the point of the image, of the book, the object, or the wall. Architecture enhances the book or whatever it adorns without representing anything in it or about it. The late antique, early Christian, or medieval Christian examples exist in sufficiently large numbers that nearly all of them are reflections of types, of real or imaginary models that inspired those examples which have been preserved. Because they are unique, the Sanʿa pages cannot be assumed to derive from types. But all of these initial pages in manuscripts, Christian ones as well as the Sanʿa ones, can be considered simply as illuminations serving exclusively to provide sensory attraction. Their absence, as in the exaltation of the emperor Otto III found in his Gospel book, immediately creates the impression of an event that is not grounded on earth, but which floats in some other substance, altogether a radically different impression from the one given by all other examples.[31] How and why do these architectural settings operate in such a peculiar way?

The Optisemic Level

To answer this question, let me introduce a third level of arguing about our two pages, a level pertinent to any visual document and whose elaboration should in fact have preceded the consideration of illustration and of illumination. The only reason for not considering it first was to show how traditional approaches to the problem, while perfectly valid and logical, are insufficient to identify the possible ways in which architectural features operate. It is as though something was still missing. What it is may emerge from considering a different level of understanding, which I would like to call "optisemic" (meaning dealing with the visual perception of signs). It is a level at which the eye recognizes a broad category of experience—a crowd of men or women, blue or reddish colors, landscape, and, in our case, architecture—without necessarily being aware of specific details.[32]

Within this context, the San'a images (pls. 16, 17; figs. 127, 128) show primarily a sequence of elevations, six or seven frontal views, set above each other but meant to be behind each other, according to a convention of representation that goes back to ancient Egyptian times.[33] There are two certain and one possible departures from this simple sequence. One departure is the disappearance of outer walls, even though gates have remained. The doorways seem closer to the first arcade than to the alleged ablution area, which seems to be in a different scale from the rest, as the jars, if correctly interpreted, are much too large and too obvious. Side walls and back wall are gone and have been replaced by an ornamental vegetal band. The small scale of this band, its colors, and its continuous repetitiveness are completely unrelated to anything else in the two images. The only function it seems to serve is that of establishing the edges of the building without indicating or even suggesting the likely character of these edges. The contrast is striking with the highly ornamented doorways whose designs have been kept to the scale of the building and whose specificity seems almost "portraitlike." The arbitrariness of the decorative band is further strengthened by the fact that the arcades abut against it in a sudden and highly improbable way, as though the impression was meant of a fragment from a building extending laterally even further.

The second departure from a simple sequence of elevations lies in what was interpreted as a "court" in the second building (pl. 17, fig. 128) The square frame cannot be interpreted as an elevation of anything. Whether it is a plan or a bird's-eye view remains moot to my mind, but in either case there would be a shift, in the "optisemic" character of this feature, from the norm of the image, as it is not comparable in manner of presentation with anything else in the image.

Another possible departure from the norm consists in the vegetation in the upper part of each representation. In the logic of the composition, it should depict some sort of garden in the back of the building, but the presence of this vegetation on both images in nearly identical fashion makes one wonder whether we are not dealing with a type element normally associated with buildings, large arches, or the upper edges of architectural motifs, something related to the pastoral or bucolic scenes on the Christian canon tables mentioned earlier and, therefore, derived from a process of designing rather than from the desire to represent something.

Why is it, however, that we so easily agree to seeing successive planes above each other rather than understanding the miniatures, for instance, as depictions of two-dimensional facades or of arbitrarily composed designs using built forms instead of vegetal or geometric ones? One answer is internal to the images. The entrances, by the specificity of their function and by the oblique steps in front of them, compel a sequential movement in space. Another answer derives from something in the viewer. The parts of the compositions, as perceived by him, register in the mind in terms that mean arcades, mosques, and so on, because these features are already images present in memory. They are there in varying degrees of concreteness and specificity, as some only see arches and others identify the Great Mosque of Damascus. And yet nothing here is like any mosque or building I know or anyone else has seen. In other words, it is simply because we claim to know the language in which these representations were coded that we assume the right to decode them. What allows anyone to make this claim? What is the language involved? The language of architectural representation or the history of the early mosque? Even supposing that I am right in arguing that these are images of early mosques, why would anyone have wanted to make representations of mosques? To teach someone else how to compose a mosque? Is it a sketch for building? To commemorate a particular building? Is it the souvenir of *a* building? To give an attractive face to a manuscript? Is it then simply an expressive and expensive book jacket?

THUS, FROM THIS particular "optisemic" point of view of understanding how images lead to interpretation, our two pages from Yemen raise all sorts of problems of meaning, of purpose, of the conceptualization and encoding of the visible and of the known by an artist, and of the return to the visible and to the built by the viewer and user. These problems and questions cannot be answered on the basis of these images alone. They require an expansion of the field of reference, which I propose to do in two areas. One is the area of architectural representation in general and especially in the medieval world and its classical background. The other area, which will evolve from the first one, is of a more general and more theoretical character and lies in the very nature of the architectural experience, as I shall try to suggest that the hybrid and intermediate nature of architecture itself has found a reflection in our two representations.

One distinction that can legitimately be made within the huge number of *re*creations of architecture on something else is between several methods of presenting buildings.[34] There is, first of all, the plan, the transformation of a building into a series of lines, dots, and other conventional signs that identify the location and character of most built elements found at any one horizontal level across the building; the most common level is the one found on the floor (fig. 148). Known in the ancient Orient and in Egypt, assumed for Hellenistic

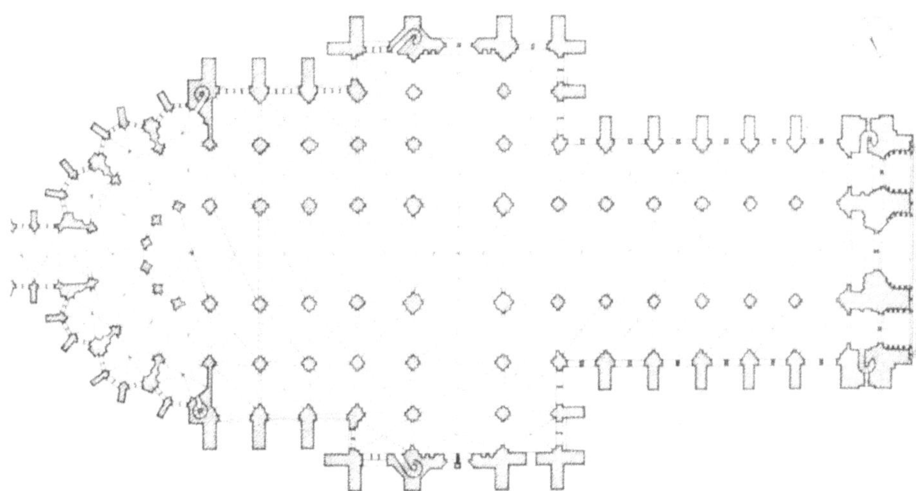

Fig. 148. Amiens, cathedral, plan.

times, the plan appears in a perfectly clear way in the *Forma Urbis Romae* commissioned between 203 and 211 (fig. 149), and reappears in equally striking form in the celebrated plan found in the Saint Gall monastery (fig. 150) and datable to the first quarter of the ninth century. Alike in so many specifics in their ways with signs for built forms, the *Forma Urbis* and the Saint Gall plan have been interpreted in very different ways. One is correctly seen as the reflection of something, the actual city of Rome, which existed independently from it, whereas the Carolingian work has been explained as an ideal plan type for monks to follow in building a new monastic establishment.[35] My aim is not to contradict or defend these interpretations, only to point out that the same kind of perceived scheme can lead to such divergent explanations, as between something that existed or did not.

Then, even though there are minor but fascinating additional exceptions throughout the Christian and Muslim Middle Ages,[36] it is only after the thirteenth century that diagrams and other schematic techniques of presenting the built structure of a building became common in western Europe.[37] The earliest remaining examples in the Muslim world are from the sixteenth century, although it is probable that plans existed as early as the fourteenth.[38] They are, I believe, unknown in southern and eastern Asia until a much later time.[39] To these examples of plans on materials like paper, parchment, or stone, which can be preserved and which in most cases were meant to be preserved in order to be seen and used more than once, there are examples of ad hoc plans made for a single practical use, most of the time to help in the

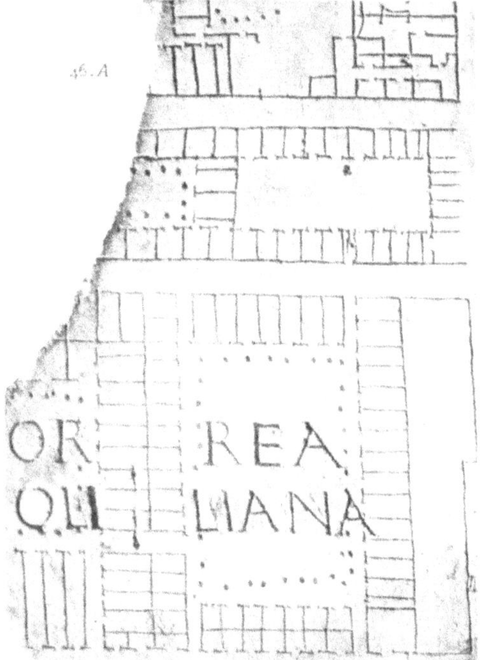

Fig. 149. *Forma Urbis Romae,* detail.

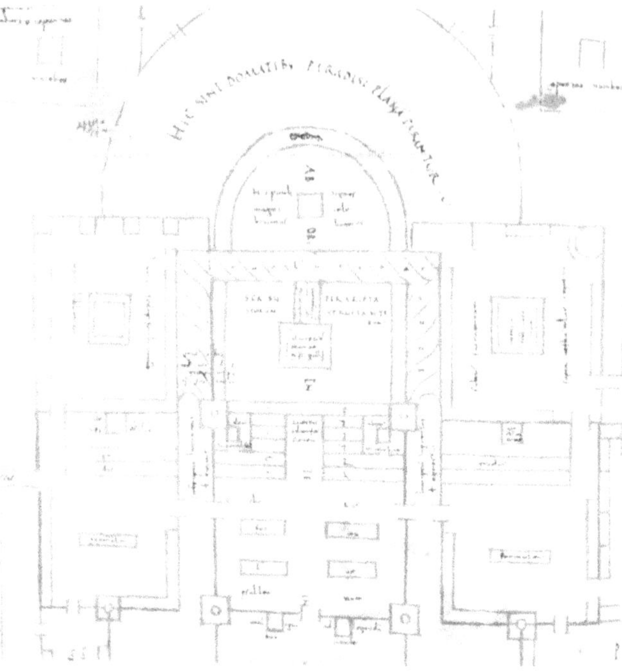

Fig. 150. Saint Gall plan, detail.

process of construction. Such are ancient sketches found on the podium walls of Apollo's temple in Didyma or the stone floor of the Holy Cross basilica in Rusafah.[40] They were visual aids in the process of construction or of instructing those responsible for a project, and these combinations of lines and dots were not meant to survive as objects, not even as ornaments.

Whatever specific, immediate, or long-range functions any one plan may have had, the problem for us is to understand how it operates. It is like a musical score whose sequence of arbitrary conventional signs is transformed into sound by those who know the conventions and who are able to transfer that knowledge into a world of sound within their mind and then into a practical expression of that sound through instruments. Those who listen *and* know the code can then reverse the process and return to the original lines and dots of a score. The sound of the instruments or even the sound in the mind, however, had nothing in common with the initial visual experience of seeing dots and lines. Similarly the bare notations of an architectural plan only make sense if one already knows more or less what a building was meant to be. The plan of Sanit Gall (fig. 150) is interesting in this respect. It is remarkable for the fact that its signs were accompanied by a considerable number of written explanatory notations and it is these notations that led the visual imagination and technical competence of scholars to reasonable proposals for what the monastery was meant to look like. At the same time the dozens of imagined reconstructions (fig. 151) are remarkably skinless. Their severity may be explained on religious grounds, as the Cistercian order did not approve of ornamentation or luxury, but I suspect that it is mostly because plans are unable by themselves, as images, to convey more than a minimum of information about the nature of a building. However much they tried by adding furniture or standing monks and seated visitors that are not in the original "score," the interpreters of Saint Gall's plan still could not make their reconstructions vibrate with any kind of life. In this sense plans are far less than musical scores; they only set a stage for a building by identifying its components, its instruments. Written instructions, a numerical scale, or a modular principle are needed to do more than sketch a monument through one's imagination.

What, then, is the point of these plans? It *is* to feed the imagination, to trigger an immensely varied series of responses, but to check or control these responses only in the most general way. Eventually, the High Renaissance transformed plans into drawings, into objects, even works of art, in their own right. Until then, the plan was but the simple intermediary between a memory, a dream, or a wish, on the one hand, and a range of possible buildings, on the other. It could be treasured because of the wealth of ideas it could lead to.

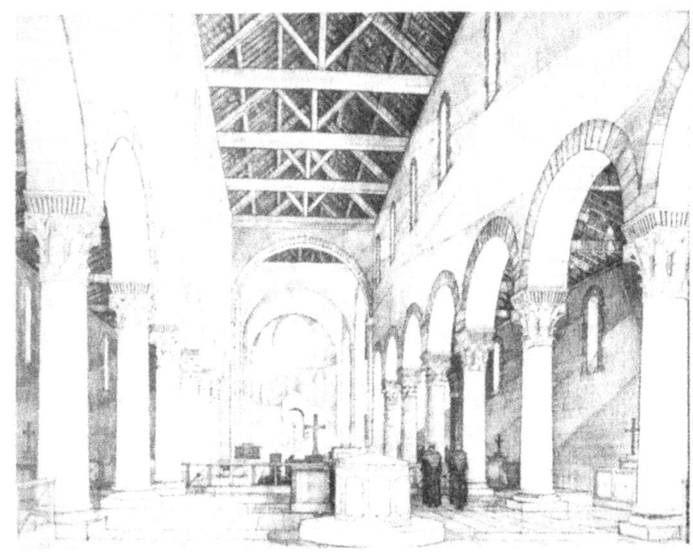

Fig. 151. Saint Gall monastery, reconstruction.

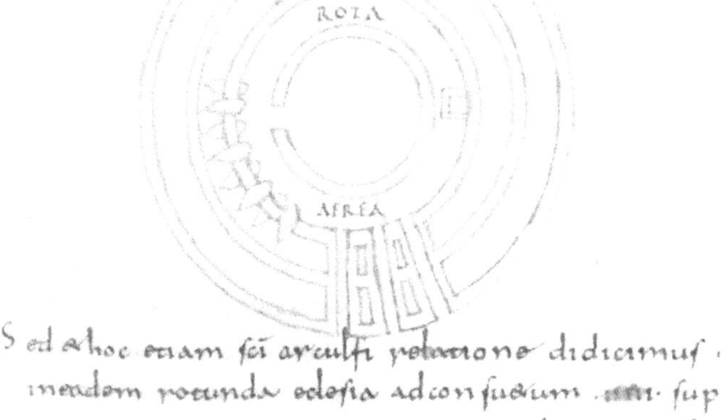

Fig. 152. Drawing of Church of the Ascension, Adamanus account. Zurich, Zentralbibl. Cod. Rh. LXXIII.

This may well have happened to Adamanus's drawings of the Holy Sepulcher or of the Church of the Ascension (fig. 152) on the basis of the probably orally transmitted information from Arculfus, who had traveled to Jerusalem.[41] For, as Krautheimer has shown in a celebrated article,[42] medieval drawings of the Holy Sepulcher never represented or suggested a single truth in their potential incarnation, and many alternate constructed versions could be meant to descend from any one of them. Just as the sight of a musical score only means to me that it depicts some music but can exhilarate a musician by its brilliance, Adamanus's drawing is utterly uninspiring, unless one's faith and probably various verbal accounts of the Holy Sepulcher can translate the drawing into a church.

A second method of presenting buildings is the two-dimensional elevation of a built form. At its most common, it is the frame around a personage or an event, and the variations of this particular genre are truly astounding, as they can be just an arcade as in the Canon tables or a whole building whose parts, as on our initial miniatures, are set above each other, as in a tenth-century Greek manuscript in Athens attributed to southern Italy.[43] The immediate origin of this manner of depicting architecture lies certainly in classical Roman mural painting with whole walls divided into sections by an architectural composition (pl. 19), which usually did not correspond to a building as it had done in the early versions of two-dimensional architecture found in Egyptian tombs. In the latter, the nature of the building, house, or temple is usually clear because the concreteness of the religious experience avoided possible uncertainties of interpretation. But in the immense array of antique, late antique, Christian medieval, or Islamic medieval and premodern examples, the building is only very rarely identifiable, and, when it is, the mechanism of identification is an inscription. It is as though architectural signs alone were not enough to identify a specific building. The point could be put more forcefully. Most instances of two-dimensional architectural images are not representations of buildings nor are they necessarily evocative of architectural complexes, although the variants there are considerable.

The third way of showing architecture leads to the nearly similar conclusion of apparent lack of purpose. Combinations of elevations set at various angles to each other succeed—in a celebrated mosaic from Tabarka in Tunisia (fig. 153), in dozens of examples from the floor mosaics of Antioch, in the Utrecht Psalter (fig. 154), on countless ivory panels and architectural spandrels, and in masses of manuscript illustrations from later Iranian paintings—in evoking churches, palaces, houses, and even whole cities.[44] I use the verb "evoke" on purpose, since the relationship between what one sees and what one understands, in all these examples, is as varied as it is complex. Two

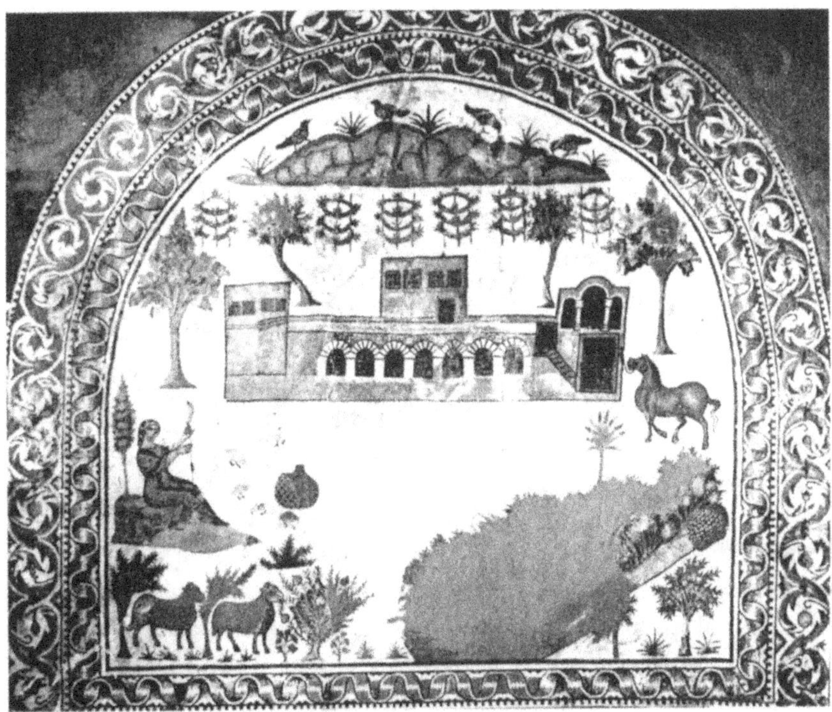

Fig. 153. Representation of house, Tunisia, Tabarka, floor mosaic, fifth or sixth century.

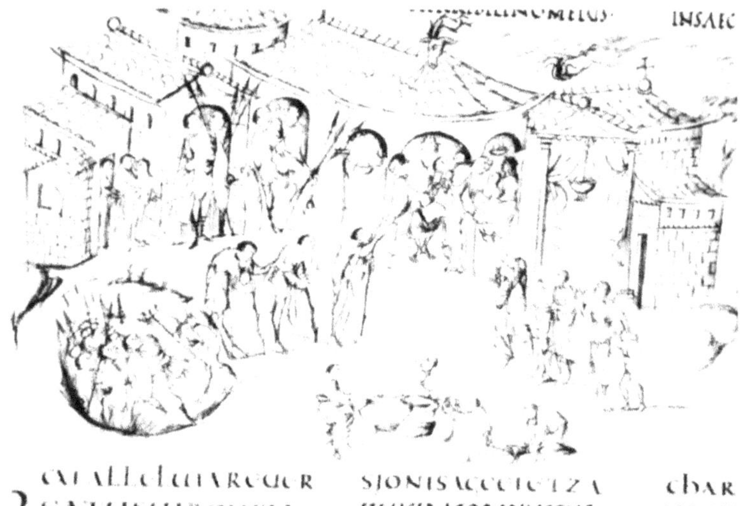

Fig. 154. Psalter, ninth century. Utrecht, Bibliotheek der Rijkuniversiteit, Script. Eccl. 484, fol. 65v (Psalter 111/112).

examples will clarify my point. The celebrated early eighth-century mosaics on the walls of the Great Mosque of Damascus (figs. 155, 156) have been a subject of controversy ever since they were uncovered some sixty years ago. They have been interpreted as specific representations of the oasis of Damascus as well as visions of Paradise according to the tenets of the Muslim faith. Reasonable arguments can be made for both of these explanations as well as for several others that conciliate the extremes of visionary buildings or cartographic depictions. The point is, however, that no explanation will be demonstrated to the exclusion of any other, as was probably the case in the eighth century,[45] until an external referent is found. In the slightly later (circa 760) mosaics recently discovered at Umm al-Rassas in Jordan, very specific cities like Nablus (Neapolis) are identified through inscriptions set next to or below repetitive types of elevations of cities (fig. 157).[46]

The point is important for my argument, for it illustrates a fascinating apparent paradox. On the one hand, an inscription identifies something specifically as Theodoric's palace (as in Ravenna's San Apollinario church) or as a city (Neapolis, Nablus, in Jordan and elsewhere). On the other hand, the visual features of the buildings so identified can be shown to have been used for hundreds of representations that are not Neapolis nor Theodoric's palace. It is not by their physical specificity that Neapolis or Theodoric's palace are identified, but the image of a city or of a palace becomes more forceful, more pungent, if it is identified as a specific town or palace. Even the buildings and cityscapes that adorn so many later Flemish paintings are there for complex evocative reasons rather than for precise denotational and iconophoric ones.[47]

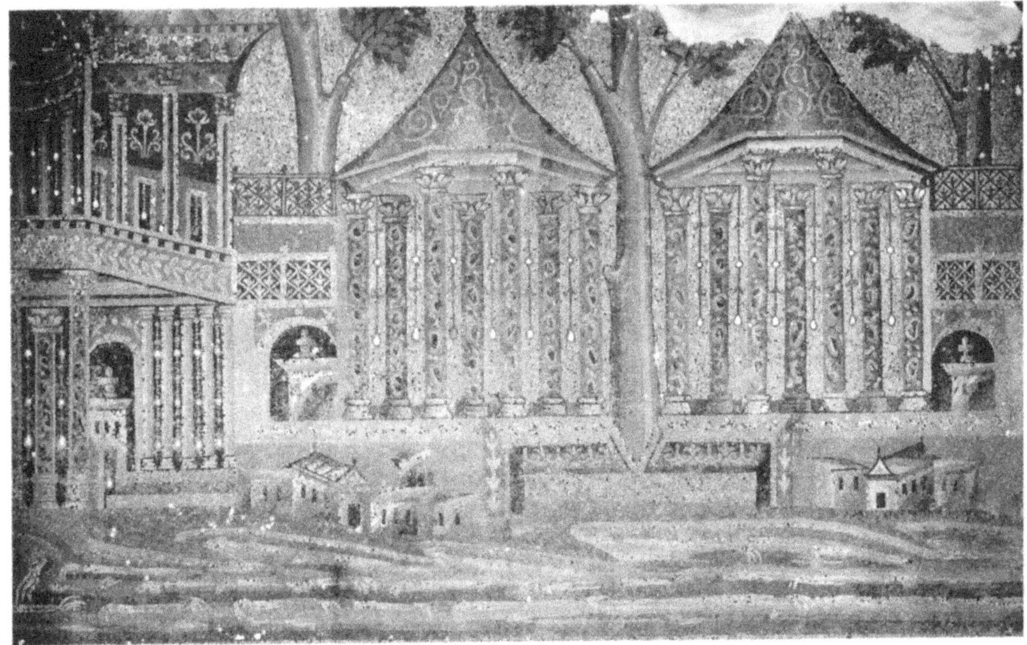

155

Fig. 155. Damascus, Great Mosque, mosaic in west portico, detail, early eighth century.

Fig. 156. Damascus, Great Mosque, mosaic in west portico, detail, early eighth century.

Fig. 157. Representation of cities, Umm al-Rassas, mosaics in church, circa 760.

157

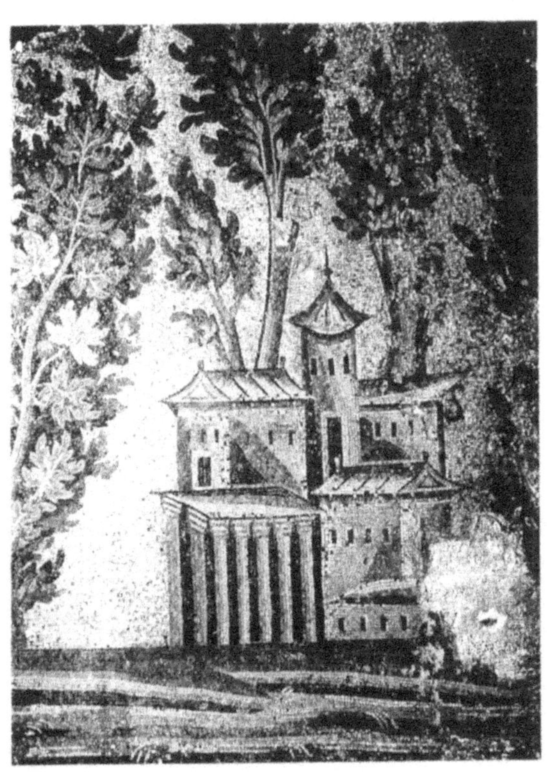

156

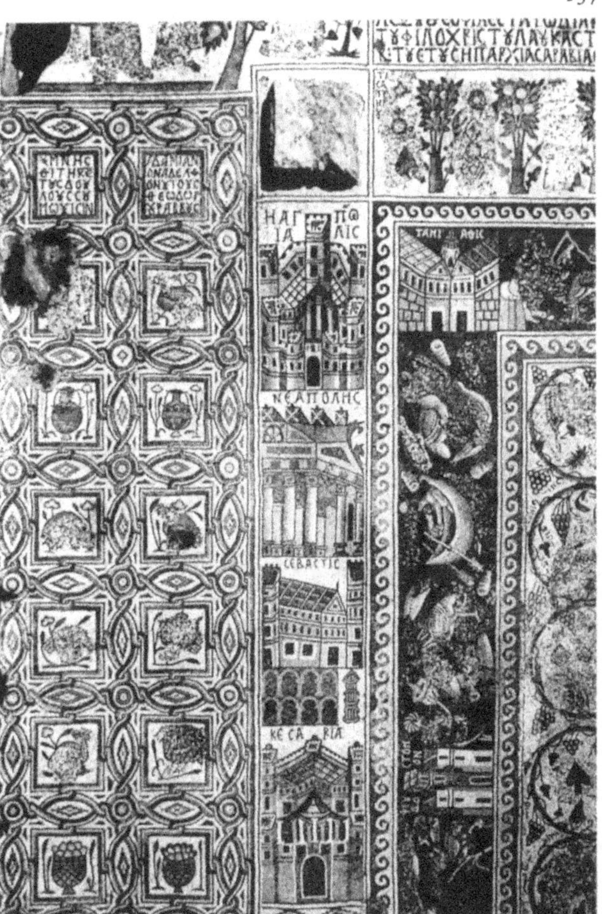

Thus, like the simple elevation, this more complex type hovers between general meanings and specific ones, but the latter always require an outside referent or a vector.

The fourth way of representing architecture is to attempt to show its full three-dimensionality. Roman illusionist painting, as in the Boscoreale frescoes now in the Metropolitan Museum or in many other examples (fig. 158), first developed ways to represent buildings by themselves, in landscapes, or in other combinations, which make fully visible the space around the building and the appearance of the building from a single point of view, as in the bird's-eye view of an amphitheater in a city from the National Museum in Naples (fig. 159), a particularly striking and complicated example of a fairly common type of image.[48] It would be easy to assume that such illusionist images represented actual buildings and often indeed they did, especially from the late Middle Ages onward, culminating, among thousands of examples, in the visually precise (and, therefore, supposed to be accurate) images of Venice by Guardi and Canaletto. Yet what is remarkable is that already in Rome, throughout the Middle Ages, in Persian miniatures, and even in later Mughal examples or in Claude Lorrain's fantasies, precision of spatial and structural illusion is no guarantee for the actual existence of buildings. Conversely, representational conventions that can hardly be called illusionistic have been

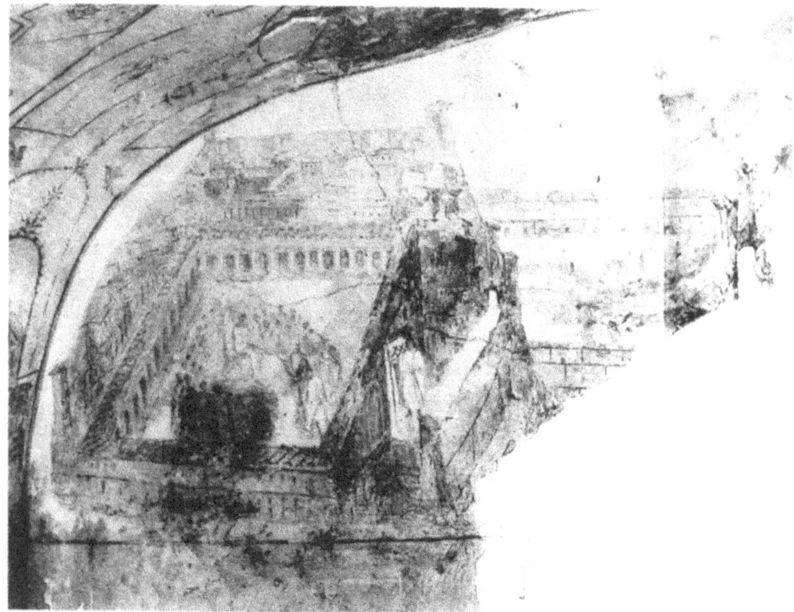

159

Fig. 158. Architectural landscape, first century A.D. Naples, National Museum.

Fig. 159. Bird's-eye view of architecture, hypogeum of Aurelius, second century A.D. Naples, National Museum.

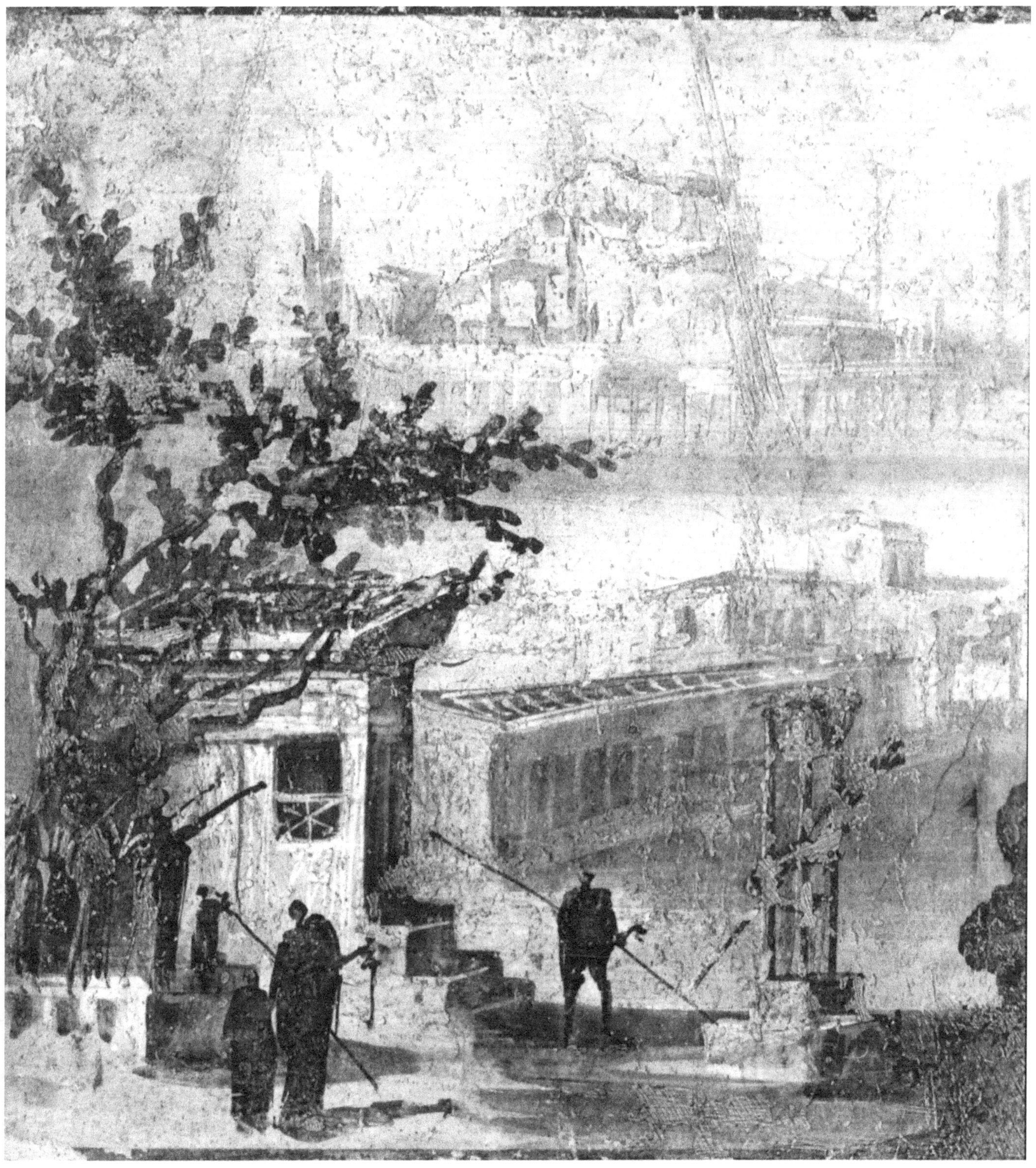

shown to exemplify and even to depict very specific buildings, as in Matrakci's celebrated depiction of cities in western Asia (fig. 160).[49]

One may wonder, in fact, whether the same conclusion can be drawn about the representation of people—that is to say, that a thoroughly realistic portrait may be of someone who never existed and a conventional one of someone who had been very much alive. The elaboration of this point is beyond the concerns of this essay, yet it illustrates, I believe, a central theme of the approach I am proposing. The theme is the existence of a peculiar and ill-defined boundary between image and reality, whereby reality remains unreal or rather untrue in architecture or in the representation of man unless certain signs are put into its image. These signs could be images of generally known buildings that provide immediate recognition, like the endless depictions of

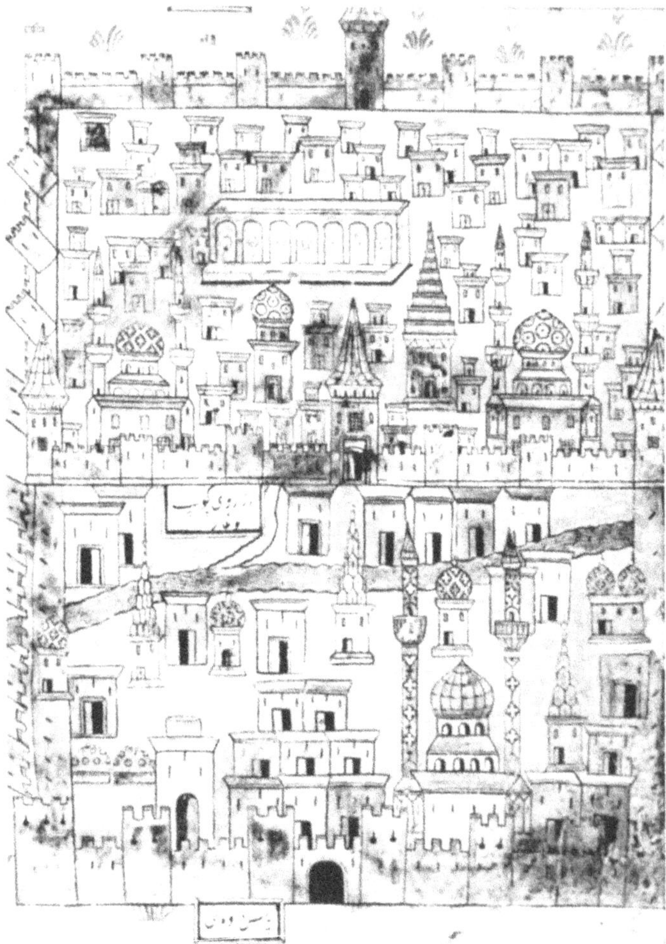

Fig. 160. Matrakci, *Travel Book*, representation of Erzerum.

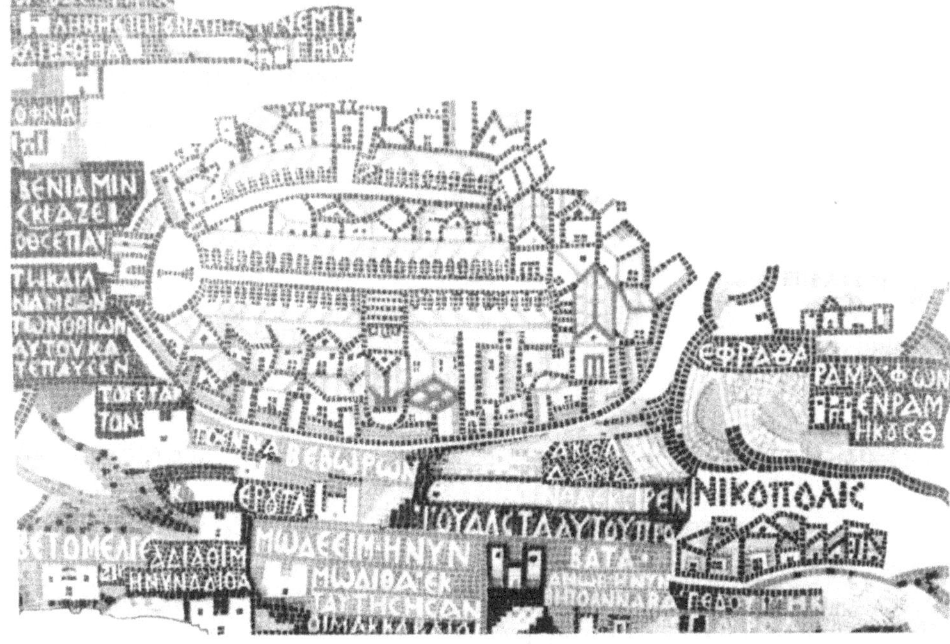

Fig. 161. Representation of Jerusalem, mosaic map in Madaba church (Jordan), sixth century.

the Piazza San Marco by Venetian painters or views of the Eiffel tower. They can also be inscriptions or other means of labeling buildings. Just to push the point in a direction I will not pursue but which is philosophically fascinating, Monet's depictions of the Rouen cathedral are only images of this particular cathedral because he said so, for, just as in a medieval practice of using architecture for other purposes than the architecture itself, the place of the cathedral is not as pertinent as the effect of color and light it makes, or rather the painter strives to suggest.[50] For, in addition to a conflict or contrast between image and reality, there is also another contrast between reality and truth, between the validity of something seen and the actual state of that something.[51]

Each one of these manners of showing architecture deserves, no doubt, additional elaboration and refinement. But even the brief sketch given to each one allows me to argue that, whatever manner of representation was chosen, whether a plan or an almost unmistakable (even if fantastic) image, the *same* modes of showing buildings were meant to have two possible meanings. One is centered on the building, which, through inscriptions or whatever other means were used, becomes concrete. It can be a type, a mosque as in another illustration (pl. 20) from the Cairo Bustan or a church as with Saint Gall's plan (fig. 150). It can also be a place or a monument. Such is the case with the early Christian mosaics and paintings in Rome showing an idealized Jerusalem or an equally fancy Bethlehem, while the more or less contemporary Madaba map in Jordan shows a mixture of architectural signs that depict Jerusalem (fig. 161).[52] The latter have iconographic meanings and do not concern these essays. They belong to the same order of investigation as the images of man or the illustration of stories in antique or post-Renaissance art; all of them are narrative in the sense that there is behind them a story, a real account, a fiction or a fantasy, perhaps even a true space in which man lives.

But the overwhelming majority of architectural images found in every technique and in thousands of examples do not refer to a type of building, purpose, or function, or to specific buildings. They do not tell a story; they do not even necessarily suggest a space or a place. They are outside of that part of the visual discourse known as iconographic because it is replete with external referents.

Before trying to explain this passion for showing buildings and parts of buildings in so many different contexts and in so many different places, let me try to make as precise as possible and as clear as possible how, in my judgment, architecture operated in all representations except the obviously iconographic ones. Two functions seem to be particularly evident. One is that architecture bounds something, it separates it from something else; whatever is circumscribed by architecture is separated from that which is outside of it. The second function is restricted to those instances, numerous though they may be, when architecture appears together with some other topic such as writing, as in canon tables, or personages, like Evangelists or heroes of sacred or profane stories. In these examples, in addition to serving as a boundary, the architectural element also compels attention to the main subject, focuses on it, provides it with its frame, and, so to speak, gift wraps it for the viewer. The key attribute of both functions—separating and wrapping better to present—is that they do not focus attention on the carrier of the function, namely, architecture, but on something else.

In most cases the "something else" is clear enough. It is the personages and events surrounded by the architecture, as in the grandiose sixth-century mosaics of Saint George in Saloniki (fig. 162),[53] with architecture as a powerful and compelling backdrop to a prophetic vision. How should one, however, interpret the architectural paintings on the walls of Roman houses (pl. 19, fig. 158), the buildings in the borders (never in the center except for specific iconographic purposes) of mosaics from Antioch, of mosaics again on the walls of the Great Mosque of Damascus (figs. 155, 156) and a few of their latter imitations, in the tower tombs of Kharraqan (fig. 163), in the fifteenth-century sanctuary of Gazur Gah in Afghanistan (fig. 164), even on the walls of Mughal forts? To this list of well-known examples of late antique and Medieval architecture or architectural features covering walls of buildings, it may be appropriate to add a totally different mode of expression, the composed orders of Gothic or post-Palladian facades in which architectural elements

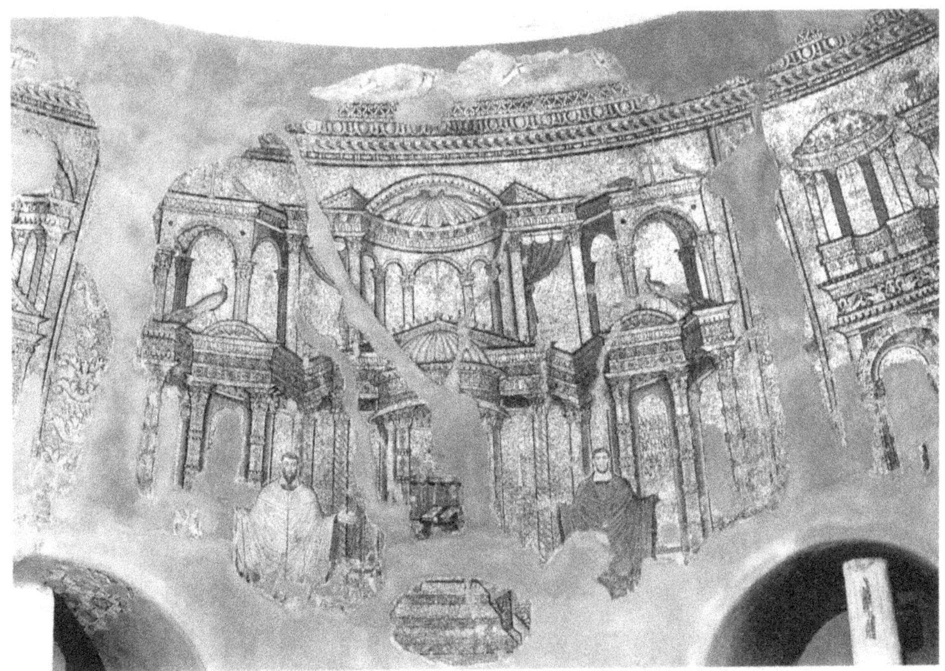

162

Fig. 162. Saloniki, St. George, mosaics, sixth century.

Fig. 163. Iran, Kharraqan, tomb tower, paintings, late medieval.

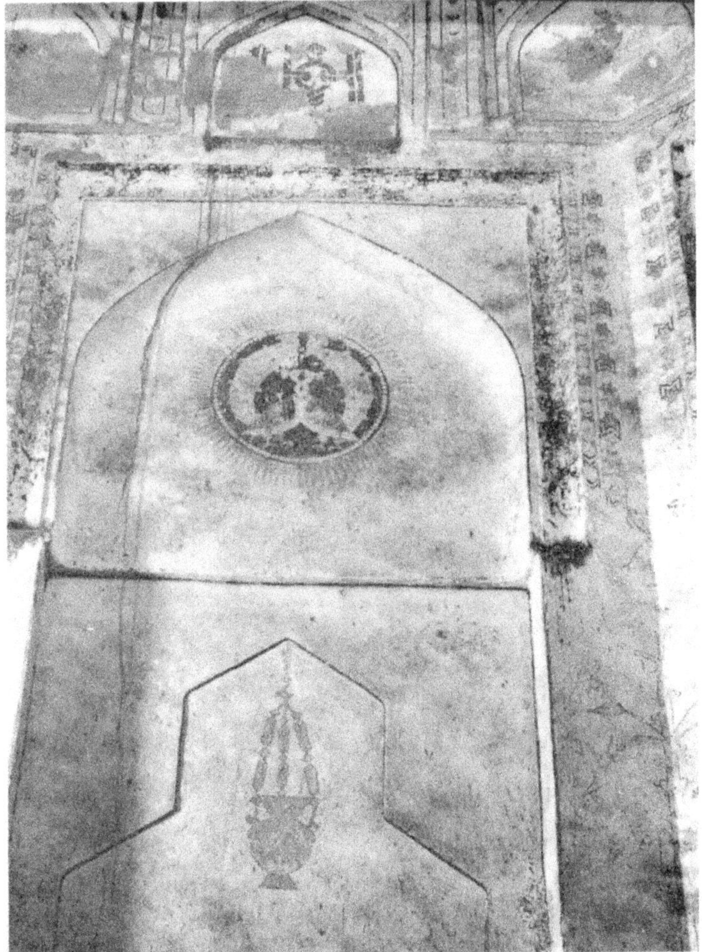

163

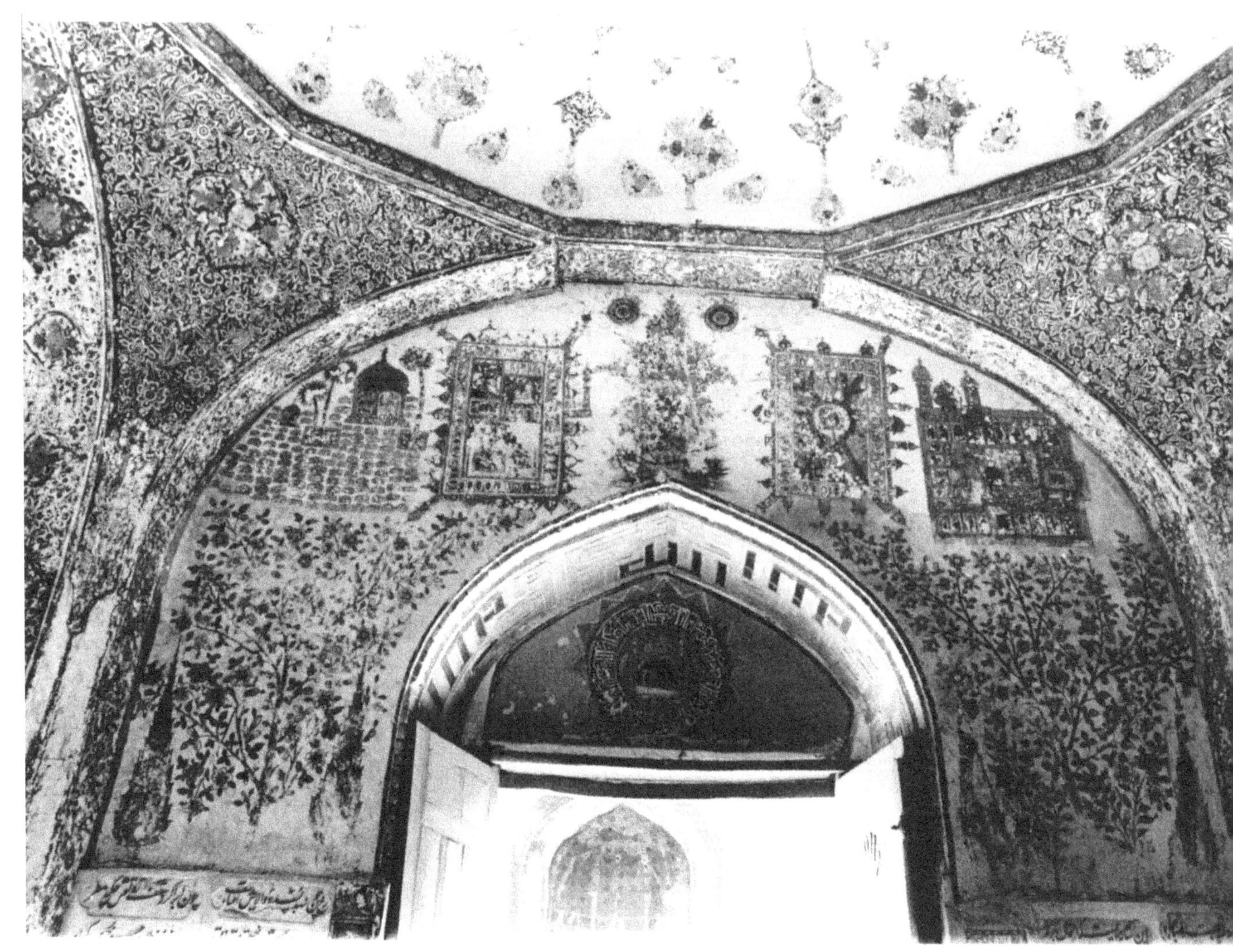

Fig. 164. Afghanistan, Gazur Gah, mausoleum, fifteenth century, later paintings.

form the face of a building and whose proportions, at least in post-Renaissance architecture, have led to so many learned studies.[54] In *all* these cases, I want to argue, separating and wrapping for announcing are the central function of the architectural decoration. The point is obvious enough for the facades of churches, cathedrals, or the exterior palatial ensembles, but do the same functions operate inside a building, as in the mosque of Damascus, for instance, the shrine at Gazur Gah, or in a Roman villa? There, I believe, architectural representation removed the actual building, the real architecture, and replaced it with a vision, with an intimation of some other order, some other expectation for the interior of the building. The degree of specificity of a message without iconographic precision remains to be seen, but the fact of a message of "difference" seems assured. Whatever is introduced by architecture is different from or more precious than whatever is outside. Although the examples just given are connected with buildings, the point can be made for ivories and for a striking monument like the huge Pala d'Oro in Venice, a huge altarpiece put together in the early fourteenth century, with its rows of arcades set above each other to frame holy images (fig. 165).[55]

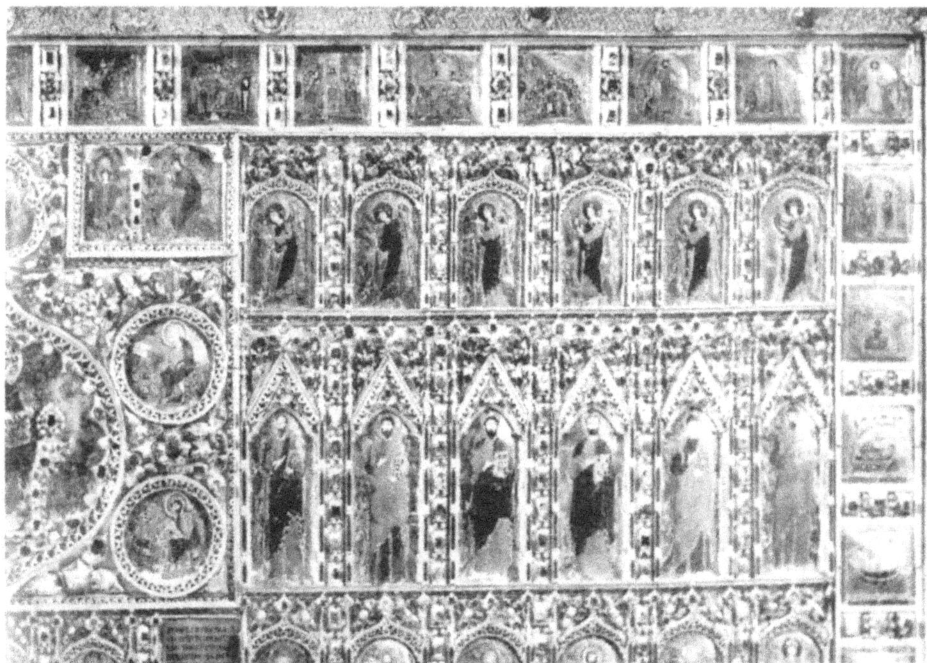

Fig. 165. Pala d'Oro, San Marco Cathedral, Venice, thirteenth century, detail.

We can thus come back to the representations of mosques with which this chapter began (pls. 16, 17; figs. 127, 128). I still do not know whether these were representations of specific buildings or not. They are certainly not type buildings like the Saint Gall plan nor obvious sanctuaries like the Haram in Mekka which began to be represented as early as in the eleventh century.[56] But the main function they fulfilled in a codex of the Koran is clear. They wrapped it, like frontispieces and, more rarely, finispieces in a number of later secular manuscripts;[57] they signaled its importance and uniqueness by physically and visually separating it from its surroundings or by inciting in the user a sentiment of awe, perhaps of holiness, certainly of anticipatory and sensory pleasure, as he opened the book.

It is not quite enough to propose an explanation of *how* these architectural features operated. An indication must be given of *why* they worked. The answer is in part provided by the notion of order argued at great length by Sir Ernst Gombrich. In ways that belong to yet uncharted aspects of perceptual intelligence, the intimation of building or of a building provides a force of presence and a solidity of power or of authority that is transmitted to whatever is connected with it—the king under an arch as on the celebrated plate of Theodosius or the "philosopher" Dioscorides in front of a peculiar, probably palatial, tower (fig. 166). But order and authority are only two of the attributes of architecture as an intermediary. Architectural images, especially if accom-

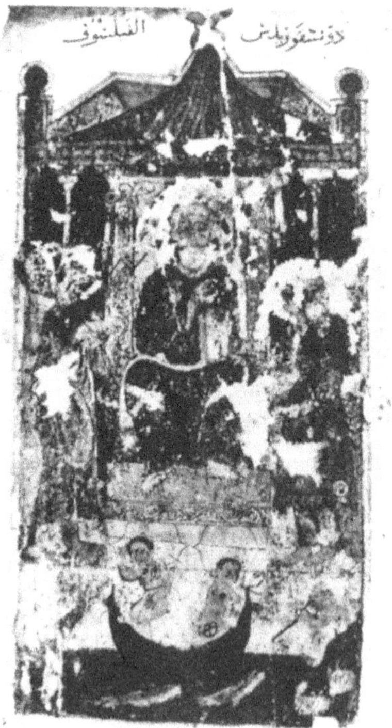

Fig. 166. "Dioscorides as Philosopher," *Materia Medica,* Istanbul, Top Kapi Seray Museum, Ahmet III 2147, fol. 2.

panied by bits of landscape, have often been seen as images of paradise as was mentioned at the beginning of this chapter. Put that simply and directly, this interpretation is certainly wrong because, whatever complex attitudes man has developed toward Paradise, in true Christian and Muslim doctrine, Paradise is part of the eschatological hope for the end of time and the afterlife, not something to be enjoyed, even vicariously, on earth. Exceptions existed no doubt, as with the troubling and mysterious Taj Mahal in Agra,[58] but they could not be as numerous as pictures of architecture without iconographic purpose.

But, if one imagines all these architectural compositions as evocations and as intermediary filters that modify the spaces in front or ahead of them—the sanctuary of a mosque or a book—then one can indeed propose to see them as covering with beauty and well-being their mundane or sacred environment. They are not images of Paradise, but feeders of a dream, the dream that life can be as beautiful as one imagines Paradise to be and as sacred texts have said it is. They succeed, or at least they were meant to succeed, because they evoke rather than represent. Precision of depiction is needed for them to be buildings, but the specificity of that precision is secondary to their power of evocation.[59]

Two additional remarks are needed before concluding. One is that this interpretation of architecture used as ornament is justified for a wide world extending from Indian-inspired Buddhism to the Atlantic. It may also be reasonable for Pre-Columbian American art, but I am less certain that it is valid with the same consistency in Far Eastern art where a representational architecture combining elevations, as in the third type discussed earlier, seems to predominate almost exclusively. There is a fundamental question here as to whether these special concerns and attributes of architecture are not concerns developed primarily in the cultures issued from the Mediterranean, western Asia, and the Indo-Gangetic valleys and, as a consequence, whether they have no universal value in the ways of geometry or, as we have yet to see, vegetation. The second point is that, in addition to a represented architecture used as ornament, there are objects shaped as buildings from China to the West. Whether Chou bronze vessels, Christian candlesticks, Islamic inkwells or lamps (fig. 167), and incense burners (fig. 168) in the Muslim and Christian Middle Ages,[60] objects of industrial art have appeared occasionally in the shape of buildings. They can be treated iconographically, typologically, or else, as I am now proposing, as intermediaries modifying, by their very shape, the quality or the value of whatever they contained and thereby affecting one's

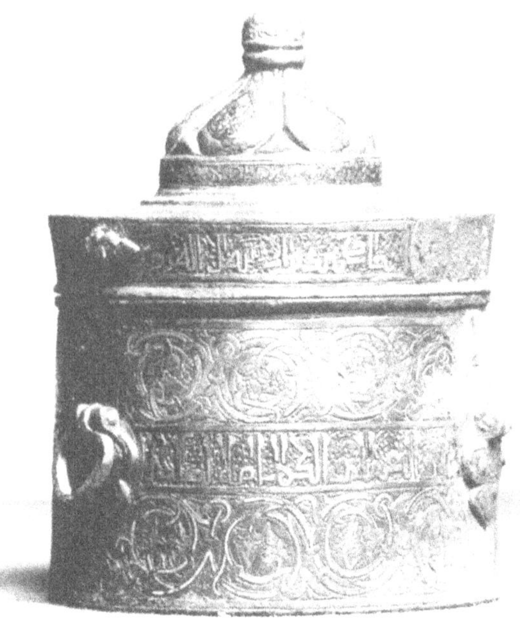

Fig. 167. Bronze inlaid inkwell, twelfth century. Baltimore, Walters Art Gallery, 54.514.

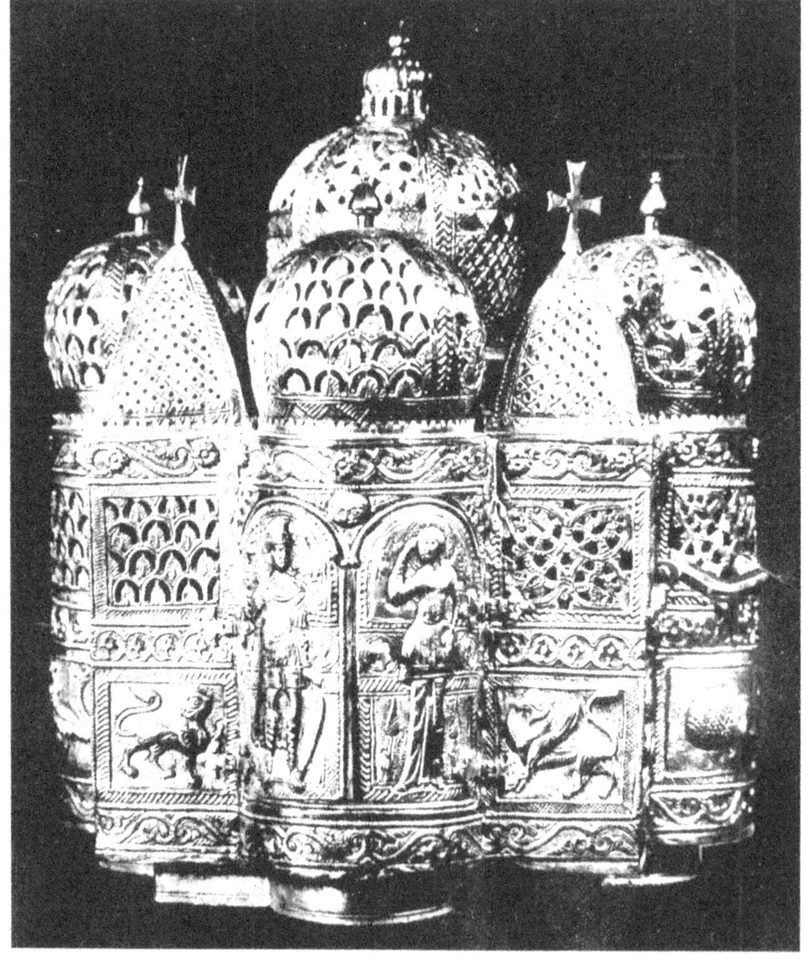

Fig. 168. Incense burner in the shape of a building, twelfth or thirteenth century. Venice, San Marco Treasury.

behavior toward what was in these objects or toward their function. A fascinating recent study of Iranian medieval inkwells with domical covers has argued that they were paradisiac pavilions (fig. 167),[61] but the argument, while partly justified, takes too concretely what is in fact an evocation rather than a representation. The more important point is that nearly all functions can be transformed into buildings. To put it differently, architecture is, in these architecturally fashioned objects, a visual access to an action, to a way of behaving, and is not restricted to representing something or evoking it.

To SUM UP, two recently discovered representations of buildings from the early Middle Ages in the Islamic world became an excuse to roam over the issue of images of architecture other than specifically iconographic ones and to argue that, in many places, at least since classical times, images of architecture became a means of access to other topics. Architectural images colored other topics, feasted on them, cuddled them, at times perhaps even overwhelmed them, but they always remained separated from the reality or the truth of whatever it was they adorned. This paradox may not be surprising if we push it one step further. After all, the perception of a work of actual architecture is not the end of one's relationship to it, as it is of a painting. Good architecture is always meant to be an invitation to behave in certain ways; it always adorns life, and, some exceptions notwithstanding, does not require the emotions surrounding whatever one does *in* a building, including looking at works of art. By understanding ornamental architecture as a charged intermediary between user or viewer on the one hand, and some action on the other, we are perhaps simply acknowledging the more profound truth of architecture in general, that it is always at the service of man and has no greater purpose than to adorn his manifold activities, something as simple and prosaic as eating or listening to a lecture and something as glorious as worshiping God or contemplating a work of art. Architecture is a true ornament in the sense I have been developing in these essays. Without it, life loses its quality. Architecture makes life complete, but it is neither life nor art.

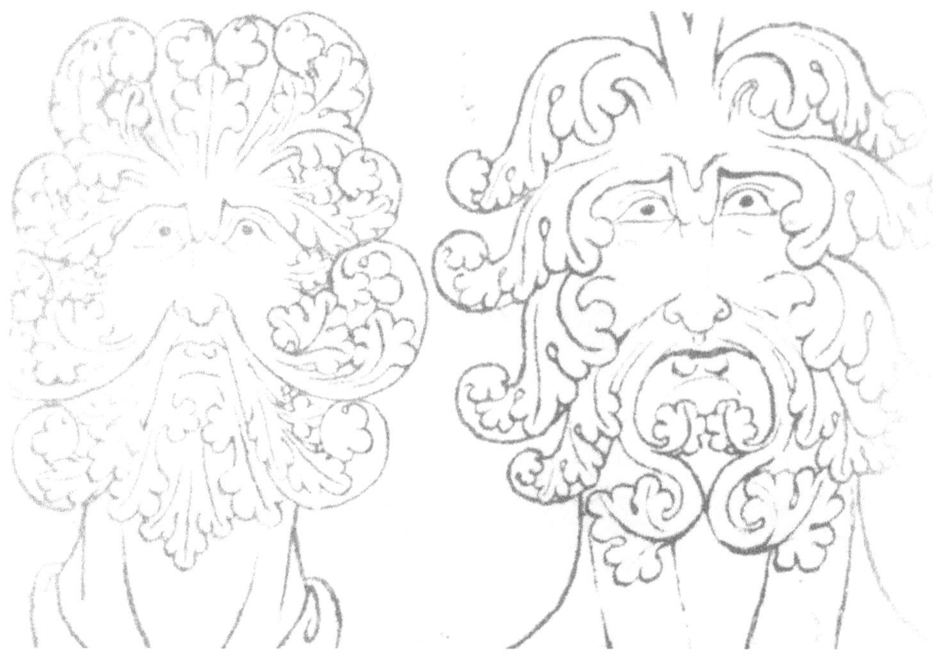

Fig. 169. Head in vegetation, early thirteenth century.

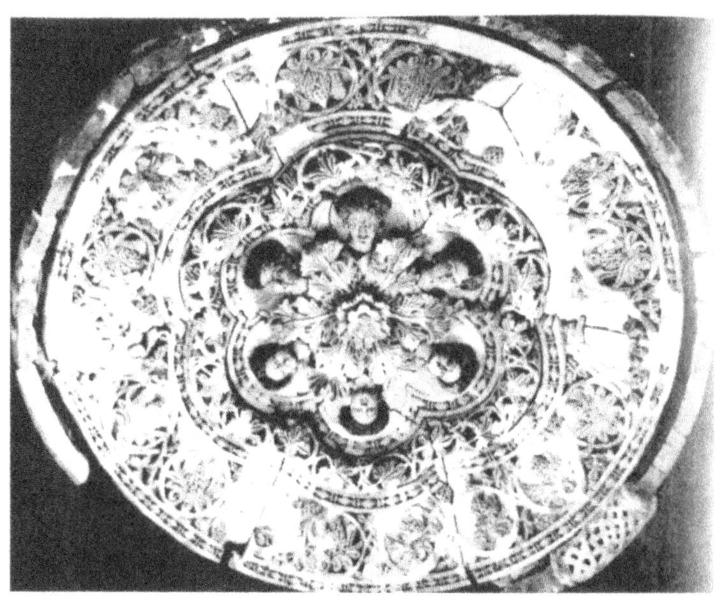

Fig. 170. Khirbat al-Mafjar, stucco ceiling, eighth century.

CHAPTER V

The Intermediary of Nature

AMONG Villard de Honnecourt's celebrated sketches from the early thirteenth century, a particularly strange one shows a head emerging from or transforming itself into a vegetal capital (fig. 169). In the eighth-century ceiling of an early Islamic palace male and female heads are alternately sculpted on a bed of leaves, which looks suspiciously like a fancy head of lettuce artfully laid open in a fancy Parisian *marché* (fig. 170). In the Roman Ara Pacis, the great Augustan monumental altar of the first century already mentioned in the first chapter of this book, half of the relief decoration is of elegantly composed leaves and flowers (fig. 22). On medieval Iranian or Mesopotamian metalwork, ceramics, or architecture, letters often end with flowers or leaves, and a whole style of writing has been called "floriated" Kufic, because of the flowers that emerge out of or transform letters (figs. 41, 57). In the earliest examples of Indian temples or in the Buddhist art of Gandhara from today's Afghanistan, the latter possibly with Mediterranean memories, a luxuriant vegetation emerges with some of the visual functions of organizing space I have discussed in dealing with architecture (fig. 171) Jessica Rawson has quite convincingly argued that Buddhism brought vegetal motifs into Chinese art.[1] This importation had spectacular results, as can easily be demonstrated through much later blue and white wares (figs. 172, 173), which flooded the world with plants and flowers arranged *à la chinoise*.[2] Altogether, it would seem, all artistic traditions on the Eurasian land mass developed designs based directly on the representation of nature, of plants and animals arranged in all sorts of ways and with varying degrees of approximating reality.

It would be nearly impossible to make a coherent list or a simple analysis of all the techniques used to represent plants and animals, of all the times and places when such representations occur, and of all the ways in which they appear. It is, in fact, difficult even to identify the edges or boundaries of the presence of nature or of natural features in artistic creativity—that is to say, to

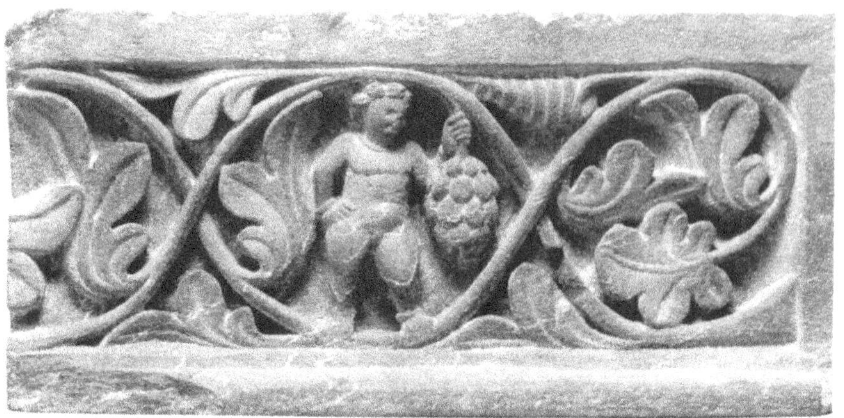

Fig. 171. Stone Relief, Gandhara, British Museum, 1951. 5–8.1.

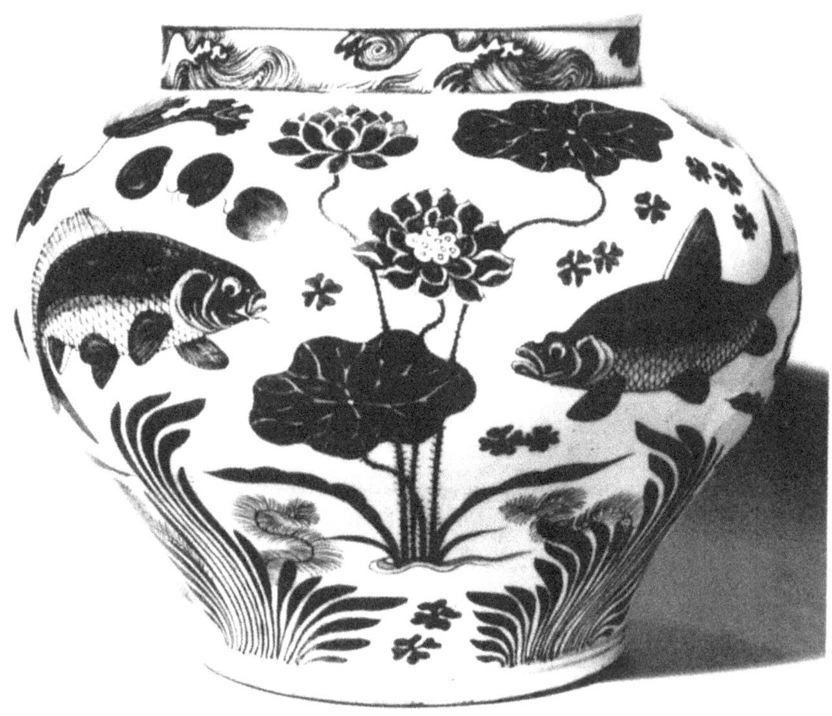

Fig. 172. Wine jar, China, Yüan period (1280–1368). Brooklyn Museum, 52.87. Gift of the Executors of the Estate of Augustus S. Hutchins.

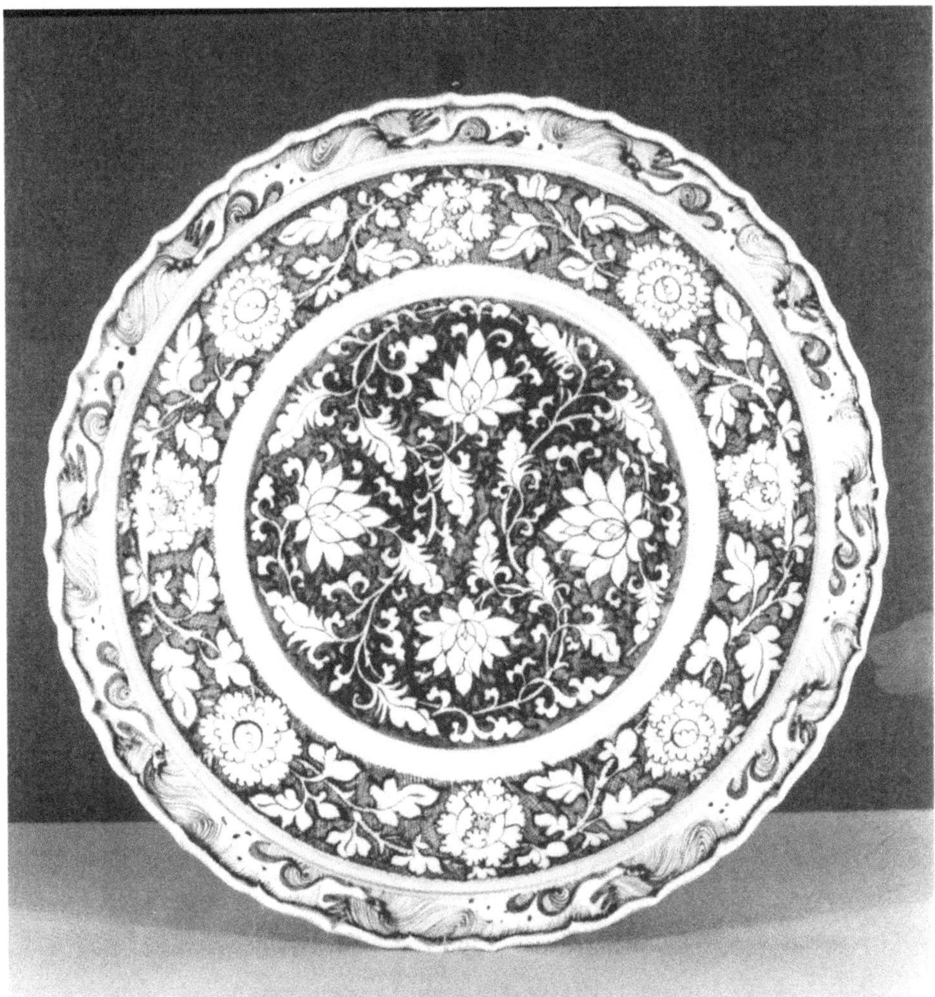

Fig. 173. Blue and white plate, China. London. Victoria and Albert Museum, 786–1894.

distinguish between a motif to be understood as representation of something and the simple addition of a floweret to a letter or to a building.

Let us consider the animation of scrolls in late antique mosaics or ivories (fig. 174), thirteenth-century metalwork in western Asia (fig. 60), and on Persian or Mughal rugs (see pls. 21–23, fig. 186). Whole or partial people and animals are overwhelmed by the vegetal setting, at times almost transformed into flowers or leaves.[3] They pop out, often unexpectedly, from stems, petals, and leaves, or, like so many trophies, are hanging on a vegetal net. The modifications brought to a presumably coherent natural world are startling enough to make us wonder whether nature or incoherence is the subject of these motifs.

Architectural space, whether constructed or imagined, is another domain for unexpected appearances of natural themes that are difficult to understand. Nearly all buildings that exemplify the grand traditions of supports on

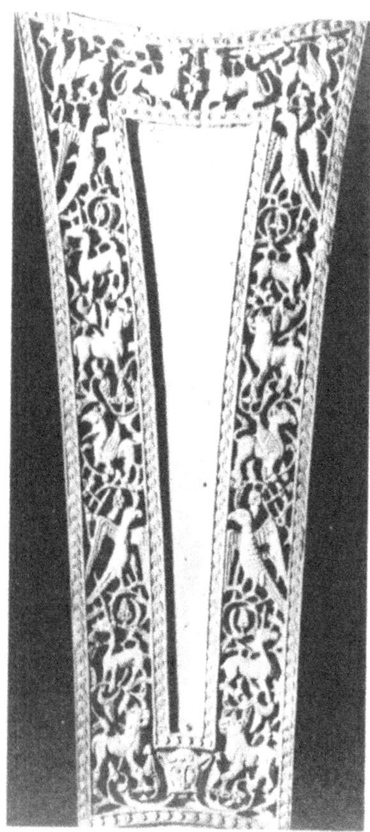

Fig. 174. Arm of Processional Cross, end of tenth century. Madrid, Museo Arquelogico Nacional.

columns and of elaborate two-dimensional facades begun many millennia ago in ancient Egypt never ceased to elaborate on and to refine capitals or friezes with perennial acanthus leaves, vine rinceaux, and lotus flowers drawn and redrawn according to endlessly honed canons.[4] After the Middle Ages, when images of men and of a mimetic nature predominate, a glorious garden of imaginary nature serves as a rug or as a platform for the Madonna of Stefano da Zevia (fig. 175), while one of Leonardo's most beautiful Madonnas sits in the midst or in front of rocks.[5] During the same sixteenth century, the small mosque of Rustem Pasha in Istanbul is almost entirely covered with polychrome tiles that transform some segments of walls into majestic carriers of trees in gardens (fig. 176), while others are covered with running or repeated scrolls or leaves (fig. 177).[6] And, if geometry seems to predominate in nonrepresentational floor mosaics of Roman or late antique times, vegetal themes are close seconds, as they are in the earliest monument of Islamic architecture, the Dome of the Rock. There, just as in Rustem Pasha, large trees (fig. 178) are

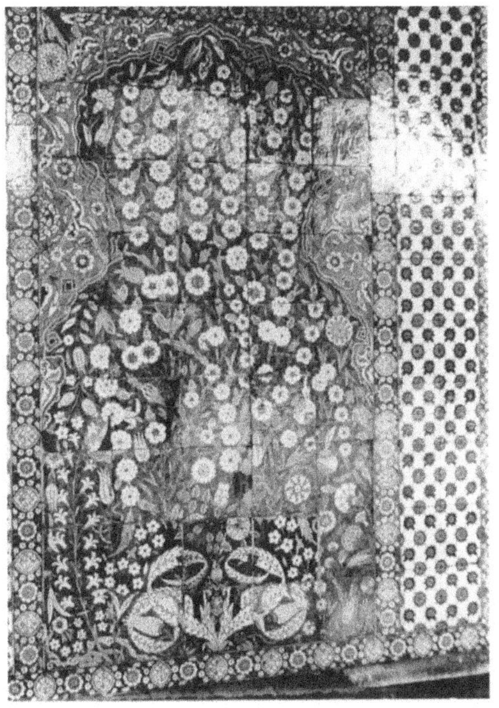

176

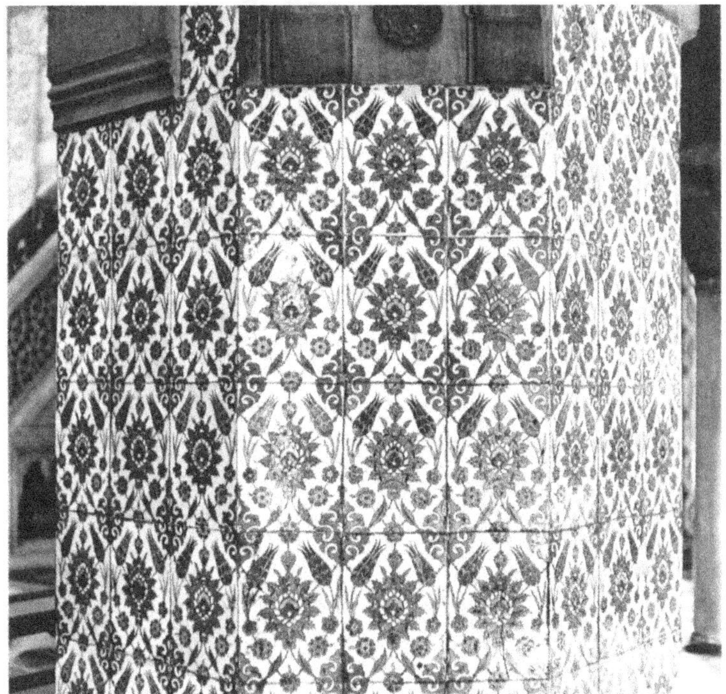

177

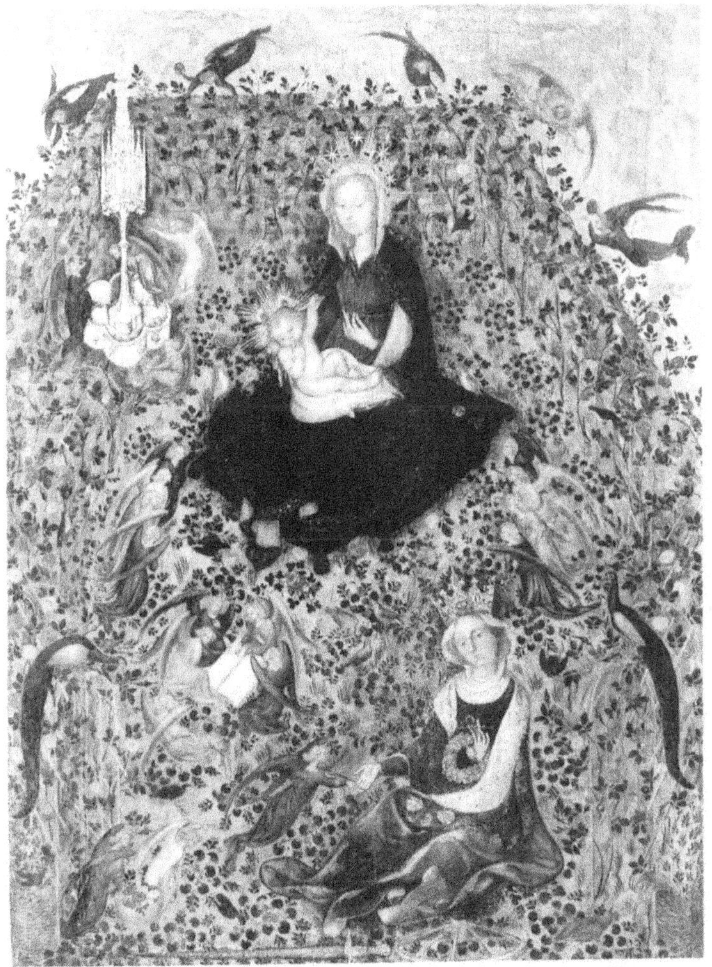

175

Fig. 175. Stefano da Zevia, *Madonna in a Garden*. Verona, Museo di Castelvecchio.

Fig. 176. Istanbul, Rustem Pasa Mosque, sixteenth century, tile decoration.

Fig. 177. Istanbul, Rustem Pasa Mosque, sixteenth century, tile decoration.

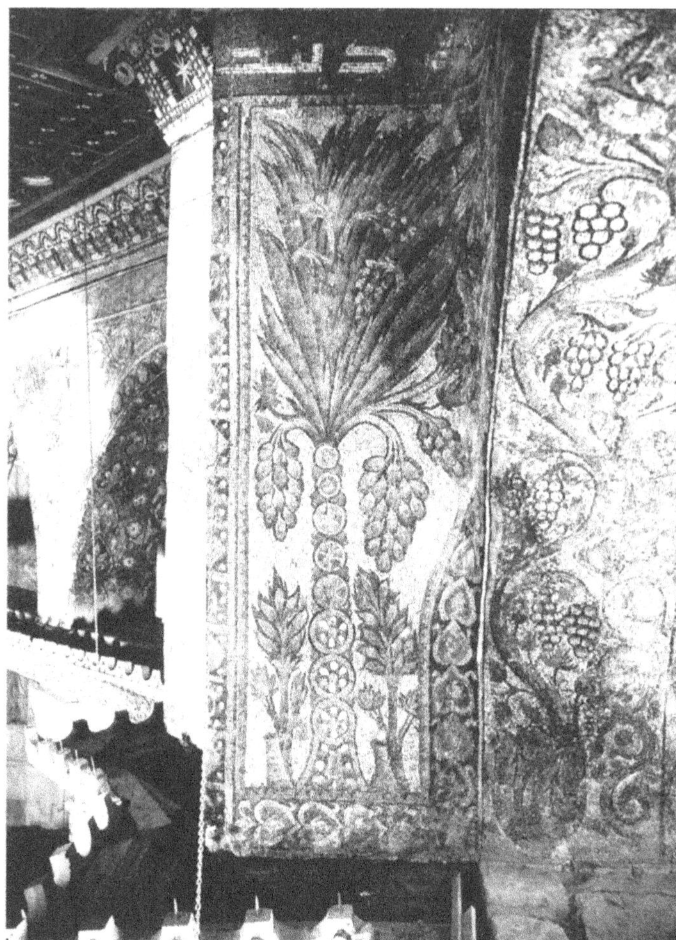

Fig. 178. Jerusalem, Dome of the Rock, mosaic decoration, trees.

found alongside scrolls and other combinations (fig. 179) adapted to the spaces provided by the builders.[7]

These last examples from Istanbul and Jerusalem are unique major works of art and, therefore, not entirely appropriate for the statement of a general problem, but they do illustrate the ubiquity of nature in the most varied of settings. Nature is found in single paintings or in whole buildings but, most of the time and certainly at first glance, is not an essential part of the monument's narrative purpose or expected use. If we add to these examples of formally recognized works of art the myriads of chairs, clothes, curtains, china cups, book covers, or wallpaper that surround us now, as they have for centuries, with constant reminders of flowers, stems, or leaves, it is difficult not to be overwhelmed by these waves of natural features, absent only from the most severe creations of "modern" artists, decorators, and architects.

In grammars of ornament, types of vegetal ornament are on a par with geometric ones. There are seventy-nine of them as against seventy-one for geometry in Lucia Valentine's book on ornament in Western medieval manuscripts,[8] a statistic not entirely accurate, as the categories into which motifs are

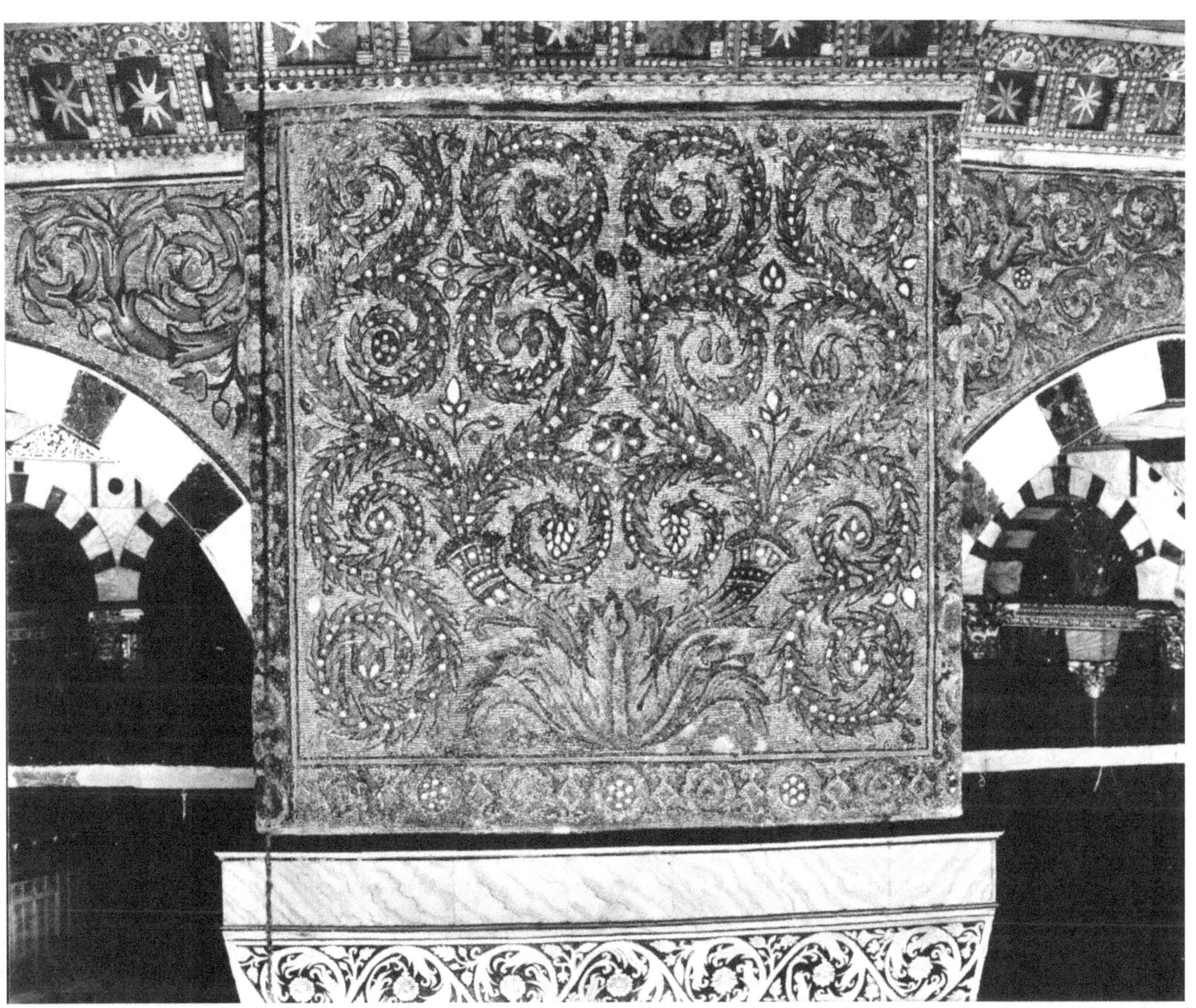

Fig. 179. Jerusalem, Dome of the Rock, mosaic decoration, scrolls.

divided are not always clear, nowhere near as clear as the geometric shapes so neatly identifiable by algebraic formulas. The point, however, is clear enough, that flowers, leaves, and stems—copied from nature or modified from natural examples, at times even totally invented, and all of them composed in thousands of different ways—are a truly universal occurrence. To all these traditional and historical examples, one can even add contemporary ones in advertising. In the supplement to a rock and roll magazine published in 1988, an interior decorator portrays himself draped in wallpaper of lush vegetation and stuck like an antique bust on another wallpaper design (fig. 180).[9]

How does one handle this immense amount of data? And what does it mean? How can one know what it means? Its very richness and variety explains why so much of the scholarly effort spent on vegetal ornament has consisted of taxonomic identifications of elements, of endless classifications, occasionally the establishment of derivations and sources, thereby illustrating the traditional art historical assumption that the genetic makeup of works of art or of individual motifs suffices to explain them. In the instance of themes issued from nature, the genetic approach has also been affected by the regional, at times even racial, associations made with these themes.[10] Without necessarily agreeing with these particular conclusions, the existence of families of natural motifs with a diachronic history is, of course, largely true and all the pursuits after further and more elaborate origins are worthy indeed and should be continued. But the query and the argument of these essays are different, as I am trying to understand the way or ways in which a generalized and often repetitive fabricated world of forms issued in this case from nature serves the comprehension, the use, or the perception of a given object. I am not so much interested in excerpting a motif and examining its variants as in knowing what an existing ornament based on vegetation has done to its carrier, at least in the eyes and feelings of the viewer. In line with the arguments developed so far with writing, architecture, and geometry, the theoretical argument or assumption of this book is that all the transformations of nature I have listed briefly are psychologically and visually related to each other and that *in their use* they form an intermediary zone between user or viewer and work of art. Is it reasonable to draw this conclusion and to hypothesize that certain ways of handling and showing nature are also intermediaries in the perception and understanding of visual forms?

AT ONE END OF the spectrum of nature in art, there lies the representational landscape that transforms nature and vegetation into a subject matter. These landscapes can be of something that exists and can otherwise be identi-

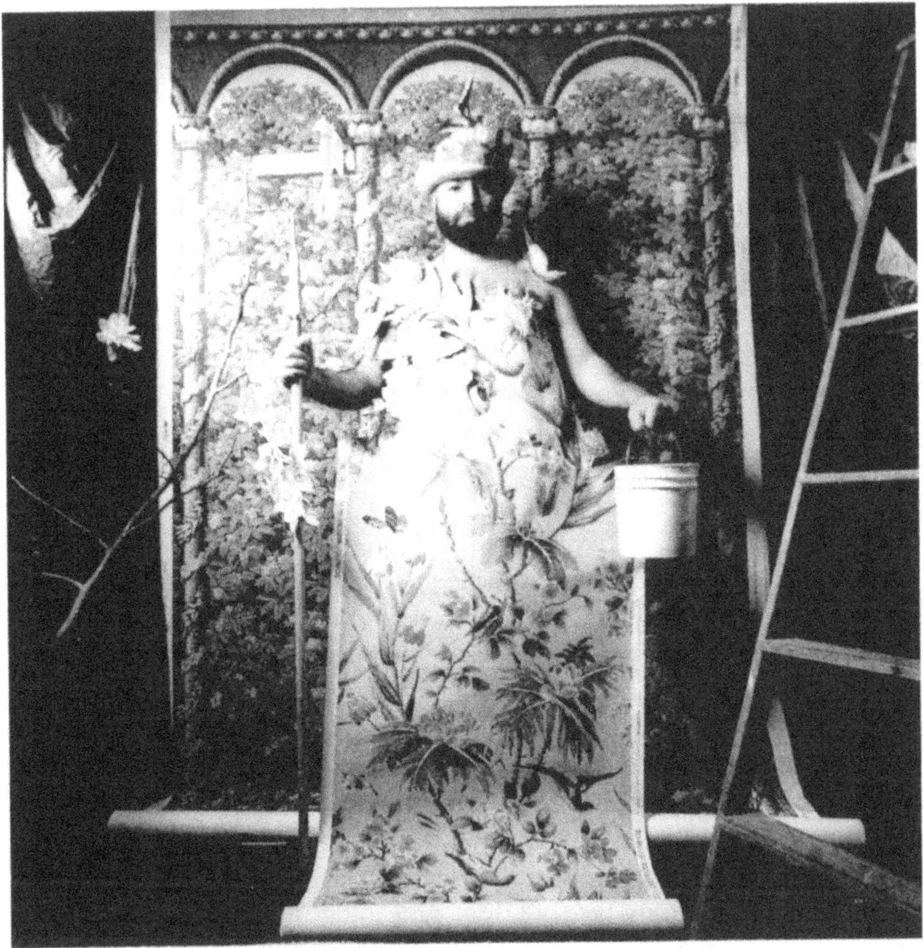

Fig. 180. Advertisement from a magazine of the 1980s.

fied, like Monet's garden at Giverny or the Mont Ste. Victoire so often depicted by Cézanne; they can also be fictional or imaginary, as with seventeenth-century rustic or noble landscapes filled with huts of peasants or with magnificent ruins. They can be creatively mythological, as with representations of Paradise in Christian art or of the colorful settings for Persian epics or lyrical meetings of lovers. What is created in all these examples is an entity that is totally completed and closed both visually and intellectually or psychologically. One can imagine another haystack in a painting by Monet or in the landscape that inspired him, and there can be another cow in a peaceful bucolic scene by Troyon or by Constable or else another pinkish rock at the edges of Persian land. But these additions, while possible, are not necessary to the paintings we see. Haystacks, cows, or fancy rocks are essential to the paintings, but the paintings do not lead the viewer back to a specific bucolic place in time, to a scene of harvest, or to an imaginary mountain. If there are values in and expectations of these paintings, they do not lie in the reenactment of a depicted moment, but in something else, the play of colors, the technique of showing a detail, the arousal of imagination. Even if natural settings may have appeared to express these values best, the values themselves are not exclusive privileges of nature alone.

Other uses of nature are very precisely iconographic. Trees, grass, or flowers are often needed to identify a setting or to support an event. The story of Adam and Eve in Paradise requires a tree, and thirteenth-century illustrators of Arabic secular manuscripts liked to keep their personages standing or seated on a thin band of grass, whether the text required a natural setting or not.[11] In a more general and much fuzzier way, a more or less hypothetical idea of a Tree of Life has been proposed (I would not say demonstrated) as an explanation for the image, fairly frequent since ancient Mesopotamian times, of single trees on buildings, miniatures, or textiles.[12] The example of the tree with the serpent in the garden of Eden is a straightforward instance of the necessary identification of a nature-derived topic through a single and non-negotiable referent. The Tree of Life illustrates a more elusive symbol, whose connotative rather than denotative power is often in the eye or mind of the beholding scholar rather than in the understanding of the user or maker. True symbolic interpretations are difficult to maintain without many more references and arguments than we usually possess. The same doubts can be expressed about a ubiquitous Tree of Life as a meaningful and consistent subject that were argued earlier about geometric forms like the circle requiring cosmic and solar explanations. But it is possible to grant that there is with vegetation, as with architecture and geometry, a peculiar zone of low charge, whereby certain formal units—a tree, a flower, the intimation of a garden—can, under certain conditions, be given evocative meanings, but these meanings are not necessary attributes of these forms.

Two examples may make my point somewhat clearer. In an often quoted but little-read book published over thirty years ago, the Finnish scholar Lars-Ivar Ringbom argued for the pervading presence, through late antiquity and the Middle Ages, of the myth of Paradise as a usually mountainous garden with animals romping in a setting of real or imagined vegetation (fig. 181).[13] This myth or belief would have inspired large-scale architectural or landscape compositions. Ringbom imagined that the original Paradise would have been located in the striking site of Takht-i Sulayman in Iranian Azerbayjan, where indeed air photographs brought out a stunning monumental settlement around the lake of an extinct volcano. Excavations neither confirmed nor

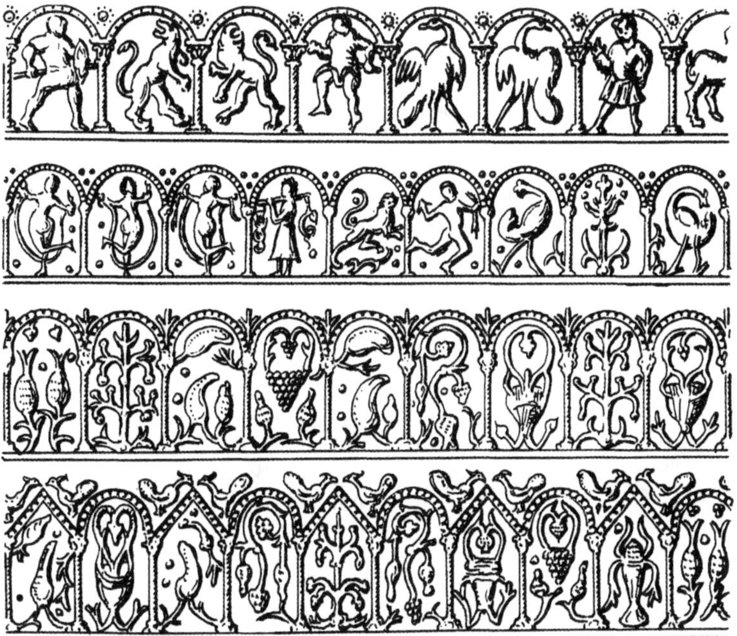

Fig. 181. "Paradisiac" type of scene on a silver or bronze plate.

denied Ringbom's hypothesis, as a huge Zoroastrian temple was discovered but, to my knowledge, without information about landscape.[14] The more exciting aspect of the hypothesis was, however, that the theme of Paradise would be visible in objects, especially in the midst of the strange and still not very well understood "Oriental" metalwork (fig. 182).[15] This myth may have had ancient Mesopotamian sources, it may have affected Roman art, but it is during the confused centuries from the fifth to the tenth in northern and western Asia that images allegedly related to the myth would have slipped into the palaces of kings, the objects of princes, sarcophagi for everyone, drinking cups or chalices.[16] Every scroll became a Tree of Life if it was vertical, as at Taq-i Bustan (fig. 183), and every bird or horned beast was eating at the source of eternity if set symmetrically around a tree and in the vicinity of a pond or of a river.[17]

It is easy enough to parody these interpretations, as all allegorical images can be made into jokes, especially if their original contexts are lost or if one no longer believes in whatever inspired them. Occasional parodies should not hide the more fundamental fact of the possibility, perhaps even likelihood, for paradisiac interpretation. There are enough references in religious texts, in secular poetry, in pious or worldly oratory and narrative literature, and in official statements like inscriptions or titles to justify an all-pervasive associa-

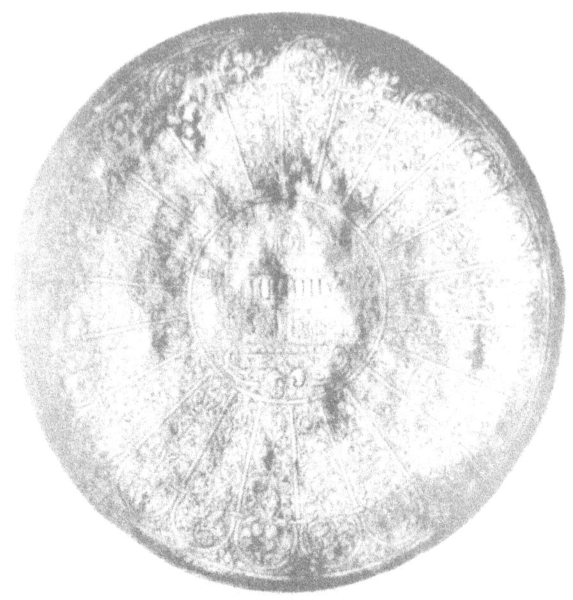

Fig. 182. Bronze plate, seventh–ninth centuries. Berlin Museum.

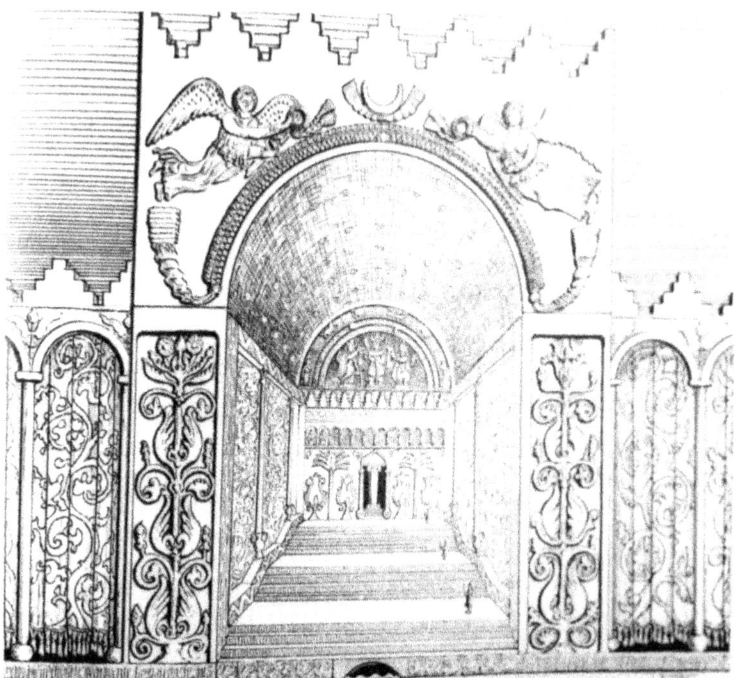

Fig. 183. Taq-i Bustan, "tree" on the side of facade, Iran, sixth or seventh century.

tion of nature, inhabited or not by animals, with the external referent of Paradise.[18] In line with the argument I developed in the previous chapter with architecture, I would call this function an evocative one. It recalls meanings without compelling them. It transfers the decision of how to understand a work of art to its viewer or user.

It may be useful to recall at this stage the distinction made earlier between a game and a liturgy. Both have prescribed rules of behavior and of utterance from which one should not deviate, but in a liturgy the outcome is always known in advance, whereas in a game it is not. A purely iconographic interpretation with general agreement and no need for further discussion is a liturgical procedure for artistic creativity, whereby the organization and operation of forms lead to a result known in advance. Evocative manipulation is, on the other hand, like a game and the outcome is never quite known. There are rules for representation or, in general, for making available and visible whatever topic was chosen, but the probability of a paradisiac (or any other) meaning can never be demonstrated.

The argument can, of course, be made that such uncertainties of interpretation are merely the result of contemporary ignorance, itself created by insufficient information. In reality, according to this argument, all those images on silver or bronze objects from northern Europe and Asia and spaces like Taq-i Bustan were culturally valid and meaningful as precisely as Christian or Buddhist spaces and imagery. It is only that we can no longer read them properly. This may well be true, and yet there is much about the character of this evidence, both visual and literary, in western and northern Asia before the eleventh century, that makes one wonder about the likelihood of a purely iconographic explanation. For instance, almost every example is nearly alone of its kind, which argues for an absence of commonly accepted types. Or else many details lack in the clarity one usually expects of an iconographically focused representation. Contemporary written sources tend to work by allusion rather than to describe spaces or buildings. It may indeed be that the remote and scattered cultures of this vast area had not reached the critical mass of artistic and intellectual activities needed for more than an art evocative of more general concepts.[19]

My second example of themes from nature with a low charge of meaning is quite different. One of the many exciting absurdities of Romanesque art is the manner in which the capitals of its columns, especially in cloisters like Silos or Moissac (fig. 184) were decorated.[20] Within a sequence of consecutive capitals, perfectly clear or very obscure references to sacred texts or to pious narratives and powerful symbolic summaries of the Christian faith are inter-

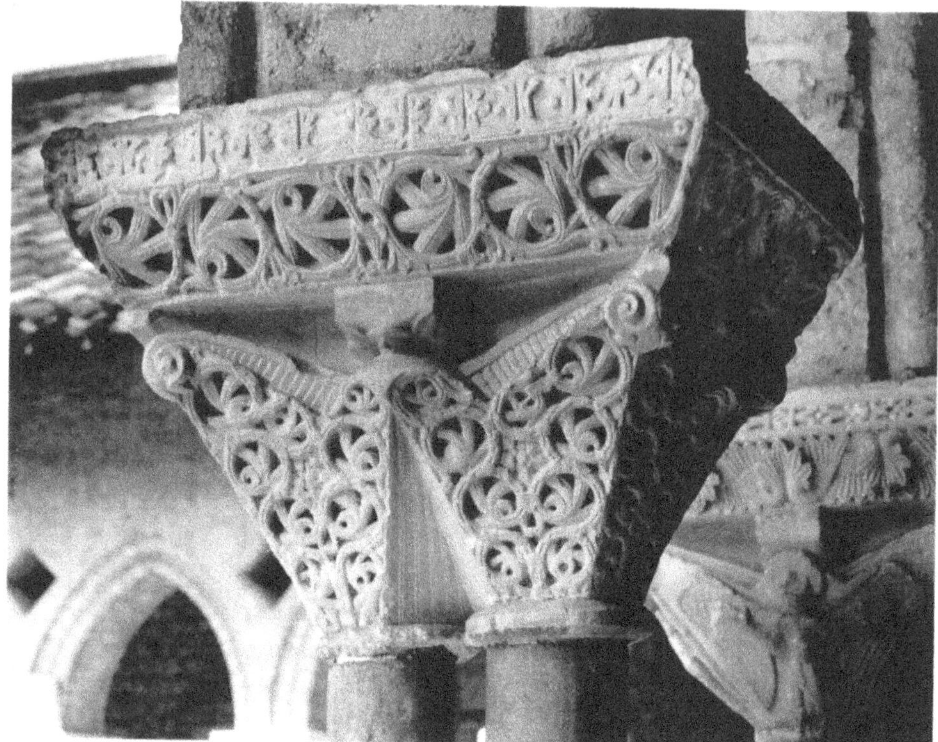

Fig. 184. Moissac, cloister, twelfth century, capital.

rupted by floral designs, which seem to be *mere* ornament, to have no external referent except at best a model book (fig. 185). If concrete meanings are given to the decoration of some capitals, should one not assume comparable meanings for all of them? Or else, perhaps, the location of all these themes, both narrative and ornamental, in places other than those of liturgical purpose diminishes their value or their charge, and it is the iconographic capitals that would have lost some of their specificity. *All* of them, regardless of subject, are more important for what they do to the three-dimensional space of the cloister, to the ways in which behavior is to be regulated in that space, than for any specific topic depicted of them. For instance, at Moissac the capitals accompany the action of someone walking and the speed of the walk affects the perception of the capitals. Like signs on highways, they are constant reminders of things already known or expected, with occasionally a novelty or an anomaly, a surprise that may even require a stop. Vegetal or other themes issued from nature could simply be flashing warnings for more concrete statements, or perhaps signs in their own right, such as intimations for rest and respite. For reasons entirely different from the ones affecting allegedly para-

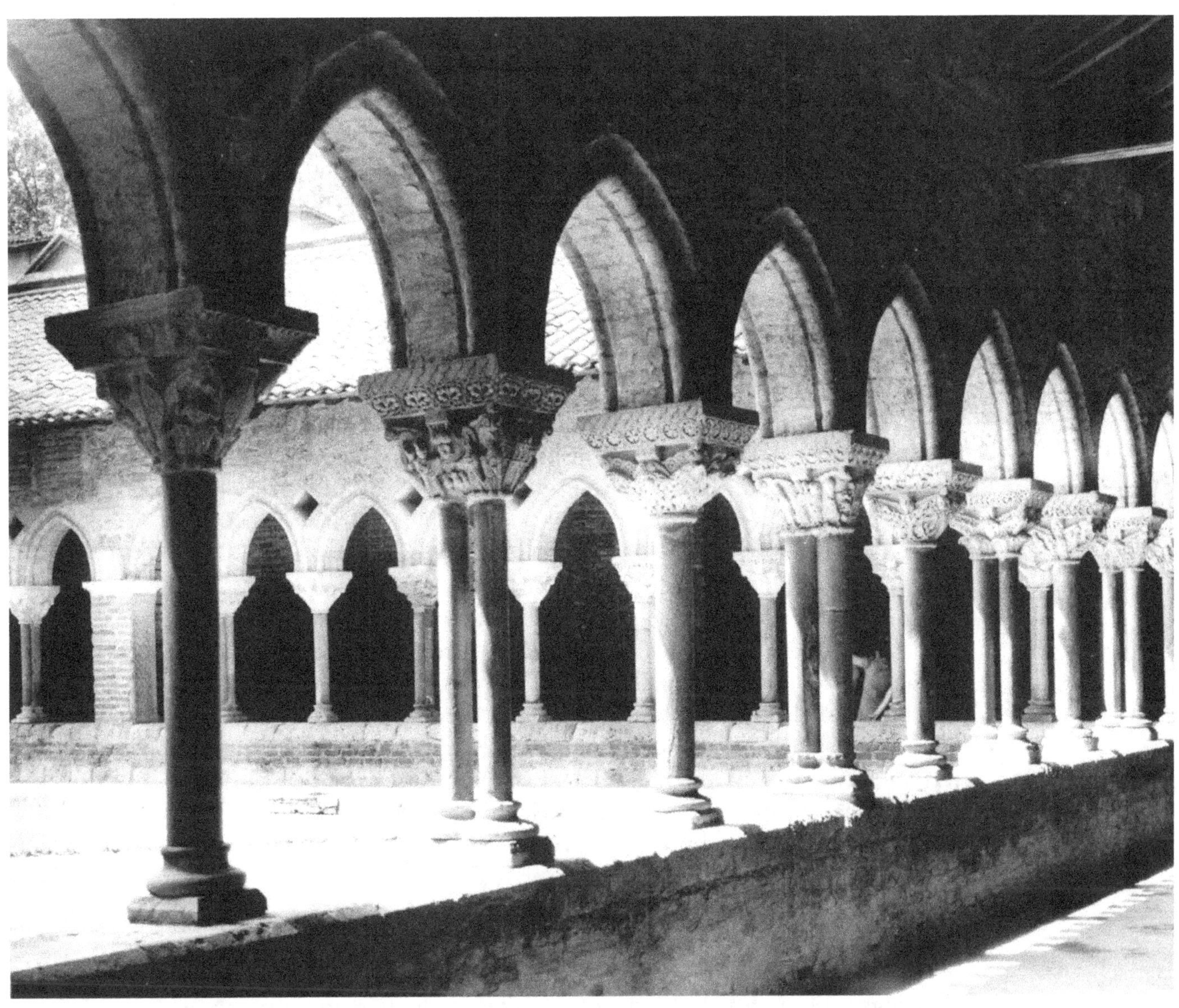

Fig. 185. Moissac, cloister, general view.

disiac trees and other plants, the natural elements of the Romanesque cloisters also appear with uncertain meanings. Their association with deeply charged images lifts their potential, while their location modifies the point of view from which they, as well as the iconophoric ones, should be understood.

For as ubiquitous a theme as that of nature, it, thus, becomes essential to understand properly the issue of "points of view." There is the common and obvious art historical principle that every work of art creates and demands for its greatest effectiveness awareness of one or more levels for viewing and appreciation. The apparent but not necessarily accurate corollary is that the quantity of points of view is indicative of the depth of meaning of the monument.[21] Whether acceptable or not, this is not the methodological direction that pertains to the reasoning of this chapter. What does matter is that, whereas architecture, geometry, and writing were always (or almost always) identifiable as such and could be focused on immediately, images of nature or of vegetation can with equal ease vanish into patterns or impose themselves as concrete and forceful things. Pattern is clear in the ways in which tendrils transform themselves into circles on the eighth-century Mshatta facade (figs. 23, 24) or surround a medallion, and even in the representation of living beings on a thirteenth-century inlaid ewer or cup (figs. 25 or 72). But it is not an exclusively Islamic phenomenon, as similar patterns existed in classical antiquity (fig. 22) and in Gothic windows (fig. 19). Alternately, monumental capitals and friezes can occasionally provide a breeze of fresh air in a darkened interior, as can be imagined for the so-called windswept capitals of northern Syria in the sixth century and for so many friezes outlining or framing architectural forms or sculpted ensembles in Gothic cathedrals.[22] These examples all imply that the operative point of view is quite literally the place from which one views the motif (as opposed to a place created in order to view it) and thus, consciously or not, that location and the activities connected with it (sitting or walking, for instance) determine the meaning of that which one sees.

Altogether, we are faced with something perplexing. Vegetal or natural decoration is found everywhere. It may have meanings, but the charge of these meanings varies a great deal and is often quite low. It often breaks monumental logic in buildings and there is some uncertainty about how to look at it, how to see it, and, therefore, how to interpret it.

THE DISCUSSION of four specific objects, very different from each other as objects and in their ways of handling vegetal decoration, will serve as an introduction to a more general hypothesis about nature as ornament. The objects are a celebrated rug in the Boston Museum of Fine Arts (fig. 186, pls.

Fig. 186. Silk "hunting" carpet, sixteenth century. Boston, Museum of Fine Arts, 66.293.

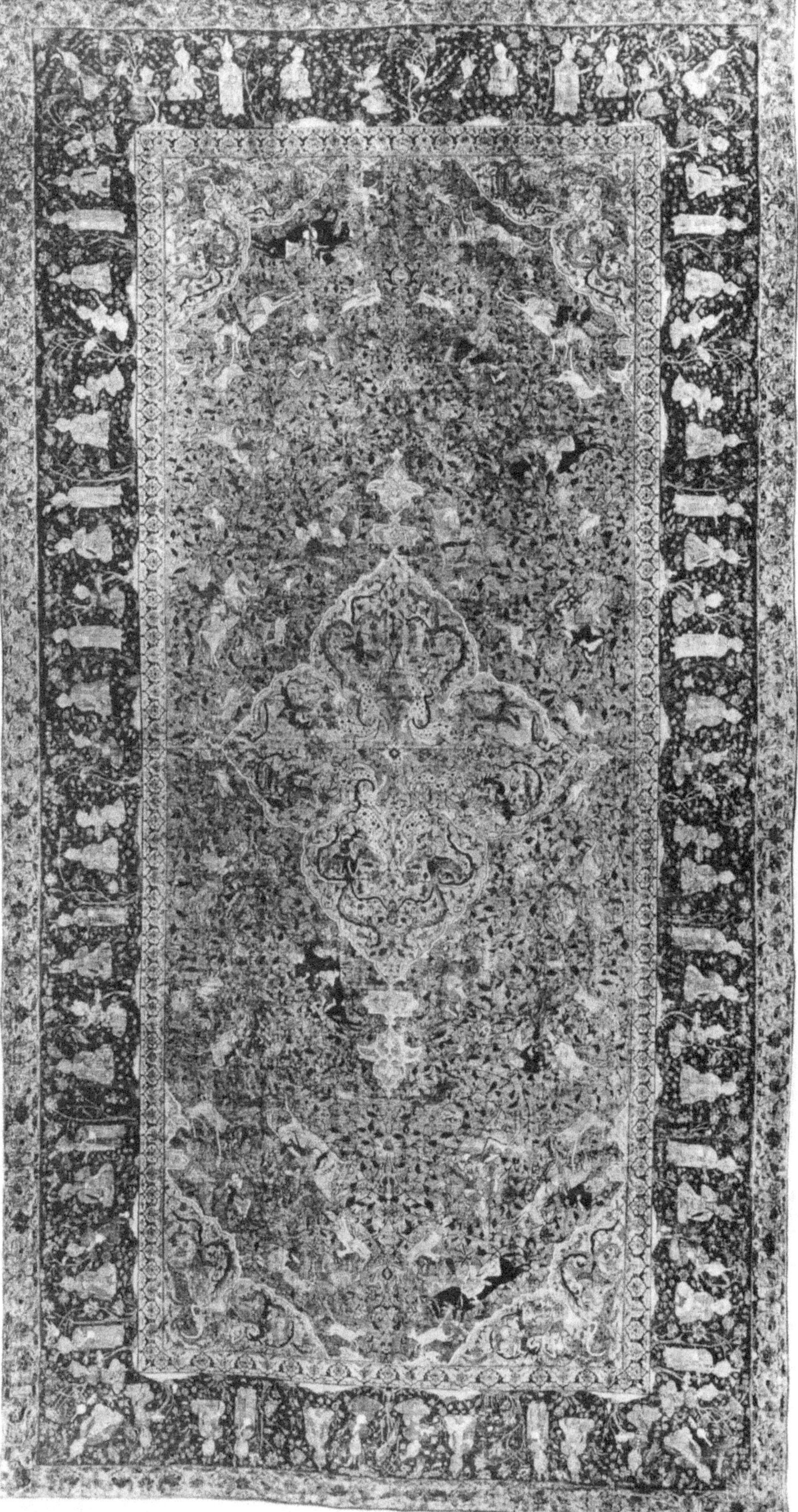

21–23), a group of blue and white ceramics from China and the Ottoman world (figs. 188–90), a few pages from manuscripts (figs. 191–93), and finally the facade of Mshatta (figs. 23, 24, and 195), the perennial standard-bearer of any discussion of ornament derived from nature and a monument mentioned more than once.

The so-called hunting carpet in the Boston Museum of Fine Arts is one of the major masterpieces of Safavid art in its heyday in the middle of the sixteenth century.[23] It is 15 feet, 9 inches long (4.80 meters) and 8 feet, 4 inches (2.55 meters) wide. It has three borders (or a border divided into three parts) serving the purpose of framing (fig. 186) so skillfully analyzed by Sir Ernest Gombrich in his work on ornament. The first and narrower border consists of a continuously repeated design of flowery stems creating a rinceaux with a large central artificial arrangement of leaves and petals framed by birds turning their heads away from the axis of each unit (pl. 21). The second border, over a darker red background, has elegantly clad figures in or over a field of trees, leaves, and flowers; they look like Persian leprechauns hiding in or stepping on a fantasylike nature. The figures are standard types of Persian painting: drinkers, cup or food bearers, conversationalists. Wildly colored birds fly around or perch on trees and occasionally a pitcher appears abandoned or forgotten near a tree (pl. 22). The third border is more repetitively rigid than the first one, with its continuous light and dark stems interlaced with each other in almost geometric precision and rhythm.

The central part of the rug contains a huge medallion with a highly symmetrical and geometricized structure of stems and leaves carrying fabulous birds and dragons (pl. 23). In the four corners a less rigid structure of more flexible stems and more natural leaves, if not flowers, hides riders hunting animals, at times involved in hand-to-hand combat with them. Additional dragons fill the very tips of the corners. To assess the rug, it is essential to note that the central section reverses the color scheme of the border. In the latter, lightly colored trees or people contrast with a dark red background, whereas the central design had a light, today slightly discolored, yellowish background with natural features, dragons, animals, or people in darker, often red, colors.

There is more than one way to interpret these mesmerizing designs and the rug that carries them. We can, for instance, follow the model of Schuyler Cammann's work on Iranian and Chinese rugs[24] and see in this rug the evocation or even the representation of an idealized and eternally beautiful and eternally composed setting, something akin to Paradise. In it the life forces of what Cammann calls the Sun-Gate are symbolized by the dragon-birds in the corners, which, so to speak, proclaim the vision of God's real Paradise. It is easy enough to find in the Koran and in Persian mystical literature citations to justify a vision of Paradise in natural terms.

The most compelling examples for the purposes of this particular rug are Koran 76:5–6 and 12–22:

> Surely the pious shall drink of a cup, whose mixture is camphor,
> a fountain whereat drink the servants of God,
> making it to gush forth plenteously
> . . . .
> and [God] recompensed them for their patience with a garden,
> and silk;
> therein they shall recline upon couches
> therein they shall see neither sun nor bitter cold,
> near them shall be its shades, and its clusters hang meekly down
> and there shall be passed around them vessels of silver, and
> goblets of crystal,
> crystal or silver that they have measured very exactly.
> And therein they shall be given to drink a cup whose mixture is
> ginger,
> therein a fountain whose name is Salsabil.
>
> Immortal youths shall go about them;
> When thou seest them thou supposest them scattered pearls,
> When thou seest them thou seest bliss and a great kingdom.
> Upon them shall be green garments of silk and brocade; they are
> adorned with
> bracelets of silver, and their Lord shall give them a pure
> draught.[25]

It is easy enough to imagine the figures around the border as "immortal youths" holding "vessels of silver and goblets of crystal" and contemplating the "fruits, and palm-trees, and pomegranates" (Koran 55:59) of Paradise. Jalaluddin Rumi and Attar, the great mystical poets of the thirteenth century within Iranian Islam, portrayed trees and shrubs, and especially flowers as eternally praising God or praying to Him. "See the upright position from the Syrian rose," writes Rumi, "and from the violet the genuflection, the leaf has attained prostration: refresh the call to prayer!" Or, in an even more striking passage, Rumi proclaims that "grace is from God, but the worldly people do not find grace without the veil [of a] 'garden.'"[26]

Finally, two of the four carpets known to have belonged to the same group as the Boston one were given originally to the Safavid dynastic shrine at Ardebil in northern Iran. It could thus be argued that a religious or holy purpose was required for this carpet and that it was an expression of piety associated with appropriate behavior in a shrine.

But there are two overwhelming arguments against interpreting the decoration of this carpet as the iconographic or even evocative representation of religious feelings or ideas. The first argument is that this type of interpretation is based on the assumption of a very particular kind of religious structure, one without a divinity and full either of dragons and demons or of abstractions like the *Tao*, the Way of Chinese philosophers and sages. This kind of religion is, I believe, quite alien to the Islamic faith, in Shiʿite Iran or elsewhere. Islam was always strongly based on the proclamation of the Word and of a divine Message, and it developed a relatively small number of religious or pious signs, none of which are present in this rug.[27] The second argument is that both the composition of the rug and its structural components serve to defuse and to diffuse the attribution of concrete, strong, meanings to any part of it. Repetition, whether by symmetry as in the middle of the rug or by sequential adjunction as on its border, diminishes the impact of that which is repeated, even if the repetitions are not always identical. The absence of thematic hierarchy between the constitutive "morphemes" (or smallest identifiable units) of the rug leaves only contrasts, as between colors or background and design, as easily perceptible fixtures. It requires a great deal of sophistication to see the divine in abstract contrasts—and neither the pattern of likely use nor the users themselves suggest the presence of this sophistication on or around the rug. Thus, even if genetically related to some religious theme, the actual carpet has little to do with any faith, because its motifs are so unhierarchical and so equalized across the field of vision, and because no sign or symbol clearly associated with the faith is apparent on it.

A second interpretation for the Boston carpet was provided during the colloquium held twenty years ago shortly after its purchase. I shall state this interpretation in a somewhat more forceful way than appears in the published record of the colloquium or in my recollection of it. It is a functional interpretation that imagines members of the court of Shah Tamasp and the emperor himself so to speak "alighting," as one speaker put it at the time, on the rug. They land in a decorous space in which personages like themselves are watching, as in a movie or rather in an old-fashioned diorama, an elegantly absurd hunt. Wherever they land, they know that their experience is the same as everyone else's, because the segment of the object that they are able to see contains items like borders or corners that imply a symmetrical arrangement and therefore a repetition in mood, if not actually in kind. This practical interpretation is appealing in the sense that it makes the rug common, almost trivialized. To understand the border as a series of fancy place names at a contemporary reception for elegant courtiers ready to drink and eat, perhaps to converse and to listen to poetry, certainly befits the sensuality of the rug and makes it accessible both visually and as an actual object for practical use. Forms of secondary significance, like courtiers in various activities, or plants, are treated so as to enhance the pleasure of conviviality, to recall or to compel specific actions.

There are many fifteenth- and sixteenth-century miniatures to substantiate a practical, aristocratically social, interpretation for this and other similar rugs, as there are literally hundreds of examples of personages seated on rugs, eating, drinking, listening to music or the recitations of various types (fig. 187).[28] This second explanation is far more satisfying to a historian than the

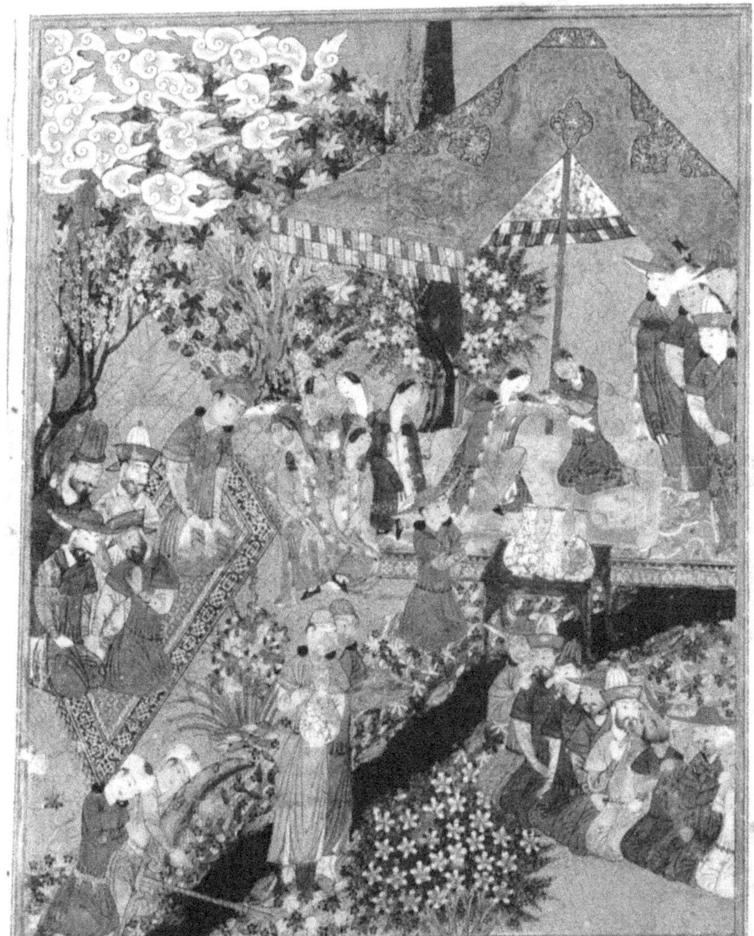

Fig. 187. Frontispiece, *Shahname,* Iran, circa 1444, half of double page. Cleveland Museum of Art, Purchase from the J. H. Wade Fund, 45.169.

first one, as it is confirmed by external sources, both written and visual, and we can easily exercise our imagination in inventing a life of pleasure on a carrier of pleasure. Yet I remain skeptical of this interpretation almost as much as I was of the first one. For, like the first explanation (or perhaps only slightly less so), the second one picks a few, primarily mimetic, elements out of the rug, develops an interpretation of these elements, and then puts them back into the rug with a vague iconographic explanation extended to the whole rug. This is not, I believe, the right way to look at this or any other carpet, neither as a contemporary exercise to satisfy the impact made by the rug nor as a proposed reconstruction of an elusive past.

The first striking feature of this rug is the visual and, in general, sensory power of its physical components, what may be called its materiality. I do not mean by that the number and kind of knots found on each one of its square inches, but the physical excitement of its fabric, even worn. Its silver threads are meant to shine and, quite independently of its designs, the fabric of the rug breathes with the life of its constituent parts (pl. 23). The rug's second feature is the peculiar nature of the perception we get of it. It can be the luscious general view of something colorful but, seemingly, always somehow out of focus because distance diminishes the precision of what one sees (fig. 186) or else it is a mass of wonderfully detailed flowers, animals, and schematically cutout people strewn on red or yellow grounds (pls. 21–23). Each viewer or user decides on his or her own at what stage of approaching the rug satisfaction, pleasure, perhaps satiation, even saturation occur within one's understanding of the object, or, better yet, one's involvement with it. In reality several stops are possible in handling the Boston rug. The viewer can stay with the stems delicately swerving around and suddenly eliciting out of nowhere a flower, a horse's head, a human, or a bird; he can travel through the rug, observing it in time, like a narrative experience without a story. Or else the eye or the hand (in fact even the foot) can pick up a whole section of the rug and feel its arrangement. With great difficulty, at least the eye can try to see the whole rug from above and at a distance. Each one of these possibilities is visually incompatible with any other one and there is no way of encompassing all parts of the rug, so to speak optisemically, to use the term coined earlier.

Next to sensory materiality we have, thus, a choice of possible but incompatible ways of focusing. And the third feature of the rug is that the viewer-user penetrates into the object, both literally, as rugs are meant to be walked on, and perceptually, as the eye meanders its way through its design. He becomes part of its structure and begins to play with its forms, to follow rinceaux or to decompose flowers. At this stage it no longer matters much whether kings and courtiers played here or whether some mystical message is encoded, for in reality it is only the sensory pleasure of seeing, feeling, composing, and recomposing that dominates. And it does so, because of a setting taken from nature that has nothing to do with any real nature, just as the people or animals are not common beasts or men in common activities. They are all in a dream, they are an imaginary fantasy. They are totally unreal and yet they are stems, leaves, animals, and flowers.

One could argue, of course, that these characteristics are all deeply bound to the culture that produced them and that poetry or even social customs and modes of social exchange also exhibit artificial and contrived expressions that use terms or gestures from common life.[29] Stems and personages would be two-dimensional and simplified because they are meant to be seen as unreal and because the natural world is to be perceived as fragmented and, therefore, as an invitation to something else, to another experience. The objection I have to this position is its assumption or implication that the value of a design can be—even should be—understood independently from the object on which it occurs. Any explanation of the rug that lessens the value of its materiality is likely to be inaccurate.[30]

Rugs and other textiles used for clothing or for thousands of household or ceremonial purposes are particularly consistent users of themes from nature. But other practical industrial arts are equally rich in such themes, as appears in ceramic objects of premodern times, for instance the celebrated blue and white pottery from China (figs. 172, 173) and western Asia (fig. 188), and a few examples of Ottoman ceramics relatable to but also very different from Chinese and Iranian counterparts (figs. 189, 190). Much has been written about the classification of these objects, about the origins of the technique, and about the relationship between series in different lands. Occasionally, an iconographic motif has been analyzed.[31] But it does not really help much to know that a specific plate is dated circa 1560 and that its decoration shows a series of stems originating from a single tuft of grass, organizing the circular space through their swerving growth, with large or small red flowers punctuating, almost randomly, the space around them, and a single long leaf, almost like a peapod or an insect, with a number of small red and white dots (fig. 194). Such a description is almost meaningless or rather without purpose; even if it is accurate, its only point is to be an exercise in transfering what one sees into a written discourse. Like all such transfers (rather than translations), it is meaningless in the same way that a Hungarian text is meaningless but legible to someone ignorant of the language, because phonetic accuracy can only be reproduced, not described.[32]

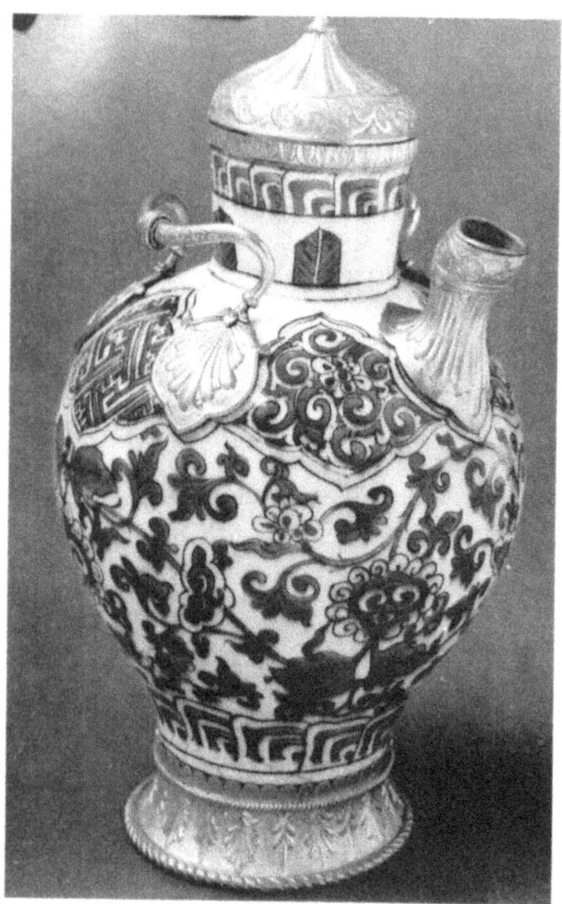

Fig. 188. Blue and white ceramic, Iran.

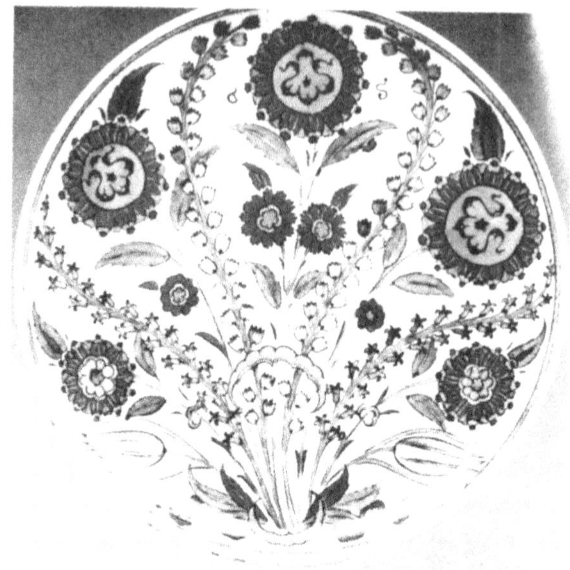

Fig. 189. Iznik plate, Ottoman, sixteenth century.

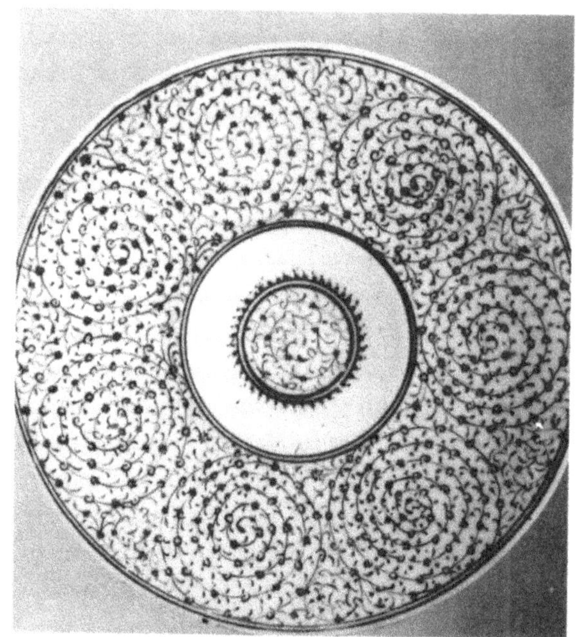

Fig. 190. Iznik plate, Ottoman, sixteenth century.

Once again, the issue is, in this particular object or in any collection of comparable objects from all over Asia, not in the identification of a motif, but in the sensory reactions to order and plan or to a perpetual circular motion (fig. 190), to dark colors, to a festival of lines, to contrasts between colors—in short, to a translation of the vegetal world of the design into definitions of being or of becoming, not to a transfer of forms from one arbitrary code to the even more arbitrary one of speech. A given ceramic *has* reds and greens, its design *becomes* a whirl or else it *is* asymmetrical. The distinction is a grammatical one as verbs of being and becoming are different from verbs of action, the latter being either descriptive (the leaf touches the flower) or iconophoric (a tulip means love). But it is not enough to agree that a statement of being or becoming is an appropriate attribute of these designs. For the designs themselves only fulfill *their* purpose if they lead the viewer or the user to behave in some way or other toward the object, to fill it with fruits, to bring some pastry on it, or to hang it on a wall. The decisions to use the object and perhaps how to use it derive from the interpretation of natural features compelled by its design and it is some properties of natural forms that made these escapes from them possible, even necessary.

I shall return shortly to what these properties may be. But a few additional examples taken from other realms than those of the industrial arts are still important in order to corner the issue better. Let us look at two pages from a mid-fifteenth-century *Shahname* preserved in the Gulbenkian Collection in Lisbon (figs. 191, 192),[33] chosen from among hundreds of possible examples. The text is written in elegant *nastaʿliq* script and is quite legible once one has learned to handle the script. As happened often, titles of sections are set out in gold in narrow rectangular tablets and decorated in a rather simple-minded and not particularly exciting way. These routine, high-quality texts are then framed by a broad margin in which several layers of ornaments occur without necessarily appearing on both pages: a thick-lined geometrically defined link or backbone, which blossoms occasionally and always ends with flowers or leaves; a miniaturized, almost invisible, rinceau of stems with flowers of many different shapes and colors; a thicker rinceau with very realistic animal heads, not unlike what we have seen earlier among rugs (fig. 186); two elaborate cartouches with clearly written but quite unnecessary mentions of the title of the book; and, on one of the two pages, a group of angels engaged in most unusual and hitherto unexplained activities. These angels need not occupy us in the context of these essays, however curious they are. Our concern is what this ornamentation of the margins has accomplished or is accomplishing for the pages of a book. Visually it is distracting, as it di-

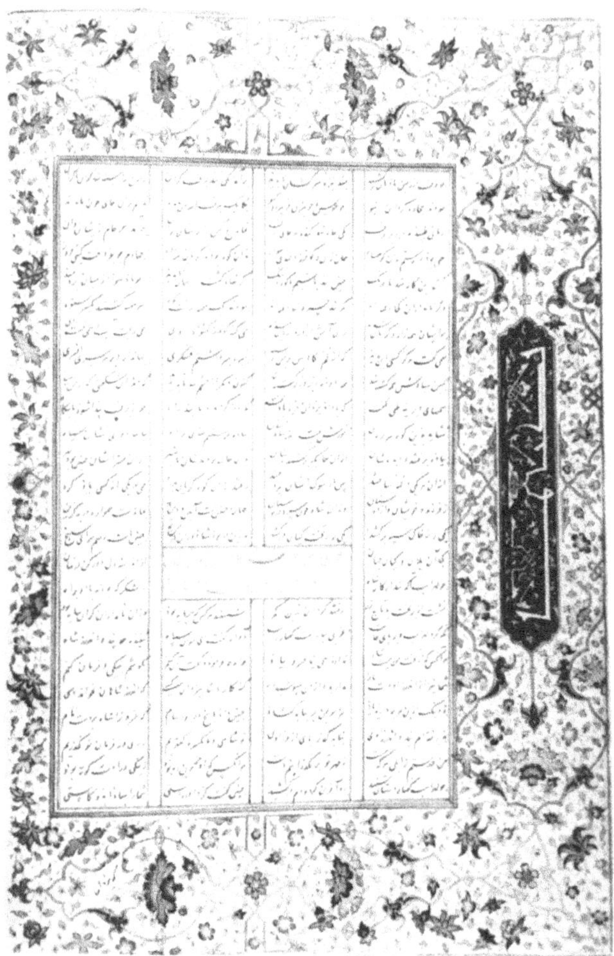

Fig. 191. *Shahname* page, fifteenth century. Lisbon, Gulbenkian collection.

Fig. 192. *Shahname* page, fifteenth century. Lisbon, Gulbenkian collection.

minishes the immediacy and accessibility of the text. Like some of the architectural settings in Christian manuscripts that were discussed in the previous chapter, this orderly natural border may well have been meant as a means to honor a text, but there is nothing unusual about the text on this particular page and we have, therefore, to assume that a whole book had been (or was meant to be) decorated in this elaborate fashion. The natural ornament, thus, served to enhance the book, not a page. It proposes the pleasure of holding, viewing, or owning a book by suggesting a ruglike setting that can be perceived at once rather than experienced piecemeal. The texture of the ornament diminishes the potential to read, but emphasizes correctly the book and not the text as a work of art.

Such natural motifs were often mixed with geometry, although the neutrality of geometric forms helped to reduce the naturalness of the vegetal ornament. The point is of some philosophical interest if one recalls Worringer's ancient theory that original geometrical designs were "naturalized" over the centuries, especially in classical times, only to be liberated again by traditional Islamic art.[34] I hesitate, of course, by temperament and belief, to accept a type of reasoning that attributes ethnic meanings or associations to forms, but Worringer may have recognized a relationship between geometry and the representation of natural ornament that may well deserve further thought. For it is true for Lenôtre's gardens in Versailles as well as for Persian manuscripts that one way of taming nature and natural forms is to force them into the artifice of geometry. Such a transformation increases the impact of every part of nature that is represented.

In all comparable cases, as in the magnificent front pages of the Ibn al-Athir manuscript in the Chester Beatty Library (fig. 193),[35] in many Timurid

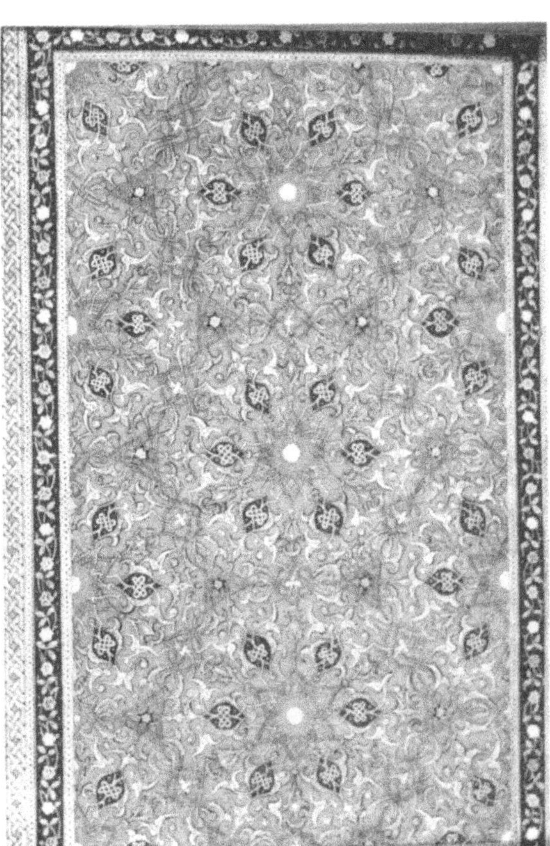

Fig. 193. Ibn al-Athir, *History*, frontispiece. Dublin, Chester Beatty Library.

metal objects (fig. 194),[36] or for vegetal ornament in or on objects of relatively small size, perceived at one glance, the eye is more rarely than with rugs concerned with the mass of details, the movement of a stem, or the shape of a leaf. It is for technical reasons that these motifs are also different from those of ceramics, for, as Jessica Rawson has pointed out,[37] errors in design are almost impossible to correct on ceramics and therefore standard types are more frequently repeated and the almost infinite minification of details is less frequent than on metalwork or manuscripts. In the latter mistakes in manufacture, errors in design, and clumsy repairs usually abound.

Thus, in addition to the taxonomy of motifs found on the designs, the appreciation of the nature of vegetal ornament requires the consideration of such characteristics as density, points of view, and size, probably among many other features of a work of art. Nowhere are all the issues of vegetal ornament better expressed than in the celebrated Mshatta facade, the eighth-century monument from the Jordanian steppe now preserved in the east Berlin Mu-

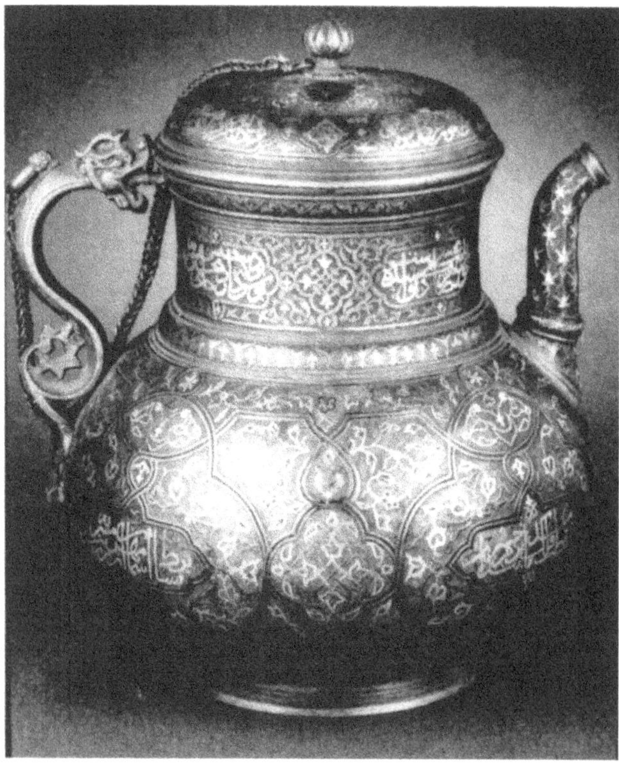

Fig. 194. Brass jug inlaid with silver and gold, 1467, Herat (?). Istanbul, Museum of Turkish and Islamic Art, no. 2961.

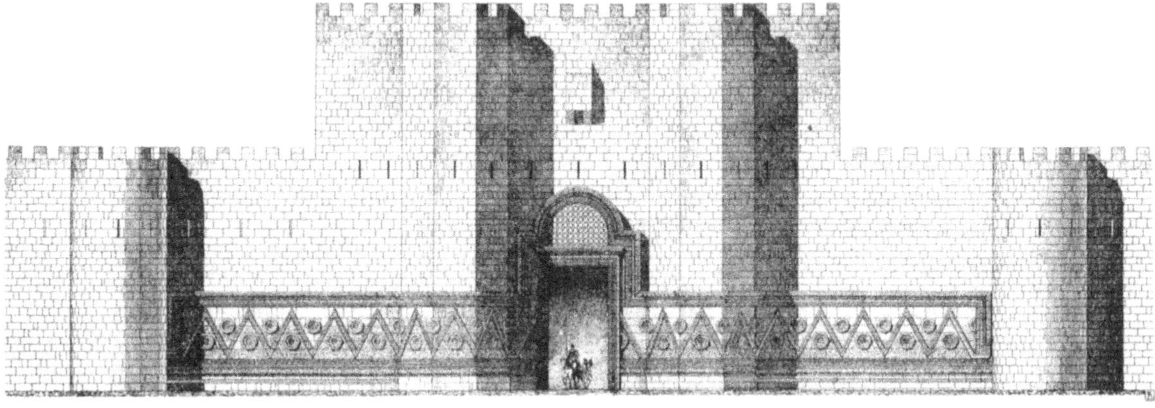

Fig. 195. Mshatta, facade, reconstruction.

seum and mentioned already at the beginning of this book.[38] Here twenty immense (3.5 meters high) stone triangles (figs. 23, 195) are carved across the front of a palace, like an immense arbitrary band signaling some rank, some importance, some value to the building behind. In spite of many efforts, no one has been able to discover a valid iconographic theme for the facade, and scholarship has dwelt mostly on the taxonomy of vegetal and other forms on it and on their origins. Ultimately, regardless of the usefulness of these descriptive and genetic studies, it is necessary to face the broader point of how the facade was seen and what did vegetal ornament do to it that other types of ornament would not have done. Just as with the ceramics, where the impact is immediate, vegetal ornament in Mshatta is a means to create from a distance the effect of luxurious texture, of orderly coherence, of light and shade on a facade facing the brilliance of the Near Eastern sun. There may have been other effects as well. None of them pertain to specific elements of the design; all are essentially abstractions outlining the sensory impact on and pleasure of the eye. It is the result that was achieved with writing and geometry in fifteenth-century Iran, primarily with geometry in the Alhambra, with architecture in Christian canon tables, or in Palladian facades.

But why vegetation? Is it simply *one* of the intermediate forms from which a patron, an artist, a craftsman, or a time can choose the one best fitted to a time, to a monument, or even to the taste or competence of an individual, patron or artisan? The answer to this question must be negative. Vegetation is too ubiquitous and too consistent to have been simply one of the alternatives available over the centuries. A better answer is, I believe, that vegetation had one attribute not available to any of the previously discussed intermediaries. It suggests or evokes life. Without *representing* life, it provides a sense of growth and movement, a feeling of those life forces on which traditional and contemporary Chinese art critics dwell so much when they talk about art.[39] It is precisely because it was life that it had so often to be tamed, by geometry for instance (fig. 111). But it always burst out, for vegetation or nature is at the same time the most common and most recalcitrant of all intermediaries. It transforms everything it touches into something else than itself or than the object on which it is found. It always leads elsewhere and yet hauntingly comes back as an evocation of life, as a form that, most of the time, appears in movement, as though, like life, it had a beginning and an end. Some of Ruskin's or of Focillon's most eloquent pages proclaim their joy at the sight of acanthus leaves adorning a capital.[40] Both writers were unusually sensitive to those aspects of artistic creation in which neutral and cold stones or bricks, simple wooden beams, two-dimensional wall surfaces, or modest capitals are made to vibrate because of flowers, stems, animals, even fabulous monsters from a fantasy nature.

The ornament issued from nature is perhaps a true demon in the special sense of active and essential intermediary given to the word *daimōn* by Plato. Chinese artists and their imitators in Iran, Turkey, or the West were aware of its demonic quality as they gave dragonlike writhing shapes to vegetal scrolls or perhaps saw a dragon in every scroll (fig. 196).[41] For ornament from nature, however and wherever it is perceived, always leads elsewhere than toward itself, it mediates between the viewer and the work of art or else between the user and the actions he or she may undertake.

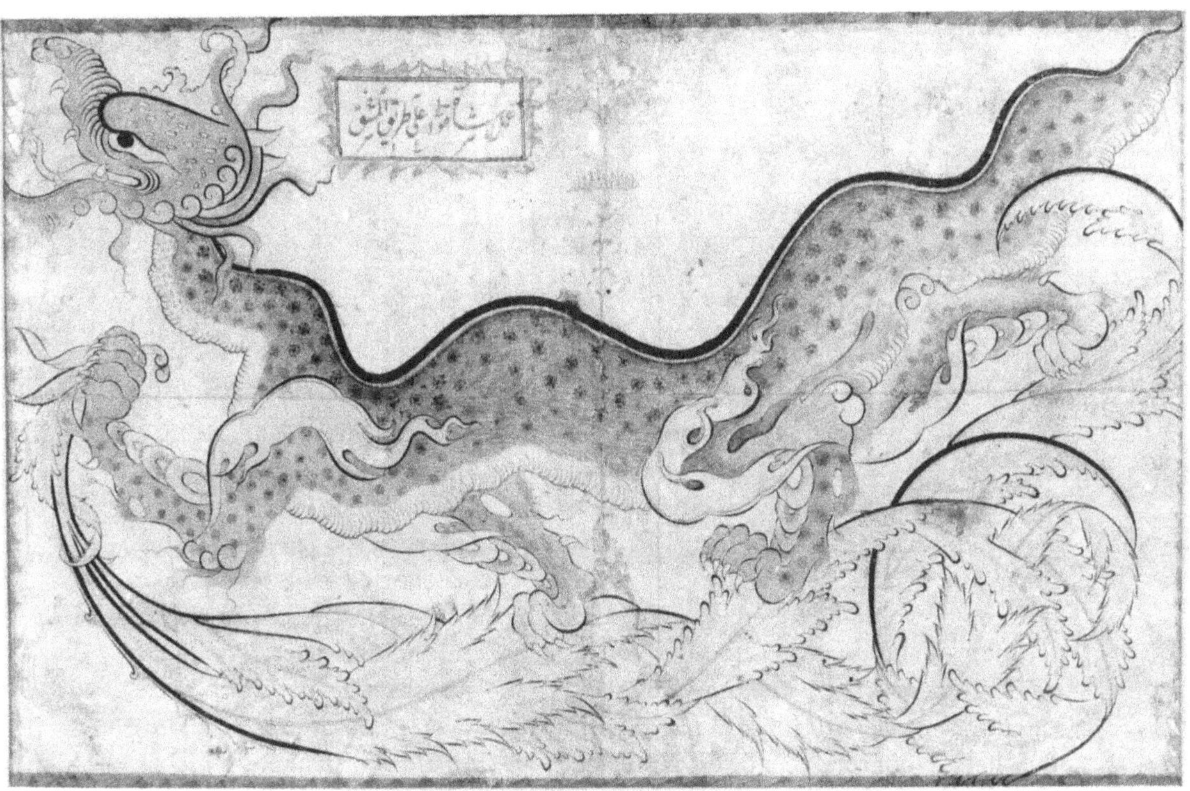

Fig. 196. Shah Kuli, drawing of a dragon, Ottoman, sixteenth century. New York, Metropolitan Museum of Art, bequest of Mrs. Cora Timken Burnett, 1957 (57.51.26).

CONCLUSION

Some Implications

THERE WERE three premises to these essays and each premise or assumption implied a number of questions. One initial assumption was that most of the traditional approaches to ornament tend to be taxonomic. They order and classify, as in large tables of forms with names that occur in so many grammars of ornament (fig. 26) or else they argue about categories of functions like framing or linking defined, among others, by Gombrich. These approaches are all in reality ways to identify certain technical functions operative in the perception or in the making of works of art and of artifacts. What these categories of classification and of description state is nearly always accurate, but they do not reflect an often expressed characteristic of ornament, which is that, in the logic of esthetic hierarchies, it alone among the forms of art is primarily, if not uniquely, endowed with the property of carrying beauty and of providing pleasure.[1] Such, at least, seems to be the consensus of books and encyclopedias about the function of ornament. How can one reconcile such a high ambition with the Linnaean classificatory character of most work on ornament?

The second premise was a more hypothetical one, that ornament (or whatever we call ornament) does not really consist of tangible and identifiable forms, because all forms can be manipulated into meaning and the most specific of iconophoric subjects can be drowned in ornament. The case of the swastika, a fairly common geometric form for decoration (fig. 116) in many cultural traditions, illustrates how presumably innocuous forms can acquire deadly associations, while the so-called "Antioch chalice" or other similar late antique, early Christian, and medieval Islamic objects bear examples of highly charged images almost transformed into ornament. If ornament does not lie in the specificity or precision of forms, yet exists and has alleged esthetic values, it, I proposed, consists in a number of probably but not necessarily finite intermediaries between the object, the work of art, on the one hand, and the viewer, the patron, maybe even the maker, on the other. These intermediaries, which I compared to the "demons" of a celebrated Platonic passage, are included in the work of art even though they are not truly part of it. They are instead filters through which messages, signs, symbols, even probably representations are transmitted, consciously or not, in order to be most effectively communicated. The major part of the book was devoted to the further analysis of four of these intermediaries—writing, geometry, architecture, and nature—with the ultimate expectation of identifying and explaining a particularly important, or so I argue, aspect of the ways of making and perceiving works of art.

There was a third assumption underlying my lectures, the assumption that there are universal modes and values in the perception and appreciation of the visual arts, even though nearly infinite variations occur in different places and at different times. The point of this assumption is that those times or places which, for whatever reasons, make particular use of certain intermediaries—like geometry, for instance, in the case of the Muslim world—do lead to conclusions or judgments valid for other areas and other times. The passage from one area or period to a different one seems always difficult to the professional who feels secure in the coziness of factual information he or she controls alone. But the public who buys books or goes to exhibitions acquires knowledge and impressions from many fields and times and truly partakes of all artistic achievements. There is a discourse about the arts, rarely written and at times unspoken, which is neither that of historians so deeply tied to time and space nor that of critics concentrating on personal views about the arts or on contemporary judgments about whatever it is that they see. It is the discourse of sensibilities affected by the excitement of visual impressions, it is a discourse of love. The choices and the judgments made in this discourse also depend on visual or intellectual and emotional intermediaries, which may or may not be those of history. Could they be the same as those of ornament? Do they operate in the same fashion? And how justified is it to argue for universal principles when judgments of pleasure or of dislike are not made according to formal scales or curves but according to other psychological, emotional, and intellectual criteria?

Writing turned out to be an incredibly complex mechanism of visual transmission. Several different terms were proposed, other than calligraphy, for its manifold uses and, most particularly, the conclusion was reached that writing can be a neutral intermediary to a text, a collector's item, an ideological means for physical and thought control, a symbolic intermediary for any number of purposes with cultural variables, and occasionally a work of art that is an end to itself. Geometry appeared as a true mediator, rarely significant on its own as an object of visual expression (except for esoteric purposes like magic), but, precisely because of its lack of consistent associations, favored and exploited by the historically marginalized world of women, frontiers, poverty, and other deprived patrons, makers, and users of art and artifacts. Images of architecture, on the other hand, were shown to be unusually rich in their variants, but also psychologically and emotionally active as protectors of the holy and of the valuable, organizers into hierarchies, and glorifiers of the powerful, the rich, or the significant. Perhaps, I suggested at the end, architecture itself, the very act of building, is an intermediary form, which always circumscribes and at times enhances behavior, but which is rarely an end in itself. A somewhat similar set of conclusions was derived from a survey of ornamental themes inspired by nature, probably the most common type of ornament. But, unlike architecture with its emphasis on power and strength, natural features, I suggested, evoke life itself and thereby uplift the value and the vibrancy of whatever is associated with them.

These summaries and whatever more specific hypotheses and explanations occur in the body of the previous chapters are only partial answers to the broad questions raised by my original premises. For, in reality, the discussion of the four themes of these essays shifted questions and answers away from the simple queries of what is ornament, how it creates that beautification which is its sole purpose, and whether universal principles underlie its effectiveness. In this conclusion, I would like to outline four directions for thought that derive from the preceding pages but which extend their arguments into different and perhaps novel intellectual directions for the study of the arts. I do not try to propose full systems of visual analysis, because I believe such systems to be premature, and I have not tried to fit whatever observation I make within the theoretical and philosophical discourses with which they may eventually belong, because of my conviction that the study of the arts, historical or other, needs to analyze itself in depth before joining up with the numerous theories of understanding and interpretation that have been floating around the humanities during the past two or three decades. Some of the notes to this conclusion, as well as to earlier chapters, testify to the approaches I have preferred, linguistics and semiotics for instance, and to the ones I have avoided like social determinism and psychology. These decisions are matters of individual choice and of degrees of competence, which need no justification, since the whole point of my essays is to propose some comments on the arts in order eventually, after many studies or different theories and ideologies, to develop more sophisticated means of understanding the arts than the prevailing ones.

The four directions I will identify are mediation and intermediaries, the limits of cultural interpretations, the boundaries of ornament and reality, and the implications and some extensions of a theory of mediation for the history of art in general. They are very different from each other as well as in the potential for thought that they suggest. The first two are, in a way, extensions of conclusions that have already been drawn, whereas the last two are more tentative developments of ideas.

Mediation and Intermediaries

The basic question analyzed in this book can be summed up through a fascinating passage at the very beginning of Charles Dickens's *Hard Times*. A pompous official is visiting a school and interrogates the students about their knowledge and ideas.

> "So you would carpet your room—or your husband's room, if you were a grown woman, and had a husband—with representations of flowers, would you?" said the gentleman. "Why would you?"
>
> "If you please, sir, I am very fond of flowers," returned the girl.
>
> "And is that why you would put tables and chairs upon them, and have people walking over them with heavy boots?"
>
> "It wouldn't hurt them, sir. They wouldn't crush and wither, if you please, sir. They would be the pictures of what was very pretty and pleasant, and I would fancy . . ."
>
> "Ay, ay, ay! But you mustn't fancy," cried the gentleman. . . . "You are to be in all things regulated and governed . . . by fact. . . . You must discard the word Fancy altogether. You have nothing to do with it. You are not to have, in any object of use or ornament, what would be a contradiction in fact. You don't walk upon flowers in fact; you cannot be allowed to walk upon flowers in carpets. You don't find that foreign birds and butterflies come and perch upon your crockery; you cannot be permitted to paint foreign birds and butterflies upon your crockery. You never meet with quadrupeds going up and down walls; you must not have quadrupeds represented upon walls. You must use," said the gentlemen, "for all these purposes, combinations and modifications (in primary colours) of mathematical figures which are susceptible of proof and demonstration. This is the new discovery. This is fact. This is taste."
>
> The girl curtseyed, and sat down.

Dickens characterizes an intellectual position and a pattern of taste that are still very much with us. It is that, however immediate or derivative it may be, art is, formally or functionally, judged by its relationship to concrete reality. Art does not allow for "fancy," only for "fact."

I shall return shortly to the peculiar boundaries between reality and ornament. In the meantime, I want to point out that Dickens's fatuous gentleman acknowledged that "objects of use" and "objects of ornament" are governed by the same rules. He reflects a nineteenth-century notion, not necessarily the majority's, that opposed the hierarchization of techniques and saw or sought broad principles applicable to all the arts, whatever adjustments may have to be made in certain places and at certain times. Among these principles, one cluster deals with ornament, a paradoxical order of forms that has been (and mostly still is) indispensable yet is considered ancillary to true art and which has been the subject of this book.

In order to escape the paradoxes and contradictions implied in the passages from Dickens and discussed in my first chapter, I proposed that ornament not be considered as a category of forms or of techniques applied to some media but not to others. Instead, I suggested, ornament is an unenunciated but almost necessary manner of compelling a relationship between objects or works of art and viewers or users. Such a relationship is established through what I called intermediaries, agents that are not logically necessary to the perception of a visual message but without which the process of understanding would be more difficult. This is so, because these intermediary agents facilitate or even compel access to the work of art by strengthening the pleasure derived from looking at something. In a general way they are like catalytic agents for chemical reactions, or code carriers in genetics or biology. Specifics are, as usual and appropriate with areas involving values and human creativity, much fuzzier than in biology or chemistry. But the four examples I have used—writing, geometry, architecture, nature—function as intermediaries rather than as concrete designs because they evoke (a verb with variable charge rather than symbolize or depict, much stronger verbs of action) in viewers well-defined emotions or stances: control and forcefulness of assertion with writing, order with geometry, boundaries and protection with architecture, life forces with nature, and throughout sensory pleasure, that terpnopoietic condition central to the arts.

There are, however, two further issues involved. One is how it is that one can identify such intermediaries; are there many others? There certainly are others and one major cluster consists in the ways of ordering space or images: composition, properties, shapes, colors, and so on. Just as with the group analyzed here, these ways of ordering have an iconophoric potential, as colors like purple or structural and compositional devices like cupolas can acquire imperial or holy meanings. Both the mediatory and the iconophoric possibilities of this cluster of potential mediators need investigation. Furthermore, concepts of perception, like the generic rather than specific recognitions and identifications I identified as "optisemic," may, upon further study, be also considered as intermediaries toward full comprehension of a visual message.[2]

The other issue for further thinking is more complex. Most of the argument of this book has assumed the approximate equivalence between the activity of the maker and that of the user. The former uses forms, willfully and consciously or automatically, in order to elicit from the user reactions of pleasure through attributes that, by virtue of their function, I have called terpnopoietic, bringers of pleasure. By giving such importance to sensory pleasure, however, I may have opened up yet another little-charted area for investigation. It consists in identifying what a critic has recently called "symptoms,"[3] which I understand to be aspects or attributes (primarily sensory ones in his view) of artifacts that create an impact on the user. The point is, however, that it may not be necessary to assume an equivalence in the meaning of forms between the aims of a maker and the reactions of a user. Users, especially when remote in time or space from the creation of objects, may well develop their own set of categories in acquiring sensory or other emotions from the arts. The only certain thing is that there must be an intermediate or a set of intermediates for any appreciation of a work of art, but the nature of these intermediaries is not fixed. For instance, for the centuries of Western art after the quattrocento, style became a characteristic manner of perceiving works of art, of seeing them, judging them, and of appreciating and valuing them. In a world of individual and individualized artists, patrons, and collectors or critics, style is a true intermediary to whatever we know of *a* Rembrandt or of *a* Cézanne, without being either the subject of the work of art or its function. In this sense, style is ornament.

Wittingly or not, like users of so many computers, we are all in need of disk-operating systems to make sense of the mechanisms available to us for dealing with the arts.

Limits of Cultural Interpretation

The vast majority of the examples used in this book comprises works of Islamic art, works from the vast and complex world whose ruling ethos had derived from Muslim rule. And the argument of this book is indeed that this particular experience illustrates with unique acuity some aspect of a universal quality of artistic experience.

But there is another side to any interpretation of a specific tradition. It is whether the "universal" attributes given to its artifacts are justified within the internal, diachronic or historical, constrictions of the culture itself. Even if Escher, a painter and draughtsman of the first half of the twentieth century, or Owen Jones, a Romantic northerner active a century earlier, can be fascinated by the sensual geometry of the Alhambra and even suggest a "deep" meaning to this geometry, their conclusions are not necessarily valid for the Muslim builders and users of the Granada palace. One should become satisfied that the classical culture of medieval or pre-modern Muslim societies considered the same issues and drew comparable conclusions.

Except for the example of writing analyzed in considerable detail, no clear-cut answer can be given so far to the question whether the explanations for various visual intermediaries were (or are) in fact culturally valid. At least so it seems from published studies, for I cannot claim any sort of expertise in handling philosophical and related sources. It seems clear, however, that, beyond and separately from the technical works mentioned in Chapter 2, several discourses existed within classical Islamic culture that have implications for a historical understanding and a synchronic interpretation of the monuments built, objects made, and artifacts used by Muslims. There is a discourse recently highlighted by A. I. Sabra that comes out of scientific observations, in this instance the *Optics* of Ibn al-Haytham written in the twelfth century in Muslim Spain. Ibn al-Haytham was led to his topic by his concern for the range of judgments that derive from the act of seeing. One of them is the judgment of beauty (*al-husn*) and, in very contemporary ways, Ibn al-Haytham identifies and discusses some of the attributes of man-made things like color or proportions as well as certain situations needed for value judgments like comparison (both similarity and dissimilarity), opacity, or darkness. The relativism implied in Ibn al-Haytham's arguments is interesting not because of the time and place that expressed it, but because he assumes that qualitative decisions of beauty are based on what would be called today the user's or the observer's context, not on intrinsic properties of artifacts.[4] Ibn al-Haytham was conscious of objects and he refers directly to several categories of materials used to make cloth or other practical things. Yet, throughout, his reasoning is an intellectual one based on a logic of thought—the necessity for certain kinds of judgments to be carried out because the act of seeing requires them. It is not a reasoning based on the observation of objects or of buildings.

An equally intellectualized and even more theoretical approach is provided by philosophers, whose Platonic and Aristotelian sources inspired notions of intermediary modes like shape, place, dimension, order, harmony, or structure, which are essential to the perception we have of anything as well as for the establishment of an elusive happiness.[5] The transfer of these categories of reality to the understanding of works of art is difficult to make, but the analytical necessity for intermediate categories of definition may well be compared with my contention of an intermediate zone of categories for the perception of works of art. It remains, however, to be seen whether such comparisons are valid because they correspond to actual processes of thought and behavior in traditional Islamic culture or because a contemporary visual analysis by today's scholarship discovers parallels to *its* process of understanding within the thought of the past.[6]

More successful results should be expected from such esthetic judgments as can be derived from the poetics of traditional Islamic cultures. In fact, with Jurjani in Arabic and in the eleventh century, Nizami in Persian in the twelfth, or Sharaf al-Din Rami in the fifteenth also in Persian, and probably later Turkish writers as well, medieval and postmedieval literary criticism has suggested the possibility of a formal esthetic for images, metaphors, prosody, and so on. Yet it has so far been proved very difficult to move from theory to the explanation of a specific monument or object and the only, in my judgment, successful essay was one that picked specific images in Nizami's poetry, in particular the ones dealing with mirrors, and then applied them to the art of painting.[7] In other words, it seemed easier to use the words of a poet than those of a literary critic or theoretician in order to provide something useful for the representational arts.

The issue of cultural interpretation of the arts at a different level than that of immediate social or personal context is thus far from resolved. In fact, one may even wonder whether it is appropriate to seek a philosophical explanation or even parallel for the arts of medieval and premodern times in the Islamic world. In Christian areas and in Buddhist and Hinduist ones, there were religious, pious, liturgical, and even theological connections between the work of the artist and the world of rational and practical thought. Such connections seem more difficult to demonstrate or to justify within the ethic of the Islamic world and it is in other ways than through philosophical or even literary thought practices that Islamic art must be approached. If this is indeed so, if, as I believe, even mystical sources and practices are not directly involved in visual experiences, the historian of art is given a uniquely interesting task, that of devising the appropriate contexts, historical or contemporary, within which Islamic art should be understood. But the issue is still open, as the study of written sources for the purposes of understanding the arts has barely begun.[8]

Ornament and Reality

Nearly all studies on ornament contrast its artificiality and contrived formalism with the "reality" of representations from natural or imaginable worlds. This contrast and the ideas associated with it have acquired a particular acuity in the twentieth century, when the rejection of representation was not always seen as the creation of ornaments and when discovery of nonrepresentational arts in other cultures led to all sorts of theories for magical and other nonrepresentational "incantations," as it was put by a leading historian of Irish art whenever works of northern art were discussed.[9]

A theory of intermediaries may be of some help in pursuing further the boundaries between ornament and reality, as it proposes the existence of an order of perception and, therefore, of reality between the viewer and the object. Like clothes or textiles in general, which reveal, enhance, or even diminish the reality of a person or of a place, the intermediary demons with which I have dealt exist and are real. Yet they are, extreme cases notwithstanding, neither the object nor the function of works of art. They do not live in a philosophical limbo but represent a category of relationship often overlooked in our tendency toward binary opposites. It is a category essential to the perception and very existence of a work of art, the category of sensory pleasure, which is not the same as the category of structures so beloved by contemporary theoreticians.[10] To the extent that this category is true, it exists, it is reality, it is part of the nature of a work of visual art. Yet it is not a representation of something with an independent existence, even if it takes forms like leaves, flowers, or arches that are part of an independent world of nature or of human constructs and constructions.

It is in fact possible, at this stage, to consider these intermediaries in two antithetical and possibly incompatible ways. One is to say that intermediaries have lost their relationship to physical reality. This is what makes them ornament, and they enter into the category of discourse—that is to say, of rhetorical devices for the presentation of other things. By being put down on paper, canvas, brick walls, or metal objects, these ornamental features merely illustrate an extension of Barthes's remark discussed earlier that the "scriptible"—that is, whatever is written (and it is legitimate to argue that the visual arts belong as a form of written text)—always requires one additional step in the making of objects and in their perception than that of direct translation.[11] It is a step whose possible referents are irrelevant to its function as an intermediary. Often in the past the linguistic and communication theory model of a code was used to identify this additional step. Codes are indeed used to build and represent whatever artists sought to make and viewers and users decode artifacts to deal with them appropriately. But the zone of intermediaries which I have studied differs from codes by its independence from the specifics of a work of art. At best, it could have been part of a code to the maker, but it becomes an intermediary of "pleasure" to the viewer.

The other way to consider intermediaries is to say that sensory attraction (or repellence) in whatever shape is built into the very existence of an artifact. It is part of its reality, of its truth, and its only peculiarity is that it is an attribute whose range can vary as widely as human emotions and feelings can be dissected and analyzed. Reality and ornament, in this second way, are always mixed with each other, as they correspond to differing yet always necessary attitudes on the part of a maker who would suddenly add a swerve to a drapery or a wave to a seascape or else on the part of a viewer who will imagine figures in depictions of water or schematize into a formal abstraction the personages or animals of a bucolic scene. All these visions would be, in this hypothesis, equally true.

One corollary to these observations can be that, in a sort of libertarian manner, the truth of a work of art is always relative to other considerations, either historical and synchronic ones, or contemporary and achronic. To resolve the philosophical danger of relativism of meaning and of judgment, it should be possible to separate more clearly than is usually done two areas of reality about any artifact. One is, for the most part, not negotiable and consists in accurate statements—presence of a dome or representation of a tree or of the Virgin Mary—that can be debated but for which one explanation is usually the correct one. The other area concerns such social, cultural, or personal truths that are no less real than the first kind and do affect the work of art, but are not only negotiable but by definition changeable. It is as though there were always several levels of truth or of reality, and this is a hypothesis for further exploration and further refinement.

Implications of Mediation

The celebrated Protestant theologian Paul Tillich, well versed in the world of visual forms, claimed that the modern world was constantly involved in a "search for meaning."[12] And it is indeed about meaning or meanings that most of this book revolves. But, beyond the specifics of the various issues raised here, two wider questions keep coming up. No answer can, at this stage, be provided for either, as much additional thinking and many new investigations are needed to provide a better focus for them. A few comments on their scope, however, can serve as a final statement issued from the preceding pages.

The first one is the role of the beholder or of the user in establishing the character of an object or of a building. It is reasonably common nowadays to separate from each other two sets of criteria that affect a given work of art. On the one hand, there are all the factors that prodded and helped an artist, an artisan, or a team of builders to make something; these are usually known as historical factors, but in reality they are "prehistorical," as their identification deals with a time that precedes the making of a work of art.[13] On the other hand lie the adventures of a work of art or of an object, the first feelings of awe or disgust, the endless criticisms, the many uses, and eventually the changes that transform a church into a mosque and then into a museum as happened with Hagia Sophia or else modify an object of Christian or Buddhist piety into a museum piece. These essays dealt primarily with this second set of activities as I investigated types or optisemic properties, and especially as I developed observations about taste, perception, and pleasure as forms acknowledged and judged according to categories of taste yet to be identified.[14] The main point was that each object, each monument, is mostly known through its "post history" and much remains to be done in explaining how this post history affects our own understanding and enjoyment of works of art.

The other question was already raised by Owen Jones and in many ways it goes back to Plato's concerns about the intrinsic falsehood of the visual arts. The question is a moral one. Curiously, it was Riegl who finally argued that, as the relationship to the beholder raises the "ethical purpose of art," one cannot deal with art before being deeply steeped in esthetics *and* ethics.[15] What exactly was meant by Riegl, Jones, or anyone else who claims a moral value to art still needs much investigation. I will limit myself to one point only. It is that works of art and in general the visually perceived environment have an extraordinary power in shaping the lives and thoughts of men and women.[16] According to a recent study, labyrinths are a "temptation to moral error," as emblems "of the world as an almost inextricable occasion of sin."[17] Indeed huge forums or lofty cathedrals as well as the humble geometric designs on the skirts worn by African women compel behavior and organize life because of the awe, terror, or pleasure they inspire. Representations can range from the exalted and holy to the pornographic and repulsive. The ranges of moral behavior and of moral imagination and consequently of moral choices offered by the arts are central to the effective performance of the spectacle offered by human creation to human judgment and to human behavior. Within this performance, ornament is the ultimate mediator, paradoxically questioning the value of meanings by chaneling them into pleasure. Or is it possible to argue instead that by providing pleasure ornament also gives to the observer the right and the freedom to choose meanings?

NOTES

Introduction

1. There is a curious paradox in art historical practice around these issues. On the one hand, there lies an acknowledged art whose history—that is, development through time—is consecrated by manuals and series of surveys. The latter, like the German *Propyläen Kunstgeschichte* or the *Pelican History of Art* in the English-speaking world and, in a shorter version, the two Larousse volumes edited by Albert Châtelet and Philippe Groslier under the title *Histoire de l'art* (Paris, 1985), are written by several authors specializing in different periods and concentrate, for the most part, on the art of western Europe seen in a chronological sequence beginning with ancient Egypt and the ancient Near East as vaguely acknowledged ancestors. The rest of the world is present, usually through single chapters or individual volumes, but rarely as related or relatable to periods identified in Western art. Although less obvious than in the past, the notion is still there that other cultures than the western European one do not have as defined a sense of history.

Manuals are usually written by a single individual, at best by a small team, and, for reasons peculiar to the economics of the textbook and to the nature of curricula in universities, they are by now almost exclusively an American phenomenon. The most popular of these manuals are H. W. Janson, *History of Art*, 2d ed. (New York, 1977); Frederick Hartt, *A History of Art*, 2d ed. (New York, 1985); and H. Gardner, *Art through the Ages*, 8th ed., (New York, 1986). Equivalents for architecture are Spiro Kostof, *A History of Architecture* (Oxford, 1985); M. Trachtenberg and I. Hyman, *Architecture from Prehistory to Post-Modernism: The Western Tradition* (New York, 1986); and the old standard, Banister Fletcher, *A History of Architecture on the Comparative Method*, 15th ed. (New York, 1950). The concentration of all these books except the one by Kristof is on Western art. With varying degrees of effectiveness and depth, they recognize the existence of other traditions, but rarely to argue from them some broader issue of understanding, judging, or appreciating the arts. The partial exception to this generalization is Hugh Honor and John Fleming, *The Visual Arts: A History* (New York, 1982), with the subtle introduction of several non-Western traditions around themes like religious art.

There is in short an intellectually assumed and emotionally felt attitude among art historians that the major issues of visual understanding are the ones elaborated in the grand tradition of Western art. Internal debates within the study of that tradition argue at times against the domination of Western art itself by the paradigms developed around classical Greek and Roman art or the art of the Italian Renaissance, and Svetlana Alpers has been the most vocal exponent of the problems involved with an art history centered on Italian issues, as in "Style Is What You Make It," in B. Lang, ed., *The Concept of Style*, (Ithaca, N.Y., 1979), pp. 137–62, and *The Art of Describing: Dutch Art in the Seventeenth Century* (Chicago, 1983). But there is an assumed overall unity of perception within Western art and the best other traditions can usually do is show additional "examples" of otherwise known features and approaches. Nikolaus Pevsner has made the point of a discrete and original western European tradition quite forcefully in the introduction to his *Outline of European Architecture*, rev. ed. (Baltimore, 1972) with its

NOTES

Introduction

1. There is a curious paradox in art historical practice around these issues. On the one hand, there lies an acknowledged art whose history—that is, development through time—is consecrated by manuals and series of surveys. The latter, like the German *Propyläen Kunstgeschichte* or the *Pelican History of Art* in the English-speaking world and, in a shorter version, the two Larousse volumes edited by Albert Châtelet and Philippe Groslier under the title *Histoire de l'art* (Paris, 1985), are written by several authors specializing in different periods and concentrate, for the most part, on the art of western Europe seen in a chronological sequence beginning with ancient Egypt and the ancient Near East as vaguely acknowledged ancestors. The rest of the world is present, usually through single chapters or individual volumes, but rarely as related or relatable to periods identified in Western art. Although less obvious than in the past, the notion is still there that other cultures than the western European one do not have as defined a sense of history.

Manuals are usually written by a single individual, at best by a small team, and, for reasons peculiar to the economics of the textbook and to the nature of curricula in universities, they are by now almost exclusively an American phenomenon. The most popular of these manuals are H. W. Janson, *History of Art*, 2d ed. (New York, 1977); Frederick Hartt, *A History of Art*, 2d ed. (New York, 1985); and H. Gardner, *Art through the Ages*, 8th ed., (New York, 1986). Equivalents for architecture are Spiro Kostof, *A History of Architecture* (Oxford, 1985); M. Trachtenberg and I. Hyman, *Architecture from Prehistory to Post-Modernism: The Western Tradition* (New York, 1986); and the old standard, Banister Fletcher, *A History of Architecture on the Comparative Method*, 15th ed. (New York, 1950). The concentration of all these books except the one by Kristof is on Western art. With varying degrees of effectiveness and depth, they recognize the existence of other traditions, but rarely to argue from them some broader issue of understanding, judging, or appreciating the arts. The partial exception to this generalization is Hugh Honor and John Fleming, *The Visual Arts: A History* (New York, 1982), with the subtle introduction of several non-Western traditions around themes like religious art.

There is in short an intellectually assumed and emotionally felt attitude among art historians that the major issues of visual understanding are the ones elaborated in the grand tradition of Western art. Internal debates within the study of that tradition argue at times against the domination of Western art itself by the paradigms developed around classical Greek and Roman art or the art of the Italian Renaissance, and Svetlana Alpers has been the most vocal exponent of the problems involved with an art history centered on Italian issues, as in "Style Is What You Make It," in B. Lang, ed., *The Concept of Style*, (Ithaca, N.Y., 1979), pp. 137–62, and *The Art of Describing: Dutch Art in the Seventeenth Century* (Chicago, 1983). But there is an assumed overall unity of perception within Western art and the best other traditions can usually do is show additional "examples" of otherwise known features and approaches. Nikolaus Pevsner has made the point of a discrete and original western European tradition quite forcefully in the introduction to his *Outline of European Architecture*, rev. ed. (Baltimore, 1972) with its prints and photographs, are almost never alike and no one has worked out what is appropriately "similar" to something else. At the same time, works may look very different that were meant to be alike, as physical likeness is no guarantee for similarity.

It is more curious and certainly a sign of the Western cultural domination of art historical thought that practically nothing has been written about the complex relations between Western art and the art of the rest of the world in the twentieth century. I only know of one general book on the arts of the twentieth century that even aknowledges the existence of other worlds; it is William Curtis, *Modern Architecture since 1900* (New York, 1984).

4. This important issue has not surfaced at all in Western criticism of art except a little bit in dealing with architecture; see, for instance, Kenneth Frampton, "Prospects for a Critical Regionalism," *Perspecta* 20 (1983). The issue can be defined in the following manner. To the extent to which a work of art is identified by its appurtenance to a land and a time, it partakes of the qualities of this time and/or land and these qualities are necessarily different from those of another land or place, since, in the contrary hypothesis, they would have to be the same land and place. Such absurd positions were taken or assumed in works written in the midst of wars like Emile Mâle, *Art français et art allemand* (Paris, 1916) or, to a lesser degree, Nikolaus Pevsner, *The Englishness of English Art* (London, 1956). They can be explained as observations necessary in moments of patriotic tension. But, among emerging new nations or cultures that, rightly or wrongly, have felt dominated by Western thought, the assertion of exclusive right to the making and explaining of certain forms of art has become a way to maintain self-identity and a certain type of dignity. For an example in the sciences, see Ziauddin Sardar, ed., *The Touch of Midas* (Manchester, 1984) and review by O. Grabar, "From Utopia to Paradigms," *Mimar* 18 (1986). These ideologically charged intellectual positions can easily become means of controlling judgments and opinions and especially of distributing certificates of "acceptability" for this or that interpretation. The dangers of such results are obvious within the framework of a dominating Western culture, but it is difficult not to understand the anger of so many artists and interpreters of the arts in other lands who feel excluded from a common adventure controlled by Western media.

In general, it is necessary to keep two distinctions in mind for an eventual elaboration of the issue of appropriate interpretation of works of art. One is that several equally true views of a given work of art can coexist and these truths are different from the veracity of a work of art where correct and incorrect statements are incompatible with each other. And then, as is more commonly agreed by the general public but not by experts, the synchronic views of a time need not be the diachronic ones and it is possible to approve an understanding compatible with our own times that is demonstrably wrong for older times, perhaps even to argue that visual values and interpretations can differ from place to place in the contemporary world without any one of them being wrong.

5. This distinction was first elaborated in O. Grabar, *The Formation of Islamic Art* (New Haven, 1974; 2d ed., 1987), p. 179. I am not aware of any discussion of the issue since then.

6. This statement cannot be proved without a type of statistical evidence that is shunned by historians of art, probably justifiably so. In fact the density of ornament varies enormously from one tradition or period to the other and it may be interesting to evaluate the differences between, for instance, pre-Columbian and ancient Egyptian densities with some worthy conclusion about the expectations made of visual forms in each civilization.

7. Although historical scholarship still dominates the field except for the study of twentieth-century art, where it shares the stage with criticism, thematic studies of

more detailed character than Kenneth Clark's works cited in note 3 do exist, for instance John Onians, *Bearers of Meaning* (Princeton, 1988); Joseph Alsop, *The Rarer Traditions of Art* (New York, 1982); or Lars-Ivar Ringbom, *Paradisus Terrestris* (Helsinki, 1956). Many iconographic studies are typical thematic investigations.

8. Three recent books illustrate quite well that there are new ways of thinking about the arts, even though the issues raised always go back to the philosophical and esthetic concerns of the nineteenth century. The books are: Donald Preziosi, *Rethinking Art History* (New Haven, 1989); Hans Belting, *Das Ende der Kunstgeschichte* (Munich, 1983); Michael Podro, *The Critical Historians of Art* (New Haven, 1982). Often these books argue points that have been made earlier. The important issue is, however, that each generation (perhaps even each decade) restates ways of dealing with the arts according to its own needs and in its own terms.

9. In being introduced to the use of word processors, I have been fascinated by the implication of a DOS, that is to say of a system that has nothing directly to do with one's work with the computer, but without which one could not do the work. Something comparable, it is suggested, may well exist in the making and perception of visual (and perhaps other) creativity.

Chapter I
A Theory of Intermediaries in Art

1. This fragment has been often published and often exhibited, but never studied. Latest information on it in the catalogue by Elise Anglade, *Musée du Louvre, catalogue des boiseries de la section islamique* (Paris, 1988), pp. 15–17. Appropriate bibliographical information will be found there. Examples of typologically similar panels are found in this and in any other catalogue or survey of Islamic objects. The dating of the Louvre piece is based on the assumption, probably correct, that it is later than but under the influence of decorative patterns and ways developed around the middle of the ninth century in the ʿAbbasid capital of Samarra (Richard Ettinghausen and Oleg Grabar, *Art and Architecture of Islam, 650–1250* (London, 1987 pp. 108–10). But, to my knowledge, none of the allegedly early panels found in Egypt are dated on their own and it is an area where the recently developed field of dendrochronology could be useful to check the visual sequences proposed by historians of art. Specificity of date is, however, not pertinent to the purposes of this book.

2. See, among many places, Otto von Falke, *Kunstgeschichte der Seidenweberei*, 4th ed. (Tübingen, n.d. but after 1936), figs. 18, 70, 71, 135, 136, etc. The history and iconography of this peculiar motif still need investigating. In all likelihood it belongs to the category of themes that illustrate royal wealth (birds as inhabitants of princely gardens and with many wondrous properties like carrying precious objects) or else that are supposed to suggest Paradise; see Lars-Ivar Ringbom, *Paradisus Terrestris* (Helsinki, 1958).

3. Ettinghausen and Grabar, *Art and Architecture of Islam*, p. 104. It was Richard Ettinghausen who argued in one of his classic articles that the "beveled" style, that is, a certain manner of treating diverse motifs, can be seen as an indicator of an Iraqi inspired pan-Islamic "imperial" stamp, "The Beveled Style," in G. C. Miles, ed. *Archaeologia Orientalia in Memoriam Ernst Herzfeld*, (Locust Valley, N.Y., 1952), reprinted in Ettinghausen's collected papers edited by M. Rosen-Ayalon, *Islamic Art and Archaeology* (Berlin, 1984). Most recently, Terry Allen, *Five Essays on Islamic Art* (Sebastopol, Calif., 1988), esp. pp. 1–15.

4. What complicates matters a bit is the

vagueness of the archaeological or architectural context in which the bird was found. Was the unusual and hitherto unique frame of the "bird" dictated by the decision to show a "bird" or by some other need or prescription, for instance the composition of the whole surface for which this fragment was originally meant?

5. Anglade, *Catalogue*, p. 31, fig. 15a, published this piece, without, however, giving its dimensions. Although the piece is complete, its actual use or potential use are impossible to deduce.

6. Anglade, *Catalogue*, figs. 14 and 16, also 23 and 23a.

7. There is no study of these ceramics as a coherent group (except briefly in Ettinghausen and Grabar, *Art and Architecture of Islam*, p. 225) and most discussions have been either fairly general or archaeological. The best recent introduction to ceramics in general is by Jean Soustiel, *La céramique islamique* (Fribourg, 1985), pp. 55–64, with important examples for the purposes of this book, pp. 65–76. While interesting and legitimate, the selection of illustrations in this rich book does not, in my judgment, do justice to the quality of some of the pieces remaining from this period. For archaeological reports that are somewhere between archaeology and the history of art, see Charles K. Wilkinson, *Nishapur: Pottery of the Early Islamic Period* (New York, 1976) and M. Rosen-Ayalon, *La poterie islamique, Ville Royale de Suse* (Paris, 1974). For a dry but clear-cut typological approach, see Sh. S. Tashhodjaev, *Hudozhestvennaia Polivnaia Keramika Samarkanda* (Tashkent, 1967). For an attempt at a visual analysis of a single bowl, see O. Grabar, "Notes on the Decorative Composition of a Bowl," in R. Ettinghausen, ed, *Islamic Art in the Metropolitan Museum of Art*, (New York, 1972), pp. 91–98. For wider considerations on dealing with ceramics, see O. Grabar, "Between Connoisseurship and Technology," *Muqarnas* 5 (1988), pp. 1–8. None of these books, articles, and reflections can unfortunately dispense the student from looking through exhibition or museum catalogues or through a few general manuals with good visual surveys like A. Papadopoulo, *L'Islam et l'art islamique* (Paris, 1976), esp. pp. 75 and 415–17.

8. For luster, in addition to Soustiel, see now Alan Caiger-Smith, *Luster Pottery* (London, 1985), and Oliver Watson, *Persian Luster Ware* (London, 1985). Although much progress has been made, the origins of luster as an esthetic phenomenon rather than as a technical one and the iconographic as well as stylistic or expressive peculiarities of the earliest examples in Iraq still need reflection.

9. Esin Atil, *Ceramics from the World of Islam* (Washington, D.C., 1973), pp. 36–37 for the often reproduced Freer bowl. A. Papadoupolo, *Islam*, fig. 85, for the best reproduction of the Iranian piece, published originally in the catalogue of a traveling exhibition of Iranian art: R. Ghirshman, ed., *Petit Palais, sept mille ans d'art en Iran*, (Paris, 1961), no. 904 and pl. C1.

10. The writing on these ceramics consists primarily of proverbs and of simple wishes of good feeling; it has been studied in a series of articles by O. Bolshakov published in *Epigrafika Vostoka* 4 ff. (1960–).

11. For a very tentative sketch of an explanation, see O. Grabar, "Reflections on the Study of Islamic Art," *Muqarnas* 1 (1983), pp. 11–12.

12. This striking painting was, I believe, first published in color in E. Akurgal, Cyril Mango, and Richard Ettinghausen, *Treasures of Turkey* (Geneva, 1966), p. 220. It struck many of those who flipped through the pages of this beautiful coffee-table book and found its way into the second edition of a manual like Janson's, H. W. Janson, *A History of Art* (New York, 1977), color plate 30. But, to my knowledge, it has never been really studied. I will return several times to this stunning work of art. Its date and place of origin are tied to the complex problem of dating the content of four extraordinary albums in Istanbul and one in Berlin. For the latest, unfortunately still incomplete, information, see *Islamic Art* 1 (1981), entirely de-

voted to the Istanbul albums. The Berlin album was published in a particularly cumbersome manner by M. S. Ipširoglu, *Sarayalben* (Wiesbaden, 1964).

13. A rather peculiar problem of logic on this issue has plagued the handling of all the areas and periods for which we do not possess adequate information about works of art other than an understanding of the works of art themselves. The problem can be defined through two questions. First, to what degree is a given representation or image necessarily unique in its way of showing something? Second, if, as is obviously the case, very rarely, can one extend that conclusion to times when we have no sense of the relationship between what remains and what existed? There is no way of answering these questions without investigations that are not pertinent to the topic of this book. They must, however, be kept in mind, because they maintain a factor of uncertainty about the originality of any work of art remaining from earlier time. Some scholars tend to treat all existing artifacts as a closed set whose conclusions are modified as new discoveries are made. Others prefer to imagine all sorts of "missing links." Both positions are justified.

14. The statement of that position was first formulated by Louis Massignon, "Les méthodes de réalisation artistique des peuples de l'Islam," *Syria* 2 (1921). Its more popular and more recent version is found in Papadopoulo, *L'Islam et l'art islamique*, but its impact is also visible, consciously or not, in general interpretations of Islamic art developed by Titus Burckhardt, *Sacred Art in East and West* (London, 1967); Laleh Bakhtiar and Nader Ardalan, *The Sense of Unity* (Chicago, 1973); Seyyed Hossein Nasr, *Islamic Art and Spirituality* (Albany, N.Y., 1987); and many others. The trouble is that what began as a brilliant but tentative essay was too rapidly seen as a doctrine without leading to further investigations within the rich literature on ethics and, to a smaller degree, esthetics in traditional Islamic culture. It was also unfortunate that the original essay, which was tied to medieval Islamic art, was later used without consciousness of historical evolution and changes over time.

15. K. Abu Deeb, *Al-Jurjani's Theory of Poetic Imagery* (Warminster, 1978), especially chap. 5 dealing with *isti'ara*, a complex word translated at times as "metaphor."

16. Once again we deal with an important methodological issue. The classic example of correspondence is Erwin Panofsky, *Gothic Architecture and Scholasticism* (New York, 1957), but it is as attractive a theory as it is an impossible one to prove. A parallel example for Byzantine art, with greater concern for the autonomy of images, is Henry Maguire, *Art and Eloquence in Byzantium* (Princeton, 1981).

17. Henri Matisse, *Ecrits et propos sur l'art* (Paris, 1972), pp. 159, 185, among other places. Pierre Schneider, *Matisse* (Paris, 1984), pp. 162–64. For W. Kandinsky, see K.C. Lindsay and P. Vergo, eds., *Complete Writings on Art*, vol. 1: *1901–1921* (Boston, 1982), pp. 73–76. Like Matisse, Kandinsky was strongly affected by the 1910 exhibition of Islamic art in Munich, followed by one in Paris in 1911. Fewer critics saw these connections, but it is a pleasure to recall one who died too young, Amy Goldin, who spent a semester studying with me and brought contemporary freshness to jaded antiquarians. She wrote "Beyond Style," *Art and Artists* (September 1968), and "Islamic Art: The Met's Generous Embrace," *Art Forum* 14 (March 1976), preparatory statements for ideas which, to my knowledge, never came to fruition.

18. In general, art historical reasoning is easier to develop around motifs that are concrete and can be seen as deriving from each other as well as generating each other, whereas processes, especially from more remote places and times than the contemporary West, must usually be hypothesized.

19. Although the matter still needs verification, the difference seems clear between the Muslim functionaries in today's Iran or in Wahhabi Saudi Arabia who do judge vi-

sual practice and, on the other hand, their medieval ancestors who concentrated on controlling the marketplace by developing mercantile and industrial regulations based on the Revelation rather than doctrines on art. Insofar as we know in a little-studied subfield, medieval control tended to be of measurable attributes like quality of manufacture or genuinness of material, whereas the contemporary one, in countries with a strict application of late medieval Islamic law, takes very much into consideration artistic judgments. It is probably true that, at some point in the consciousness of religious thought and practice in the Islamic world, the realization of the existence of "art" in the Renaissance sense of the word led to a wide spread of different reactions. Some are as early as the sixteenth century, others are only contemporary. But the matter needs more scrutiny for today as well as in the past.

20. See pp. 5 and 241.

21. Museum of Modern Art, New York, *Pablo Picasso: A Retrospective* (New York, 1980), pp. 190–91. E.-G. Güse and B. Rau, *Pablo Picasso. Die Lithographien* (Stuttgart, 1988), p. 24. These are publications of the lithographs. To my knowledge they have never been analyzed and explained. For sources, see Herschel B. Chipp, *Theories of Modern Art: A Source Book by Artists and Critics* (Berkeley, 1968), p. 60; Robert Goldwater and Marco Treves, *Artists on Art* (New York, 1958), pp. 363, 417, 443, 445. I am grateful to my colleague Professor Irving Lavin for showing me his hitherto unpublished study of the Picasso lithographs. His purpose and point of view are quite different from mine.

22. Furthermore, the verb "to stylize" is connected to the protean word "style," whose meanings could fill a volume. See my comments in the preface. For a classical definition, see Mayer Schapiro, "Style," in Morris philipson, ed. *Aesthetics Today* (Cleveland, 1961), and for a more contemporary view, S. Alpers as quoted in Introduction, note 1.

23. It turned out to be particularly difficult to discover when the word "abstraction" or the adjective "abstract" began to be used to describe compound forms or to identify artistic ambitions and expectations. For general introductions, see Tate Gallery, *Towards a New Art: Essays on the Background to Abstract Art 1910–1920* (London, 1980), and Maurice Tuchman, *The Spiritual in Art: Abstract Painting 1890–1985* (New York, 1985). The following components seem to have entered into the set of associations made with the words "abstract" and "abstraction": decisions by painters like Larionov or Kandinsky to use the term for their works (circa 1911); judgments by critics, as when Maurice Denis, also a painter, warned Matisse of the dangers of abstraction (1905); ideological movements like theosophy or Worringer's philosophy of history, which saw in abstract forms a higher level of interpretation of the inner soul (circa 1905–1910). See Henry G. Gardiner, ed., *Color and Form 1909–1914* (San Diego, 1981). There are additional ideas and documents in "Non-objective Art," *Encyclopedia of World Art* (New York, 1965).

24. See chapter 4.

25. I realize, of course, that this statement simplifies the more profound point that any transformation of shapes and ordering of lines, dots, and hues constitute a creative art, which may acquire a value of its own. I shall return to this question in conclusion.

26. Here is the full text: "presenting or possessing schematic or generalized form frequently suggested by and having obscure resemblance to natural appearances through a contrived ordering of pictorial or sculptural elements."

27. For Kandinsky, see references in note 23. Anna Chave, *Mark Rothko's Subjects in Abstraction* (New Haven, 1989), p. 195; I have also profited from the first version of an article by Natasha Staller on "The Ideology of Symbolist Style," which has not yet appeared. See also Ann Gibson and Stephen Polcari, eds., "New Myths for Old," *Art Journal* 42 (1988), especially the very telling

quotations from Barnett Newman. Random references to abstraction or decoration are common among critics of modern art; see, for example, Harry Rand, *Paul Manship* (Washington, D.C., 1980) or *Arshile Gorky* (London, 1981), pp. 194–95.

28. In recent years a certain amount of thinking has been directed to the uses of the past in art and history within a broader spectrum than the traditional one provided by the relationship of Western art to antiquity. Works like John Sweetman, *The Oriental Obsession* (Cambridge, 1988), D. Lowenthal, *The Past Is a Foreign Country* (Cambridge, 1985), or an exhibition like the one held in Berlin in 1989 under the title *Europa und der Orient* (with a superbly illustrated catalogue), edited by G. Sievernik and H. Budde (Berlin, 1989), are all more or less successful and more or less profound explorations of the theme that a patron, a user, or a maker of art relates the experience or the needs of his time to something older or alien. Less frequently mentioned is that often the questions of any one time define that time's judgment over the past. These issues are particularly noteworthy when one looks at the art, and especially architecture, produced in newly independent countries. In Lahore, Pakistan, for instance, the systematic use of Mughal ideas in the architecture of imperial Britain led to its rejection as a model by the first architects of independence. The latter found in a certain type of "modern" internationalism a secure base for nearly a generation until a more authentic past was searched for and the old Mughal imperial buildings were discovered. See Kamil Khan Mumtaz, *Architecture in Pakistan* (Geneva, 1987). What is implied by this example is something well known to those who have studied the "reception" of art—that the visual and other memories of observers affect their perception of any work of art. Mark Rothko even argued the point in a positive sense when he said: "If people want sacred experiences, they will find them here [in his paintings]. If they want profane experiences, they will find them too. I take no side." (Chave, *Rothko*, p. 195). Does this statement on his own work by a nearly contemporary painter, shaped by his time, justify *any* interpretations of works from the past?

29. There is no way of entering simply into the history of ornament in the nineteenth century. For a general introduction centered on much neglected German literary examples, see Frank-Lothar Kroll, *Das Ornament in der Kunsttheorie des 19. Jahrhunderts* (Hildesheim, 1987). For standard examples, see J. Bourgoin, *Théorie de l'ornement* (Paris, 1883); F. S. Meyer, *Handbook of Ornament* (New York, 1895); Richard Glazier, *A Manual of Historical Ornament* (London, 1948); A. Spelz, *The Styles of Ornament* (London, 1900); Peter Jessen, *Der Ornamentistik* (Berlin, 1920).

30. Ben Sirach quoted in Werner Foerster, *From the Exile to Christ: A Historical Introduction to Palestinian Judaism* (Philadelphia, 1964), p. 25.

31. The verb *naqqasha* is as difficult to translate as it is usually easy to understand, for it means "to do something to a surface in order to make it fancier." *Zawaqa* is more general in implying the aim to embellish. *Isti'ara* is the most complex of these terms, as it implies a transfer of meaning; see Abu Deeb, *Al-Jurjani*, esp. pp. 61 and 313. The vocabulary for esthetic and technical terms in Arabic and other languages and by Muslim communities has not been studied in much detail. See A.F.L. Beeston, *The Epistle on Singing-girls of Jahiz* (Warminster, 1980), pp. 25–26, for terms used for qualitative judgments dealing with harmony. More has been done for construction, as in O. Grabar and R. Holod, "A Tenth-Century Source for Architecture," *Eucharisterion, Harvard Ukrainian Studies* 3–4 (1979–1980), p. 314.

32. J. Gonda, *The Meaning of Vedic Bhusati* (Wageningen, 1939). See also A. Coomaraswamy, *Selected Papers: Traditional Art and Symbolism*, ed. Roger Lipsey (Princeton, 1977), pp. 241–45 (and through-

out for all sorts of exciting vistas). I owe the first reference to my colleague Professor Pramod Chandra. All of my examples except the last one came from Gonda's book. Professor Chandra gave me the quotation of the moon as an adornment of the night, but he could not recall where he had read this sentence. It is such a beautiful image that I am keeping it as the contribution of an anonymous Indian sage. It curiously fits with the following passage by E. Le Roy-Ladurie describing the relationship in premodern France between the king and the nobility: "les nobles sont groupés autour du trône comme un ornement et disent à celui qui y prend place ce qu'il est" (*L'état royal* [Paris, 1987], p. 19).

33. William Curtis, *Le Corbusier, Ideas and Forms* (Oxford, 1986), p. 24.

34. The evil of art or of beautiful objects was a topos of classical Islamic thought, as in Ibn Miskawayh, *Traité d'Ethique*, trans. Muhammad Arkoun (Damascus, 1969), pp. 301–3, who argues that the provision of pleasure makes any object a source of evil leading man astray. Philippe de la Hine, second director of the Academy of Architecture, followed its motto to "strip architecture of its vicious ornaments"; J. Ryckwert, *The First Moderns* (Cambridge, 1988), p. 15. In recent times, shortly after the Iranian revolution of 1979, the Iranian delegation of UNESCO opposed a prosaic plan to make slides on Islamic art on the grounds that true Islam is incompatible with whatever art is. More modulating and more complex views come out of mystical writing, as in the cases of Rumi and Nizami. For Rumi, see examples in Ettinghausen and Grabar, *Art and Architecture of Islam*, p. 330 with references. For Nizami, see Priscilla Soucek, "Nizami on Painters and Painting," in Richard Ettinghausen, ed., *Islamic Art in the Metropolitan Museum of Art* (New York, 1972).

35. Maurice Crampon, *La Cathédrale d'Amiens* (Amiens, 1972); Jean Bony, *French Gothic Architecture* (Berkeley, 1983); Robert Mark, *Experiments in Gothic Structure* (Cambridge, 1982). It is rather curious that the work of architectural historians is so independent from that of scholars dealing with representations.

36. For the Ara Pacis, a recent discussion with full bibliography is Peter J. Holliday, "Time, History and Ritual on the *Ara Pacis Augustae*," *Art Bulletin* 72 (1990).

37. The long bibliography on Mshatta is reviewed by K.A.C. Creswell, *Early Muslim Architecture*, 2d ed. (Oxford, 1969), pp. 604–6. For a controversial hypothesis about its date, see O. Grabar, "The Date and Meaning of Mshatta," *Dumbarton Oaks Papers* 41 (1987), where novelties of interpretation since 1969 are mentioned.

38. Metalwork is probably the most studied of all techniques of Islamic art next to architecture. The objects of the period of the illustration and earlier ones are discussed in Eva Baer, *Islamic Metalwork* (Binghamton, N.Y., 1983), with complete bibliography and especially appropriate references to the works of D. S. Rice, who did make occasional allusions to formal problems of visual judgments.

39. Examples of manuals are Owen Jones, *The Grammar of Ornament* (London, 1868; repr. New York, 1986); D. Ware and M. Stafford, *An Illustrated Dictionary of Ornament* (New York, 1974); and the works by Spelz, Glazier, Mayer, and Bourguoin in note 29.

40. There probably is something silly in pursuing ghosts of past sins, as one condemns or mocks the "orientalist" terminology of so many manuals from the nineteenth century or issued from its ideologies. The problem, however, is only in part that some of these identifications like "Moorish" or "Saracenic," which are ideologically charged in ways resented today, are still used. It is also that this kind of categorization has affected the contemporary arts of new nation-states and has been seen as reflecting modern national states and their ideologies rather than visual configurations.

41. The operation of the past becomes

apparent as monuments are scrutinized beyond their mere physical appearance and basic vital statistics or beyond an automatic acknowledgment of their existence. The study of Islamic art has only very recently reached the stage where the historicism of certain monuments is singled out, especially when it extends beyond obvious copies or revivals. An interesting Cairene example is that of the early eleventh-century mosque of al-Hakim. It reflected a ninth-century model and inspired a late thirteenth-century one. The historical concerns involved in these revivals have been brought out by Jonathan Bloom in several articles like "The Origins of Fatimid Art," *Muqarnas* 3 (1985), and "The Mosque of al-Hakim in Cairo," *Muqarnas* 1 (1983).

42. A. Riegl, *Spätromische Kunstindustrie* (Vienna, 1927), trans. Rolf Winken as *Late Roman Art Industry* (Rome, 1985). David Summer has perceptively suggested that both Riegl and Worringer preferred ornament to images "because ornament is a purer expression of form and therefore provides a less encumbered view into form's spiritual meaning." D. Summer, "Art Historical Description," *Critical Enquiry* 15 (1989), p. 376. See a good critique of Riegl by E. Gombrich, *The Sense of Order* (Oxford, 1979), pp. 180–90.

43. This method is not always explicitly identified, even in typical articles like M. Dimand, "Studies in Islamic Ornament," *Ars Islamica* 4 (1937), and "Studies in Islamic Ornament II," in George C. Miles, ed., *Archaeologica Orientalia in Memoriam Ernst Herzfeld* (Locust Valley, N.Y. 1952). But it is a method that totally permeates the dating and attributions of most museum catalogues.

44. I. Iermolieff-Schwarze, alias Giovanni Morelli, *Kunstkritische Studien über italienische Malerei* (Leipzig, 1889), pp. 1–78, esp. p. 40. See also Hayden B. J. Maginnes, "The Role of Perceptual Learning in Connoisseurship," *Art History* 13 (1990).

45. This happens, for instance, in K.A.C. Creswell's tabulation of the "influences" at work in the Dome of the Rock, *Early Muslim Architecture*, 2d. ed. (Oxford, 1969), p. 123. In a more sophisticated way, D. S. Rice's analysis of metalwork from Mossul obeyed the same principles; See "The Bronzes from Mossul," *Ars Orientalis* 2 (1957), pp. 321–25.

46. John Ruskin, *The Seven Lamps of Architecture* (London, 1880), p. 173; *The Stones of Venice* (London, 1853–1858). In general, see Kristine O. Garrigan, *Ruskin on Architecture* (Madison, Wis., 1973).

47. Henri Focillon, *La vie des formes* (Paris, 1947).

48. Gombrich, *Sense of Order*.

49. It is difficult to know where there are "hidden" motifs in vegetal ornament. I have already alluded to the Ara Pacis and to Mshatta. Another example is the so-called Antioch Chalice (K. Weitzmann, ed., *Age of Spirituality* [New York, 1979], pp. 606–8) and I shall return to the issue in Chapter 5.

50. James C. Faris, *Nuba Personal Art* (London, 1972). I was introduced to this book and to some of its ideas by the extraordinary man and mind that were the late Joseph Alsop.

51. Jacques Mercier, *Rouleaux magiques éthiopiens* (Paris, 1979), pp. 21–22, for the example I have illustrated and an explanation of its meaning.

52. E. Gombrich, *Art and Illusion* (Princeton, 1960).

53. For Mikhail Bakhtin, the most direct introduction is K. Clark and M. Holquist, *Mikhail Bakhtin* (Cambridge, 1984). The latest in an ever growing literature on Bakhtin is the translation of his early essays by M. Holquist, *Art and Answerability* (Austin, Tex., 1990), where further references will be found.

54. This point has often been denied by those who restore old buildings to their pristine state. Following the practice of philologists and of historians of painting, the assumption has been made that the earliest state of a building is always the "correct" one. Yet a building that survives is one that adapts itself to the evolution of life and the

changes of taste and a great building may indeed be one that changes, not that remains the same. Although many paintings and sculptures were occasionally changed for reasons of taste, such fig leafs are not supposed to be appropriate. One possible reason is that paintings or sculptures rarely had the useful and practical functions of architecture. And they could be stored away or painted over, if no one wished to look at them.

55. Quoted from Rycrwert, *First Moderns*, p. 37.

56. My quotations are from the translation by Walter Hamilton (London, 1951), pp. 79–95.

57. For a general statement on Plato's esthetics, see Rupert C. Lodge, *Plato's Theory of Art* (London, 1953), and Margaret R. Mills, *Image as Insight* (Boston, 1985), p. 142. For related arguments, see Gerald F. Else, *Aristotle Poetic's* (Cambridge, 1957), pp. 129ff., for ideas of pleasure. For demons, see Angus Fletcher, *Allegory: the Theory of a Symbolic Mode* (Ithaca, 1964), pp. 38 ff., and A. D. Nock, *Conversion* (Cambridge, 1933).

58. Alain Viala, "Prismatic Effects," *Critical Inquiry* 14 (1988), p. 563.

59. Henri Michaud, *Un barbare en Asie* (Paris, 1933), p. 28.

60. Sigmund Freud, *Beyond the Pleasure Principle*, vol. 18 of *The Complete Works of Sigmund Freud* (London, 1955), p. 21.

Chapter II
The Intermediary of Writing

1. See p. 18

2. For the purposes of this essay, there is no point in speculating about the reasons why this painting was made. But it is an intriguing question, as it is hardly likely that it illustrated a text and it is too complete an image to have served as a sketch or model for something like a wall panel. It might have been a frontispiece or some other kind of page enhancing a book. Maybe it was after all a devotional picture, even though this conclusion assumes a pious behavior ascertained among Christians, Buddhists, or Hinduists, but not among Muslims. A thorough study of shrines and of religious practices, especially in the wider Iranian world, could, however, show that doctrinal objects of the type of our page did exist or propose an alternate explanation. The only account known to me of a contemporary religious treasury is by Soad Maher Mohammed, *Mashhad al-Imam ʿAli fi al-Najaf wa ma bihi min al-Hidaya wa al-Tuhaf* (Cairo, 1968). It concentrates on textiles, but has information on other items.

3. Examples by Piet Mondrian are the most telling because, within one of his series of paintings, small squares or rectangles of different colors are common; Kermit S. Champa, *Mondrian Studies* (Chicago, 1985), most particularly some early paintings (circa 1918–1919) on pp. 61–68 or the celebrated *Broadway Boogie-Woogie* of 1942–1943, pp. 127–38. But several other, more recent schools of painting also used geometric units of different colors; for examples see E. C. Goossen, *Ellsworth Kelly* (New York, 1973), pp. 42–53, and Lawrence Rubin, *Frank Stella Paintings 1958 to 1965* (New York, 1986).

4. Lisa Golombek and Donald Wilber, *The Timurid Architecture of Iran and Turan* (Princeton, 1988), with interesting examples on fig. 324 (Abrandabad) and fig. 336 (Baku). The whole motif deserves a true taxonomic and interpretative study. Suggestive remarks were made on the "whorl" by Richard Ettinghausen, "The Wade Cup," *Ars Orientalis* 2 (1957), pp. 342–43.

5. There is no comprehensive study of ʿAli in history and in myth. For examples of the range of meanings he has had, see Annemarie Schimmel, *Mystical Dimensions of Islam* (Chapel Hill, N.C., 1975), and

Calligraphy and Islamic Culture (New York, 1984). For additional examples and some interesting commentaries, see G. de Fouchécour, *Moralia, les notions morales dans la littérature persane* (Paris, 1986), esp. pp. 23–24, 118–20.

6. This assumption should be tested through a truly unbiased experiment. In apparent practice, however, one may assume the existence in the minds of literate men and women of a category "written text," which can be acknowledged even without the ability to understand what is written or knowing in what language and what script. On some aspects of this "grammatological" theory, see p. 61 for the references to Jacques Derrida's work. See also p. 172 for my definition of "optisemic" as a category of perception within which seeing writing may fit.

7. The issue of when letters or forms looking like letters should be literally read as words or parts of words has been a very confused one. A. Souren Melikian-Chirvani has, in several of his recent studies, argued for a meaning to be given to most letters. See, among other places, his monumental *Islamic Metalwork from the Iranian World* (London, 1982); also, *Le bronze iranien* (Paris, 1973). But the writing of Arabic letters was at times imitative, as in so many designs known as "kufesque." The first to have noted the use of Arabic writing in ornament was Adrien de Longpérier, "De l'emploi des caractères arabes," *Revue Archéologique* 2 (1846). New definitions were offered by George C. Miles, "Byzantium and the Arabs," *Dumbarton Oaks Papers* 18 (1964), who coined the word "kufesque." See also S.D.T. Spittle, "Cufic Lettering in Christian Art," *Archaeological Journal* 111 (1954), and R. Ettinghausen, "Kufesque in Byzantine Greece, the Latin West and the Muslim World," in D. Kouymjian, ed., A Colloquium in Memory of George Carpenter Miles (New York, 1976). Spittle used the term "pseudo-Cufic," while Archibald M. Christie preferred "mock Arabic," in "The Development of Ornament from the Arabic Script," *Burlington Magazine* 40 (1922). For further thoughts on this topic, see below, pp. 102 and 259–260.

8. No topic of Islamic art has elicited more books and even articles than what is known as calligraphy. These books and studies can be divided into three categories: usually wonderfully illustrated manuals depicting the process or mechanism of writing (cutting pens, choice of ink, proportion of letters), with more or less successful examples of each type; catalogues of exhibitions; more or less learned studies that seek to provide either a history of writing, or an esthetics of it, or both.

The most successful examples, in my view, of the first group are: Hassan Massoudy, *Calligraphie arabe vivante* (Paris, 1981); A. Khatibi and M. Sijelmassi, *L'art calligraphique arabe* (Paris, 1980) (interesting examples, often careless text); Yasin H. Safadi, *Islamic Calligraphy* (London, 1978); J. Fada'ili, *Atlas Khatt* (Isfahan, 1391/1965); Naji Zayn al-Din, *Bada'i' al-Khatt al-*ʿArabi (Baghdad, 1972); Yusuf Muhammad Ghulam, *The Art of Arabic Calligraphy* (by author, 1982); Ismayil Hakki Baltacioğlu, *Türklerde Yazi Sanati* (Ankara, 1958); M. Arsel, *Das Schriftbild in der türkischen Kunst* (Ankara, 1967); Pares I.S.M. Rahman, *Islamic Calligraphy in Medieval India* (Dacca, 1979). A wonderful early example of fascination with writing in Arabic letters is E. H. Palmer, *Oriental Penmanship* (London, 1886).

The most useful catalogues are Martin Lings and Y. Safadi, *The Qur'an* (London, 1978); Anthony Welch, *Calligraphy in the Arts of the Muslim World* (Austin, Tex., 1979); David James, *Qur'ans and Bindings from the Chester Beatty Library* (London, 1980); Shen Fu et al., *From Concept to Context*, Freer Gallery of Art (Washington, D.C., 1986); Geneva, Musée d'Art and d'Histoire, *Calligraphie islamique* (Geneva, 1988).

Among studies the most important are Clément Huart, *Les calligraphistes et miniaturistes* (Paris, 1909), an intelligent paraphrase and reorganization of major nineteenth-century Ottoman compendiums based almost exclusively on sixteenth-century sources, with a consciousness of the difficult meanings of certain terms; Adolf Grohmann, *Arabische Paläographie*, 2 vols. (Graz, 1971), indispensable if for no other reason that it contains a complete list of examples of writing for early centuries as known by 1970; Annemarie Schimmel, *Islamic Calligraphy* (Leiden, 1970), and especially the wonderful *Calligraphy and Islamic Culture*, by which I was much inspired, even if I eventually took a different turn in interpreting writing in Muslim lands; Nabia Abbott, *The Rise of the North Arabian Script* (Chicago, 1939), one of the irreplacable basic books on the origins of scripts, and *Studies in Arabic Literary Papyri*, vol. 1 (Chicago, 1957), for a renewed discussion of early scripts; Hassan al-Basha, *Al-Khatt al-Arabi* (Cairo, 1968); Priscilla P. Soucek, "The Arts of Calligraphy," in Basil Grey, ed., *The Arts of the Book in Central Asia* (Paris, 1979); Janine Sourdel-Thomine, "Khatt," in *Encyclopedia of Islam*, 2d edition, and "L'Ecriture arabe et son évolution ornementale," *Centre de synthèse, l'ecriture et la psychologie des peuples* (Paris, 1963); Ernst Kühnel, *Islamische Schriftkunst* (Berlin, 1942), the only book that is moved primarily by esthetic considerations, as can be seen by the choice of illustrations, all of them masterpieces, even if the Victorian text avoids mentioning values of any sort; David James, *Qur'ans of the Mamluks* (London, 1988), an excellent example of a catalogue not tied to a collection or an exhibition, but which analyzes the document of a time and of a place; Manuel Ocana Jimenez, *El Cufico hispano y son evolucion* (Madrid, 1970), as straightforward as its title.

Other studies will be mentioned as they become pertinent to the argument of the text.

9. André Grabar and Carl Nordenfalk, *Le Haut Moyen Age* (Geneva, 1957), pp. 126–28.

10. For the earliest period and for provocative general ideas on the subject, see Carl Nordenfalk, *Die Spätantike Zierbuchstaben* (Stockholm, 1970).

11. To my knowledge there is no overall study of the history of the Latin alphabet. For partial views, see Donald Jackson, *The Story of Writing* (New York, 1981); Aliza Cohen-Mushlin, *The Making of a Manuscript* (Wiesbaden, 1983); Marc Drogin, *Medieval Calligraphy* (New York, 1989); Jacques Stiennon, *Paléographie du Moyen Age* (Paris, 1973); Berthold L. Ullman, *Ancient Writing and Its Influence* (Toronto, 1980); Samuel H. Thomson, *Latin Bookhands* (Cambridge, 1969); or, for later times, Pierpont Morgan Library, *Art of the Printed Book 1455–1955* (New York, 1984), with many examples. Manuals of paleography and of codicology bring out various aspects of the development of letters. A special case should also be made for the Hebrew alphabet, which was occasionally transformed by ornament and, at times, was used to create ornament. See Bezalel Narkiss, *Hebrew Illuminated Manuscripts* (Jerusalem, 1969), pls. 1–5.

12. Hermann Fillitz, *Das Mittelalter*, vol. 1 (Berlin, 1969), p. 139 and pl. 29. See also Rudolf Suntrup, "Te-igitur-initialen und Kanonbilder," in Ch. Meier and U. Ruberg eds., *Text und Bild* (Wiesbaden, 1980), pp. 278–382.

13. An example is the exhibition held at the Houston Contemporary Art Museum under the title: *Contemporary Calligraphers, Mark Tobey, Morris Graves* (Houston, 1956).

14. Most of the key books on Far Eastern calligraphy are catalogues of exhibitions, often with elaborate introductions and frequently with sensitive discussions of individual objects. Throughout and with one full exception and a few partial ones here and there, all the catalogues known to me emphasize either processes of manufacturing or attributions to individual penmen. The main ones are Tseng Yu-Ho Ecke, *Chinese Calligraphy* (Philadelphia, 1971) (with an interesting but short introduction); Lucy Driscoll and Kenji Toda, *Chinese Calligraphy* (New York, 1962); Shen C. Fu et al., *Traces of the Brush* (New Haven, 1977); Tonen-

Hsuin Tsien, *Written on Bamboo and Silk* (Chicago, 1962); Lothar Ledderose, *Mi Fu and the Classical Tradition of Chinese Calligraphy* (Princeton, 1979); Richard Barnhart, "Chinese Calligraphy," *Bulletin, Metropolitan Museum of Art* 30 (1972), pp. 230–41; Yoshiaki Shimuzu and John M. Rosenfield, *Masters of Japanese Calligraphy* (New York, 1984); Y. Shimizu, "The Rite of Writing," *RES* 16 (1988); Alfreda Murck and Wen C. Fong, *Words and Images* (Princeton, 1991); for works by John Hay, see my note 126. An interesting survey of Asian calligraphy from East to West whose subtitle shows fear of its own topic is Shen Fu, Glenn D. Lowry, and Ann Yonemura, *From Concept to Context: Approaches to Asian and Islamic Calligraphy* (Washington, D.C., 1986).

15. Driscoll and Toda, *Chinese Calligraphy*, p. 1, for quotations and comments.

16. Quoted in Tseng Yu-Ho Ecke, *Chinese Calligraphy*, introduction (no page number).

17. Joseph Needham, *Science and Civilisation in China*, vol. 4, p5. 2 (Cambridge, 1965), p. 33, among many places. Baltimore Museum of Art, *2000 Years of Calligraphy* (Baltimore, 1972), is a good introduction to so-called calligraphy after Gutenberg. Since the Muslim world did not really acquire printing until the nineteenth century, the issue of mechanical reproduction occurred in completely different social and cultural conditions from the Western or Chinese ones. To my knowledge, it has never been studied in any complete way within the Muslim traditions.

18. For examples of scripts and minimal comments or texts on writing, see A. S. Osley, *Scribes and Sources: Handbook of the Chancery Hand in the Sixteenth Century* (London, 1980); S. Knight, *Historical Scripts* (New York, 1984).

19. Baltimore, *2000 Years*, p. 104.

20. J. Milton, *Colasterion*, as quoted in *Oxford English Dictionary*, s.v. "Calligraphy."

21. Abbott, *Rise*, p. 41. The source of the story is the late polygraph Ibn Khalliqan, but it represents a typical image of taste, even if of a later date than alleged by the story.

22. Jacques Derrida, *De la grammatologie* (Paris, 1977), esp. pp. 1–30, and then p. 68.

23. The term was first introduced by the late Ignace Gelb, *A Study of Writing: the Foundations of Grammatology* (Chicago, 1952; rev. ed., 1964), but Gelb's otherwise fascinating book ends up once again by being a "history" *of* rather than a discourse *on* writing. He thus illustrates a dilemma we are constantly facing in this study, which lies in the implications of parallelisms between chronology and judgment. So very often a sequence in time establishes values: the older the better or else everything tends toward a precise moment, which is the pinnacle of success and which is followed by decline. Antiquarianism and simpleminded Darwinism both end up by being moral positions, whether they were meant to be or not.

24. In this, as in many other things, the twentieth century has been revolutionary. Records and tapes can preserve sounds, just as events can be preserved on films. The implication of all of this for the future is outside of my concern, but it does seem reasonable to expect that esthetic and other attitudes toward the arts will over time be radically modified by the new ranges and rates of availability of all arts. In fact, history itself may be modified.

25. Erica Dodd, "The Images of the Word," *Berytus* 18 (1969), was the initial statement, which eventually became a book with the same title (with Shereen Khairallah [Beirut, 1981]).

26. These have been recognized for some time; see Richard Ettinghausen and Oleg Grabar, *Art and Architecture of Islam, 650–1250* (London, 1987), pp. 28–30, and O. Grabar, *The Formation of Islamic Art* (2d ed., New Haven, 1987).

27. Muhammad b. Ishaq al-Washsha, R. Brünnow, ed., *Kitab al-Muwashaha* (Leiden, 1886), pp. 151 ff. Schimmel, *Calligraphy and*

Culture, pp. 25–26; R. B. Serjeant, "Materials for a History of Islamic Textiles," *Ars Islamica* 16 (1951), p. 67.

28. Plural of *majlis*, usually translated as "audience hall" or "reception hall." In his 1987 dissertation at MIT., Hazem Sayyed argued that the word had a more technically specific meaning, at least from the tenth century onward, "The Rab' in Cairo" (P.h.D. diss., Massachusetts Institute of Technology, 1987).

29. Mas'udi, *Muruj al-Dhahab*, ed. and trans. Barbier de Meynard and Pavet de Courteille (Paris, 1861–1877), vol. 7, pp. 192–94.

30. Alessio Bombaci, *The Kufic Inscription in Persian Verses* (Rome, 1966); Mehdi Bahrami, *Gurgan Faiences* (Cairo, 1949); and several articles by L. T. Giuzalian in *Epigrafika Vostaka* 2–6 (1951–56); Melikian-Chirvani, *Metalwork*, pp. 260–65; L. T. Giuzalian, "Bonzovoi kuvshin 1182g," in *Pamiatniki Epohi Rustaveli* (Leningrad, 1938); P. B. Cott, *Siculo-Arab Ivories* (Princeton, 1939); Gaston Wiet, *Soieries Persanes* (Cairo, 1948).

31. These are the so-called *tiraz* textiles assumed to have been manufactured under government auspices. Their inscriptions are listed in epigraphical repertories, but they have rarely been studied, only catalogued. See E. Kuhnel and L. Bellinger, *Catalogue of Dated Tiraz Fabrics* (Washington, D.C., 1959).

32. See p. 14 and notes 7–11 for Chapter 1.

33. This is not to say that words alone were examples of taste. It may just be, for instance, that many of the sources with which I have dealt concentrate on poets and on chanceries, milieus that prized the word. There were exceptions, as with the statues erected by Khumarawayh b. Ahmad b. Tulun in his palace within the present complex of Cairo; Maqrizi, *Khitat* (Cairo, 1853), vol. 1, pp. 316–17. Khumarawayh's palace was of the latter part of the ninth century. In the following century in Afghanistan, the Ghaznevid Mas'ud also had figures this time painted on the walls of a palace; Bayhaqi, *Ta'ikh-i Mas'ud* (Tehran, 1945), trans. A. K. Arends, as *Istoria Mas'uda* (Tashkent, 1962), p. 132 of translation, p. 121 of text. These are just examples drawn from written sources. Actual remains of representations on monuments are in fact more numerous than what remains of writing, but they have never been assembled as a corpus.

34. Kuwait National Museum, *Masahif San'a'* (Kuwait, 1983) and Werner Daum, ed., *Yemen* (Frankfort, 1988), pp. 178–87. See also my Chapter 4. François Deroche, *Catalogue des manuscrits arabes, les manuscrits du Coran*, 2 vols. (Paris, 1983–1985). A major written source for the interpretations I am proposing is Ibn al-Nadim, *Kitab al-Fihrist*, ed. G. Flügel (Halle, 1872; repr. Beirut, n.d.) trans. B. Dodge, as *The Fihrist of al-Nadim* (New York, 1970), pp. 4–12 and 10–22 respectively.

35. The best introduction to the word within the context of this essay is the entry "Khatt" by Janine Sourdel-Thomine in the *Encyclopedia of Islam*, but it would be interesting to have a full study of this root, as, for example, students of early Islamic urbanism deal with it quite differently; J. Akbar, "Responsibility and the Traditional Muslim Built Environment" (Ph.D. diss., Massachusetts Institute of Technology, 1984), pp. 152–70, and, "Khatta and the Territorial Structure of Early Muslim Towns," *Muqarnas* 6 (1989). It would be interesting to relate all these meanings together.

36. There is no simple and immediately accessible introduction to the rich coinage of the Islamic world except through the catalogues of major collections like John Walker's for the British Museum (*Catalogue of Muhammedan Coins*, 2 vols. [London, 1951–1956]) or studies on specific areas or periods, with G. C. Miles, *The Numismatic History of Rayy* (New York, 1938), as a model.

37. Ibrahim Shabbuh, *Sijill qadim li-maktabah Jami' al-Qayrawan* (Cairo, 1957), p.

7; Jonathan Bloom, "The Blue Koran," in *Les Manuscrits du Moyen-Orient* (Istanbul, 1988), and "Al-Ma'mun's Blue Koran," in L. Kalus, ed., *Revue des études islamiques: Mélanges Dominique Sourdel* (Paris, 1989).

38. Grohmann, *Paläographie*, is the only one to have paid some systematic attention to these motifs. See, however, D. S. Rice's study cited in note 42.

39. Significant examples in Grohmann, *Paläographie*, pp. 52–54. On tombstones in general, see now the first volume of A. Abd el-Tawab and S. Ory, *Stèles islamiques de la néropole d'Assouan* (Cairo, 1983–1986); Khaled Moaz and Solange Ory, *Inscriptions arabes de Damas*, vol. 1 (Damas, 1977); see also various reviews by Y. Ragheb, as in *Studia Islamica* 72 (1990).

40. The close relationship of all the techniques involved in making a book appear clearly in the manual of Ibn Badis, studied and translated by Martin Levey, "Medieval Arabic Bookmaking," *Transactions of the American Philosophical Society* 52 (1962). For more recent studies and full bibliographies, see Gulnar Boseh et al., *Islamic Bindings and Bookmaking* (Chicago, 1981). For a useful survey of techniques of bookmaking with a particular concern for traditional terminology, see A. In. Kaziev, *Hudozhestreno-teknicheskie Materialy* (Baku, 1986). For a classical analysis of book binding as an art historical document, see Richard Ettinghausen, "Near Eastern Book Covers," *Ars Orientalis* 3 (1959).

41. After years of service in government, he fell into disgrace, had his hand and then his tongue cut out by order of one of the new breed of military rulers, and died shortly thereafter in prison. It is said that, after the loss of his right hand, he learned to write beautifully with the left one. For further references see D. Sourdel, "Ibn Mukla," in *Encyclopedia of Islam*. There is some question as to whether Ibn Muqla ever wrote a manual for writing, inasmuch as some later manuscripts (for example, quoted in Massoudy, *Calligraphie*) attributed to him do exist. My preliminary understanding is that later manuscripts are historical forgeries. For a typical late text in Arabic, see Edward Robertson, "Muhammad ibn ʿAbd Ar-Rahman on Calligraphy," *Glasgow University, Studia Scientifica et Orientalia* (Glasgow, 1920).

42. The manuscript is Istanbul, Topkapi Sarayi, Bagdat 125. It is published and discussed by D. S. Rice, *The Unique Ibn al-Bawwab Manuscript in the Chester Beatty Library* (Dublin, 1955).

43. Best examples of scripts are found in the first group of sources in note 8. They can be divided into three early angular scripts (*mashq*, Kufic, eastern Kufic) soon to be refined after the digestion by scholarship of Yemeni discoveries; the six cursive styles (*thuluth, naskhi, muhaqqaq, rayhāni, rawqīʿ, riqāʿ*); three Persian scripts used in many other lands as well (*ta'līq, nastaʿlīq, shikasteh*); and a number of regional variants like the *maghrebi* script of North Africa and several scripts in the Indian subcontinent, whose original names have not been identified. The easiest introduction is in Y. H. Safadi's book. For Bangladesh, see now M. Y. Siddiq, "An Epigraphical Journey," *Muqarnas* 7 (1990).

44. See James, *Qur'ans of the Mamluks*, for the best, by far, discussion of these magnificent volumes. There is no study of *Shahnama*'s as such, but a sense of their quality emerges by just perusing the appropriate plates in exhibition catalogues like Glenn Lowry, *A Jeweler's Eye* (Washington, D.C., 1988) or T. Lentz and G. Lowry, *Timur and the Princely Vision* (Washington, D.C., 1989).

45. For all these Iranian scripts, as developed in the late fourteenth and fifteenth centuries, the best introduction is Soucek, "The Arts of Calligraphy," in Gray, *The Arts of the Book in Central Asia*.

46. There are many examples of several scripts together on the same page, book, object, or work of architecture, although the predominating pattern is that of one cursive and one angular script next to each other. It would be interesting to plot examples of

several scripts and figure out whether ideological, esthetic, or other constraints affected these examples.

47. This manuscript is known as the "Qarmatian" Koran because, I suppose, some dealer tried to sell leaves from it as coming from a Shi'ite source. For the latest on this manuscript, see Beatrice St. Laurent, "The Identification of a Magnificent Koran Manuscript," in F. Deroche, ed., *Les manuscrits du Proche-Orient* (Istanbul and Paris, 1989).

48. I am not aware of any formal publication of this manuscript (40, 164, 2a). The page illustrated here was published in color in S. C. Welch, *The Arts of Islam* (New York, 1987): When it was exhibited in the museum some years ago, the following label entry accompanied the page: "The manuscript strains to the limits of stylistic coherence without ever actually going too far." The sentence is peculiar but it is clear that its author recognized the unusual quality of the page he described.

49. In the absence of an ecclesiastical structure, Islam has not preserved easily accessible or formally codified liturgical or pious practices and, therefore, it is very difficult to understand or to imagine the actual uses of books with holy subjects and, in fact, of objects as well that have been associated with the faith. The practice of reading the Holy Script according to certain sequences and the recitation of litanies and of prayers exist in Islam, as they are present in Christianity, Buddhism, or Judaism, but religious books have not been organized in groups like books of hours or lectionaries typical of Christianity. All this merits further investigations, just as it would be interesting to know what was meant by chant in the references to chanters of the Koran found in later endornment (*waqf*) documents. It would also be important to find out something about the development of a pious behavior requiring recitation.

50. Franz Rosenthal, "Abu-Haiyan al-Tawhidi on Penmanship," *Ars Islamica* 13–14 (1948), p. 11; reprinted in his *Four Essays on Art and Literature in Islam* (Leiden, 1971), p. 35.

51. al-Washsha, *Kitab*, p. 160, among many places; Schimmel, *Calligraphy and Culture*, p. 256.

52. See p. 63.

53. The issue has been brought up by Jonathan Bloom in his remarks on the "blue" Korans. On a much broader level, it is remarkable that the opposite seems to have occurred in Renaissance Europe with translations of the Bible into vernacular language. There the traditional assumption is that access to the Biblical text in the vernacular led to freer and more varied interpretation. In the Muslim world of the eleventh or twelfth centuries, easy access to the text of the Revelation meant a fuller assertion of its rules in every little detail.

54. Ahmad B. ab-Qalqashandi, *K. al-Insha'* (Cairo, 1967), esp. part 3; Walther Björkman, *Beiträge zur Geschichte der Staatskanzlei im islamischen Ägypten* (Hamburg, 1928). The issue is complicated by the orientalist sin of easy generalization. Thus, Huart's sources (see my note 8) are exclusively Ottoman with the exception of a single Persian source of the early fourteenth century. A survey of the manuscripts gathered in Carl Brockelman, *Geschichte der arabischen Literatur* (Leiden, 1943–), and Fuat Sezgin, *Geschichte der arabischen Schriftum* (Leiden, 1967), failed to elicit the existence of technical manuals in Arabic earlier than the Mongol invasion. Is it an accident? Or is it just possible that the formalization of writing was primarily a post-Mongol, Iranian and Ottoman, phenomenon projected into the past for mythic justification? I believe it to be unlikely that the novelties of the tenth and then thirteenth centuries were not accompanied by manuals of some sort, but the whole matter of chronology does require some more systematic study of manuscripts than has happened so far.

55. The best catalogue is Ayşegül Nadir, *Imperial Ottoman Firmans* (London, 1986).

56. Ettinghausen and Grabar, *Art and Architecture of Islam*, pp. 209 ff.

57. See pp. 12–18; among the few important studies on the ways rather than topics of writing on ceramics, see Lisa Volov (Golombek), "Plaited Kufic," *Ars Orientalis* 6 (1966).

58. The Iraqi examples are mostly of ceramics that contain almost the same range of values as in northeastern Iran. The most easily accessible examples are found in Helen Philon, *Early Islamic Ceramics* (London, 1980), esp. figs. 107 ff. In Egypt there are also ceramics with varieties of writing, although apparently fewer than elsewhere, as well as tombstones and woodwork; illegibility and imitations of writing seem to be rarer in Egypt than in Iran or Iraq, but this impression may be based on an unsystematic survey. Yet, in general, it may be quite worthwhile to prepare statistical tables of the occurrence of kinds of writing in different areas and different techniques.

59. This is particularly striking in some of the miniatures from a Dioscorides manuscript dated 1224 found in many collections. See H. Buchthal, "Early Islamic Miniatures from Baghdad," *Journal of the Walters Art Gallery* 5 (1942), figs. 1, 4, 18, 20, 23. As to animation in metalwork, its main features were first outlined by D. S. Rice, *The Wade Cup in the Cleveland Museum of Art* (Paris, 1955).

60. Examples abound throughout the books on Timurid architecture by Golombek and Wilber, *Timurid Architecture*, and B. O'Kane, *Timurid Architecture in Khorasan* (Costa Mesa, Calif., 1987), which have been quoted earlier.

61. For Isfahan, see Anthony Welch, *Shah Abbas and the Arts of Isfahan* (New York, 1973), p. 65; for Meshhed, Mosque of Gawhar Shad, see Golombek and Wilber, *Timurid Architecture* pp. 37 and 328; O'Kane, *Khorasan*, pp. 119ff. The practice is also true for the Ottomans, as in Karahisari's drawings for several of Sinan's mosques, Huart, *Calligraphistes*, p. 116, and for the Mughals, as in Wayne Begley, "Amanat Khan and the Calligraphy of the Taj Mahal," *Kunst des Orients* 12 (1978–1979).

62. There is, for instance, an early tradition that seems to have been bureaucratic and formal, as with Qalqashandi (see note 54). There is a second tradition based on the names of calligraphers set like a sort of biographical dictionary; Qadi Ahmad's treatise translated by V. Minorsky as *Calligraphers and Painters* (Washington, D.C., 1959) is the most available example. There are actual manuals, (several have been published by Abdullah Chaghatai and others remain unpublished) with their practice designs. There are also florilegia of opinions for educated and cultured elite, as with Tawhidi's opuscule mentioned earlier. Finally, stories or judgments about writing and scribes as well as metaphors and images using writing are found in nearly every genre of literature in the Muslim world, from poetry to austere sociological manuals like Ibn Khaldun's. Yet, so far, there has not come out of all these sources and resources any reasonable historical or interpretative explanation of writing.

63. See note 54 for the curious absence of works on writing in Sezgin or Brockelman. See V. Minorsky's introduction to Qadi Ahmad, *Calligraphers and Painters*, pp. 17–18, for a statement on the difficulty of knowing what exists that is pertinent to the topic. Difficulties are further compounded when translations, even excellent ones like Minorsky's, are provided, because new questions and new approaches require the knowledge of what specific, Arabic or Persian, term was used for judgments. For an example of the problems involved in understanding terms, see Nabia Abbott, "Arabic Paleography," *Ars Islamica* 8 (1941), pp. 102–3, where the potential confusions between technical descriptive and judgmental meanings of the same words are illustrated, if not discussed on a theoretical level.

64. I have used the following sources: Joseph Sadan, "Nouveaux documents sur scribes et copistes," *Revue des Etudes Islamiques* 45 (1977); Franz Rosenthal, *Ars Islamica* 13–14 (1948), reproduced (without the Arabic text) in his *Essays*; Qalqashandi, *K. al-*

Insha', part 3; Qadi Ahmad, *Calligraphers and Painters*; and quotations from many of the books listed in note 8.

65. Soucek, "The Arts of Calligraphy," in Gray, *The Arts of the Book in Central Asia*.

66. Tawhidi, no. 43, in Rosenthal *Essays*, p. 38. I have modified, and inelegantly so, Rosenthal's translation by writing "handwritten piece" rather than "handwriting," because I understood the text to refer to something concrete, which "handwriting" does only in part.

67. Ibid., no. 85, p. 46.

68. Qadi Ahmad, *Calligraphers and Painters*, p. 49. More on cypresses and writing in Annemarie Schimmel, "Schriftsymbolik im Islam," in R. Ettinghausen, ed., *Aus der Welt der islamischen Kunst, Festschrift für Ernst Kühnel* (Berlin, 1959), p. 249.

69. As from Schimmel, *Calligraphy and Culture*, p. 136; the whole book is a treasure of fascinating quotations. Another book on the subject of images of beauty is Sharaf ul-Din b. Muhammad Rami's *Anis al-ʿUshshaq*, trans. with comments by Clément Huart, *Traité des termes figurés relatifs à la description de la beauté* (Paris, 1875). Its fascinating images of the manifold beauties of the body's nineteen parts should become the starting point of a whole series of studies on esthetic judgments in the Timurid and later periods.

70. Qadi Ahmad, *Calligraphers and Painters*, p. 64.

71. Oversize manuscripts of the Koran were common in the fourteenth century. A more peculiar phenomenon is that of oversize illustrated books or alleged books like the Safavid *Falnama*, a book of religious lore or the huge *Hamzanama* made for Akbar in India. On these works, see the forthcoming thesis by Julia Bailey and the recently completed dissertation by Zohra Faridani (Harvard University, 1989).

72. Şevket Rado, *Türk Hattatlari* (Istanbul, n.d.), pp. 235ff. Schimmel, *Calligraphy and Culture*, p. 24; Huart, *Calligraphistes*, p. 101.

73. Huart, p. 258.

74. Qalqashandi, *K. al-Insha'* part 3, pp. 21–23; cf. Björkman, *Staatskanzlei*, a useful introduction to Qalqashandi, but not to our topic.

75. Ibn al-Haytham, *The Optics*, trans. A. I. Sabra (London, 1989), vol. 1, pp. 200 ff.; very important commentary, which is a whole introduction to esthetics, appears in vol. 2, pp. 97–105.

76. Tawhidi, no. 49; in Rosenthal, *Essays*, p. 39.

77. Examples are *Tarifah* or the ten *taf'il* forms listed by Tawhidi at the beginning of his essay; *taswir* and *naqsh* (Ibn Durustawayh); Qadi Ahmad, *Calligraphers and Painters*, pp. 116 ff., for a whole set of such words in a poem. Huart also has noted the importance of this issue of vocabulary and occasionally given Ottoman technical terms, as with the identification of parts of letters and of their composition, *Calligraphistes*, pp. 352 and 244.

78. Qadi Ahmad, *Calligraphers and Painters*, p. 87.

79. In addition to the several books and articles by Professor Schimmel which have already been mentioned several times, see F. Rosenthal, "Significant uses of Arabic Writing," in *Essays*, p. 50.

80. Oleg Grabar, *The Illustrations of the Maqamat* (Chicago, 1984), pp. 79–81; Dr. Irene Bierman has been working on the meanings and variants of the *lam-alif* but, to my knowledge, has not yet published her findings. On the *lam-alif* as a separate letter, see Robertson in *Glasgow Studia Orientalia*, p. 83.

81. For the inscriptions, largely pious, on the Ottoman "boat" at the Boston Museum of Fine Arts, see Miroslav Krek, "Uthman's Ark of Noah," *Archives of Asian Art* 24 (1970–1971), p. 84.

82. Huart, *Calligraphistes*, pp. 267–70. The issue is a complicated one, as being a bureaucrat does not prevent one from being a mystic. From at least the thirteenth century onward mystical images may well have permeated all levels of society without implying allegiance to mystical orders and movements. It is in this fashion that many

representations on ceramics were explained; Ettinghausen and Grabar, *Art and Architecture of Islam*, p. 328.

83. Schimmel, *Calligraphy and Culture*, p. 108.

84. Tha'alibi, *Kitab Thimar al-Qulub* (Cairo, 1326 A.H.), p. 49.

85. Rosenthal, *Essays*, pp. 34, 36, 37.

86. Qadi Ahmad, *Calligraphers and Painters*, p. 122; Schimmel, *Calligraphy and Culture*, pp. 80 ff., for other examples.

87. Schimmel, *Calligraphy and Culture* pp. 80–81, for a discussion of the Iranian-Islamic notion of the Primordial Pen.

88. The concept involved—that of the *niyah*, "intent," as it exists behind an act—is defined in the Traditions (not in the Koran) as the basis on which to judge an action.

89. A great deal has been written about the institutions at the courts of Muslim princes, which, especially from the Mongol empires of the late thirteenth century onward, manufactured fancy illustrated manuscripts and, for instance under the Ottomans, served as general purveyors of beautiful things or gadgets in many different techniques. See Esin Atil, *The Age of Suleyman* (Washington, D.C., 1986) and, for Iran, Lentz and Lowry, *Timur*, or Wheeler Thackston, *A Princely Vision* (Cambridge, 1988), pp. 346–48, among many places. That matters were in fact more complicated than is generally assumed through the simple model of artisans and artists attached to court ateliers has been suggested by M. S. Simpson's reconstruction of the making of an admittedly unusual manuscript ("The Production and Patronage of the *Haft Aurang* in the Freer Gallery of Art," *Ars Orientalis* 13 [1982]), and by Allan and Carol Fischer, "A Note on the Location of Royal Ottoman Ateliers," *Muqarnas* 3 (1985). What happened before the Mongols is far less clear and is tied to the issue of the royal "treasures," of which the only well-known ones are in the Fatimid in Cairo; see my note 91. For general issues of patronage seen in more traditional ways, see the contributions by O. Grabar, E. Whelan, J. Bloom, S. Blair, and W. Denny to Esin Atil, ed., *Islamic Art and Patronage: Treasures from Kuwait* (New York, 1991).

90. There is no coherent history of collecting in the traditional (or contemporary) Muslim world. For a general introduction to the whole issue, see Joseph Alsop, *The Rarer Traditions of Art* (New York, 1982), esp. pp. 253–56, 418, 423. For the Mughals, see Abdul Aziz, *The Imperial Treasury of the Indigan Mughals* (Lahore, 1942), who shows how dependent the Mughals were on the practices of earlier Indian rulers. Similarly, the Ottomans had been affected by the organization of Byzantine court treasures. Much less is known about Safavid treasures, mostly because the information has not been put together.

91. The main studies on these treasures are Paul Kahle, "Die Schätze der Fatimiden," *Zeitschrift der deutschen Morgenlandgesellshaft* 89 (1935), and M. Zaky Hassan, *Kunuz al-Fatimiyin* (Cairo, 1937). The major new source is al-Rashid b. el-Zubayr, *Kitab al-Dhakha'ir wa al-Tuhaf*, ed. M. Hamidullah (Kuwait, 1959), trans. into English by Ghada Qaddumi (Ph.D. diss., Harvard University, 1990).

92. Maqrizi, *Khitat*, vol. 2, pp. 408–25.

93. Ibid., p. 409.

94. The point of collecting is seen by Alsop too much in the mercantile terms of the value of a work of art (see *The Rarer Traditions of Art*) and there is no doubt that such a view is supported by the popular press. But, without denying the paramount importance of money in art seen as a sort of investment, there are other factors involved in collecting: greed, power, lust, arbitrary choices. Contemporary millionaires and kings of old were at times motivated by other feelings than exposure of and to wealth.

95. A fascinating example is that of the parchment in a private collection in Beirut with an alleged autograph of the letter sent by the Prophet to the Persian emperor Khosroes II, partly published in Musée Ibrahim Sursock, *Art islamique* (Beirut, 1974). It has been added as a supplement of

these pages inserted between the Arabic and French versions of the catalogue. Most other pious forgeries known to me remain unpublished.

96. There is as yet no real attempt at explaining the phenomenon of albums and most interest has been devoted to the images *in* albums rather than to the complete collection of items in any one of them. For preliminary notes on the earliest and very different albums of the fifteenth century, see Lentz and Lowry, *Timur*, p. 171. Dr. Massumeh Farhad is preparing a study of some of the major Safavid albums in Istanbul with new information about their manufacture.

97. Huart, *Calligraphistes*, p. 97.

98. Atil, *Age of Suleyman*, but see also my note 89.

99. There lies there yet another subject that needs investigation. Only a thorough statistical analysis of major holdings of manuscript collections within a defined time and area could truly justify the conclusion proposed here.

100. The topic of public writing has been tackled by Professor R. Bierman in a work which has not yet appeared but which I could see at the request of the author. My approach to the issue is in this book totally different from hers without in any sense contradicting it. In the meantime research in the direction of explaining a public use of inscriptions with ideological content has been accomplished by Jonathan Bloom, "The Mosque of al-Hakim in Cairo," *Muqarnas* 1 (1983) and "The Mosque of Baybars," *Annales Islamologiques* 18 (1982).

101. See note 61. Some of the issues of writing with messages on objects were brought up by various articles and books by Melikian-Chirvani, including those quoted earlier in note 7, and by Linda Komaroff, "The Timurid Phase in Iranian Metalwork" (Ph.D. diss., New York University, 1984).

102. The Isfahan panel was published by L. Hunarfar, *Ganjineh-i Ta'rikh-i Isfahan* (Isfahan, 1344 AH), p. 110. See also Oleg Grabar, *The Great Mosque of Isfahan* (New York, 1988), pp. 34–35.

103. Max van Berchem, *Matériaux pour un Corpus Inscriptionum Arabicarum: Jérusalem* (Cairo, 1927), pp. 368–91, among several places.

104. G. Necipoglu, "The Life of an Imperial Monument: Hagia Sophia after Byzantium," in Robert Mark, ed., *The Structure of Hagia Sophia* (Princeton, 1991).

105. Sherban Cantacuzino, ed., *Architecture in Continuity* (New York, 1985), pp. 103–9. The building has been often discussed in the architectural press.

106. See note 59.

107. Very little has been written about the visual esthetics of the Ka'bah and of its transformation through textiles. For early times, see O. Grabar, "On Reading al-Azraqi," *Muqarnas* 3 (1985). For a fascinating glimpse of Mekka in Ottoman times, see Suraiya Faroqhi, *Herrscher über Mekka* (Munich, 1990).

108. L. T. Giuzalian, "A Bronze Qalamdan of 542/1148," *Ars Orientalis* 7 (1968), pp. 95–119.

109. However important they have been, studies of the decoration of metalwork other than writing have rarely succeeded in personalizing an object. A partial exception is the study of the unique and extraordinary Baptistère de St. Louis, by Doris Behrens-Abouseif, "The Baptistère de Saint Louis," *Islamic Art* 3 (1989). See also Jonathan Bloom, "A Mamluk Basin," *Islamic Art* 2 (1986).

110. B. Moritz, *Arabic Palaeography* (Cairo, 1905; repr. Osnabrück, 1986). It is also interesting that this book only contains plates. Its "text" came much later with the works of Grohmann under the same title cited earlier in note 8.

111. With varying degress of commitment, and depth, esoteric implications of writing have been argued in various works, often quoted, of S. Melikian-Chirvani and A. Schimmel. A more prosaic approach has been argued by Grohmann as in his "Die bronzeschale M. 388–1911 im Victoria and Albert Museum," in R. Ettinghausen, ed., Aus der Welt der islamischen Kunst,

(Berlin, 1959). His way can be contrasted with Schimmel's article in the same volume entitled "Schriftsymbolik im Islam."

112. Examples: Rado, *Hattatlari*, pp. 235ff.

113. This is yet another topic for further elucidation. A study of manuals of writing would provide a sense of how types of scripts were judged and a survey of monuments and of albums would give an idea of which ones prevailed. As a result, we could come up with the kind of history that seems available for Chinese scripts—that is to say, one in which the synchronically specific meaning and purpose of a written piece, on paper or on an object, can easily be fitted into the diachronic evolution of a script.

114. The issue is a fascinating one, as one relates to each other the situation in the Soviet Union where Arabic scripts have been replaced by Cyrillic, in Turkey or Indonesia where Latin letters are used for national languages, in China where there is a dominant pictographic language, in Africa struggling between Arabic and Latin characters, and then in the core lands of Arabic, Persian, Urdu, Bengali, and Malay languages where the Arabic script is known and tends to predominate especially with the growth of fundamentalist identity.

115. There are a few variations occasionally about both rhythmic verticality and right-to-left direction. In the mass of examples, these variations are insignificant, although, once again, an awareness of the psychological definition of how scripts operate is necessary before an esthetic evaluation can be justified.

116. Kjeld von Folsach, *Islamic Art: The David Collection* (Copenhagen, 1990), p. 84; Sonia Seherr-Thoss and Hans Seherr-Thoss, *Design and Color in Islamic Architecture* (Washington, D.C. 1968), pl. 50, p. 114.

117. One of the issues involved is that of the degree of meaningful recognition that can legitimately be given to fragments of words. Only Souren Melikian-Chirvani has, at least indirectly, dealt with the issue by asserting a syndechdocal meaning to letters standing for whole words; see my note 7. Magical meanings are also likely because of the numerous examples of books or pieces of paper with letters used by seers of all sorts. For metalwork examples, see G. Wier, *Catalogue du Museé Arabe du Caire: Objets en Cuivre* (Cairo, 1932), pls. 40–43.

118. Examples abound as a *sic* in parenthesis indicating errors in Arabic characterizes the publication of many objects. See Ettinghausen, "Kufesque in Byzantine Greece." Errors of that type are made more common with the "populist" streak than among major works of official art.

119. This panel is often illustrated; see Seher-Thoss, *Design and Color*, pl. 65; also, L. Golombek, *The Timurid Shring at Gazur Gah* (Toronto, 1969), fig. 110.

120. Chahriyar Adle, "Recherches sur le module et le tracé correcteur dans la miniature orientale," *Le Monde Iranien et l'Islam* 3 (1975).

121. Atil, *Age of Suleyman*, pp. 194–98; O. Grabar, "An Exhibition of High Ottoman Art," *Muqarnas* 6 (1990).

122. The identification of frontier cultures within medieval Islamic civilization still requires investigation. It is possible that Africa should be added to the list. In inscriptions in another frontier culture, Michael Rogers recognized the existence of a "genre between calligraphy and common script." M. Rogers, "Calligraphy and Common Script," in P. Soucek, ed., *Content and Context of Visual Arts in the Islamic World* (University Park, Penn., 1988).

123. Although never analyzed in all of its formal and other implications, the assumption of two strands within classical Persian painting from the late fourteenth century onward underlies studies by R. W. Robinson (as in *Persian Drawings* [New York, 1965]), E. Grube (among several places, *The Classical Style in Islamic Painting* [New York, 1969]), and S. C. Welch (for instance, *Wonders of the Age* [Cambridge, 1979]), among others. Massumeh Farhad, in her doctoral dissertation, "Safavid Single Page Painting, 1629–1660" (Harvard University, 1982), has

dealt with the last decades of that double direction in the late seventeenth century.

124. To the works quoted in note 12, add Richard Barnhart, "Wei Fu-jen's *Pi Chen T'u* and the early Texts on Calligraphy," *Archives of the Chinese Art Society of America* 18 (1964).

125. Y. Shimizu and John M. Rosenfield, *Masters of Japanese Calligraphy* (New York, 1984).

126. John Hay, "The Human Body as a Microcosmic Source of Macrocosmic Values in Calligraphy," in S. Busch and Ch. March, eds. *Theories of the Arts in China* (Princeton, 1983), among several pertinent articles.

127. The use of Arabic letters in the art of non-Muslims, especially Western ones, deserves more reflection than it has received so far. See references in note 7, and O. Grabar and Richard Ettinghausen, "Art and Architecture," in J. Schacht and C. E. Bosworth, eds., *The Legacy of Islam*, 2d ed. (Oxford, 1974), pp. 244–320, with lengthy bibliographies to that time. For more examples from a totally different point of view, one may profit from the wonderful illustrations in the catalogue of the exhibition *Europa und der Orient* (Berlin, 1989). Specific medieval examples are discussed by George C. Miles, "Classification of Islamic Elements," in *Actes, XIIème Congrès des Etudes Byzantines* (Belgrade, 1964), or L. Pavlovič, "Contributions à l'étude de l'épigraphie iconographique," *Recherches sur l'art* (Novi Sad, 1984). In general, there seem to be sufficient differences between regions and periods in the use of borrowed Arabic letters or words that any generalization is probably inadequate.

128. There are, to my knowledge, no discussions or statements on uses or potential of writing in the contemporary art of Muslim countries. But there are examples from which a critical theory could be formulated in time. Some random examples: B. Ben Hossain Alaoui, *Art contemporain arabe*, Institut du Monde Arabe (Paris, 1988), esp. pp. 77, 81, 82, 97, 103, 133. On a different level, see the exhibition, also organized by the same Institut du Monde Arabe, *Mémoire de soie* (Paris, 1988), p. 212, with political uses of writing.

129. M. Falamaki and K. Adle, "Al-Ghadir Mosque, Tehran," *Mimar* 2 (1988).

Chapter III
The Intermediary of Geometry

1. The issue of a hierarchy within reasonable interpretations and explanations of works of art requires further discussion. It is an issue of particular importance in any consideration of the arts of "others," as incorrect or incomplete explanations are often seen as cultural slurs or slights. Over the past century, the problem of "correct" or "incorrect" approaches has come up with respect to national or ethnic identifications for the arts. Specialists in Islamic art, for instance, have been criticized for being too Irano-centered or, on the contrary and by different groups of people, for subsuming Iranian art under a Muslim veneer. When confined to labels, this level of criticism is usually rather silly, even if great figures in the history of art like Emile Mâle and Nikolaus Pevsner contributed to it (see note 4 to Introduction). The real problem lies elsewhere. Different needs and different responses to works of art will always occur and some of them are bound to be at variance with the original "truth" of an object.

A particularly striking example of that is the Dome of the Rock in Jerusalem; for basic bibliography, unfortunately without interpretation, see "Kuds" in the *Encyclopedia of Islam*, 2d ed., and for a partial explanation see O. Grabar, "The Meaning of the Dome of the Rock," in M. J. Chiat and K. L. Reyerson, eds. *The Medieval Mediterranean*, (St.

Cloud, Minn., 1988); the topic is far from exhausted. The original meaning to the Muslim patrons of the building was already lost in the Middle Ages and replaced by a pious one more satisfactory to the majority of believers. But the Muslim meaning or meanings were never the ones adopted by Christians or Jews, who themselves varied over the centuries about the meaning of the monument. The unique situation and history of Jerusalem made the Dome of the Rock equally unique, but it is probably only so in the extreme range of its varieties. In general, how does one define an acceptable equilibrium between the authenticity of a work of art in its original state and the history of its use over time?

2. Arthur Loeb, *Color and Symmetry* (New York, 1971); Thomas W. Wielting, *The Mathematical Theory of Chromatic Plane Ornaments* (New York, 1982); Branko Grünbaum and G. C. Shepherd, *Tilings and Patterns* (New York, 1987). These are books I have consulted without necessarily understanding them. They are themselves based on centuries of documented research going back to the Middle Ages and formalized in the Renaissance in Italy. Every year brings out a new crop of books on geometric patterning.

3. Owen Jones, *The Grammar of Ornament* (London, 1856; repr. New York, 1987), pp. 5–6. David Van Zanten, *The Architectural Polychromy of the 1830's* (New York, 1977).

4. For studies, see Bernard Schweitzer, *Greek Geometric Art* (London, 1971) and J. N. Coldstream, *Greek Geometric Pottery* (London, 1968); for pictures P. E. Arias and M. Hirmer, *A History of Greek Vase-Painting* (New York, 1962). For scholarly detailed discussion, see J. L. Benson, *Horse, Bird and Man: The Origins of Greek Art* (Amherst, Mass., 1970).

5. Among many places, Arthur U. Pope, ed., *A Survey of Persian Art*, vol. 1 (London, 1938), pp. 171–94, esp. 176–77; Edith Porada, *The Art of Ancient Iran* (Baden-Baden, 1962), pp. 23ff.; any of several versions of exhibitions with catalogues that circulated in the 1960s. The likelihood of ceramic decoration to have simplified mimetically inspired topics has been the subject of some discussion. My own views on the subject have wavered a lot. At the time of writing, I tend to question the process of simplified representation of the visible as the first step toward naturalism, being perhaps overly affected by D. Collins and J. Onians, "The Origins of Art," *Art History* 1 (1978).

6. George Kubler, *The Art and Architecture of Ancient America*, 3d ed. (London, 1986), pp. 174, 184, 437, 468–9, among many examples.

7. Any survey of Chinese art has good examples of bronzes, or see John A. Pope et al., *The Freer Chinese Bronzes* (Washington, D.C., 1967), nos. 29, 83. George W. Weber, Jr., *The Ornament of the Late Chou Bronzes* (New Brunswick, N.J., 1973), is an excellent example of the struggle between a taxonomy convincingly argued out and the objects themselves, which are almost throughout transformed into partial drawings in order to make the taxonomy work. See, in a different but rather exciting vein, Joseph Lee Koerner, "The Fate of the Thing: Ornament and Vessel in Chou Bronze Interlacery," *RES* 10 (1985).

8. Karl Jettmar, *Art of the Steppes* (Baden-Baden, 1964), and E. Bunker et al., "Animal Style," *Art from East to West* (New York, 1970), are reasonable introductions to a rich material. They do not entirely replace basic studies by S. I. Rudenko, *Kultura Naseleniia Tsentralnogo Altaia* (Moscow, 1960) or M. I. Artomonov, *Sokrovicha Sakov* (Moscow, 1973).

9. Jettmar, *The Steppes*, pp. 16–17.

10. Metropolitan Museum of Art, *From the Lands of the Scythians: Ancient Treasures from the Museums of the USSR* (New York, 1975), pl. 8.

11. James C. Faris, *Nuba Personal Art* (London, 1972); also see my p. 41.

12. David Heathcote, *The Arts of the Hausa* (London, 1976).

13. For contemporary geometric paint-

ing as by Frank Stella, E. Kelly, R. Anuskiewicz, and many others, see H. H. Aronson, *History of Modern Art*, 3d ed. (New York, 1986), esp. chap. 2. Linda D. Henderson, *The Fourth Dimension and Non-Euclidian Geometry in Modern Art* (Princeton, 1983). Most books on art do not even mention M. C. Escher, considered by most to be too much of a popular illustrator; see, however, *The Graphic Work of M. C. Escher* (New York, 1984) and Caroline H. MacGillavry, *Fantasy and Symmetry* (New York, 1976).

14. The study of the arts of India is in some turmoil and exhibits uncertainty of purpose, as can be seen in the several articles that have appeared in *Art Journal* 49 (1990) (Donald M. Studtner, guest editor). The relationship between architecture and a culturally expressed geometry has affected much of Michael Meister's writings (*Art Journal* 49 [1990], pp. 399–400). See in particular "Geometry and Measure in Indian Temple Plans," *Artibus Asiae* 44 (1983) and "Mandala and Practice," *Journal of the American Oriental Society* 99 (1989). For the mandala as a more universal principle, see N. Ardalan and L. Bakhtiar, *The Sense of Unity* (Chicago, 1973).

15. For the purposes of these essays I would like to reiterate a key distinction between signs and symbols as they appear in the visual world. Signs have always a direct and immediate, denotative, relationship to a subject, which can be known (even if it is actually obscure because of ignorance or for other reasons). A symbol connotes something that may be quite independent of what it is; symbols are usually short-lived without constant recharging.

16. Jystona S. Kilambi, "Toward an Understanding of the *muggu*," *RES* 19 (1985).

17. Peter S. Stevens, *Handbook of Regular Patterns* (Cambridge, 1984), for a very comprehensive and, to the uninitiated, lucid survey of patterns of their transformations; he uses consistently examples drawn from world art. See also D. K. Washburn and D. W. Crave, *Symmetries of Culture* (Seattle, 1988). A more specific topic is engaged, in a much more profound way, by Hermann Weyl, *Symmetry* (Princeton, 1952); it involves crystals and other primary expressions of the natural world and leads to what could be called a metaphysics of geometry. More recently, various social scientists and even a few historians and critics of art have become fascinated by the designs discovered or created by the late A. Mandelbrojt through fractal geometry; among other places, see H. Jürgens, H.-O. Peitgen, and D. Saupe, "The Language of Fractals," *Scientific American* 263 (1990), pp. 60–67.

18. Stevens, *Patterns*, pp. 332–35; Gombrich, *Sense of Order*, pp. 67–83.

19. The five most accessible ones for Islamic regular geometric patterns are J. Bourgoin, *Arabic Geometrical Pattern and Design* (New York, 1973, without text), a pioneering book published in Paris in 1879 under the title *Les éléments de l'art arabe* and based almost exclusively on the monuments of Cairo; Issam El-Said and Ayşe Parman, *Geometric Concepts in Islamic Art* (London, 1976), a very lucid statement of forms with excellent drawings but a debatable interpretation, to be discussed further on; the same critique applies to Keith Critchlow, *Islamic Patterns* (London, 1976); E. H. Hankin, "The Drawing of Geometric Patterns in Saracenic Art," *Memoirs, Archeological Survey of India* 15 (Calcutta, 1925), which is based on examples from India; and David Wade, *Patterns in Islamic Art* (London, 1976), another example of matching patterns on existing objects with theoretical schemes, which is mercifully skimpy on historical or religious interpretations. Keith Albarn et al., *The Language of Pattern* (London, 1974), includes an interesting extension of Islamic models into a wider and at times exciting speculation on form making as a manner of organizing space. In their context, the cultural component is just about gone.

There are less accessible publications on geometry in Islamic art that show, however, that questions about it are asked everywhere: Haresh Lalvani, *Coding and Generating Islamic Patterns* (Ahmedabad, 1982); a whole issue of *Marg* 34 (1983) was devoted to *The Impulse to Adorn*; A. A. Sultan, "Notes on the Divine Propositions in Islamic Architecture," *Process Architecture* 15 (1980), published in Japan; and the work of A. Bulatov, especially *Geometricheskaya Garmonisatzia v Arhitektury Srednei Azil, IX–IIVV*, 2d ed. (Moscow, 1988).

It is more intriguing to know when model books of geometric forms, as distinguished from manuals of geometry, made their appearance. The earliest known so far are from the fifteenth century. The key text is al-Kashi, *Miftah al-Hisab*, ed. Nabulsi Nader (Damascus, 1977), trans. with important comments by L. Bretanitsky and B. Rosenfeld, "Arhitekturnaia Glava," *Iskusstvo Azerbaijana* 5 (1956). For preliminary studies, see G. Necipoglu, "Plans and Models," *Journal of the Society of Architectural Historians* 45 (1988), and Renata Holod, "Defining an Art of Architecture," in *Aga Khan Award, Architectural Education in the Islamic World* (Singapore and Geneva, 1986), and "Text, Plan and Building," in *Aga Khan Program: Theories and Principles of Design in the Architecture of Islamic Societies* (Cambridge, 1988). See also R. Lewcock in G. Michell, ed., *Architecture in the Islamic World* (London, 1970).

20. For Ottoman ceramics, see Walter Denny's chapter in Esin Atil, ed., *Turkish Art* (Washington, D.C., 1980), and especially N. Atasoy and J. Raby, *Iznik Pottery* (London, 1989), figs. 323–24, for example. The origin of the motif I am illustrating is usually given as the *tughra* designs accompanying Ottoman imperial signatures (fig. 52). This may well be true, but it is a historical and genetic statement, not a visually critical one, as only taxonomic historians of art think of Ottoman signatures when looking at these ceramics.

21. Alexander Papadopoulo, *L'Esthétique de l'art musulman: La peinture*, 6 vols. (thesis, University of Paris I, 1972; available in mimeographed form from Lille). His views are found in a less forceful way in his monumental *L'Islam et l'art musulman* (Paris, 1976). It is, of course, unlikely that a single geometric procedure affected centuries of artistic creativity, but the notion of a sort of geometric substratum in many shapes with specific cultural affinities may not be as wild as I had thought earlier.

22. This little known monument, like this whole forgotten province of Islam's frontier with China and the North, deserves more thinking than it has received. See Nagim-Bek Nurmuhammedov, *Iskusstvo Kazakhstana* (Moscow, 1970), pp. 45–49.

23. The classical statement for the Renaissance is Rudolph Wittkower, *Architectural Principles in the Age of Humanism* (New York, 1971). For central Asia, it is Bulatov, *Geometricheskaia*. To my knowledge, there is no introduction to the place of geometry in traditional Muslim society. Hints of its importance appear as one looks at the works of al-Farabi (I. Madhkour, *La place d'al-Farabi dans l'école philosophique musulmane* [Paris, 1934]; al-Farabi, *Rasa'il* [Alma-Ata, 1970], esp. pp. 159–62; Omar Khayyam, *Traktaty*, ed. B. A. Rosenfeld [Moscow, 1961]. In the West geometry became the core of a conception of education, which culminates in Viollet le-Duc's wonderful account of rational education through the learning by a bright young boy of natural geometry, *Histoire d'un dessinateur* (Paris, 1879), esp. pp. 32 and 286.

24. The issue of "regular" geometry in objects is a rather interesting one, even though only a few of the writers mentioned so far have dealt with it (Papadopoulo, es-Said). It can, for instance, be argued that the decoration of plates and bowls is always a problem of the decoration of circles, a basically geometric problem, and that the division of the cylindrical body of a bronze candlestick into six or twelve panels required a practical knowledge of geometry. How this was actually done remains unknown.

25. There is a considerable bibliography on these ornaments. More or less complete lists with good individual descriptions are

found in K.A.C. Creswell, *Early Muslim Architecture*, 2d ed. (Oxford, 1969), brought up to date by James Allen, *A Short History of Early Muslim Architecture* (London, 1989), or, less monographically, in Richard Ettinghausen and Oleg Grabar, *Art and Architecture of Islam, 650–1250* (London, 1987), chap. 2. A more interpretative essay is in O. Grabar, *The Formation of Islamic Art*, 2d ed. (New Haven, 1987), esp. chap. 4. Other pertinent recent studies or essays are by Robert Hillenbrand, "La *dolce vita* in Early Islamic Syria," *Art History* 5 (1982), F. A. Touqan, *Lilha'ir* (Amman, 1979), and H. G. Franz, *Palast, Moschu und Wüstenschloss* (Graz, 1984).

26. This point has been primarily suggested by O. Grabar, *Formation*, 2nd ed., supplementary chapter, pp. 196ff., and several articles on the paintings of Qusayr Amrah, "La place de Qusayr Amrah," *Cahiers Archéologiques* 36 (1988), and "Une nouvelle inscription," *Revue des Etudes Islamiques* (1989). A Mediterranean (or, as was preferred by some, "Hellenistic") background for Umayyad secular art was implicitly recognized by an older (pre–World War I) generation of scholars who assumed for whatever they knew of Umayyad art that it illustrated what had remained of secular art everywhere and who were convinced of classical origins for nearly everything.

27. Robert Hamilton, *Khirbat al-Mafjar* (Oxford, 1959). Hamilton has more than once returned to "his" palace, the latest foray being the wonderful *Walid and His Friends* (Oxford, 1988), which puts together a, for the most part, most plausible explanation of the building. Fascinating, even if not entirely acceptable, hypotheses were provided by Richard Ettinghausen, *From Byzantium to Sasanian Iran and the Islamic World* (Leiden, 1972), with a reply by Hamilton, "Khirbat al-Mafjar," *Levant* 10 (1978). Most of the argument lies around images on floor mosaics in the bath, which are so unique that their meaning is almost impossible to provide.

28. Creswell and Allen, *Early Muslim Architecture*, pp. 135–40. The masses of fragments partly reconstructed in the Damascus National Museum still await the investigator.

29. Hamilton, *Mafjar*, p. 280.

30. The relatively few studies published so far on Khirbat al-Mafjar (Hamilton) or Qasr al-Hayr West (D. Schlumberger, "Kasr al-Heyr," *Syria* 20 [1939]), or even Qusayr Amrah, about which more has been written, allege, for the most part, a Mediterranean background for the motifs, with a significant input from places east. All of this is explained (Grabar, *Formation*, pp. 195–202) by the new political configuration of western Asia after the Muslim conquest which made accessible to the rich Arab ruling aristocracy of Syria-Palestine (and probably parts of Western Arabia as well) ideas and motifs from the whole Eurasian world except for China. Unfortunately this shopping-center explanation of the history of the arts does not seem to me any longer to deal adequately with the concrete reality of any one monument.

31. For those who may wish to seek esoteric meanings in the first half of the eighth century and who agree with the very plausible attribution of Mafjar to al-Walid II, the eccentric prince-poet and bon vivant, it could be possible to investigate whether being called a *zindiq*, a heretic, as he frequently was, and being interested in astrology and in occult sciences may have been translatable into geometric forms in the early eighth century.

32. An alternate explanation would be the historical-genetic one of the transfer to Palestine and Syria of a technique of wall covering with stucco developed for completely different reasons in Iraq, Iran, and central Asia. There are numerous problems in dating stucco panels attributed to the Sasanian period in Iran, but there is an assumption that walls were covered with decorated stuccos, at least in fancy establishments; J. H. Schmidt, "L'expédition de

Ctésiphon," *Syria* 15 (1934); D. Thompson, *Stucco from Chal Tarkhan* (Warminster, 1976); V. A. Shiskkin, "Architekturnaia Dekoratsiia Dvortsa v Varakhshe," *Trudy Otdela Vostoka Ermitage* 4 (1947).

Initially and for many years this was also my preferred explanation, as it fitted better with the art historian's obligation to provide chronologically linear explanations; Grabar, *Formation*, pp. 180–82; Ettinghausen and Grabar, *Art and Architecture of Islam*, pp. 58–59. I feel now that explanations which require the transmission of esthetic ideas and of technologies over thousands of miles require a better-articulated cultural explanation than I am able to provide for the eighth century. For examples of how to use the little evidence that is available for later times, see the studies mentioned in note 19.

33. Much of this has to be assumed without ethnographic investigations probably no longer possible or without analyses of pre-Islamic poetry. The only clear document is that the sanctuary of the Kaʿbah in Mekka, the holiest shrine in Arabia, was covered with expensive and multicolored silks; Azraqi, *Akhbar Makka* (Beirut, 1970?), vol. 1, pp. 173ff., a reprint of F. Wüstenfeld's original *Geschichte der Stadt Mekka* (Göttingen, 1858). M. Gaudefroy-Demombynes, "Le voile de la Kaʿba," *Studia Islamica* 2 (1954). The notion of a textile esthetic was introduced by L. Golombek, "The Draped Universe of Islam," in P. Soucek, ed., *Content and Context of Visual Arts in the Islamic World* (University Park, Penn., 1988).

34. I do not know who first coined the term "brick style," but the earliest dated (circa 943) building exhibiting these new features is the Samanid mausoleum in Bukhara; Ettinghausen and Grabar, *Art and Architecture of Islam*, pp. 217–224. For eleventh- and twelfth-century monuments, see pp. 272–75.

35. Ibid., pp. 278, 290. Both of these monuments also used plaster decoration, at times imitating brick.

36. There are examples in Iraq (Baghdad, Irbil, Mossul), Syria (Ruqqah), and Turkey (Dunaysir, Malatga). All these places can be located through Ettinghausen and Grabar, *Art and Architecture of Islam*, or through the catalogue in Michell, *Architecture in the Islamic World.*

37. The clearest statement of these principles is in El-Said and Parman, *Geometric Concepts.* The Golden Mean has, of course, been the subject of numerous studies since the discovery, already in antiquity, of its uniquely pleasing properties on the one hand and irrational structure on the other. See M. Cleyet-Michaud, *Le nombre d'or* (Paris, 1974).

38. Examples can easily be found in two kinds of books:

first, regional and temporal surveys associated in particular with Soviet scholarship in Azerbayjan and in central Asia (various books by G. A. Pugachenkova and L. I. Rempel), with recent works on fifteenth-century architecture in the broader Iranian world (O'Kane, and Golombek and Wilber), and with most works on Mughal architecture in India (G. Michell or R. Nath);

second, wider and usually ahistorical surveys, mostly of photographs, as in D. Hill and O. Grabar, *Islamic Architecture and Its Decoration* (London, 1954), and Sonia Seherr-Thoss and Hans Seherr-Thoss, *Design and Color in Islamic Architecture* (Washington, D.C., 1968).

39. See references in note 19. The only fairly thorough study of the issues is the one by Bulatov, *Geometricheskaia* who does move from a small number of texts (not always fully understood) to theoretical drawings and to specific buildings. What is missing everywhere is an adequate explanation or even hypothesis on how, at different times and in different places, technological knowledge was transmitted to craftsmen.

40. This sort of hypothesis emerges from the recent gatherings that surrounded an exhibition of Timurid art put together at the Sackler Museum in Washington and the Los Angeles County Museum; see T. Lentz and

G. Lowry, *Timur and the Princely Vision* (Washington, D.C., 1989). The exhibition inspired the invaluable gathering of sources done by Wheeler Thackston, *A Century of Princes* (Cambridge, 1988), with a mine of information. Papers from a seminar held at Toronto will be published by Lisa Golombek and Maria Subtelny, *Timurid Art and Culture,* supplement 6, *Muqarnas* 8 (1992). The coincidence of the exhibition and of the nearly simultaneous appearance of two books on Timurid architecture is bound to lead to much rethinking about Islamic art.

41. Whatever (and it is very little) has been done about the esthetics of Islamic art based on original sources has centered on a few Safavid documents dealing primarily with literary esthetics. For the earlier medieval period, I only know of three studies: Richard Ettinghausen, "Al-Ghazzali on Beauty," in M. Rosen-Ayalon, ed., *Islamic Art and Archaeology* (Berlin, 1984); Bishr Farès, *Essai sur l'esprit de la décoration islamique* (Cairo, 1952), Ibn al-Haytham, *The Optics,* trans. A. I. Sabra (London, 1989), esp. pp. 97–100.

42. There is an interesting study to be made of the rate of presence of geometric ornament in buildings with different functions.

43. The entry "Fann" in the *Encyclopedia of Islam* only deals with its contemporary meaning for the arts. It would be interesting to have a linguistic history of the root with no significant Koranic significance, as it is only used once in the Revelation.

44. The literature of the *muqarnas* is both lengthy and so far inconclusive. Most pertinent references are found in the latest attempt at an explanation by Yasser Tabbaa, "The Muqarnas Dome," *Muqarnas* 3 (1985). For technical matters, see the very different views of M. Ecochard, *Filiation aux monuments grecs, byzantins et islamiques* (Paris, 1977), and U. Harb, *Ilkhanichiche Stalaktiten gewölbe* (Berlin, 1978). For an analysis of the *muqarnas* in a precise historical context, see Jonathan M. Bloom, "The Introduction of the Muqarnas into Egypt," *Muqarnas* 5 (1988).

45. O. Grabar, *The Great Mosque of Isfahan* (New York, 1989).

46. Grabar, *Great Mosque,* following Sheila Blair, *Arabic Inscriptions in Iran* (Leiden, 1991).

47. For an initiation to science in the late eleventh century, see E. S. Kennedy, "The Exact Sciences," in J. A. Boyle, ed., *The Cambridge History of Iran,* vol. 5 (Cambridge, 1968), pp. 663–66.

48. See pp. 153–154.

49. The issue underlying this paragraph is the extent to which a small number of examples that struck Western imagination relatively early on with particular vigor did not receive undue importance in scholarly thinking. For the Mamluks, see the articles in *Muqarnas* 2 (1981). For the Maghrib, see books on geometry like P. Ricard, *Pour comprendre l'art musulma* (Paris, 1924), and, more recently, André Paccard, *Traditional Islamic Crafts in Moroccan Architecture* (Saint Jorioz, France, 1980).

50. O. Grabar, *The Alhambra* (London, 1978), pp. 140–150.

51. E. Müller, *Gruppen theoretische Untersuchunger aus der Alhambra* (Rüschlikon, 1944).

52. The problem does, however, remain of whether a correlation can be established between quantity of objects made, buildings built, paintings painted, and the variety of stylistic or thematic ideas in them.

53. For instance Critchlow, *Patterns,* pp. 56 and ff., in which perfectly legitimate and true arithmetic observations are set in a cultural context compressed to the point of unintelligibility or downright falsehood. A more sophisticated view, although also criticized for scholarly inadequacies, was developed over a decade ago by S. H. Nasr, *Science and Civilization in Islam* (London, 1976). His views have changed in part, as in *Islamic Art and Spirituality* (Albany, N.Y., 1987).

54. I should add that it is quite reasonable to consider that architectural planning with

cosmological implications can indeed have geometric forms, because there has always been a close relationship between urban and living planning and cosmology. Y. I. Allawi, "Some Evolutionary and Cosmological Aspects to Early Islamic Town Planning," in M. B. Sevcenko, ed., *Theories and Principles of Design* (Cambridge, 1988). But town planning is an exercise different from and more portentous than wall decoration. Also eighth- or tenth-century examples cannot be used for later centuries.

55. H.S.M. Coxeter et al., eds., *M. C. Escher: Art and Science* (Amsterdam, 1987), p. 16. The whole volume is an interesting argument for the impossible—that is, for a matching of art and science.

56. *Le Nouvel Observateur*, December 14, 1984, pp. 66–67.

57. See, for instance, Margaret Courtney-Clarke, *The Art of West African Women* (New York, 1990); Lamia Doumab, *Architecture and Women* (New York, 1988); Isabelle Arescombe, *A Woman's Touch: Women in Design from 1860 to the Present Day* (New York, 1984). As an example of folk art using geometry in a particularly successful and monumental fashion, I would cite the paintings in Yemeni mosques, which are slowly beginning to emerge from obscurity. A particularly striking example in B. Finster, "Die Freitagmischee von Šibam," *Baghdader Mitteilungen* 10 (1979). In fact it is reasonable to try to study the contemporary vocabulary of craftsmen for an understanding of the past. So far, however, I have not been able to figure out what can be gained beyond an accurate terminology of geometric or geometricizing forms.

Chapter IV
The Intermediary of Architecture

1. The basic facts about the discovery and the largest number of photographs are most easily accessible through the catalogue of an exhibition held in Kuwait's National Museum, *Masahif Sanʿa* (Kuwait, n.d.). See also Werner Daum, ed., *Yemen* (Frankfurt, 1988); Hans-Caspar Graf von Bothmer, "Frühislamische Koran-Illuminationen," *Kunst und Antiquitaten* 1 (1986). The technical task of untangling the folios and of studying them has been entrusted to a German team from the University of Saarbrücken.

2. The history of the mosque of Sanʿa has not yet been entirely unraveled. For a careful assessment of texts as well as of the archaeological evidence, see R. B. Sergeant and Ronald Lewcock, *Sanʿa, An Arabian Islamic City* (London, 1983), pp. 323–50, but also the wonderful poems on mosques, pp. 313–14; Paolo Costa, "La Moschea Grande di Sana," *Annali Ist. Orientale di Napoli* 34 (1974); Barbara Finster, "Die Grosse Moschee von Sanʿa," *Baghdader Mitteilungen* 9 (1978) and 10 (1979); *Archaeologische Berichte aus dem Yemen* 1 (1982) and 3 (1986).

To imagine the removal of these manuscripts as a Qarmatian gesture or as the result of a Qarmatian threat makes some cultural sense, as the Qarmatians fed on a puritanical streak in the population of Sanʿa (a streak actually present in every center of a revealed religion) and these books were indeed beautifully decorated and could easily be seen as unethical. But so many other possibilities exist that speculation is idle until more concrete evidence comes about.

3. The problem of dating parchment pages with passages from the Koran consists of a set of unresolved issues: relationship between existing fragments and several known recensions only codified in the tenth century; history of scripts (partly dealt with in Chapter 2); establishment of an acceptable history for the recension of the text. For these problems, see the survey with good bibliographies in A. T. Welch, "Kur'an,"

Encyclopedia of Islam, 2d ed; see also Carl Brockelman, *Geschichte der arabischen Literatur*, vol. 1 (Leiden, 1943), pp. 38–39 for frauds attributed to Ali, and F. Sezgin, *Geschichte der arabischen Schriftum*, vol. 1 (Leiden, 1967), p. 18. But even these excellent surveys do not take into account the earliest "text" of the Scripture found in the late seventh-century inscriptions of the Dome of the Rock; see E. Combe, G. Wiel, J. Sauvaget, et al., *Répertoire chronologique d'epigraphic arabe* (Cairo, 1931–), no. 9. In the light, however, of all recent discoveries on parchment, this inscription also needs a new and more accurate checking. In short, it seems to me very difficult to propose early or late dates for any page from this group without many paleographic and technical studies.

4. See, in particular, the article by L. Jenkins in *Masahif* for a Syrian origin, the implications of the *Yemen* exhibition in Germany for a Yemeni one. A possible Arabian meaning or origin is suggested in a brief note by Jonathan Bloom, *Minaret: Symbol of Islam* (Oxford, 1989), p. 177.

5. The key study so far is by Hans-Caspar Graf von Bothmer, "Architekturbilder im Koran," *Pantheon* 45 (1987), which has discussed nearly every one of the questions and puzzles raised by these pages. My emphases are different from von Bothmer's and I am less certain of a date for the manuscript as early as the one he proposes. On some details I have different views. His article, however, is an excellent example of what should happen when a new and unusual discovery takes place: to make it available as soon as possible for further discussion. In the secretive world of connoisseurship, the case is rare enough to deserve praise. Furthermore, during a long conversation in April 1991, Professor von Bothmer provided further information about the manuscript. Much of it was incorporated in the text and I am grateful to him for additional generosity.

One question, which is not directly pertinent to my argument in this book but that is otherwise important for codicological purposes, is whether one can imagine a single volume of 520 folios or whether, as will often happen in later times, several volumes must be assumed. The latter makes the text so much easier to use that it must be more likely than a single codex whose sheer weight (especially if we consider its size) would have been unwieldy for anyone to carry.

6. von Bothmer, "Koran-Illuminationen," fig. 1. For the Vienna Dioscorides, see the facsimile edition, *Codex Vindobonensis med. Gr. 1 der Österreichischen Nationalbibliothek* (Graz, 1965–1970).

7. Once again, as we saw in Chapter 2, the history of the script is not sufficiently well developed to allow for dating the pages on any other basis than that of the ornaments and diacritical marks in the text. In an evolutionary scheme according to traditional Darwinian principles, pages with a large number of added ornaments should be later than plain pages. But it is also possible, even likely, that distinctions of taste or of expense took priority and that they operated differently from paleographical ones.

8. There is no easily accessible list of sizes for medieval manuscripts, especially from the Muslim world. See Graham Pollard, "Notes on the Size of the Sheet," *Library*, 4th ser., 22 (1941); paper Korans acquired large dimensions in the more exhibitionist Mongol and Mamluk periods. But one of the largest Mamluk manuscripts was forty-eight by thirty-two centimeters, considerably smaller than the Yemen one; David James, *Qur'ans of the Mamluks* (London, 1988), p. 34.

9. First of all, while I cannot really propose a different explanation than that of a tower with a spiral inside, too little has remained to make towers the only possible explanation. The second difficulty is that towers were very rare in early Islamic times and, with a minimal number of exceptions, did not begin to appear in a consistent way

until the tenth century, with the exception of the sanctuaries in Mekka and especially Medina, which did have eighth-century towers, for reasons that are not quite the liturgical ones of later minarets. See Bloom, *Minaret*, esp. p. 48.

10. It is on purpose that this sentence is so convoluted. To my great surprise, in two instances of showing these pages to groups of Muslims—one, a highly sophisticated group of engineers in Kuwait, the other one, young students of architecture in Cambridge, Massachusetts—the drawings were not immediately recognized as images of mosques, whereas nearly every historian of Islamic art sees them as such. Similar experiments with historians of other arts than Islamic art or simply with text-based historians led to equally unsettling results in the sense that it is only with reluctance that images of physical mosques were seen. See p. 193 for further implications of this point.

11. See Corning Museum of Glass L55.1.125, apparently an unpublished object. Its shape is like that of the objects on the San'a representations and it has two hooks for hanging. The problem is that it is molded and covered with vegetal and animal motifs and thus unsuitable for a mosque. Comparable vessels are found in the David Collection in Copenhagen (K. von Folsach, *Islamic Art* [Copenhagen, 1990]), no. 227, dated cautiously between the ninth and twelfth centuries, or the Metropolitan Museum (L. Jenkins, "Islamic Glass," *Metropolitan Museum of Art Bulletin* 44 [1986]). The basic shape itself, in the conservative world of glassmakers, goes back to the antique, and finds its culmination in the thousands of Mamluk and Ottoman "mosque lamps." There is, to my knowledge, no evidence until the San'a illustrations to assume that early examples like the Corning one were lamps hung in buildings. This is an area where, for once, statistical information so liked by archaeologists could be put to use if found in a proper urban context. A new function, lighting mosques, must have led to the massive manufacture of new objects or to a change in the proportional number of traditional ones.

12. For all the buildings mentioned in the text (except the mosque of San'a), see Richard Ettinghausen and Oleg Grabar, *Art and Architecture of Islam, 650–1250* (London, 1987), pp. 35ff. and passim; for the mosque of San'a, see B. Finster and others quoted in note 2. It must be stressed that the specific interpretation of the illustrations as representations of *a* building poses all sorts of problems but would also transform them into truly unique sources for history.

13. By the word "codicological" I mean something akin to, but a little wider than, the usual sense of the word, as in manuals of codicology. I mean those aspects and attributes of any one book that are exclusively that particular book's privilege and would not exist in the shape in which they appear if it had not been for the particular context of that book. These aspects and attributes can be classified in terms of orders or possibly modes, such as illustration (adding images to enhance a text), design (organization of individual pages), or economics (making a book look expensive). In general more thought needs to be devoted to the ways in which the huge information available about any one book or manuscript should be organized.

14. The most easily available selection of texts is in Klaus Brisch, "Observations on the Iconography of the Great Mosque at Damascus," in Priscilla P. Soucek, ed., *Content and Context of Visual Arts in the Islamic World* (University Park, Penn., 1988), pp. 14–21. An important earlier discussion of these same texts is in Barbara Finster, "Die Mosaiken der Omuygadenmoschee von Damaskus," *Kunst des Orients* 7 (1972). I am still troubled by an interpretation of the mosaics of the Damascus mosque as representations of Paradise, and this for two reasons. One is that this conclusion is based on fragments remaining in relatively secondary parts of the court; can one assume that the whole mosque was Paradise? The other one is that the idea of "representing" the Paradise

is contrary to Muslim practice, especially when contrasted to Christian ways in iconoclastic times. It is, however, true that Damascus could have been an exception, since the whole building had a meaning in relationship to the Christian population of the city as well as an internal Muslim one. For a recent formal analysis that claims a paradisiac interpretation on more formal grounds, see G. Hellenkempa Salies, "Die Mosaiken der Grossen Moschee von Damaskas," *Universita degli Studi di Bologna, XXXV Corso . . . sull-arte Ravennate e Bizantina* (Ravenna, 1988).

15. The latest study of these manuscripts is P. Klein, *Beatus-Kodex* (Hildesheim, 1976) and John Williams, ed., *The Illustrated Beatus* (Oxford, 1991). For suggestive historical explanations of architecture in the Beatus manuscripts and elsewhere in Spain, see J. Dodds, *Architectural Ideology in Early Muslim Spain* (University Park, Penn., 1990), esp. pp. 76–77.

16. O. Grabar, "The Illustrated Maqamat of the Thirteenth Century," in A. H. Hourani and S. M. Stern, eds., *The Islamic City* (Oxford, 1970). The unique manuscript with a fascination for strange architecture is London, British Library oriental 9718 (circa 1310); O. Grabar, *The Illustrations of the Maqamat* (Chicago, 1984), esp. p. 13.

17. B. Moritz, *Arabic Palaeography* (Cairo, 1905; repr. Osnabrück, 1986), pls. 3–11. These extraordinary pages have never been studied since their publication without commentary nearly a hundred years ago. It is regrettable that I was unable to obtain new photographs of these pages.

18. Robert Hamilton, *Khirbat al-Mafjar* (Oxford, 1959), pl. LXV, 1.

19. It is indeed curious that significant architectural features appear in several versions of the *Materia Medica* of Dioscorides (in particular the Bologna and Istanbul examples); see E. Grube, "Materialen zum Dioskurides Arabius," in R. Ettinghausen, ed., *Aus der Welt der islamischen Kunst* (Berlin, 1959). The other striking example is the frontispiece of the Vienna Galen, K. Holter, "Die Galen-handschrift," *Jahrbuch der Kunsthistorischen Sammleungen Wien*, n.s. 2 (1937).

20. A particularly striking transformation of an architectural frontispiece with a narrative is Behzad's celebrated first two pages of Sa'di's *Bustan* in Cairo (dated 1488) with its court scene as a *tableau vivant*; see T. Lentz and G. Lowry, *Timur and the Princely Vision* (Washington, D.C., 1989), pp. 260–61.

21. Yani Maimaré, *Katalogue of Arabic Gospels in Mt. Sinai* (Athens, 1985), figs. 5 and 4.

22. For Evangelists, the classical study is A. M. Friend, Jr., "The Portraits of the Evangelists," *Art Studies* (1927 and 1929). There is, to my knowledge, no single survey of authors' portraits, although K. Weitzmann has often alluded to the topic, as in "The Greek Sources of Islamic Scientific Illustrations," in G. C. Miles, ed., *Archaeologia Orientalia in Memoriam Ernst Herzfeld* (Locust Valley, N.Y., 1952). For canon texts, the classic study is by Carl Nordenfalk, *Die Spätantiken Kanontafeln* (Güteborg, 1938).

23. The most accessible Hebrew examples are in Bezalel Narkiss, *Hebrew Illuminated Manuscripts* (Jerusalem, 1969), pls. 1, 2, 5, 7. For Slavic examples, see V. N. Lazarev et al., *Drevnerusskoe Iskusstvo* (Moscow, 1963), pp. 140–4.

24. Examples are too numerous to require mentioning. For a general survey and discussion, see Otto Pächt, *Book Illuminations in the Middle Ages* (Oxford, 1986), esp. chap. 7 dealing with the "architectural structuring" of miniatures. See also Hermann Fillitz, *Des Mittelalter*, vol. 1 (Berlin, 1969), pls. 17 and 32, among many others.

25. Alba Bible (Madrid, Casa de Alba, Palacio de Liria, fol. 25v), as in Jean Glénisson, *Le livre au Moyen Age* (Paris, 1988), p. 150.

26. G. Wilpert, *I Sarcophagi Cristiani* (Rome, 1929–1935), pls. XI and so on. E. Kitzinger, *Byzantine Art in the Making* (Cambridge, 1977), pls. 23–24, 33–48.

27. H. Schlunk, *Untersuchungen im frühchristlichen Mausoleum von Centcelles* (Berlin, 1959). For other uses of architecture in medieval Spanish art and especially for the striking paintings at Santullano de Prades, see H. Schlunk and M. Berengner, *La pintura mural asturiana de los siglos IX y X* (Madrid, 1957).

28. J. Garber, *Die Karolingische St. Bendiktkische in Mals* (Insbruck, 1915); Nicoló Rasmo, "Note Preliminazi," *Stucchi e Moraici Acto Medivevali* (Milan, 1959).

29. Glénisson, *Le livre au Moyen Age*, fig. 39.

30. Marie-Hélène Rutschowcaya, *Coptic Fabrics* (Paris, 1990); Dorothee Renner, *Die koptischen Textilien in den Vatikanische Museen* (Wiesbaden, 1982); Deborah Thompson, *Coptic Textiles in the Brooklyn Museum* (New York, 1971); Klaus Wessel, *Coptic Art* (London, 1965). For ivories see any manual of Byzantine art like W. F. Volbach and J. Lafontaine-Dorogne, *Byzanz und der christliche Osten* (Berlin, 1968), pls. 87–88.

31. F. Dressler, *Das Evangeliar Otto III* (Frankfort, 1978).

32. Both visual perception and semiology are well developed fields and the more recently popular field of cognition has also dealt with how one knows whatever one remembers and with how one remembers. I am aware of many of these endeavors, but I am deliberately avoiding them in the text of my essays, in order to see how historical analysis of visual material will lead to larger issues on its merits rather than as adaptations of theories developed elsewhere.

33. Alexander Badawy, *Le dessin architectural chez les anciens Egyptiens* (Cairo, 1948). This is a rich and informative book, but the interest of its author was primarily in what drawings tell about Egyptian architecture, not in the technique of representation.

34. It is altogether rather surprising that there is no systematic study of the representation of architecture, as there are books or other scholarly efforts on landscape or on human beings, admittedly by the same individual, Kenneth Clark, *The Nude* (Princeton, 1956) and *Landscape into Art* (New York, 1949; repr. 1976); even on apes (H. W. Janson, *Apes and Ape Lore* [London, 1952]) or on fantastic beings (Jurgis Baltrusaitis, *Le Moyen Age fantastique* [Paris, 1981]). The closest to my topic is Spiro A. Kostof, *The Architect* (Oxford, 1977), but there too the principal emphasis is a different one.

35. Henri Jordan, *Forma urbis Romae*, (Berlin, 1874); G. Carettoni et al., *La Pianta Marmorea di Roma* (Rome, 1955–60). The main edition of the Saint Gall plan is W. Horn and E. Born, *The Plan of St. Gall* (Berkeley, 1979). See W. Eugene Kleinbauer, "Pre-Carolingian Concepts of Architecture Planning," in Marilyn J. Chiat and Kathryn L. Reyerson, eds., *The Medieval Mediterranean* (St. Cloud, Minn., 1988), for an excellent summary of the issues and of the various opinions about the Saint Gall plan.

36. Horn and Born, *St. Gall*, pp. 53–56, for Carolingian example.

37. Villard de Honnecourt is the earliest example of a recorder of architecture who used plans systematically for whole monuments or for details. Theodore Bowie, *The Sketches of Villard de Honnecourt* (Bloomington, Ind., 1959); François Bucher, *Architector* (New York, 1974); H. Hahnloser, *Villard de Honnecourt: Kritische Gesamtausgabe* (Graz, 1972). On a different level, see also Carol Heitz, *L'architecture religieuse carolingienne* (Paris, 1980), esp. pp. 212–20, and his earlier *Recherches sur les rapports entre architecture et liturgie* (Paris, 1963), pp. 113–18. For both works, drawings from the Middle Ages are used.

38. G. Necipoglu-Kafadar and Renata Holod as quoted in Chapter 3, note 19. See also the interesting later examples studied by Hassan al-Basha, "Ottoman Pictures of the Mosque of the Prophet," *Islamic Art* 3 (1989).

39. See Nancy S. Steinhardt, *Chinese Imperial City Planning* (Honolulu, 1990), for a study of various types of Chinese representations. Although it is written from a differ-

ent perspective, much is always gained from Joseph Needham, *Science and Civilisation in China* vol. 3 (Cambridge, 1959), esp. pp. 497–50.

40. L. Haselberger, "Werkzeichen am jüngeren Didymeion," *Istanbuler Mitteilungen* 30 (1989); I. Bayer, "Architekturzeichnungen auf dem Boden der Basilika," in T. Ulbert, ed. *Die Basilika des Heiligen Kreuzes in Resafa-Sergiopolis* (Mainz, 1986).

41. Adaman, *Arculf's Narrative*, trans. James Macpherson (London, 1889); Carol Heitz, "Renonveau de l'architecture," *Dossiers de l'Architecture* 30 (1978).

42. R. Krautheimer, "An Introduction to an Iconography of Medieval Architecture," *Journal of the Warburg and Courtauld Institutes* 5 (1942).

43. K. Weitzmann, *Die byzantinische Buchmalerei* (Berlin, 1935), fig. 580 and p. 22.

44. A manuscript like the Utrecht Psalter (E. de Wald, *The Utrecht Psalter* [Princeton, 1953]) is full of examples of churches or palaces or of all sorts of other buildings. So are many Byzantine marginal psalters like the Orlerdoff one; see M. V. Shchepkina, *Miniatary kludovskoi Psaltyry* (Moscow, 1977). See André Grabar, "Quelques notes sur les psautiers," *Cahiers Archéologiques* 15 (1965).

45. The bibliography and all key references are in note 12. Compromise explanation in Ettinghausen and Grabar, *Art and Architecture of Islam* pp. 42–45. The assumption of contemporary scholarship is that a single explanation must be assumed for the time when the mosaics were created. In theory, this is a correct assumption and certainly valid for the sponsors of the mosaics. On the other hand, in the visually complex world of the first century of Islamic rule, it is possible to imagine that interpretations by viewers varied considerably. This possibility is strengthened by the variations in later accounts of these mosaics.

46. M. Piccirillo, "Le Iscrizioni di Um er-Rasas," *Liber Annuus* 37 (1987), and "The Mosaics at Um er-Rasas," *Biblical Archaeologist* 51 (1988).

47. Typical examples in James Snyder, *Northern Renaissance Art* (New York, 1985), pl. 22, figs. 130 and 104.

48. Bianchi-Bandinelli, *Le centre du pouvoir* (Paris, 1969), fig. 70; for illusionism in general, see A. Maiuri, *Roman Painting* (Geneva, 1953); H. Joyce, *The Decoration of Walls, Ceilings and Floors* (Rome, 1981), with a new set of categories of analysis.

49. Matrakci, *Beyan-i Menazil-i Sefer-i Irakeyn*, ed. H. G. Yurdaydin (Ankara, 1976), esp. pl. 105b.

50. The point could be pushed even a point further to argue that, at the same time, the effects of color and light could not be effective without an identified but not identifiable topic. There is, in other words, a curious equilibrium at work between subject and manner of showing it, out of which even contemporary "abstract" art has failed to emerge.

51. The issue here goes much beyond the scope of these essays, but it involves the celebrated Platonic view of mirrors of truth, which are never the truth, unless it is the mirror that is the object of art, as was implied in my conclusion to Chapter 2.

52. For Roman mosaics, see W. Oakeshott, *The Mosaics of Rome* (New York, 1967), pl. IX, fig. 135. The Madaba map was published and studied by M. Avi-Yonah, *The Madaba Mosaic Map* (Jerusalem, 1959), pl. 7. See also D. Levi, *Antioch Mosaic Pavements* (Princeton, 1947) and Irving Lavin, "The Hunting Mosaics," *Dumbarton Oaks Papers* 17 (1963).

53. Known for many decades, these mosaics have been the subject of some controversy in recent years. See Theocharis Pazaras, *The Rotunda of St. George* (Thessaloniki, 1985), and W. E. Kleinbauer, "The Iconography and the Date of the Mosaics," *Viator* 3 (1972), with bibliography; J.-M. Spieser, *Thessalonique et ses monuments des IVe au VIe siècle* (Athens, 1984).

54. The classical one is R. Wittkower,

Architectural Principles in the Age of Humanism (London, 1988), esp. pp. 70–93.

55. H. R. Hahnloser, *Il Tesoro di San Marco: La Pala d'Oro* (Florence, 1965), is the basic publication.

56. The earliest representation known to me is on an early twelfth-century small steatite in the Baghdad Museum; V. Strika, "A Ka'bah Picture in the Iraq Museum," *Sumer* 32 (1976). For a general survey of the available evidence, see Paolo Cuneo, *Storia dell' urbanistica: Il Mondo Islamico* (Rome, 1986), chap. 2. It is apparently in the fourteenth century that these religious images began to proliferate, but why?

57. Frontispieces are common. Finispieces are rarer, but they did occur in the early Koran manuscript discovered in Chapter 3 and in at least one thirteenth-century illustrated manuscript, the *Mukhtar al-Hikam* of al-Mubashshir (Top Kapi Seray Ahmet III 3206); Richard Ettinghausen, *Arab Painting* (Geneva, 1962), pp. 74–79.

58. Wayne Begley, "The Myth of the Taj Mahal," *Art Bulletin* 61 (1979); with Z. A. Desai, *Taj Mahal* (Cambridge, 1989). The interpretation by Begley of the Taj Mahal as an actual recreation of the garden of Paradise with the Throne of God has not been accepted by all, even though I tend to subscribe to it. But, even if partly correct, its implication for the building is that of a slightly blasphemous ensemble.

59. This is yet another question that extends the remarks of this essay into broader theories of perception for visual forms, as it suggests two ways for works of art to affect their viewers and users. One is through the direct communication of information and the other one through various kinds of evocations. The relationship between the two needs yet to be worked out. For a preliminary statement on the subject, but with very different implications, see A. Grabar, "Quelques notes sur les psautiers," *Cahiers Archéologiques* 15 (1965). For a still underdeveloped view on the subject, see O. Grabar, "A Note on the Chludoff Psalter," *Harvard Ukrainian Studies* 7 (1983).

60. A study should some day be devoted to the uses of fancy boxes and containers and to the shapes they took across cultures and times: Tang ceramic containers, medieval reliquaries, incense burners, places to store holy books, and so forth. Throughout, it seems, a domes top predominated, thus suggesting a relationship to royal and religious parallels.

61. S. Melikian-Chirvani, "State Inkwells in Islamic Iran," *Journal of the Walters Art Gallery* 44 (1986).

Chapter V
The Intermediary of Nature

1. For Villard de Honnecourt, see H. Hahnloser, *Villard de Honnecourt: Kritische Gesamtausgabe* (Graz, 1972), pl. 10, or Theodore Bowie, *The Sketches of Villard de Honnecourt* (Bloomington, Ind., 1959), pl. 26. The Khirbat al-Mafjar ceiling has been often reproduced since its original publication in R. W. Hamilton, *Khirbat al-Mafjar*, pl. LIV, 7. For the Ara Pacis, see p. 33. Examples of vegetation on medieval Islamic objects are everywhere; for floriated Kufic, the original studies are that of S. Flury, as in *Islamische Schriftbänder: Amida* (Basel, 1920). For India and the Far East, I have relied primarily on Jessica Rawson, *Chinese Ornament: The Lotus and the Dragon* (London, 1984).

2. J. Soustiel, *La céramique islamique* (Paris, 1985), esp. pp. 2, 8, 9, and 11; B. Gray, "Blue and White Vessels in Russian Miniatures," *Transactions of the Oriental Ceramic Society* 24 (1948–1949); Y. Crowe, "Aspects of Persian Blue and White and China," *Transactions* 53 (1979–1980); John Pope, *Fourteenth Century Blue and White* (Washington, D.C., 1952); John Carswell, *Blue and White Chinese Porcelain and Its impact*

on the Western World (Chicago, 1985); Regina Krahl, *Chinese Ceramics in the Topkapi Saray Museum* (New York, 1986).

3. As examples more or less chosen at random, see T. Kraus, *Das Römische Welt* (Berlin, 1967), pl. xxib; W. F. Volbach and S. Lafontaine-Desognes, *Byzanz und der christliche Osten* (Berlin, 1968), pls. 3a, 87, 116b, among many places. See also my pp. 33–36 for examples from Islamic art. For Mughal art, see Marthe Bernus-Taylor et al., *Arabesques et jardins de paradis* (Paris, 1990), nos. 112–14.

4. Capitals have played a curious diagnostic role in the historiography of architecture. They have been used as means to date buildings, on the assumptions that, for rarely explored reasons, they automatically reflected changes and differences from period to period or area to area and that they possess dialectal continuity in the sense that the same or similar capitals were used in the same areas at the same time. The masterpiece of this kind of taxonomic capitalology is Rudolf Kautzsch, *Kapitellstudien* (Berlin, 1936). More sophisticated explanations of capitals occur in works such as one already mentioned by John Onians, *Bearers of Meaning* (Princeton, 1988), where capitals are integrated within the structure of orders. Romanesque capitals have generally been studied as independent carriers of images rather than as parts of a building's artistic or technical structure, as, for instance, in Meyer Schapiro, *Selected Papers: Romanesque Art* (New York, 1977).

5. Additional examples and discussion from a different point of view are found in Kenneth Clark, *Landscape into Art* (New York, 1949; repr. 1976).

6. W. B. Denny, *The Ceramics of the Mosque of Rüstem Pasha* (New York, 1977). For more general views on the mosque and on ceramics used in mosques, see various parts of E. Atil, ed., *Turkish Art* (Washington, D.C., 1980).

7. The nearly complete publication of these mosaics is by M. van Berchem in K.A.C. Creswell, ed., *Early Muslim Architecture*, 2d ed. (Oxford, 1969), with, however, some errors in captions. The possible iconography and meaning of these mosaics is still a subject of discussion; the latest contribution is by M. Rosen-Ayalon, *The Early Islamic Monuments of al-Haram al-Sharif* (Jerusalem, 1989).

8. Lucia Valentine, *Ornament in Medieval Manuscripts* (London, 1965) or D. Ware and M. Stafford, *An Illustrated Dictionary of Ornament* (New York, 1974), among many examples. For an excellent example of pure taxonomy in handling this ornament, see G. Schneider, *Pflanzliche Bauornamente der Seldschuken in Kleinasien* (Wiesbaden, 1984).

9. Several years later, a certain amount of searching has failed to discover the original location of this photograph.

10. These assumptions permeate a lot of nineteenth-century studies of ornament; see Chapter 1, notes 14, 29, 46. They are still present whenever national calls are made on the prestige of works of art. It would be wrong to discard and deny a method of analysis simply because it is occasionally misused. My only major point is that the genetic explanation of a work of art provides only one of its many facets.

11. The most obvious examples are in the illustrations of the *Maqamat*. See O. Grabar, *The Illustrations of the Maqamat* (Chicago, 1984), esp. pp. 119–20 where the character of this support is discussed.

12. H. Frankfort, *The Art and Architecture of the Ancient Orient* (London, 1955), esp. pp. 67–68. P. A. Underwood, "Fountain of Life," *Dumbarton Oaks Papers* 5 (1950); also, in a different vein, J. Dickie, "The Iconography of the Prayer Rug," *Oriental Art* 17 (1972), for a specifically Islamic interpretation of the Tree. See "Arbore della Vita," in *Encyclopedia dell'Arte Medievale* (Rome, 1991).

13. Lars-Ivar Ringbom, *Paradisus Terrestris*, vol. 2 (Helsinki, 1958). The book is important for the theory it proposes, even if there are many uncertainties about it, but it is especially important for the documentation Ringbom put together of objects, im-

ages, and holy places that can be given a symbolic meaning within a certain time and space, the first nine centuries of our era, primarily in and around the Mediterranean.

14. The excavations carried out at Takht-i Sulayman have not been completed and now are unlikely ever to be. For a preliminary survey, see Rudolf Naumann, *Die Ruinen von Takht-e Suleiman* (Berlin, 1977), with a bibliography on work done until then.

15. The notion of "Oriental silver" was coined by J. Smirnov in a celebrated album with that title, *Vostochnoe Serebro* (St. Petersburg, 1909). His album is a treasure of data, which lead to discoveries almost every time its plates are perused. At the present time, the only scholar who has been systematically working on these objects is Boris Marshak, whose latest work is *Silberschätze des Orients* (Leipzig, 1986). For bronze, see his "Ranneislamskye bronzovye bliuda," *Trudy Ermitaga* 19 (1978).

16. For example, Marshak, *Silberschätze*, pls. 82–85, 97, 126.

17. The most celebrated example is that of the plate in the Hermitage Museum in Leningrad with two animals on the side of a tree: I. A. Orbeli and K. Trever, *Orfèvrerie sassavide* (Leningrad, 1935), pl. 32. The theme is related to that of the snake-eating stag, for which see R. Ettinghausen, *Islamic Art and Archaeology*, ed. M. Rosen-Ayalon (Berlin, 1984). For Taq-i Bustan, see E. Porada, *Art of Ancient Iran* (New York, 1962), pp. 192ff. and S. Fukai and K. Horiuchi, *Taq-i-Bustan* (Tokyo, 1969).

18. This is a very complex issue, as gardens and Paradise are often automatically confused. See, as a latest example, G. Bellafiore, "I giardini Paradiso," *Argumenti di Storia dell'Arte* 1 (1983).

19. The issue is a vast one and cannot be dealt with in the context of these essays. I only want to suggest, first, that there probably is a correlation between consistency of cultural meaning and quantities of examples; second, that remaining documents, however few, are probably a reasonable random proportion of what existed unless a systematic destruction can be demonstrated; and, third, that it is difficult to make history out of unique objects. But all of this needs much reflection.

20. Schapiro, *Romanesque Art*; *The Romanesque Sculpture of Moissac* (New York, 1985); C. Alarno Martinez, *El Claustro Romanico de Silos* (Madrid, 1983).

21. There is so much to say about the Ghent Altarpiece, a single monument with masses of "events" depicted requiring lengthy descriptions and analyses. By contrast, there is so little to say about a piece of gold jewelry except that it is expensive or looks attractive when worn. It is easy then to conclude that the respective values of the two creations are to be evaluated differently and that the Ghent Altarpiece is richer than a piece of jewelry. Reality may well be quite different, as the jewelry has a depth of personal life usually absent from an item of church furniture.

22. For windswept capitals, see, for instance, Richard Krautheimer, *Early Christian and Byzantine Architecture* (Baltimore, 1965), pl. 45 B and C, pp. 113ff. Any Gothic cathedral has laced sculpture of vaguely vegetal origin in the finials of its buttresses or surrounding its windows.

23. A seminar on this carpet was held in Boston in March 1970 and the talks were published in *Boston Museum of Fine Arts Bulletin* 69, nos. 355–56 (1971). That issue also contains a careful and detailed technical description of the carpet.

24. Schuyler v.R. Cammann, "Symbolic Meanings in Oriental Rug Patterns," *Textile Museum Journal* 3 (1972), and "The Interplay of Art, Literature, and Religion," *Journal Royal Asiatic Society* (1978).

25. For a further discussion, see Annemarie Schimmel, "The Celestial Garden in Islam," in Elizabeth B. MacDougall and Richard Ettinghausen, eds., *The Islamic Garden* (Washington, D.C., 1976), pp. 13ff.

26. Quoted by Schimmel, ibid., p. 25.

27. The relationship between art and faith has not been a significant issue of schol-

arship or of any other kind of thinking in recent decades. For only partial exceptions that do try to deal with religion and art, see Margaret R. Mills, *Image as Insight* (Boston, 1985), and Paul Tillich, *On Art and Architecture* (New York, 1987). There always is the special case of Orthodox, especially Russian, icons with a constant stream of literature. Even when significant, the question was almost always one of relating a specific faith (or aspect of a faith) to a form. A more interesting and more fruitful direction could be taken by relating types of behavior within different faiths with works of art.

There are actually very few identified Muslim visual signs with a clearly religious or pious meaning. The most obvious one is the mihrab form used in mosques and tombs. It may be shown on so-called prayer rugs, but that is yet another topic of uncertainty when the prayer was really the purpose of what dealers called prayer rugs. A similar shape was used as decoration in religious or secular buildings. While Nuha Khoury's exhaustive study on the subject is being completed, see G. Fehervari, "Tombstone or Mihrab," in R. Ettinghausen, ed., *Islamic Art in the Metropolitan Museum of Art* (New York, 1972). Other motifs with religious implication, such as the "eye" or the "hand" of Fatimah, seem to be folk interpretations and folk topics that are not accepted at all levels. But there again further research may change these conclusions.

28. Examples abound. For instance Basil Gray, *Persian Painting* (Geneva, 1961), pp. 102–3, 132, 137. See my note 33.

29. All people familiar with the Arab and Iranian worlds are aware of the plethora of formulas accompanying greetings as well as news of important or mundane events in one's life. To my knowledge, no serious work has dealt with an analysis of those greetings or of official and other formulas as reflections of emotional attitudes and social habits. On a different but pertinent level of analysis, see Marilyn Waldman, *Toward a Theory of Historical Narrative* (Columbus, Ohio, 1980), which deals with a Persian historical text and its structure. Even work on poetry has, at least as far as I know, been more technical than theoretical.

30. Exceptions would be rugs or other textiles with a clear image and, as a result, a clear iconography. These are instances where the image represented takes over the physical quality of the object. In the West, such would be the case with the large tapestries with historical or mythological topics; for instance, Edith A. Standers, *European Post-Medieval Tapestries in the Metropolitan Museum of Art* (New York, 1985); Daniel Meyer, *Gli Arazzi del Re Sole* (Florence, 1982); Francis P. Thomson, *Tapestry Mirror of History* (New York, 1980). In the Muslim world, textiles with the representation of rulers are mentioned in texts; Maqrizi, *Khitat* (Cairo, 1853), vol. 2, pp. 410–12; Ibn al-Zubayr, *Kitab al-Dhakha'ir wa al-Tuhaf*, ed. H. Hamidullah (Kuwait, 1959), pp. 304–46. For the contemporary world, rugs or textiles with the representation of the Dome of the Rock or of the Taj Mahal or else of political and spiritual leaders are common.

31. See note 2.

32. The point is an important one whenever one deals with descriptions of paintings and perceptive remarks on the issue by Michael Baxandall, *Patterns of Intention* (New Haven, 1985), esp. chap. 1.

33. T. Lentz and G. Lowry, *Timur and the Princely Vision* (Washington, D.C., 1989), pp. 128–29. After studying these pages carefully, I am no longer convinced that their illuminations are contemporary with the text, or that they came from the same original manuscript. But these issues of connoisseurship are not pertinent to my essays.

34. W. Worringer, *Abstraction and Empathy: A Contribution to the Psychology of Style* (1908; repr. London, 1953), esp. pp. 74–76.

35. Lentz and Lowry, *Timur*, pp. 200–201.

36. Linda Komaroff, "The Timurid Phase in Iranian Metalwork" (Ph.D. diss., New York University, 1984).

37. Rawson, *Chinese Ornament*, p. 26.

38. See p. 247 for a basis bibliography on Mshatta.

39. See pp. 115–117.

40. J. Ruskin, *The Stones of Venice* (New York, 1853), p. 60, on the capitals in Torcello or M. Focillon, *L'art des sculpteurs romans* (Paris, 1964), pp. 88–89, among many examples.

41. A different but comparable interpretation of these dragons is found in S. C. Welch, "Two Drawings, a Tile, a Dish, and a Pair of Scissors," in R. Ettinghausen, ed., *Islamic Art in the Metropolitan Museum of Art* (New York, 1972).

Conclusion
Some Implications

1. The often violent reaction against ornament that raged in some nineteenth-century circles and among flag-bearers of modernism ("less is more") can easily be explained in psychological terms as an acknowledgment of ornament's values.

2. Even though the author was quite unaware of ideas such as have been developed in this book, see the analysis on *topoi* as intermediaries to specific events in the lives of saints carried by Cynthia Hahn, "Picturing the Text," *Art History* 13 (1990). The whole issue finds wonderful illustrations in contemporary attempts at visual iconography in new countries or in countries trying to create a new art of power. For a fascinating, even if deeply prejudicial and personal, account, see Samir al-Khalil, *The Monument, Art, Vulgarity, and Responsibility in Iraq* (Berkeley, 1991), esp. chaps. 8–10.

3. This point and the ideas from it came from perusing works of Georges Didi-Huberman, for example, *Devant l'image* (Paris, 1990) and *Fra Angelico* (Paris, 1990). I owe these references to Isabelle Frank to whom I am most grateful (see her review in *Times Literary Supplement*, January 11, 1991).

4. Ibn al-Haytham, *The Optics*, trans. A. I. Sabra (London, 1989), vol. 1, pp. 209ff., and the exemplary commentary, vol. 2, pp. 97–105. See also my pp. 86–87 for an earlier use of al-Haytham.

5. For instance, al-Farabi, *Idées des habitants de la cité vertueuse* (Cairo, 1949), *Eticheskie Traktaty* (Alma-Ata, 1973), and *Fusul al-Madani*, ed. and trans. D. M. Dunlop (Cambridge, 1961), esp. for notions of pleasure (p. 39) and love (p. 53) or else with intermediate activities (pp. 40 and 48–49). In general, see "al-Farabi" in *Encyclopedia Islamica*, and M. Mahdi, *The Philosophy of al-Farabi* (New York, 1962).

6. Similar issues were alluded to in my earlier reference to atomism as an explanation for certain types of abstraction in Islamic art (p. 19). An interesting avenue for further work lies probably in the esoteric literature of the ninth and tenth centuries. Writings like those of *Ikhwan al-Safa*, "The Brethern of Purity," contain all sorts of tantalizing ideas, which seem almost to explain or to recall themes of the arts. In reality, no real connection between these tractates and the visual world have so far succeeded, but this is not a reason not to try. See, for summaries, Yves Marquet, *Les philosophies des alchimistes et l'alchimie des philosophes* (Paris, 1988).

7. See note 69 in Chapter 2 and note 15 in the Introduction. The one successful use of literary images for art is by Priscilla Soucek, "Nizami on Painters and Painting," in R. Ettinghausen, ed., *Islamic Art in the Metropolitan Museum of Art* (New York, 1972).

8. It is important to realize, for instance, that the big surveys of sources like those of C. Brockelman, F. Sezgin, and O. Pareja, or even the multiauthored *Handbuch der Orientalistik* offer practically no help for someone seeking sources useful to the arts and crafts.

9. Sir Ernst Gombrich's whole book is a

reaction to contemporary trends and to a contemporary taste; see my pp. 40–41. The quotation about incantations is from Françoise Henry, *Irish Art in the Early Christian Period* (London, 1947), p. 188, but see from p. 185 onward.

10. See above pp. 45–46, and Jonathan Cullen, *Theory and Criticism after Structuralism* (Ithaca, N.Y., 1982), esp. p. 152 for philosophical binaries or p. 133 for intermediaries. I am leaving aside as unresolved the question whether a written text can exist without a language.

11. See pp. 61 and 63. Good survey of these theories and approaches in Cullen's book, *Theory and Criticism.*

12. Paul Tillich, *Theology of Cultures* (New York, 1959), p. 108.

13. It is interesting to note how much more comfortable Gombrich is with his own evidence whenever he can provide a *pre*-history to something; as in *The Sense of Order* (Oxford, 1979), pp. 245 and 284.

14. Thomas A. Sebeok, *The Tell-tale Sign: A Survey of Semiotics* (Lisse, 1975), and esp. pp. 27–36 for the essay by Hubert Damisch on "Semiotics and Iconography." This is just one of many places where issues are debated of what is seen and how it is interpreted.

15. More on this topic in M. Olin, "Forms of Respect: Alvis Riegl's Concept of Attentiveness," *Art Bulletin* 71 (1989).

16. For an aspect of this power, see David Freedberg, *The Power of Image* (Chicago, 1989), esp. pp. 374ff. Also various works quoted earlier by M. Baxandhall.

17. Penelope R. Doob, *The Idea of the Labyrinth* (Ithaca, N.Y., 1990), pp. 144–45.

INDEX

GPSR Authorized Representative: Easy Access System Europe - Mustamäe tee 50, 10621 Tallinn, Estonia, gpsr.requests@easproject.com

www.ingramcontent.com/pod-product-compliance
Lightning Source LLC
LaVergne TN
LVHW081257100826
845148LV00005B/899

* 9 7 8 0 6 9 1 2 5 2 7 6 6 *